# Logic, Argumentation & Reasoning

## Interdisciplinary Perspectives from the Humanities and Social Sciences

## Volume 22

Logic, Argumentation & Reasoning (LAR) explores links between the Humanities and Social Sciences, with theories (including decision and action theory) drawn from the cognitive sciences, economics, sociology, law, logic, and the philosophy of science.

Its main ambitions are to develop a theoretical framework that will encourage and enable interaction between disciplines, and to integrate the Humanities and Social Sciences around their main contributions to public life, using informed debate, lucid decision-making, and action based on reflection.

- Argumentation models and studies
- Communication, language and techniques of argumentation
- Reception of arguments, persuasion and the impact of power
- Diachronic transformations of argumentative practices

LAR is developed in partnership with the Maison Européenne des Sciences de l'Homme et de la Société (MESHS) at Nord - Pas de Calais and the UMR-STL: 8163 (CNRS).

Proposals should include:

- A short synopsis of the work, or the introduction chapter
- The proposed Table of Contents
- The CV of the lead author(s)
- If available: one sample chapter

We aim to make a first decision within 1 month of submission. In case of a positive first decision, the work will be provisionally contracted—the final decision about publication will depend upon the result of an anonymous peer review of the complete manuscript.

The complete work is usually peer-reviewed within 3 months of submission.

LAR discourages the submission of manuscripts containing reprints of previously published material, and/or manuscripts that are less than 150 pages / 85,000 words.

For inquiries and proposal submissions, authors may contact the editor-in-chief, Shahid Rahman at: shahid.rahman@univ-lille3.fr, or the managing editor, Juan Redmond, at: juan.redmond@uv.cl

More information about this series at http://www.springer.com/series/11547

Teresa Lopez-Soto
Editor

# Dialog Systems

## A Perspective from Language, Logic and Computation

Springer

*Editor*
Teresa Lopez-Soto
Speech and Phonetic Sciences Lab
University of Seville
Seville, Spain

ISSN 2214-9120 ISSN 2214-9139 (electronic)
Logic, Argumentation & Reasoning
ISBN 978-3-030-61437-9 ISBN 978-3-030-61438-6 (eBook)
https://doi.org/10.1007/978-3-030-61438-6



This Springer imprint is published by the registered company Springer Nature Switzerland AG
The registered company address is: Gewerbestrasse 11, 6330 Cham, Switzerland

# Contents

# Chapter 1
# Introduction

**Teresa Lopez-Soto**

**Abstract** This volume represents a multidisciplinary effort in the study of dialog considering multiple research fields, including linguistics, logic and computation. The incorporation of one more monograph into the series that directly tackles language use demonstrates an increasing interest on the disciplinary approach to language. All in all, language and mind, rational thinking and spontaneous conversations are all part of the same highly sophisticated system that characterizes human beings. This monograph is an invitation to consider new methods from various disciplines that can help develop progress in understanding logic, argumentation and reasoning.

**Keywords** Linguistics · Logic · Philosophy of Language · Automatic Dialog Systems · Computer-Mediated Communication · Pragmatics · Cognitive Linguistics

This monograph is divided into 3 parts, namely: Part I *Some Preliminaries on Dialog from the Perspective of Logic and Cognitive Linguistics;* Part II *Dialogical Approaches: Contextualism, Enrichment and Abduction Revisited*; and Part III *Dialog in Real Life: The Internet, Multimodal Communication and Automatic Dialog Systems*.

**Part I Some Preliminaries on Dialog from the Perspective of Logic and Cognitive Linguistics** deals with issues in dialog from the crossover between Logic and Cognitive Linguistics. Chapters in this part offer a review of the concept of dialog arguing that all human communication is dialogical in nature. Dialog here is defined as a linguistic-cognitive mechanism that is the basis of our thinking and supports the unilateralist conception that is established between logical affirmation and negation. This part begins with Chap. 2 – *Inner Dialogues: Typology, Uses and Functions* – with attention to "monologism" and "dialogism" that helps us understand the origins of dialog itself. Monologic vs. dialogic features of human dialog are

T. Lopez-Soto (✉)
Speech and Phonetic Sciences Lab, University of Seville, Seville, Spain
e-mail: teresals@us.es



T. Lopez-Soto (ed.), *Dialog Systems*, Logic, Argumentation & Reasoning 22,
https://doi.org/10.1007/978-3-030-61438-6_1

also discussed in Chap. 3 – *The Cognitive Construction of Dialog: Language and* Mind – but from a cognitive perspective that presupposes all human communication is dialogic in nature. Both chapters entail a description of (inner) dialogs being some sort of linguistic-cognitive mechanisms that involve thought and discourse planning processes, but Chap. 3 specifically refers to dialog being a dynamic system physiologically wired within the memory systems of the brain which can be constantly enriched and reshaped according to the individual's life experiences. Chapter 3 always refers to dialog as verbal communication (the written text being just a direct transfer from the spoken text) while Chap. 2, interesting enough, posits that the mental dialogs that we recreate in our minds have in common with other verbal discursive structures the same kinds of benefits and are, therefore, based on the same causes. If we are to accept a more cognitive/neurological description of these benefits, dialogs ultimately serve to promote the individual's integration into their social group while gaining more information of the outer world through perception and along our lifespan. This chapter reminds us of the impact of dialog on the life experiences of the individual from its physiological connection with the memory systems in the brain, and also in its impact on social skills. The latter is one of the most current and interesting topics in Neuropsychology.

Inner dialogs also involve, through argumentation, a reflective exercise that aims to convince the (future) listener. In this sense, there is a coincidence in the assumption made from Narrative Theory and Cognitive Linguistic model of Current Discourse Space and the "Construal Hypothesis" that assumes all communication being dialogic in nature even when apparently monologic (as could be the case of inner dialogs). Furthermore, construals represent ongoing cognitive definition through dialog that may be transferred to permanent memory store even in monologic mode, which is defined as "initiating" dialogic. That is to say, monologism for recent models in Cognitive Linguistics is merely the preliminary stage of dialogism where the initiator triggers the global process of communication, but which can be overturned (thus, the initiator would become the recipient) at any time. In light of the Narrative Theory, initiation is seen as "responsibility", with a distinction between "announcer" and "annunciator" meaning that the latter is responsible for what has been said.

Chapter 4 – *In Defense of Unilateralism* – complements the first 2 chapters by reviewing the notion of meaning from the approach of inferentialism. The author defends the idea of meaning being determined by its use and this can be inferred from the meaning of surrounding elements. The idea is also assumed by Psycholinguistics in the sense that meaning is mentally constructed as a complex network of binomial items (phonological and semantic in nature) that are integrated within higher nodes (categories) which are connected in terms of their common attributes. Still, from the perspective of logic, the author defends the idea of bilateralism from two applications: first, an interpretation of logical constants whose premises are assertions/denials, and conclusions are denials/assertions. The chapter proceeds with a discussion of truth-value gaps and gluts to distinguish between denying a sentence and asserting its negation.

Dummett's interpretation of unilateralism implies assertion being first, denial being second. Therefore, answering a propositional question negatively implies the possibility of doing so but positively. Rumfitt, on the other hand, understands assertion/denial as having a bilateral relationship still some issues are left for discussion. All speech acts cannot be said to remain entirely independent, considering that Rumfitt himself also argues that certain principles coordinate assertion and denial. Questions to be answered here would be to what extent can bilateralism maintain the contradiction of assertion/denial being independent. Besides, if coordination principles hold dependent, what relationship can they establish with independent speech acts?

**Part II Dialogical Approaches: Contextualism, Enrichment and Abduction Revisited**, further deals with the theory of discourse but more from the perspective of the Philosophy of Language and Logic. In its Part II, the authors review contextualism, enrichment, and the problem of abduction, from a dialogical approach. The topics covered are the following: meaning and knowledge from dialog; CTT and Immanent Reasoning for the enrichment and composition of meaning; Mirativity; Dynamic Formalism; and Parallel Reasoning in Jurisprudence. In Chap. 9 – *Parallel Reasoning by "ratio legis" in Contemporary Jurisprudence. Elements for a Dialogical Approach* – the authors provide further evidence of a quite innovative trend in legal reasoning that uses analogy, more specifically inferences by parallel reasoning, in the area of Spanish Civil Law. Interesting enough, the use of parallel reasoning in texts have been disseminated especially by researchers in Artificial Intelligence that seek to develop suitable software-support in the area (automatic analysis of case studies, for example, in comparative jurisprudence for sentence parsing). More is said on jurisprudence in Chap. 5 – *Proverbs as Reasons under the Talking-Tree: the Dialogical Articulation of Proverbs within the Baule Tradition* – which revisits the creation of meaning (and reality) through verbal argumentation. The *Talking-Tree* is a designated location in African communities around which members of the community gather to pass law. This space for interactive communication is seen as a democratic and peaceful forum where conflicts are resolved through dialog. Conflict management shows several patterns of argumentation justified by a collection of traditional proverbs that are orally passed from generation to generation. This approach to the interpretation of meaning finds similarities in Chap. 3, which states that meaning serves the final purpose of the individual's social integration within the community. Also, the cognitive approach to dialog sees oral interaction as a two-directional cognitive activity: semantic memory is both accessed to and reshaped according to the (possibly) new meaning that can be created during oral interaction. The correlation with argumentation via proverbs in the Talking-Tree tradition seems evident. Citing the authors, "meaning and knowledge are constituted during dialogical interaction", also "this research should set the basis for a larger epistemological research on the structure of argumentation patterns born and developed in Africa, where meaning and knowledge are constituted during dialogical interaction". This also suggests a wide range of very interesting questions about the understanding of reasoning within our own Western philosophical tradition. Currently, the logics cultivated by traditions such as the

Muslim or African ones are being studied and rescued. It is a subject of great cultural interest, and —in particular— to the Philosophy of Logic.

Chapter 7 – *How Surprising! Mirativity, Evidentiality and Abductive Inference* – revisits complex mirativity and compares it with inferred evidentials and deferred realizations. Mirativity was initially proposed by Scott Delancey as a grammatical category or a linguistic strategy that encodes the speaker's surprise. Contrastive studies give evidence of different mirativity strategies but share the assumption that mirativity is originated in something that has been seen, heard or inferred. The authors analyze this grammatical category in relation with evidentiality and abduction and provide further evidence of mirativity to explain how speakers express commitment (the "annunciator" in Chap. 2) or responsibility of the words being said.

Chapter 8 – *Two Convergences to Dynamic Formalism: Bakhtin's Dialogism and Brouwer's Creating Subject* – argues around recent research of the dialogical framework incorporating materiality in dialog through Bakhtin's criticism of literary formalism. The authors propose a dialogical reading of Kripke's schema, traditionally granted as not constructive, towards a new understanding of its constructive content. Chapter 6 – *What the Weatherman Said: Enrichment, CTT and the Dialogical Approach to Moderate Contextualism* – deals with *Immanent Reasoning,* Martin-Löf's dialogical approach to the constructive Type Theory (CTT) as a form to distinguish Recanati's process of *free enrichment* and *saturation.* The author tackles the issue of pragmatic modulation, where "the speaker-receiver interaction is integrated into the notion of enrichment" and refers to anaphora and time/location grammatical categories as referential elements in the model.

Finally, **Part III Dialog in Real Life: The Internet, Multimodal Communication and Automatic Dialog Systems**, is more specific: it discusses the problem of discursive materiality, the nature of representations and the impact of multimodal communication in the interaction of tourism users; it analyses the potential and challenges in the use of conversational interfaces (computer programs) for the specific area of mental health; and, most interestingly, this part offers a novel approach to dialog that takes into account its non-verbal aspects, not only the paralinguistic characteristics (gestures, body language, gaze), but also the external elements such as signals, location, geographical distribution and behavioral social norms.

This Part III begins with a very novel approach to dialog in which all multiple variables are taken into consideration: non-verbal here involves not only paralinguistic features (gestures, body language, gaze) but external elements to both speaker and listener (signals, location, geographical distribution and norms/rules of societal conduct). In Chap. 10 – *Communication in Tourism: Information Technologies, the Human User, Visual Culture and the location* – the authors take tourism as a general setting (the location variable) and, using a pragmatic approach, analyze multiple discursive practices both at the local, national and international levels within an integrative model of dialog and communication. A whole set of elements are analyzed from turn-takings, pictures/images of cultural artefacts, street signs, etc. together with non-verbal linguistic communication artefacts. The result is an array of strategies of intercultural communication that compel complex communicative competence: linguistic (lexical, syntactic), discursive, sociocultural and pragmatic. Sensory interaction with the touristic resort evokes retrieval of mental imagery and emotional load that allows for a complex meaning construction. Location is a very powerful component in the creation of meaning and, without making implicit use of the term, they also get inspiration from Cognitive Linguistics in order to build their own proposal. The chapter is a good introduction for readers interested in Ecolinguistics. Chapter 11 – *Conversational Agents for Mental Health and Wellbeing* – and Chap. 12 – *Internet Conversations: the New Challenges of Digital Dialogue* – review some of the most updated trends in both Automatic Dialog Systems (with special attention to applications on health management) and Computer-Mediated Communication (with special attention to dialog in social networks). They give way to a new challenge in dialog studies that have to do with Engineering and Corpus Linguistics, respectively.

Overall, this monograph aims to demonstrate that the problem of dialog is vastly rich, it involves many aspects of our rationality (mental, cognitive, social, behavioral, logical, etc.) through which we deal with the world. Indeed, the authors in the volume address rich issues of contemporary, multidisciplinary and philosophical nature. The focus is, therefore, in line with a broad perspective on the problem of dialog.

# Chapter 2
# Inner Dialogues: Typology, Uses and Functions

**Jesús Portillo-Fernández**

**Abstract** In this paper we analyse "inner dialogues" as linguistic-cognitive mechanisms involved in thought and discourse planning processes: decision making, resolution of moral dilemmas, conversational positioning, prospective and retrospective emulation of discourse, refutation of an idea by emulating a tribunal, self-convincing and self-deception, prediction of future contexts through discourse, etc. Starting from the review of discursive structures (monologues, dialogues, polyphonic discourses and their respective subtypes), we will analyse the facets of speaker, the mental staging, monological and dialogical perspectives and types of intervention in these, with the aim of defining the "inner dialogue" concept. Finally, we will propose a theoretical approach to the most frequent uses and main benefits of the use of inner dialogues.

**Keywords** Inner dialogues · Mental emulation of discourse · Discursive polyphony · Thought planning

## 2.1 Inner Dialogues and Truth Value

A theoretical approach to the "inner dialogue" concept can be understood as a linguistic-cognitive mechanism involved in thought and discourse planning processes. Interested in the human capacity to imagine conversations, we analyse under what circumstances we do it, focusing our attention on the truth value that we grant it (veracity), benefits that it gives us (or we think it gives us) and the purpose that it pursues. We present a study about the inner experience of the conversation as an exercise of introspection to analyse "backstage" and to understand how we create mental/fictional stages capable of recreating discursive alternatives.

J. Portillo-Fernández (✉)
Universidad de Sevilla, Sevilla, ESPAÑA
e-mail: jeporfer@us.es

 
T. Lopez-Soto (ed.), *Dialog Systems*, Logic, Argumentation & Reasoning 22,
https://doi.org/10.1007/978-3-030-61438-6_2

First, we will analyse in detail the concepts of "dialogue", "monologue" and "discursive polyphony" and their subtypes to understand what these discursive structures consist of and how they work. We focus our attention on the degree of intervention of the narrator, the origin and the function of each subtype, the degree of transformation of words by the narrator, the vehicle of expression used (voice or thought), the degree of freedom and emancipation of the psychic intimacy of the character, syntactic characteristics of each structure and the use of theatrical techniques to carry them out. Starting from this review, we will remember functions of the two facets of speakers (announcer, the person who enunciates or emits the act of speech; and annunciator, the person who takes responsibility for what has been said, referred speech or assertion) and we will approach the distinction between monologism and dialogism to understand the nature of each type and subtype of discursive structures (according to the number of announcers and annunciators).

We will review various polyphonic constructions and we will stop at the analysis of emulation and simulation processes to understand what it is we do when we generate inner dialogues in our minds. The second parameter must be the types of situations we imagine in dialogue form, if there is a tendency to mental recreation of (conversational) situations based on inner dialogues and where the need to create inner dialogues arises. We will return to the distinction between monologism and dialogism to study the double nature of inner dialogues and we will analyse the two forms of intervention that the author has of inner dialogues in relationship with them.

We should wonder about the main benefits of inner dialogues in everyday life and here we analyse their most frequent uses: resolution of moral dilemmas (through observation or participation), re-evaluation of a position or opinion by means of the generation of a (mental) tribunal, strengthening an idea through refutation before making it public, exercises of empathy and understanding of the other, finding solace or recreation of pending conversations through a retrospective use, verification of the degree in which a conversation is feasible or avoidance of improvisation in them through a prospective use and self-convincing (for benefits or for self-deception).

## 2.2 Theoretical Framework – Discursive Constructions: Monologues, Dialogues and Discursive Polyphony

To begin with, we clarify the meaning of "dialogue" concept, distinguishing it from terms such as "monologue" or "polyphonic structure" (see Fig. 2.1). A dialogue (from Latin *dialŏgus* and from Greek *διάλογος*) is a conversation between two or more people who alternatively manifest their ideas or affections. It is a communication or discussion in which information about one or more topics is exchanged. A dialogue is an external utterance between at least two people that requires oral, signed or written interaction. To be able to speak about dialogue two interlocutors are necessary, a sender and a receiver who exchange their roles in the conversation in turn. Valles Calatrava (2002, p. 296) defines the dialogue as the canonical form of

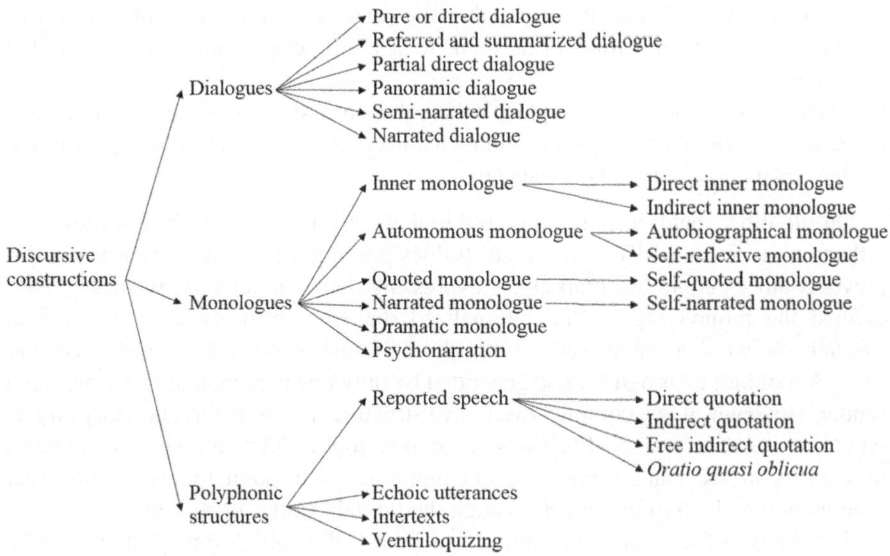


**Fig. 2.1** Discursive constructions

verbal interaction of the enunciative and communicative act between speaker and listener (I-You) with permanently reviewable roles. It is a strategy opposed to narration, description and monologue.

According to its origin and function, several types of dialogues can be differentiated: (1) dialogues linked to the dialectical problem of the search for truth (for example, platonic dialogues); (2) heuristic dialogues, in which the interlocutors provide arguments susceptible to conclusion. This kind of dialogue has as its main objective the discovery, the inquiry; and (3) eristic dialogues, in which objective is to defeat the adversary, not to complement their arguments. Bobes Naves (1992, 1993) presented in her works a classification of the dialogues according to the intervention of the narrator in them:

- Pure or direct dialogue (also called abruptive dialogue): it consists of the exact reproduction of words and voices of the actors, where the narrator disappears. Pure dialogues do not use tags or interpolations from the narrator.
- Referred and summarized dialogue: it is a summary relating to a dialogue scene that the narrator makes, narrating gestures and movements of the characters.
- Partial direct dialogue: it is the direct intervention of the characters, with their own voice, used to enunciate their own words, after having been previously reproduced by the narrator in the referred and summarized dialogue.
- Panoramic dialogue: it is the summary, offered by the narrator, of numerous and possible identical scenic dialogues. It offers a panorama where the temporal frequency is iterative (repetitive).

- Semi-narrated dialogue: it occurs when the narrator assumes the words of two or more characters and transforms them to a minor degree than in the narrated dialogue.
- Narrated dialogue: it takes place when the narrators completely assume and transforms the words of two or more characters to the maximum degree through their own enunciation and perspective.

On the other hand, a monologue (etymologically μονολόγος, from Greek) is a reflection made internally or out loud. It does not require an explicit answer and it prevents other people from talking or expressing their opinions. Benveniste (1966) defined the monologue as "an internalized dialogue, formulated in an internal language between a sender self – often the only one who speaks – and a receiver self". A monologue is a discourse generated by only one person, that is, it only has a sender. However, it is a complex discursive structure due to its directionality and its typology. According to the directions of the monologue and their respective vehicles of expression we can differentiate (1) monologues through the voice (external monologue) and (2) monologues through the thought (inner monologue).

The theory of the narrative, authors such as Cohn (1978) and Beltrán (1992), following this line, propose a classification of the monologues regarding the greater or lesser degree of autonomy or dependence of the monologue in relation to the narrator.

- Inner monologue: inner monologue concept, "flow of consciousness" in the Anglo-Saxon tradition, is the modality of direct discourse and not said, without interlocutor and without narrative guardianship in which their inner thoughts are reproduced in an analogical way and with basic syntax. Its objective is to mimic the subconscious thought process.
  - Direct inner monologue: it is a subtype of the inner monologue in which the narrator does not appear, and the mental process of the character is directly reproduced. Cohn (1978) called it "autonomous monologue" and Genette (1991) "immediate discourse". This type of monologue is always formulated in the first person.
  - Indirect inner monologue: it is the other subtype of inner monologue, expressed in the third person through an omniscient and heterodiegetic narrator. It is the midpoint between the cited monologue (formula with greater autonomy) and psychonarration (formula with greater dependence).
- Autonomous monologue: it is the expression with the greatest degree of freedom and emancipation of the psychic intimacy of the character (it is always formulated in the first person), its flow of consciousness, without depending on any frame or narrative guardianship.

  - Autobiographical (autonomous) monologue: it is a subtype of autonomous monologue in which the character is the narrator and relates its own thoughts in an orderly manner and in the first person. It generates, textually, the illusion of the existence of an interlocutor although not explicitly.
  - Self-reflexive (autonomous) monologue: it is a variant of the autonomous monologue proposed by Beltrán (1992) in which the character's thinking is directly reproduced but it uses the second person in a formal way to favour, through ungrammaticality and discursive anomalies, alogicity.

- Quoted monologue: in this type of monologues the narrator directly reproduces the flow of consciousness of the character as a soliloquy. Unlike the narrated monologue and the psychonarration, the quoted monologue does not use the third person.

  - Self-quoted monologue: it is a monologue subtype in which the narrator-character directly reproduces its own thinking through the formal use of the first person and, normally, marking or quoting the text itself.

- Narrated monologue: also called free indirect discourse, it is the intermediate step between quoted monologue and psychonarration. The thoughts of the character are exposed in a relatively faithful way by a heterodiegetic and omniscient narrator, maintaining numerous features of the actor's speech, although with certain transformations.

  - Self-narrated monologue: it is a variant of narrated monologue in which the perspective of the narrator self (present) and the character self (past) converge. It reproduces the thought indirectly and in the first person.

- Dramatic monologue: it really is a variant of dialogue in which only the voice of one of the characters is reproduced and uses blank lines or dotted lines to represent the voice of the speaker without expressing speech.
- Psychonarration: it is the most indirect technique of reproduction of thought (flow of consciousness) in which an omniscient narrator relates the psychic life of the characters with its voice and discursive features.

Valles (2002, p. 442) states that monologue is a type of discourse in which a character speaks (soliloquy) or thinks (inner monologue) for itself, expressing its most intimate thoughts and feelings with authenticity and disinhibition. In addition to the types of monologues described by Narrative theory, there is a theatrical technique called "comical monologue" or "stand-up comedy" in which the interpreter exposes a situation or a topic on which it makes observations from a comical point of view (dubitative repetitions, decontextualization, sudden interruptions, irony, absurd communication and contexts, free indirect style, inclusion of thoughts of the character in the story of the narrator, etc.).

We carefully review the types of dialogues and monologues described previously to analyse the relationship between them and to be able to understand the "monologism" and "dialogism" concepts. Both terms classify utterances depending on the number of perspectives and the control the author has over the voices in the discourse (Bajtín 1929).

- Monologism refers to a single vision of the world, a discourse in which the use of different voices is subordinated to the controlling purpose of the author of the story.
- Instead, dialogism does not intend characters to be simple objects in the author's universe, but rather subjects of their own significant world; that is, there is a free and independent contrast of words and conceptions of the characters not subordinated to the author of the story.

It is important to understand the difference between both concepts because one and the other, monologues and dialogues, can create monologisms and dialogisms. A speaker can basically play two facets (Fuentes 2004, p. 129):

- Announcer: the person who enunciates or emits the act of speech (complement of the discursive enunciation and reformulation, complement of enunciation and modality).
- Annunciator: the person who takes responsibility for what has been said, referred speech or assertion.

When we distinguish monologism from dialogism, we consider the number of annunciators involved in the discourse, that is, the number of people who assume responsibility for what has been said, regardless the number of announcers. However, in principle, when we differentiate monologue and dialogue, we consider the number of announcers involved in the locutionary act. For this reason, we will review the polyphonic structures and their types, with the purpose of defining the object of our investigation: the "inner dialogues". Bajtín (1989) takes up the musical term "polyphony" (from Greek πολυφωνία) related to the harmonic composition of a voice from many, to explain a social and dialogical linguistic self. He establishes the concept of polyphony to designate the presence of numerous voices in the fictional text, intimately connected with its plurilingualism or social dimension and, especially, with dialogization. The author defines it as a plural situation where different voices and points of view are not vehicles of truth, nor are subordinated to a conceptually dominant idea potentially embodied in the voice of the material author of the message. He understands it as the dialogical configuration of the relations of multiple voices in the same discourse in which each voice involved does it with independence (a principle respected by the announcer), being the notion of absolute truth logically impossible.

Bajtín (1929, 16–17) explains it as the "plurality of independent and unmistakable voices and consciences, the authentic polyphony of autonomous voices", as a singularity due to the integration of different discourse, languages and social voices. From the studies by Bajtín, as we analysed in detail in Portillo-Fernández (2012, 2018), multiple studies on discursive polyphony have taken place, such as those by Benveniste (1966, 1974), Goffman (1974), Authier-Revuz (1982), Ducrot (1984, 1986), Sperber and Wilson (1986), Reyes (1984, 1987), Roulet (1987), Clark and Gerrig (1990), Nølke (1994), Tordesillas (1998), Günthner (1999), Donaire (2000,

2008), Espuny (2008) or Bango and Prieto (2008), among others, that shaped the traditional distinction between reported speech (direct quotation, indirect quotation, free indirect quotation and *oratio quasi oblicua*), echoic utterances, intertexts and ventriloquizing.

As we have previously seen, the discursive constructions (monological, dialogical or polyphonic) can be classified from the level in which they are made (voice-external or thought-internal). Up to now we have focused our attention on analysing the external discursive constructions (the utterances). Nevertheless, the inner discursive constructions (mental), constitute an interesting field of study of discursive planning, of decision making and even of the modification of thought or opinion.

## 2.3 Understanding "Inner Dialogue" Concept

In this section, we will attempt to develop a definition of "inner dialogue" by following the structure portrayed in Fig. 2.2. Among the many capacities of the human mind (to reason, calculate, remember, etc.) we will focus our attention on the ability to emulate. From Latin *aemulāre*, to emulate is to imitate the actions of others trying to match them and even exceed them. The emulation does not imply falsification or pretence, that is, it tries to make a replica. A similar term to emulation, sometimes confused with this, is simulation. To simulate (from Latin *simulāre*) is to represent something, faking or imitating what is not.

We often emulate dialogues in our mind (inner dialogues) in which we imagine and plan conversations. Inner dialogues constitute an emulation mental exercise based on the knowledge, the experience, the emotions and the will (expectations) of the person who generates them. The purpose of the person who imagines them is to emulate the conversation as it would really happen, however, the inner dialogues simulate conversations adapted to the author's vital coordinates (knowledge, experience, emotions and expectations). Inner dialogues are not only based on

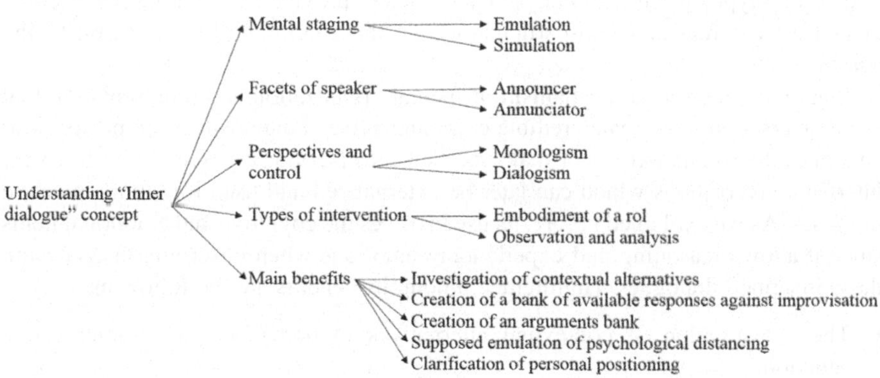


**Fig. 2.2** Understanding "inner dialogue" concept

imagination or fantasy (which they also are, as we will explain later), but on the theoretical-practical heritage, the desires and the fears of who generates them. It is a versatile linguistic-cognitive mechanism, capable of carrying out multiple functions: making explicit latent information, making reasoning based on emulation of dialogues, planning a conversation and anticipating possible discursive alternatives, etc.

One of the most interesting aspects of inner dialogues is their double nature: dialogism (as purpose) and monologism (in reality). When we create inner dialogues in our minds, we intend to generate dialogic discourses in which each voice is independent. However, it is inevitable that these voices participate in expectations, emotions, experiences and knowledge of who imagines them.

Nevertheless, inner dialogues have a great potential for reasoning since they try to emulate conversations by means of voices that represent different roles with the aim of positioning, making a decision, clarifying doubts, trying to predict events, etc. They are based on the staging of the imagined communicative situation, from which a discursive polyphony with different perspectives (voices/roles) is generated. The main difference between these and the traditional types of polyphonies is that the inner dialogues do not have phonation (they do not need to be pronounced, since they take place in the mind) although the voices of the conversation make quotes, use echoic utterances or ventriloquize.

We can differentiate two types of inner dialogues according to the intervention of the person (author) who generates them:

- Inner dialogues in which the author is one of the interlocutors of the conversation. In this case the author embodies one of the roles of dialogue and directly interacts with the rest of the speakers.
- Inner dialogues in which the author is not one of the interlocutors of the conversation but stays on the sidelines observing and analysing the imagined conversation to draw conclusions from a (theoretically) more objective point of view.

The first type tries to emulate conversations in which the author intervenes with the intention of anticipating the words of its interlocutors and be prepared to answer. The second type, as we will analyse later, aims to provide an impartial perspective, or at least external and non-participatory, of the communicative situation to the author.

Inner dialogues are a mechanism of mental organization and representation that use conversation to recreate credible communicative situations (for the person who generates them) and extract or make explicit information. It is the ability to create internal conversations which can later be externalized and used for communicative purposes. As we explained before, its use involves the cognitive and emotional fields since it allows reasoning and experiencing emotions when observing or analysing these imagined dialogues. Highlighted among its benefits are the following:

- The investigation of contextual alternatives to understand a communicative situation.
- The creation of a bank of available responses against improvisation.

- The creation of an arguments bank to convince the interlocutor or himself (persuasion/self-persuasion).
- The supposed emulation of psychological distancing to get a more objective perspective.
- The clarification of personal positioning in a specific situation.

Inner dialogues, unlike the flow of consciousness described by inner monologues (direct discourse, without interlocutor, without narrative guardianship, alogical reproduction and basic syntax), use the dialogical structure to mentally create a communicative situation (that substitutes or complements the flow of consciousness) with the intention of taking distance and being a participant or spectator of the scene. The polyvalence of inner dialogues is also observed in the ability to integrate echoic utterances in their construction, to make direct, indirect quotes and any types of reported speech, to establish implicit and explicit intertextual relationships, and even to mentally use ventriloquizing. Bellow, we will analyse some of its most frequent uses.

## 2.4 Inner Dialogues – Analysis of the Most Frequent Uses

Considering that it is impossible to describe all uses of inner dialogues, we will analyse some frequent ones, as a propaedeutic study that will serve as a basis for future research. The creation or recreation of polyphonic communicative situations capable of staging the author's thought makes imagining the future possible, modifies memories, predicts events, puts oneself in the place of another (empathy), raises a moral dilemma discursively, etc. Occasionally, the author of the inner dialogue participates as one of the interlocutors of the mentally recreated conversation and, other times, they only act as spectators extracting information from the possible discursive variants, information that could later be used in real conversations (see Fig. 2.3).

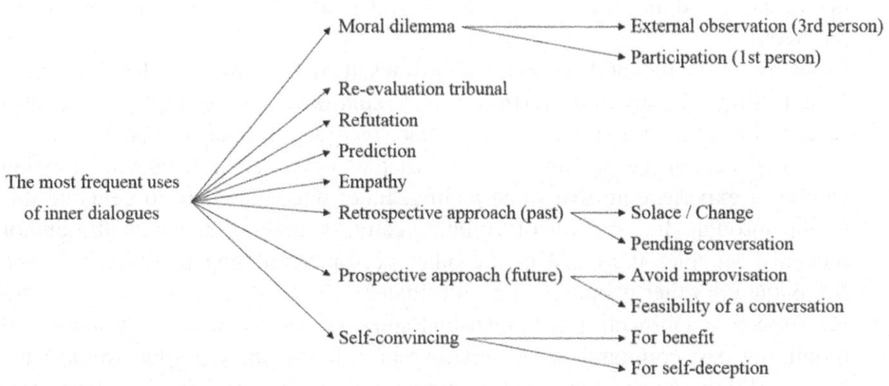


**Fig. 2.3** The most frequent uses of inner dialogues

- Moral dilemma: a dilemma is an argument formed by two opposing propositions disjunctively in such a way that, denied or granted either, a certain conclusion is demonstrated. A moral dilemma occurs in situations in which a person is forced to choose between two options, usually contrary or incompatible. Inner dialogues allow to stage moral dilemmas through two simple ways: (1) through observation of the conversation between two people who represent the options of the dilemma, or (2) through mental participation in a conversation with another person who has the second option raised by the dilemma. The analysis of the moral dilemma can allow extraction of conclusions, the prediction of consequences of each of the positions and the consequent positioning. Its function is to decide between exclusionary options.
- Re-evaluation tribunal: the emulation of a tribunal capable of evaluating a situation or behaviour, constitutes a very useful polyphonic resource to remember opinions already heard, to imagine others and to contrast them with the point of view of the author's inner dialogue. The purpose of the tribunal is to collect information and different opinions, stored or generated by the author about a behaviour or situation, to distance themselves from their own opinion and re-evaluate their position.
- Refutation: refutation, as a scientific term, is the criterion of truth that seeks to reinforce a theory trying to deny it; that is, the author of the theory becomes the main enemy of it, with the aim of finding its weak points, before making it public. The more times the author tries to deny it without success, the stronger its theory will be. Inner dialogues allow generating a list of interlocutors who present objections to an idea in order to correct possible failures. We usually use refutation to verify the correctness and authenticity of our ideas or arguments before presenting them to others.
- Prediction: it consists of the announcement by revelation, founded knowledge, intuition or conjecture, that something must happen. Inner dialogues, through the discursive staging of a given situation, can be used to expose, as premises, the known information about a situation and draw conclusions by means of inductive, deductive or abductive reasoning. Its function is to anticipate events before they occur, using a dialogical structure as an explanatory engine of the premises of prediction.
- Empathy: it is the ability to identify oneself with someone else and share their feelings. Its etymology (from Greek ἐμπάθεια / πάθος) tells us about a relationship of trust and the ability to share passions. Empathy is an exercise of transcendence, the emulation of feeling what the other person feels without being certain of experiencing that same feeling. Inner dialogues help to generate this fiction through the creation of communicative situations in which the author mentally occupies the place of the other person, emulating the responses and behaviours of other people's vital coordinates.
- Retrospective approach (past): inner dialogues are capable of reconstructing and modifying past communicative situations in order to find out what would have happened if there had been different interactions among speakers. This retrospective modification allows us to conform and to find solace through the creation of

credible discursive versions to give the author a chance to change what happened in its memory. Another habitual use of inner dialogues with retrospective approach is to generate conversations that never took place (because the interlocutor has died, because we have no relationship with them, etc.) with the intention of living, in some way, that pending experience.

- Prospective approach (future): likewise, and as we have already described before, inner dialogues are capable of imagining future contexts caused by conversations. Its main functions are to avoid improvisation in an important conversation (which is going to take place) and to prepare responses for possible discursive alternatives. They can also be used to study how feasible a conversation is (which is not predicted in principle) and to decide if it is profitable or advisable to realise.

Finally, we would like to focus our attention on the capacity of self-convincing or self-persuasion of inner dialogues. Persuasion (from Latin *persuasio, −ōnis*) is the exercise of inducing, moving or forcing someone with reasons to believe or to do something. Self-persuasion implies offering arguments to oneself and becoming convinced, even changing one's mind. Aristóteles (2005), in the fourth century B.C. in his work *Rhetoric*, already distinguished between arguments linked to *ethos* (authority, credibility and honesty of the speaker), to *pathos* (emotions and feelings) and to *logos* (logical and rational arguments). He conceived rhetoric as a branch of dialectics which does not require any particular knowledge of science and could be used by any intelligent person, as "the ability to see all possible ways to persuade people in any matter" (Rhetoric I, 1. 1355 b26), including ourselves. The classic distinction between being convinced (having a firm position towards an idea or opinion which is born from within) and being persuaded (being externally induced, moved or forced to believe or do something; a psychological process linked to communication). This distinction presents the ability of inner dialogues to self-convince as a tool capable of generating fictitious speakers who make us change our mind, as if they were real external persuasive sources.

Despite not having the opportunity, at this moment, to delve into the prolific research on argumentation and persuasion made since the mid-twentieth century to the present to be very extensive [Cf. Ducrot (1983, 1986), Van Eemeren and Grootendorst (1984), Perelman and Olbrechts-Tyteca (1989), Cialdini (1990), Plantin (1990, 1998), Weston (1993), Anscombre and Ducrot (1994), Eggs (1994), Lo Cascio (1998), Vega Reñón (2003), Fuentes and Alcaide (2005, 2007), Marafioti (2005), Walton (2006), Toulmin (2007), Marafioti and Santibáñez (2010), Vega Reñón and Olmos (2011), Guastini and Álvarez (2014) and Claramonte (2016), among many other reference works], it is pertinent to analyse the function of inner dialogues in terms of self-convincing.

Firstly, when we talk about self-convincing, we are referring to the mental exercise of giving us arguments to believe, think or do something that we originally did not believe, think or plan to do. In other words, self-convincing is an inner discursive process that seeks to change the will, opinion or beliefs of the person by argumentation. It is a reflective exercise in which the argumentator and the person whom one wants to convince coincide. Inner dialogues, as we explained before, can mentally generate communicative situations in which self-convincing shaped as soliloquy (monologue) is reinforced by interlocutors who argue in favour of the idea which they intend to adhere. Self-convincing is a complex mental mechanism in which the person is not always able to differentiate self-persuasion to real benefit or to self-deception. Research studies such as those by Goleman (2004), Trivers (2013) o Mele (2016) deal in depth with self-deception from psychological and philosophical perspectives, one of the facets of self-convincing based, sometimes, on the discursive mental polyphony staged by inner dialogues.

Self-deception, when it comes to using inner dialogues, goes through the confusion between the voices generated by the person (announcers) and the real independence of these affirming or denying a certain position (annunciators). That is to say, when instead of gathering heard and real voices (announcers and annunciators) in our mind, we mentally use the voice of another person (announcer) to listen to our own ideas (annunciator), we falsify the conversation by using the voices of others as a vehicle to express ourselves. It is a kind of mental ventriloquizing by means of which we create false interlocutors, with their respective voices and physical aspect that actually embody our own perspective. This type of inner dialogues generates a false discursive polyphony in which there are several voices but only one annunciator responsible for everything that is said.

## 2.5 Conclusions

The main purpose of this research was to understand the functioning of conversations that we imagine in our minds, their causes, benefits they bring us, characteristics they have in common with the rest of spoken discursive structures, their idiosyncrasies and their most frequent uses. We have called this type of conversations "inner dialogues" and we have analysed them from an exhaustive review of types of monologues, dialogues and polyphonic structures of discourse.

Inner dialogues constitute a versatile linguistic-cognitive mechanism capable of carrying out multiple functions, a mental emulation exercise based on the knowledge, the experience, the emotions and the will (expectations) of the person who generates them. They are based on imagination, fantasy, theoretical-practical heritage, the desires and the fears of who generates them. Inner dialogues have a double nature: dialogism (as purpose, since we intend to generate dialogic discourses in which each voice is independent) and monologism (in reality, since it is inevitable that these voices participate in expectations, emotions, experiences and knowledge of who imagines them).

Inner dialogues have a great potential for reasoning since they try to emulate conversations by means of voices that represent different roles, they are based on the staging and generate a discursive polyphony with different perspectives (voices/roles). Despite not having phonation (since they take place in the mind), we can differentiate two types of inner dialogues according to the intervention of the person (author) who generates them: (1) inner dialogues in which the author embodies one of the roles of dialogue and interacts directly with the rest of speakers and (2) inner dialogues in which the author stays on the sidelines observing and analysing the imagined conversation to draw conclusions from a (theoretically) more objective point of view.

They represent a mechanism of mental organization and representation whose use involves cognitive and emotional fields. We highlight, among its main benefits, the clarification of personal positioning in a specific situation, the supposed emulation of psychological distancing to get a more objective perspective, the creation of an argument bank to convince the interlocutor or oneself (persuasion/self-persuasion), the creation of a bank of available responses against improvisation and the investigation of contextual alternatives to understand a communicative situation.

Among its most frequent uses we highlight the following: (1) the discursive approach of a moral dilemma through observation or mental participation in a conversation; (2) the emulation of a tribunal capable of evaluating a situation or behaviour in order to re-evaluate its positioning; (3) the generation of a list of interlocutors who present objections to an idea in order to correct possible mistakes (refutation); (4) anticipation through the use of a dialogical structure as an explanatory engine of prediction premises; (5) the creation of communicative situations in which its author mentally occupies the place of the other person; (6) the ability to reconstruct and modify past communicative situations in order to find out what would have happened if there had been different interactions, to find solace through the creation of credible discursive versions for the author or to generate conversations that never took place with the intention of living, in some way, that pending experience; (7) the study of how feasible a conversation is, to decide if it is profitable or advisable to be carried out; and (8) the capacity of self-convincing or self-deception.

The theoretical and introductory nature of this research invites to delve into the human capacity to change one's perception of reality through the creation of alternative versions of it, to build bridges between psychological and linguistic studies on self-convincing and self-deception, to analyse implicit contents that are involved in this type of mental-discursive constructions and its relationship with verbal courtesy.

## References

Anscombre, J. C., & Ducrot, O. (1994). *La argumentación en la lengua*. Madrid: Gredos.

Aristóteles. (2005). *Retórica*. Madrid: Gredos.

Authier-Revuz, J. (1982). Hétérogénéité montrée et hétérogénéité constitutive: éléments pour une approche de l'autre dans le discourse. *DRLAV, 26*, 91–151.

Bajtín, M. (1929). *Problemas de la poética en Dostoievski* (p. 1986). México: F.C.E.

Bajtín, M. (1981). *The dialogic imagination*. Texas: University of Texas Press.

Bajtín, M. (1989–1991). *Teoría y estética de la novela*. Madrid: Taurus.

Bango, F. M., & Prieto, V. (2008). Las locuciones a /dia / poli – fonía. In Bango de La Campa et al. (coord.), *Intertexto y polifonía* (Vol. 2, pp. 773–780). Oviedo: Universidad de Oviedo.

Beltrán Almería, L. (1992). *Palabras transparentes*. Madrid: Cátedra.
Benveniste, É. (1966 y 1974). *Problemas de lingüística general I y II*. México: Siglo XXI.
Bobes Naves, Mª. C. (1992). *El diálogo*. Madrid: Gredos.
Bobes Naves, Mª. C. (1993). *La novela*. Madrid: Síntesis.
Cascio, L. (1998). *Gramática de la argumentación: estrategias y estructuras*. Madrid: Alianza.
Cialdini, R. B. (1990). *Influencia: ciencia y práctica: cuáles son los factores determinantes para que una persona diga sí a otra persona*. Barcelona: Secretariado de publicaciones de la Universidad de Barcelona.
Claramonte Sanz, V. (2016). *Pensamiento crítico y argumentación*. Valencia: Tirant lo Blanch.
Clark, H., & Gerrig, R. (1990). Quotations as demonstrations. *Language, 66*, 764–805.
Cohn, D. (1978). *La transparence intérieur. Modes de representation dans la vie psichique dans le roman* (p. 1981). Paris: Seuil.
Donaire, M. L. (2000). Polifonía y punto de vista. *Revista Iberoamericana de Discurso y Sociedad, 2*, 73–88.
Donaire, Mª. L. (2008). Dialogismo constitutivo de la lengua. In Bango de La Campa et al. (coord.), *Intertexto y polifonía* (Vol. 2, pp. 923–929). Oviedo: Universidad de Oviedo.
Ducrot, O. (1983). Opérateurs argumentatifs et visée argumentative. *Cahiers de Linguistique Française*. Genève Université de Genève, Unité de Linguistique Française.
Ducrot, O. (1984). Esquisse d'une théorie polyphonique de l'énonciation. In O. Ducrot (Ed.), *Le dire et le dit* (pp. 171–237). Paris: Éditions de Minuit.
Ducrot, O. (1986). *El decir y lo dicho. Polifonía de la Enunciación*. Barcelona: Paidós Comunicación.
Eggs, E. (1994). *Grammaire du discours argumentatif: le topique, le générique, le figure*. Paris: Kimé.
Espuny, J. (2008). Polifonía discursiva y/o lingüística. In Bango de La Campa et al. (coord.) *Intertexto y polifonía* (Vol. 2, pp. 931–934). Oviedo: Universidad de Oviedo.
Fuentes Rodríguez, C. (2004). Enunciación, aserción y modalidad, tres clásicos. *Anuario de estudios filológicos, 27*, 121–145.
Fuentes Rodríguez, C., & Alcaide Lara, E. R. (2005). *Mecanismos lingüísticos de la persuasión*. Madrid: Arco-Libros.
Fuentes Rodríguez, C., & Alcaide Lara, E. R. (2007). *La argumentación lingüística y sus medios de expresión*. Madrid: Arco-Libros.
Genette, G. (1991). *Ficción y dicción* (p. 1993). Barcelona: Lumen.
Goffman, E. (1974). *Frame analysis-an essay in the organization of experience*. Boston: Northeastern Press.
Goleman, D. (2004). *El punto ciego: Psicología del autoengaño*. Madrid: B de Bolsillo.
Guastini, R., & Álvarez Medina, S. (2014). *Interpretar y argumentar*. Madrid: Centro de Estudios Políticos y Constitucionales.
Günthner, S. (1999). Polyphony and the `layering of voices´ in reported dialogues: An analysis of the use of prosodic devices in everyday reported speech. *Journal of Pragmatics, 31*, 685–708.
Marafioti, R. (2005). *Temas de argumentación*. Buenos Aires: Biblos.
Marafioti, R., & Santibáñez, C. (2010). *Teoría de la argumentación: a 50 años de Perelman y Toulmin*. Buenos Aires: Biblos.
Mele, A. R. (2016). *El autoengaño desenmascarado*. Madrid: Cátedra.
Nølke, H. (1994). *Linguistique modulaire: de la forme au sens*. París: Peeters. Lovaina.
Perelman, C., & Olbrechts-Tyteca, L. (1989). *Tratado de la argumentación: la nueva retórica* (p. 1958). Madrid: Gredos.
Plantin, C. (1990). *Essais sur lárgumentation*. Paris: Kimé.
Plantin, C. (1998). *La argumentación*. Barcelona: Ariel.
Portillo-Fernández, J. (2012). Polifonía y yuxtaposición: voces de conciencia en la animación. In L. Fernández Moreno et al. (Eds.), *Ensayos sobre lógica, lenguaje, mente y ciencia* (pp. 163–178). Sevilla: Ediciones Alfar.

Portillo-Fernández, J. (2018). Ventriloquización: Estudio del fenómeno discursivo y sus usos. *Revista de Filología y Lingüística de la Universidad de Costa Rica, 44*(2), 237–252.
Reyes, G. (1984). *Polifonía textual: la citación en el relato literario*. Madrid: Gredos.
Reyes, G. (1987). Polifonía textual: variedades lingüísticas en la narrativa hispanoamericana reciente. In María T. Vaquero de Ramírez (aut.), Humberto López Morales (aut.). *Actas del I Congreso Internacional sobre el español de América* (pp. 1067–1076). Puerto Rico: Academia Puertorriqueña de la Lengua Española.
Roulet, E. (1987). Complétude interactive et connecteurs reformulatifs. *Cahiers de Linguistique Française, 7*, 193–210.
Sperber, D., & Wilson, D. (1986). *La relevancia: comunicación y procesos cognitivos* (p. 1994). Madrid: Visor.
Tordesillas, M. (1998). Esbozo de una dinámica de la lengua en el marco de una semántica argumentativa. *Signo y seña, 9*, 349–978.
Toulmin, S. (2007). *Los usos de la argumentación*. Barcelona: Ediciones Península.
Trivers, R. (2013). *La insensatez de los necios: la lógica del engaño y el autoengaño en la vida humana*. Madrid: Katz.
Valles Calatrava, J. R. (2002). *Diccionario de Teoría de la Narrativa*. Granada: Alhulia.
Van Eemeren, F. H., & Grootendorst, R. (1984). *Speech acts in argumentative discussions: A theoretical model for the analysis of discussions directed toward solving conflicts of opinion*. Berlín: De Gruyter Mouton.
Vega Reñón, L. (2003). *Si de argumentar se trata*. Barcelona: Montesinos.
Vega Reñón, L., & Olmos, P. (2011). *Compendio de lógica, argumentación y retórica*. Madrid: Trotta.
Walton, D. (2006). *Fundamentals of critical argumentation*. New York: Cambridge University Press.
Weston, A. (1993). *Las claves de la argumentación*. Barcelona: Ariel.

# Chapter 3
# The Cognitive Construction of Dialog: Language and Mind

**Teresa Lopez-Soto**

**Abstract** The rapid spread of interdisciplinary methods on the study of language has provoked a massive reconfiguration of the concept of dialog in research. Likewise, computer-based communication and the large data that it provides has completely changed our notion of what language entails: we have moved away from written text to spoken conversation, from a sentence-based approach to large corpora and from monologic to an increasing dialogic view of language. This chapter reviews the human memory system and establishes a connection with some theories in the field of Cognitive Linguistics in order to shed some light in understanding the final purpose of human communication and how it connects our most social nature with knowledge and information across our lifespan. Interactions are described as being dialogic in nature having the ultimate goal for the initiator of the communicative interaction to collect information from the outside, and the recipient of that interaction in the role of instantiating that objective. Dialog is seen as specific (the present time frame determines meaning construction), focused, prominent and dynamic (users alternate roles during dialog from initiator to recipient and viceversa). Communicative interaction ("usage events" according to Cognitive Linguistics) is so important in our lives that it shapes the way the brain is wired and posits some interesting theories on how language usage is constructive *per se*. The chapter finally draws on the correlation that exists between these usage events ("construals" in Current Discourse Space), the subjects of conceptualization, the objects of conceptualization and cognitive mapping, more in particular Working Memory, as the main engine that allows for repetitive stimulation and Long-Term Memory (Semantic and Episodic Memory) which finally stores complex semantic networks made up of form (phonological load) and meaning (semantic load). These sophisticated cognitive patterns stand for knowledge as we know it and represent permanent structures from which users can retrieve, reshape and extend along life experience.

T. Lopez-Soto (✉)
Speech and Phonetic Sciences Lab, University of Seville, Sevilla, Spain
e-mail: teresals@us.es



T. Lopez-Soto (ed.), *Dialog Systems*, Logic, Argumentation & Reasoning 22,
https://doi.org/10.1007/978-3-030-61438-6_3

**Keywords** Neuropsychology · Working memory · Long-term memory · Semantic memory · Episodic memory · Cognitive linguistics · Current discourse space · Construal hypothesis

## 3.1 Introduction

Speech and language innately describe human beings in as much as it defines, not only the way we interact with the outer world, but also how we internally organize our rational thinking. Yet, it is still unknown what mental processes participate and how they are defined in terms of physiology and organization in the brain. In the last decades, a huge interest in the field of neuroscience has led to significant progress in understanding language comprehension and production. Most of the growing body of work on language and brain processes are articulated within the fields of psycholinguistic models and cognitive psychology that have increasingly incorporated more experimental models of study and modern tools that have favored new data to ponder. Also, the introduction of powerful tools in electrophysiology and neuroimaging have made it possible to retrieve an increasing body of data that has been used to develop more complex and complete theories that aim to understand how the human being perceives and produces linguistic interaction. In addition to this, advances in the area of Theory of Discourse and Cognitive Linguistics have evolved into a more integrated study of human language, with two solid parameters: the spoken value of language (with the integration of intonation and gestures studies) and a more dialogic rather than monologic analysis of language that has led into new theories in Conversation Analysis.

There is growing consensus around the idea that the interactive nature of language is based on a negotiation process between two or more participants. This has been treated as an inherent part of cognitive models of language in the last two decades. This interactional view on cognition and language has led to an emergence in new grammatical theories, too. For example, Construction Grammar has witnessed a new awareness of encoding of this interactional meaning (Boogaart et al. 2014) or the pragmatic use in spoken language (Fried and Östman 2005). The research made from this usage-based paradigm highlights interaction, with spontaneous face-to-face interaction as the central mode. Thus, new priorities include the development of non-verbal structures (gesture, posture, gaze) into the scope of analysis, with the implication of a non-static concept of linguistic construction of meaning (Deppermann 2011): language is meaning and meaning is always under creation, deletion and transformation.

Much of the studies and models within the scope of the so-called "Interactional Constructional Grammar" has been placed under those assumptions (Auer 2009; Brône and Zima 2014; Fischer 2010; Günthner et al. 2014): meaning is expected and that set of expectations draws a general interactional setting to which all agents quickly adapt. Meaning is created throughout transaction and there exists a whole collection of endogenous variables (lexical, morphological, phonetic, syntactic, pragmatic, gestures, gaze) together with some other exogenous elements (experience, object of the negotiation process, socio-cultural characteristics of the communicative situation, among others). Interaction, on the other hand, has neatly escaped the realms of dialogic framing with the expansion of online communication, where the monologic analysis of the speaker's message posits the object of negotiation to be one-sided: the message is to be repeated, highlighted, appraised or reproduced but rarely replied to (Brône and Coulson 2010; Coulson 2000, 2006; Fauconnier and Turner 2002).

As stated, the complexity of the interactional (whether monologic or dialogic) linguistic exchange (whether spoken or written) has expanded to exogenous variables of a more sociocultural nature. Langlotz (2015), for example, defines the *Ethnography of Communication* as an interaction that depends on the physical presence of specific linguistic structures (location, physical signs, weather, time, date) coupled with cognitive expectation in the mind of participants that shape meaning and interpretation of the linguistic exchange considering spatial, temporal, cultural, visual and auditory signals surrounding the purely linguistic exchange of sounds, gestures or gazes. The study, replicated by many more authors, is rooted in the analysis of communication for tourism (e.g. typical exchanges between tourist agents and visitors/customers). Tourism has increasingly been used as a common framework to understand a series of new variables needed for the definition of meaning as such: where you are, what you see, what you want, etc. in an environmental setting that makes the interactional exchange unique in contrast with normal and more routine-like conversations (the participants are positioned in a privileged location that highlights all these variables in terms of the sensory stimulation they experience, the fact that they have been "transposed" to an entirely new natural setting away from their natural linguistic biosystem). Langlotz defends the idea of language as a negotiation between the agents and meaning that can be created or destroyed at any time with constraints imposed on allowable speech turns, the lexical choice at hand, syntax and speech style that are exclusively associated with the objectives of such negotiation (in the study by Langlotz, booking hotel rooms). Here lies the idea that dialog just follows a prescheduled, institutionalized procedure, in words of Heritage (2005), a pre-structured construction that is subject to conventional expectations in both form and meaning (and, thus, interpretation).

In this chapter, I will review some basic aspects of psycholinguistic theories of language, more specifically, the mental lexicon and lexical access, that aim to define the way our brain may organize linguistic information, beginning with lexical information (that entails both semantic and phonological encoding, that is, meaning and form, whether spoken or orthographic). One may believe that meaning directly derives from linguistic interaction, which may come to say that the mere exposition to the spoken or written form of language is enough to assimilate meaning. Some authors, however, have argued that this is an illusionary creation that is possible because of the tremendous speed at which our sensory systems operate. However, access to memory (experience, repetition of the same stimuli, among other variables) are partly responsible of the way we interpret dialog. Baggio (2018) posits a multilevel theory of semantics to explain how meaning is generated at both perception (comprehension) and production. His theory draws on recent advances in semantics and pragmatics, more in particular vector-space semantics (Zwarts 1997, 2001; Zwarts and Winter 2000), discourse representation theory and signaling game theory. Such complex theories have emerged in the absence of a unified theory that could explain an increasing body of data available due to the appearance of electro-physiological and neuroimaging methods. Baggio goes deep into the ideas of meaning, consciousness, sociality and action, a multi-layered approach that seems to be common ground in understanding meaning in dialog from a more cognitive perspective.

On the other hand, studies on memory (sensory memory, working memory and long-term memory) from a neurophysiological point of view have given rise to a new interpretation of meaning in terms of storage and retrieval properties. Meaning seems to be constantly refreshed and re-created through life experience in normal language situations. Still, studies on pathological language (Alzheimer, aphasia, etc.) have also shed light on important issues related to the way we symbolize reality through words, phrases and conversations.

The second part of this chapter will concentrate on some pragmatic and discoursal theories of dialog that have been developed in the area of Cognitive Linguistics, more specifically, those related to meaning, such as the Construal Hypothesis that tries to explain how conceptualization (the "viewer" in Langacker's terms) prototypically extends to the speaker and hearer, who coordinate in order to construct the object of conceptualization, insisting on the idea of meaning as being an element of creation, deletion and modification through the re-elaboration of the message at the very time it is being delivered and received. Some ideas will also shed light on usage events as well as a brief review of the interpretation of the metaphor and metonym inspired by Langacker's model of Current Discourse Space (CDS).

## 3.2 Psycholinguistic Theories of Language

### *3.2.1 The Mental Lexicon*

The concept of mental lexicon refers to the mental storage of words that includes semantic, syntactic and form (both orthographical and phonological). Most psycholinguistic theories agree on the existence of this mental lexicon in language, but some propose a different model for language comprehension and production, while others agree on a central storage structure for both input and output. Theories that account for our mental lexical capacity (Miller 1991) speak of a database that goes from 50,000 to 100,000 words in a normal adult speaker. This amount clearly demonstrates that such a structure must be engineered to be organized efficiently.

Marslen-Wilson and Welsh (1978) were the first to put together a series of assumptions which later on evolved in the so-called Cohort Theory of Word Recognition. This theory is founded in 2 principles:

- Speech is processed word by word
- Word recognition is activated before the actual pronunciation of the word is completed

Additionally, it is important to make reference to the concept of semantic priming in lexical decision making.

#### 3.2.1.1 Speech Is Processed Word by Word

The authors assume that listeners recognize words in a series, one after the other. This common psychological approach to speech recognition is based on the idea that the human brain activates prediction (i.e. probability) when words are perceived in a conversation (or identically when written following the orthographical representation). This model contradicts preliminary theories (Miller 1962) strongly biased by a quantitative view of cognitive lexical processing. Miller, for example, argued that speech perception can only be understood as a collection of discrete decisions which cannot be made as fast as words are pronounced. Miller was very much adopting here a lexicographical perspective, with an obsession on the total load of lexical items that can be processed and produced by a normal speaker. Miller estimated that lexical decisions necessary to identify a word occur at about one per second while the global complex of word recognition seems to make use of less time than that.

However, Marslen-Wilson (1973) presented strong evidence for word by word recognition. He empirically presented a model that posts how words are recognized soon after the acoustic input impinges on the ear of the listener and that predictions for recognition do not limit to the acoustic identification of the word under processing but extends far beyond its phonetic limits as soon as the following word reaches our auditory perception. This assumption early established a strong connection between meaning and form (semantics and acoustics) which has later on evolved into a firm conviction according to which the Mental Lexicon is believed to contain both phonetic and semantic load into each lexical entry and that both ingredients are acquired at the same time. One might say that meaning and form are stored in a blended fashion. This assumption is logical from the perspective of language being a metaphorical/metonymical representation of language, with metaphors (sounds) coming to integrate the sensory reality (meaning).

In the same line, other authors after Marslen-Wilson came to confirm this serial interpretation of word recognition. Cole and Jakimik (1978) employed listening for mispronunciation tasks to demonstrate that the semantic information that is provided by one word can already be used to recognize the one that is immediately following. These constraints between words, semantic in nature, help predict the probability of the next word in the series.[1] Cole and Jakimik tested identification of word-pairs in

[1]Predictive techniques attributed to the way the Mental Lexicon is accessed to in normal conversation have been adopted by Artificial Intelligence in areas such as Automatic Speech Recognition (ASR). Jelinek (1997), Murphy (2012), Koehn et al. (2003), among others, have developed

which there exists strong semantic connection between the two lexical items (e.g. "gold ring", "baby cried") vs. other word-pairs in which probability of co-occurrence seems semantically lower (e.g. "old ring", "lady cried") and discovered that prediction of the second word in the pair was showing a faster latency (over 180 msec faster) than when the second word in the pair was not semantically constrained.

#### 3.2.1.2 Word Recognition is Activated Before the Actual Pronunciation of the Word is Completed

One of the main advantages of the **cohort model** developed by Marslen-Wilson (1987) is that it encompasses a psycholinguistic and neurolinguistic vision of lexical storage and retrieval that has been accepted up to our days. The model describes how the visual/auditory stimulation can be mapped into a lexical item that is stored in the so-called Mental Lexicon (for both creation and retrieval). The main idea behind the model is that (in lexical retrieval) the activation of the correct lexical item is triggered before the information has finally reached the cortical area in charge of language processing (Wernicke's area). Following a Bayesian/Hidden-Markov model approach, as more segments are being added, the probable lexical items identified are being discarded in favor of the one that matches the input. The model posits three stages: (i) during "access stage" all possible words that begin with the same speech segment are activated in the memory areas that store our "mental lexicon"; (ii) "competitors" in the second stage ("competition stage") are being discarded as new information is provided through input; (iii) the final stage ("recognition stage") takes place when a decision has finally been reached.

#### 3.2.1.3 Semantic Priming in Lexical Decision Making

One important idea that has shaped the definition of the Mental Lexicon as a semantic network is that of "semantic priming". Priming here refers to the concept of meaning coming in groups of words (or "phrases") in which one element, typically the first one, shows a priming effect over the subsequent elements, or "targets". Much of the neuropsychological testing that has been developed in the past decades comes from the idea of our brain being stimulated in the shape of a network when it comes to the storage and retrieval of lexical items (an example

statistically-based algorithms in language modeling and machine learning in general from the ideas stated by psychologists such as Marslen-Wilson and Cole (and more) 30 years earlier. This transposition of the concept of prediction (probability) in the way human beings store and retrieve lexical items (form and meaning) have evolved into inferential models in Artificial Intelligence, including (dynamic) Bayesian methods (Murphy and Russell 2002; Juang et al. 1997; Zweig and Russell 1998), hidden Markov models (Cappé et al. 2006; Juang and Rabiner 1991) or maximum entropy (Toutanova and Manning 2000; Rosenfeld 1997).

would be the triggering of related terms when a prime is elicited, as in “truck” elicited by “car” or “baby” elicited by “pacifier”). If one was to establish a connection between this concept in relationship with dialog, it is obvious that some semantic concepts stated in a conversation can trigger some other related items, thus establishing some mental imaging in the mind of the listener that could differ from the original semantic network in the mind of the speaker. To put it in simple words, human beings organize semantic concepts into sophisticated networks over time and this configuration would be supported by external circumstances that may be affected by social and cultural characteristics in the particular surrounding and clearly shaped according to the history and experience of the speaker.

As a summary of this section, we could say that speech perception involves prediction and that such prediction is mostly determined by the way the meaning carriers are networked into phrases that are mentally activated through the acoustic signal processing within a complex hierarchy of priming effects of some lexical items over other lexical items. It has generally been accepted (since Miller 1962), that our mind shows some sort of “capacity” in terms of the lexical information load that can be stored. In more recent decades, cognitive models of prediction have specifically incorporated the idea of frequency in the usage of terms/concepts in order to explain how prediction really operates. This has especially been possible thanks to the introduction of novel methods, particularly those related with empirical data, such as corpus linguistics, sociolinguistics and big data. In this line, studies in Cognitive Linguistics have made use of frequency to explain language change, both at the morphological and phonological levels (Krug 1998); semantic priming effects in lexical decision (Lupker and Pexman 2010; Tse and Neely 2007; Plaut and Booth 2000); or to explain patterns of syntactic use and lexical effects of phrases and constructions in conversation (Bybee and Hopper 2001).

However, all things taken into account, it seems that prediction alone is not enough to proceed with a final definition of how language is construed. If that was the case, information would not be possible and dialog would consist of the mere exposition of one’s ideas. However, dialog makes informational interaction possible. In cognitive models, prediction has been enriched with the idea of feedback of activation from lexical to pre-lexical processes as implemented in interactive-activation models (IAMs) (Norris et al. 2016). Feedback can enable the listener to adapt to changing input, and thus it entails the potential to modify pre-existing mental networks, more in particular the mental lexicon. Norris and colleagues highlight how this potential (the fact that the listener may recognize unusual input and reshape meaning accordingly) optimizes the performance of speech recognition using Bayesian inference. In short, meaning is built upon the frequent exposition to a particular stimulus that uses form (phonological/orthographical properties of lexical items) as a priming element that can be inferred (using Bayesian models) in an ever-increasing semantic network that can be altered on spot during dialog thanks to interaction between the participants. This non-static view of meaning presupposes the existence of a fixed location in the brain that is adaptable in terms of storage and retrieval.

## 3.2.2 *Memory and Language*

### 3.2.2.1 Working Memory

Of the three-way setting that has been used in psychology to describe memory (sensory memory, working memory, WM, and long-term memory, LTM) the one that is more relevant to understand how language is articulated is that of working memory (Baddeley 2003; Baddeley and Hitch 1974). Experimentation with children with language impairment showed a deficit in their capacity to acquire native vocabulary as compared with healthy children (Gathercole and Baddeley 1989) in an experiment that involved some rehearsing through repetition. This constant rehearsal via active articulation is fundamental to understanding WM and the process of language learning in general. This characteristic of WM puts spontaneous conversation, for example, in the view of linguistic practice where meaning is under negotiation but not necessarily learned. WM operates in contrast to LTM where the semantic, episodic and procedural systems have been identified.

WM refers to a temporary location for the storage and manipulation of information that is divided into three subsystems: (i) The "phonological loop" directly correlates with the idea presented in the sections above according to which the Mental Lexicon is composed of lexical units with acoustic attributes that are used to establish semantic interpretation with other lexical units; (ii) the "visuospatial sketchpad" would provide the visual equivalent in a way that the acoustic information primes in the direction of external realities that can be visually processed; and (iii) the "central executive" that would be in charge of making the necessary amendments during the processing of language. A fourth subsystem, the "episodic buffer" has recently been proposed in which memory seems to be loaded in a series of "episodes" that overlap with one another.

WM has been differentiated from long-term memory as being a temporary storage setting in the prefrontal cortex. Hebb (1949) already suggested this distinction and he defined LTM as that system in the brain capable of storing durable information. Brown (1958) and Peterson and Peterson (1959) later on empirically demonstrated that part of our memories can rapidly be lost in the absence of repetition (rehearsal). This two-component system was definitely demonstrated through data extracted from neuropsychological patients for whom damage to the medial temporal lobes would lead to evidence of impaired capacity for new learning while actions that would not require access to long-term storage would not be affected (Baddeley and Warrington 1970; Milner 1966) or from evidence from patients with aphasia (Shallice and Warrington 1970).

The idea of WM as a separate storing structure to hold temporary information can be understood within the so-called Modal Model (Murdock 1974) ("modal" here comes from the statistic *mode* or more repeated value in a data series). Frequency, repetition and rehearsal are key ideas in determining this two-store taxonomy, even though not only qualitative differences are used to distinguish among them but also the processing mechanisms that are involved at each stage. The main idea behind is

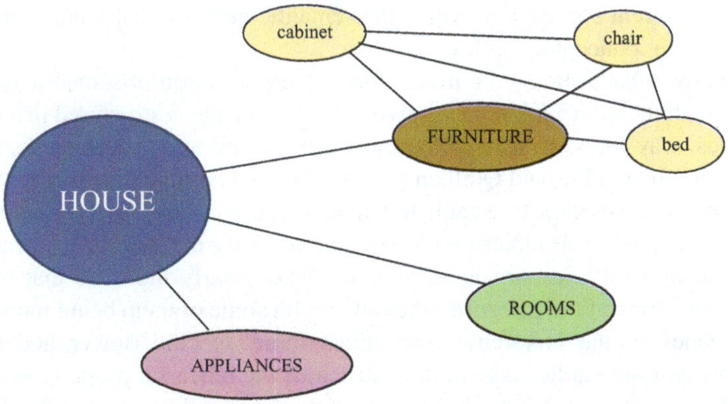


**Fig. 3.1** An example of associative semantic network in which related words are colored the same

that sensory information is transformed in some sort of lasting memory that needs to be rehearsed (repeated) and structured (categorized) in order to be maintained. This repetition takes place at the level of WM and, at some point, its significance is regarded to be prominent enough as to be directed to a more permanent register (LTM).

Cognitive studies have always been concerned with the "capacity" of memory and therefore of learning. A pioneer work is that by Miller (1956) "The Magical Number Seven, Plus or Minus Two". In his study, Miller estimated that individuals facing a learning task that implied new information could only recall a maximum of lists containing no more than 8 items. This concept of "storage limitation" is actually complemented with the idea of "multiple chunks of information": even though the human being seems to organize incoming pieces of information of a limited duration, this only happens at the level of "temporary processing" (the one where WM is responsible for) while units become higher "chunks of information" that comprise multiple elements tied by various attributes and connections, which corresponds with a more permanent construction stored at the level of LTM. As with individual units, research has also demonstrated limitations in the number of chunks that can be created (Cowan 2001).

This "way of doing things" in memory clearly correlates with existing theories of representation of (semantic) meaning. Two main currents have been developed in order to propose a semantic network model that can directly relate concepts and words. The first approach proposes that concepts are represented by their semantic properties in the brain. For example, the term *house* has several semantic features, including "is furniture", "located in room", that represent this word in the semantic network. Likewise, each semantic feature associated can further be linked (shared) with other lexical terms (see Fig. 3.1). The main idea behind this model is the existence of "linguistic universals" or some sort of universal attributes that all languages have into account in order to represent meaning. The mental lexicon is actually a different approach in which the semantic network that binds words do so by representing conceptual nodes.

Somehow, what seems to be true is that the organization of semantic terms that correlate with the information we receive from the outside is structured in a complex hierarchical way for both word recognition (perception) and lexical access (production). Studies by Collins and Quillian (1970) observed correlations between reaction times when subjects had to establish semantic relationships between some given terms. For example, participants took less time to verify the statement "a canary is a bird" compared to "a canary is an animal". This clearly indicates that terms are organized in terms of the categories they fit in with some of them being more general (parent nodes in the hierarchy) and others more specific (lower nodes in the hierarchy). Similar studies also give evidence of the rehearsal property of memory (WM) in as much as the reply of the participant would reflect a non-static or logical relationship between concepts (categories) but depending on the participant's experience. For example, Rips et al. (1973) give evidence of some data-based studies in which participants could assign "a robin is a bird" a faster verification than to statements such as "an ostrich is a bird" for being a less typical exemplar.

#### 3.2.2.2 Episodic Memory

The episodic memory is the cognitive structure that accounts for the autobiographical sequences (or episodes) than a human being can recall. Episodic and semantic memory are said to be LTM memory structures that are defined as a declarative type of memory (explicit memory) meaning that they can be consciously accessed. Episodic memory is in charge of storing past experiences (episodes of our life) while semantic memory holds factual information. Most tasks related to language involve the access to both the mental lexicon (semantic memory, as described below) and the episodic memory. Examples of episodic memory could be the following: (a) He whistled as she was leaving the house; (b) I was gladly impressed when I finally met my boss over the phone to find him extremely amiable; (c) Summers were scorching back in the time and I remember spending afternoons lying on the floor in search of some cool surface. The existence of such a structure has been strongly motivated by studies in patients with amnesia, since they can recall information semantic in nature but forget some "historical" episodes of their lives.

The importance of episodic memory for language lies in the fact that multiple studies have demonstrated that meaning (and all objects involved, both lexical items and grammatical rules) are acquired and learned through constant exposition to those stimuli in authentic life situations.[2] "Frequency" to stimulation acquires a

---

[2]Another interesting debate between the concepts of "acquisition" and "learning" is worth some time, but may escape the objectives of this chapter that attempts to be just a general review. However, much has been said about "acquisition" relating to a constant repetition necessary for "learning" in which case it would be more associated with short-term cognitive storage structures,

predominant position in cognitive studies that attempt to explain how meaning is represented. Many of these studies insist on the idea that meaning, and grammatical usage in general, is learned from birth through repeated learning episodes (Harm and Seidenberg 2004; Melby-Lervåg et al. 2012; and the "connectionist model" in Chang et al. 2006, to cite a few).

Episodic memory and semantic memory are both intertwined and have a direct correspondence with the way we learn about the world around us, which helps us integrate and survive. Even though they are both defined as being declarative types of memory (access to them can be done consciously) that intertwining characteristic is not conscious. Somehow, the brain elaborates a complex statistical machine that calculates objects (lexical items and grammatical rules) and their frequency (probability, inferential rules) through repeated exposures before such learning (and, therefore, meaning) is created (Perruchet and Pacton 2006; Turk-Browne et al. 2009; Conway et al. 2010; Misyak and Christiansen 2012).

#### 3.2.2.3 Semantic Memory

The semantic memory may be described as the structure that holds the mental lexicon, a thesaurus made up of form and meaning, conceptual associations, transitions, constraints and attributes that are inherent to such a system as explained above. In opposition to episodic memory above, semantic memory is more cognitively related, that is to say it requires some processing of the information collected through observation. In semantic memory, the relationships between semantic categories, their properties and rules must also be built along the way, mere exposition does not suffice. Examples of such data-based information could be the following: (a) I remember his birthday is 4th or 5th of August, maybe 4th; (b) You know it is too hot when butter easily melts on toasts; (c) Candles may cause the ceiling to turn gray.

As with episodic memory, semantic memory is a type of declarative memory that refers to our LTM in an integration of form and meaning. However, such structure should not be considered a simple static warehouse where knowledge is passively stored. Evidence from clinical studies (neurodegenerative diseases and aphasia) have demonstrated that semantic memory is rather a complex and interrelated system that spreads its multiple components across several cortical regions.

---

such as WM, while LTM would account for the containment of more perdurable cognition load, therefore knowledge or learning (Pagpagno et al. 1991; Hulstijn 2001; Gathercole 2006).

## 3.3 Dialog in Cognitive Linguistics

### *3.3.1 Some Preliminaries on Cognitive Linguistics*

Dialog is an exchange of messages between one and more participants that is never unidirectional in the sense that it entails complex cognitive modifications: once dialog begins, all participants somehow alter their cognition (knowledge) of the world outside. From the point of view of the linguistic theory, the structure of dialog encompasses knowledge at several substructures:

- Phonetics and Phonology
- Morphology and Lexicon
- Syntactic properties and construction rules
- Semantic relations (both intensional and extensional)
- Pragmatic properties (speech acts)
- Interaction management ("moves" and "turns")
- Socio-cultural variables

From the point of view of the cognitive theory, the structure of dialog requires at least six more areas of cognitive activation:

- Cognitive planning
- Execution
- Monitoring
- Comprehension (processing, scaffolding, creation of a cognitive structure)
- Storage
- Retrieval

Researchers working in the usage-based paradigm (Zima and Brône 2015) agree on the fact that the natural language setting is that of spontaneous face-to-face interaction and that any other types of language use (writing, monologic or computer-based) are structurally guided by this original configuration (Ibbotson 2013). This "interactional" characteristic of language seems to be the most prominent assumption in any cognitive-linguistic based approach to understanding communication and dialog in particular. Interests on interaction have come along with an increasing spread of multimodality and interdisciplinary models of language. Really fruitful research has enlarged the focus of any linguistic study to include bodily means of expression (gesture, posture, gaze), intonational features (pitch, speed, loudness), dialog management (conversation analysis), among others.

With the spread of data-based analyses (Corpus Linguistics) the limitations of Cognitive Linguistics regarded as being too much written oriented have overturned a non-dialogic orientation (Linell 1998) into a more suitable methodological approach for the research in dialog. In the last decades, Cognitive Linguistics has intensely drawn conclusions from more contextualized instances of language including corpus studies and statistical tools (Janda 2015). This usage-based approach to understanding language (Barlow and Kemmer 2000) has derived in definitions of several theories of cognitive grammar that draw on the concept of "usage events" of language (Cienki 2015). Usage events highlight the ways dialog participants build message (non-lexical sounds, intonation patterns and gesture) allowing for different degrees of specificity, focusing, prominence and dynamicity.

The theory of Cognitive Grammar developed by Langacker (1987) and Langacker and Langacker (2008) posits a general framework for the study of linguistic behavior that is inspired by the most general abilities of perception, attention and categorization. Cognitive Grammar is also based on the idea of language constituting a symbolic phenomenon in which patterns symbolize specific conceptual structures that allow for a knowledge of the world we perceive through our senses. Following De Saussure's (1959) semiotics, these symbolic structures are composed of both form and meaning (acoustic information that can be processed by mental structures, as explained above, and the meaning it recreates): phonology and semantics. These (phonosemantic) units are gradually created and the instances (experiences) where they are instantiated from are called "usage events" (Langacker 1988). Usage events here merely refer to those life experiences that are processed and accordingly stored in our memory and which are later on available to understand future events in a process of progressive understanding of the outer world.[3] The two most relevant models that have pursued exploration into these matters are Langacker's Current Discourse Space Model (CDS) and Barsalou's Dynamic Model of Situated Conceptualization (Barsalou 2005, 2015). This chapter will finish with a review of the former and a description of the so-called Construal Hypothesis.

### 3.3.2 *The Construal Hypothesis and Langacker's Model of Current Discourse Space*

According to Langacker (2001) discourse (dialog) consists of a series of frames that are seen by a group of participants at a particular moment in time and space. He coined the term *frame* to encompass where meaning can be found and how it is built upon and he made a classification of these frames from the temporal perspective (experiential approach) that determines how participants in the dialog reshape preconceptual notions of knowledge through communication. Current Discourse Space (CDS) frames are divided into the following:

---

[3]The author of this chapter would like to remind the reader of the importance of social interactions and the very social nature that characterizes us as individuals. It would be relevant to incorporate more of that social perspective in research on dialog in order to emphasize and account for the relevance of our desire to belong to a social group for which purpose language must be seen as the most important agent (Tomasello 2003).

- *Minus frame*: information that has not yet been shared between participants in the dialog and is, therefore, unknown (this would be the starting point of discourse).
- *Zero frame (focus frame)*: the frame where dialog actually takes place consisting of constant interaction and sharing of all kind of information.
- *Plus frame*: it happens when the cognitive structures of participants in the dialog have been shaped once information is known and acknowledged for by participants.[4]

Semantic research within the area of Cognitive Linguistics has extensively been done from a cross-language perspective and prominently focused on metaphorical and metonymical comparisons in order to understand how language is organized (language is to reality as much as metaphor is to a symbolic interpretation of what is perceived through our sensory system). Contrastive studies have provided very insightful conclusions on the way human beings create conceptual maps that couple with external reality. Metaphors, thus, have contributed to making discourse a dynamic area of study in which the cognitive map that the discourse space generates is under constant (re-)creation. The objects of discoursal creations have been termed as "construals" in Linguistics. Metaphors are being used to assist the processes that are needed to understand the world outside: we build a conceptual representation of that world and dialog (discourse) is the precise time where (perdurable) meaning is created.

The so-called Construal Hypothesis comes to state that meaning is not a fixed reality, but is constantly under reconceptualization and that "construal" always involves a given perspective (spatial, epistemic, etc.) that is received (i.e. "construed") through language interaction. The hypothesis entails meaning being grounded on the construal relationship that happens between the subjects (interactants) and the objects of that conceptualization (the meaning at hand). This hypothesis puts the language user as the central element in the discoursal process, as a goal in itself: dialog serves to modify the way the mind understands reality and the position of the user in the world he interacts with.

Verhagen (2005) insisted on extending the subject of conceptualization to a twofold perspective, that of the speaker (actor) and the listener (passive subject) whose roles could be exchanged at any point in time but who would act differently according to the moment in discourse their role is to be situated (whether that being active or passive). This cognitive coordination is important especially if we focus on the object of conceptualization and understand that one person takes the initiative while another one follows the trend. This has interesting applications in the area of Computer-Mediated Communication (CMC) where communication appears to be (at least, initially) more monologic than dialogic (especially in social networks where users basically post text or media without a clear intention to engage into dialog). The Construal Hypothesis, however, would describe CMC from a different

[4]From a neuropsychological point of view, the "zero frame" would require the activation of working memory while the "plus frame" would entail the information being stored in long-term memory structure.

perspective, that of the CMC user taking the role of initiator predominantly but not necessarily in a monologic fashion. Holt (2004) describes discourse on the Internet as being built on both monologism and dialogism. Monologic discourse for this author actually refers to an anticipation that the initiator makes of the future dialog, which means that they provoke meaning to be created (even though in one particular direction). That construction of meaning (the "construals" in CDS) would equally affect the initiator and the passive recipient and monologic would become only procedural while dialogism would cover all aspects of discourse ("dialogic" here meaning interaction and, thus, cognitive reshaping of all participants at hand). For Holt, "dialogic utterances are securely bound to what goes on in the world, whereas the monologic perspective encourages utterances that are disjunct from the 'messy' reality of the world" (p. 189).

The Construal Hypothesis goes away from traditional Cognitive Linguistics that seems to attribute cognition and language only to the individual, while CDS puts dialogism under a more social consideration and accounts for dialog as being both interpersonal and social (Linell 2009).

## 3.4 Concluding Remarks

(Spoken) language is a powerful tool that integrates the sensory information that we receive from the outside (through our perceptual system, mainly auditory and visual) into a complex network of semantic structures that serves us to symbolically represent the outer reality. "Spoken" here refers to the basically oral nature of language, with the written form being just a transfer of the acoustic form into an orthographical representation. "Symbolically", on the other hand, refers to the basically metaphorical perspective that our cognitive system adopts in approaching that cognitive representation. The mental system in charge of the communicative skills in human beings is a combination of processing and storage structures. Psycholinguistic theories have devised a generally accepted model according to which our storage capacity is divided into declarative (conscious access) and temporary (working memory vs. long-term memory) roughly speaking. This broad classification (for both processing and storage) implies dynamicity, meaning that we have the capacity of memory storage and retrieval. Working memory is in charge of assisting the processing modules in the brain when the input arrives and directly connects with long-term memory systems (semantic and episodic memories) when prominence is high enough as to determine a permanent storage.

Within the long-term memory, the semantic memory, a sort of mental lexicon (thesaurus) is in charge of piling up a series of lexical (semantic) units that comprise both form (acoustic information) and meaning. It is the acoustic information that establishes the triggering in the brain that allows for lexical identification. Acoustic processing can speed up the process of identification of the semantic input with a combination of some constraints and prediction rules that can point in the direction of the correct identification even before all sounds pronounced have been perceived by the listener. This is possible because the mental lexicon is not a sequential, but rather a tridimensional structure in which nodes are integrated on the basis of constraints, expectation rules, probability and categorization that makes lexical items being paired between each other in very specific lexical neighborhoods. Identification takes place using probability rules (based on previous perception) between sequences (phrases) according to which the final candidate chosen for identification is pruned out of discarding all other candidates along speech. Words are then identified in a serial way, one word, one segment at a time.

Finally, this chapter has pointed out the idea of meaning not being a permanent truth but rather a dynamic entity that receives constant feedback for reconfiguration throughout our lifespan. That makes cognitive structures (especially memory ones) particularly flexible and dynamic, allowing for reconceptualization after preliminary evaluation of ongoing interactive information. This dynamic characteristic of dialog has been defined in Cognitive Linguistics through different models. This chapter has reviewed Langacker's Current Discourse Model in combination with the "construal hypothesis". In the model, meaning is constantly being created and dialog is described in terms of a series of "usage events", each one specific enough as to focus in the direction of the most updated prominent feature that will reshape conceptualization in the brain.

Overall, the chapter combines a brief review of some relevant theories in psycholinguistic and cognitive models that describe dialog as being spoken, dynamic and inferential in nature, for frequency (and probability) is central when decisions have to be made in order to understand the reality that we perceive through our senses.

## References


Auer, P. (2009). On-line syntax: Thoughts on the temporality of spoken language. *Language Sciences, 31*, 1–13.

Baddeley, A. (2003). Working memory: Looking back and looking forward. *Nature Reviews Neuroscience, 4*(10), 829–839.

Baddeley, A. D., & Hitch, G. (1974). Working memory. In G. H. Bower (Ed.), *The psychology of learning and motivation: Advances in research and theory* (Vol. 8, pp. 47–89). New York: Academic.

Baddeley, A. D., & Warrington, E. K. (1970). Amnesia and the distinction between long-and short-term memory. *Journal of Verbal Learning and Verbal Behavior, 9*(2), 176–189.

Baggio, G. (2018). *Meaning in the brain*. New York: MIT Press.

Barlow, M., & Kemmer, S. (Eds.). (2000). *Usage-based models of language*. Stanford: Center for the Study of Language and Information.

Barsalou, L. W. (2005). Situated conceptualization. In *Handbook of categorization in cognitive science* (pp. 619–650). St. Louis: Elsevier Science Ltd.

Barsalou, L. W. (2015). Situated conceptualization: Theory and applications. In *Perceptual and emotional embodiment* (pp. 19–45). London: Routledge.

Boogaart, R., Colleman, T., & Rutten, G. (Eds.). (2014). *Extending the scope of construction grammar* (Vol. 54). Berlin: Walter de Gruyter GmbH & Co KG.

Brône, G., & Coulson, S. (2010). Processing deliberate ambiguity in newspaper headlines: Double grounding. *Discourse Processes, 47*(3), 212–236.

Brône, G., & Zima, E. (2014). Towards a dialogic construction grammar: Ad hoc routines and resonance activation. In R. Giora & J. W. Du Bois (Eds.), special issue of *Cognitive Linguistics, 25*(3), 457–495.

Brown, J. (1958). Some tests of the decay theory of immediate memory. *Quarterly Journal of Experimental Psychology, 10*(1), 12–21.

Bybee, J. L., & Hopper, P. J. (Eds.). (2001). *Frequency and the emergence of linguistic structure* (Vol. 45). Amsterdam: John Benjamins Publishing.

Cappé, O., Moulines, E., & Rydén, T. (2006). *Inference in hidden Markov models*. New York: Springer.

Chang, F., Dell, G. S., & Bock, K. (2006). Becoming syntactic. *Psychological Review, 113*(2), 234.

Cienki, A. (2015). Spoken language usage events. *Language and Cognition, 7*(4), 499–514.

Cole, R. A., & Jakimik, J. (1978). Understanding speech: How words are heard. In *Strategies of information processing* (pp. 67–116). London: Academic.

Collins, A. M., & Quillian, M. R. (1970). Facilitating retrieval from semantic memory: The effect of repeating part of an inference. *Acta Psychologica, 33*, 304–314.

Conway, C. M., Bauernschmidt, A., Huang, S. S., & Pisoni, D. B. (2010). Implicit statistical learning in language processing: Word predictability is the key. *Cognition, 114*(3), 356–371.

Coulson, S. (2000). *Semantic leaps: Frame-shifting and conceptual blending in meaning construction*. Cambridge: Cambridge University Press.

Coulson, S. (2006). Constructing meaning. *Metaphor and Symbol, 21*(4), 245–266.

Cowan, N. (2001). The magical number 4 in short-term memory: A reconsideration of mental storage capacity. *Behavioral and Brain Sciences, 24*(1), 87–114.

De Saussure, F. (1959). *Course in general linguistics*. New York: Philosophical Library.

Deppermann, A. (2011). The study of formulations as a key to an interactional semantics. *Human Studies, 34*(2), 115–128.

Fauconnier, G., & Turner, M. (2002). *The way we think: Conceptual blending and the mind's hidden complexities*. New York: Basic Books.

Fischer, K. (2010). Beyond the sentence: Constructions, frames and spoken interaction. *Constructions and Frames, 2*(2), 185–207.

Fried, M., & Östman, J. O. (2005). Construction grammar and spoken language: The case of pragmatic particles. *Journal of Pragmatics, 37*(11), 1752–1778.

Gathercole, S. E., & Baddeley, A. D. (1989). Evaluation of the role of phonological STM in the development of vocabulary in children: A longitudinal study. *Journal of Memory and Language, 28*(2), 200–213.

Gathercole, S. E. (2006). Nonword repetition and word learning: The nature of the relationship. *Applied PsychoLinguistics, 27*(4), 513–543.

Günthner, S., Bücker, J., & Imo, W. (Eds.). (2014). *Grammar and dialogism: Sequential, syntactic, and prosodic patterns between emergence and sedimentation*. Berlin/Boston: de Gruyter.

Harm, M. W., & Seidenberg, M. S. (2004). Computing the meanings of words in reading: Cooperative division of labor between visual and phonological processes. *Psychological Review, 111*(3), 662.

Hebb, D. O. (1949). *The organization of behavior: A neuropsychological theory*. New York: Wiley/Chapman & Hall.

Heritage, J. (2005). Conversation analysis and institutional talk. In *Handbook of language and social interaction* (Vol. 103, p. 47). Mahwah: Lawrence Erlbaum Associates.

Holt, R. (2004). *Dialogue on the internet: Language, civic identity, and computer-mediated communication*. Westport: Greenwood Publishing Group.

Hulstijn, J. H. (2001). Intentional and incidental second language vocabulary learning: A reappraisal of elaboration, rehearsal and automaticity. In P. Robinson (Ed.), *Cognition and second language instruction* (pp. 258–286). Cambridge: Cambridge University Press.

Ibbotson, P. (2013). The scope of usage-based theory. *Frontiers in Psychology, 4*, 255.

Janda, L. A. (2015). Cognitive linguistics in the year 2015. *Cognitive Semantics, 1*(1), 131–154.
Jelinek, F. (1997). *Statistical methods for speech recognition*. Cambridge, MA: MIT Press.
Juang, B. H., & Rabiner, L. R. (1991). Hidden Markov models for speech recognition. *Technometrics, 33*(3), 251–272.
Juang, B. H., Hou, W., & Lee, C. H. (1997). Minimum classification error rate methods for speech recognition. *IEEE Transactions on Speech and Audio Processing, 5*(3), 257–265.
Koehn, P., Och, F. J., & Marcu, D. (2003, May). Statistical phrase-based translation. In *Proceedings of the 2003 conference of the North American Chapter of the Association for Computational Linguistics on Human Language Technology-Volume 1* (pp. 48–54). Association for Computational Linguistics.
Krug, M. (1998). String frequency: A cognitive motivating factor in coalescence, language processing, and linguistic change. *Journal of English Linguistics, 26*(4), 286–320.
Langacker, R. W. (1987). *Foundations of cognitive grammar: Theoretical prerequisites* (Vol. 1). Stanford: Stanford University Press.
Langacker, R. W. (1988). An overview of cognitive grammar. In *Topics in cognitive linguistics* (p. 3). John Benjamins. ISO 690.
Langacker, R. W. (2001). Discourse in cognitive grammar. *Cognitive linguistics, 12*(2), 143–188.
Langacker, R. W., & Langacker, R. (2008). *Cognitive grammar: A basic introduction*. New York: OUP USA.
Langlotz, A. (2015). Local meaning-negotiation, activity types, and the current-discourse-space model. *Language and Cognition, 7*(4), 515–545.
Linell, P. (1998). *Approaching dialogue: Talk, interaction and contexts in dialogical perspectives* (Vol. 3). Amsterdam: John Benjamins Publishing.
Linell, P. (2009). *Rethinking language, mind, and world dialogically*. Charlotte: IAP.
Lupker, S. J., & Pexman, P. M. (2010). Making things difficult in lexical decision: The impact of pseudohomophones and transposed-letter nonwords on frequency and semantic priming effects. *Journal of Experimental Psychology: Learning, Memory, and Cognition, 36*(5), 1267.
Marslen-Wilson, W. (1973). Linguistic structure and speech shadowing at very short latencies. *Nature, 244*(5417), 522–523.
Marslen-Wilson, W. (1987). Functional parallelism in spoken word recognition. *Cognition, 25*, 71–102.
Marslen-Wilson, W. D., & Welsh, A. (1978). Processing interactions and lexical access during word recognition in continuous speech. *Cognitive Psychology, 10*(1), 29–63.
Melby-Lervåg, M., Lyster, S. A. H., & Hulme, C. (2012). Phonological skills and their role in learning to read: A meta-analytic review. *Psychological Bulletin, 138*(2), 322.
Miller, G. A. (1956). The magical number seven, plus or minus two: Some limits on our capacity for processing information. *Psychological Review, 63*(2), 81.
Miller, G. A. (1962). Some psychological studies of grammar. *American Psychologist, 17*(11), 748–762.
Miller, G. A. (1991). *The science of words*. New York: Scientific American Library.
Milner, B. (1966). Amnesia following operation on the temporal lobes. In C. M. W. Whitty & O. L. Zangwill (Eds.), *Amnesia*. London: Butterworths.
Misyak, J. B., & Christiansen, M. H. (2012). Statistical learning and language: An individual differences study. *Language Learning, 62*(1), 302–331.
Murdock, B. B. (1974). *Human memory: Theory and data*. Potomac: Lawrence Erlbaum.
Murphy, K. P. (2012). *Machine learning: A probabilistic perspective*. Cambridge, MA: MIT Press.
Murphy, K. P., & Russell, S. (2002). *Dynamic Bayesian networks: Representation, inference and learning*. PhD thesis, University of California, Berkeley.
Norris, D., McQueen, J. M., & Cutler, A. (2016). Prediction, Bayesian inference and feedback in speech recognition. *Language, Cognition and Neuroscience, 31*(1), 4–18.
Papagno, C., Valentine, T., & Baddeley, A. (1991). Phonological short-term memory and foreign-language vocabulary learning. *Journal of Memory and Language, 30*(3), 331–347.

Perruchet, P., & Pacton, S. (2006). Implicit learning and statistical learning: One phenomenon, two approaches. *Trends in Cognitive Sciences, 10*(5), 233–238.

Peterson, L., & Peterson, M. J. (1959). Short-term retention of individual verbal items. *Journal of Experimental Psychology, 58*(3), 193.

Plaut, D. C., & Booth, J. R. (2000). Individual and developmental differences in semantic priming: Empirical and computational support for a single-mechanism account of lexical processing. *Psychological Review, 107*(4), 786.

Rips, L. J., Shoben, E. J., & Smith, E. E. (1973). Semantic distance and the verification of semantic relations. *Journal of Verbal Learning and Verbal Behavior, 12*(1), 1–20.

Rosenfeld, R. (1997, December). A whole sentence maximum entropy language model. In *1997 IEEE workshop on automatic speech recognition and understanding proceedings* (pp. 230–237). IEEE.

Shallice, T., & Warrington, E. K. (1970). Independent functioning of verbal memory stores: A neuropsychological study. *The Quarterly Journal of Experimental Psychology, 22*(2), 261–273.

Tomasello, M. (2003). The key is social cognition. In *Language in mind: Advances in the study of language and thought* (pp. 47–57). Cambridge: MIT Press.

Toutanova, K., & Manning, C. D. (2000, October). Enriching the knowledge sources used in a maximum entropy part-of-speech tagger. In *Proceedings of the 2000 Joint SIGDAT conference on Empirical methods in natural language processing and very large corpora: Held in conjunction with the 38th Annual Meeting of the Association for Computational Linguistics-Volume 13* (pp. 63–70). Association for Computational Linguistics.

Tse, C. S., & Neely, J. H. (2007). Semantic priming from letter-searched primes occurs for low-but not high-frequency targets: Automatic semantic access may not be a myth. *Journal of Experimental Psychology: Learning, Memory, and Cognition, 33*(6), 1143.

Turk-Browne, N. B., Scholl, B. J., Chun, M. M., & Johnson, M. K. (2009). Neural evidence of statistical learning: Efficient detection of visual regularities without awareness. *Journal of Cognitive Neuroscience, 21*(10), 1934–1945.

Verhagen, A. (2005). *Constructions of intersubjectivity: Discourse, syntax, and cognition.* Oxford: Oxford University Press on Demand.

Zima, E., & Brône, G. (2015). Cognitive linguistics and interactional discourse: Time to enter into dialogue. *Language and Cognition, 7*(4), 485–498.

Zwarts, J. (1997). Vectors as relative positions: A compositional semantics of modified PPs. *Journal of Semantics, 14*, 57–86.

Zwarts, J. (2001). *Vectors across spatial domains: From place to size, orientation, shape and parts (1).* Unpublished ms., SIL/BTL, Kenya.

Zwarts, J., & Winter, Y. (2000). Vector space semantics: A model-theoretic analysis of locative prepositions. *Journal of Logic, Language and Information, 9*, 169–211.

Zweig, G., & Russell, S. (1998). *Speech recognition with dynamic Bayesian networks.*

# Chapter 4
# In Defense of Unilateralism

**Gonçalo Santos**

**Abstract** Assertion and denial are speech acts that play a central role in different theories of meaning, but the proper way to understand their relation remains an object of debate. We set out to identify the source of this disagreement and compare the proposals made by different theories of meaning. We also defend a unilateralist understanding of the relation between assertion and denial, according to which denying a sentence means that its assertion conditions could never be satisfied.

**Keywords** Bilateralism · Negation · Denial · Logical constants · Intuitionism · Classical logic · Non-classical logic

## 4.1 Inferentialism, Unilateralism and Bilateralism

How do certain expressions of natural language come to have the meaning that they have? While there are different approaches to explain this phenomenon, the Wittgensteinian slogan *meaning is use* has played an influential role in the development of a whole family of theories of meaning. One approach (introduced by Brandom 1994, 2000) that can be traced back to this origin is called *inferentialism.* According to the inferentialist, the meaning of an expression is determined by how we use it and its use can be described in terms of its inferential relations with other expressions.

As an illustration of the inferentialist approach, suppose that the meaning of a declarative sentence S is wholly determined by how we use it. Asserting and denying S are two different ways of using it. Its assertion conditions are the circumstances under which S is assertible, and its denial conditions are the circumstances under which S can be denied. Suppose that the only ways of using S relevant for its meaning are assertion and denial. Under these assumptions, the inferentialist could characterize the meaning of S by describing its assertion and denial conditions.

G. Santos (✉)
Faculdade de Ciências, Center for Philosophy of Sciences, University of Lisbon, Lisbon, Portugal
e-mail: gbsantos@fc.ul.pt

 
T. Lopez-Soto (ed.), *Dialog Systems*, Logic, Argumentation & Reasoning 22,
https://doi.org/10.1007/978-3-030-61438-6_4

This approach to meaning would also need to consider the relation between assertion and denial. We will consider two accounts of this relation. One claims that assertion and denial are independent speech acts, and, accordingly, the description of the assertion conditions is independent of the description of the denial conditions. The other claims that assertion and denial are not independent speech acts and, in particular, assertion has priority over denial. The characterization of the denial conditions depends on the characterization of the assertion conditions (in a sense that we describe further ahead). Following the terminology employed in the literature, we will refer to the first account as *bilateralism* and to the second as *unilateralism.*[1]

Our discussion will consider two applications of bilateralism. First, we discuss an interpretation of the logical constants, where their introduction and elimination rules have, respectively, premises that are assertions/denials and conclusions that are denials/assertions. We then discuss an understanding of truth-value gaps and gluts, which distinguishes between denying a sentence and asserting its negation.

In both cases, we argue that claiming that assertion and denial are independent speech acts raises a challenge. On the one hand, this account of their relation must differ from the sort of dependence defended by the unilateralist. On the other hand, it must also differ from complete independence. The challenge, therefore, consists of providing an account of the relation between assertion and denial that satisfies both constraints.

We claim that the absence of this account reveals a gap in the bilateralist approach. If bilateralism claims that use determines meaning and that the use of a sentence should be described in terms of assertion and denial conditions, it must also provide an accurate description of the relation between these speech acts. By contraposition, if bilateralism lacks an account of this relation, it cannot explain the meaning of a sentence in terms of its assertion and denial conditions.

The intended upshot of our argument is to reply to an objection raised by (Restall 2005):

> It is often thought that intuitionistic logic fares especially well when it comes to proof-theoretic justification of logical consequence. The justification here is seriously incomplete. The intuitionist has to do more work to explain the priority of assertion over denial and the resulting restriction of connective rules on the right.

Michael Dummett was an influential proponent of unilateralism. His theory of meaning played a central role in his philosophical account of intuitionistic logic (see Dummett 1973, 1977, 1991, 2002). While we will not discuss the relation between unilateralism and intuitionistic logic in detail (but see Santos (2018)) our

[1]We could also consider a third way of understanding the relation between assertion and denial, where denial has priority over assertion. This approach is called *falsificationism* and a recent defense is provided by Kapsner (2014). Thus, a full defense of unilateralism would not only need to consider the need of a relation between assertion and denial, but also the direction of such a relation (that is, whether assertion has priority over denial or if it is the other way around). In the present work, I only discuss the first point.

arguments could be employed as evidence in favor of the Dummettian position, offering a reply to the objection raised by Restall.

The basic structure of the reply is the following. The existence of a gap in the bilateralist approach reveals that its justification of logical consequence is incomplete. Since this gap is absent from the unilateralist approach, if we want to account for logical consequence in terms of assertion and denial and if unilateralism privileges intuitionistic logic, its proof-theoretic justification of logical consequence could indeed fare better than bilateralist justifications of other logics.

## 4.2 Rumfitt on Assertion and Denial

Bilateralism was originally put forward by Rumfitt (2000, 2002). His proposal endorses an account of assertion and denial in terms of answers to "Yes" or "No" questions, originally offered by Smiley (1996). For a declarative sentence S, its assertion conditions are those conditions under which we are entitled to answer "Yes" to the question "Is it the case that S?" When these conditions are satisfied, we can assert S. Analogously, its denial conditions are those conditions under which one is entitled to answer "No" to the same question. When these conditions are satisfied, we can deny S. Based on this account, Rumfitt (2000, p.797) argues that assertion and denial are independent speech acts and, therefore, assertion and denial conditions are not interdefinable:

> On this alternative conception, mastering the sense of an atomic sense A will involve learning methods whose deployment might entitle one *either* to affirm it *or* to reject it. Successful application of these methods, one might say, will put one in a position to answer the question whether A either by "Yes" or "No" as appropriate. Affirmative answers, however, enjoy no priority over negative ones. The acts of answering a propositional question affirmatively and of answering it negatively – the acts of accepting its content and of rejecting it – are conceived to be on all fours. I shall call this view of how a sentence's might be specified the *bilateral* conception [...].

Rumfitt's understanding of the relation between assertion and denial gives rise to a disagreement with unilateralism. As already mentioned, Michael Dummett was an influential proponent of unilateralism and this theory of meaning played a central role in his philosophical account of intuitionistic logic. According to Dummett, assertion enjoys priority over denial. Employing Smiley's terminology, the unilateralist claims that answering a propositional question negatively depends on our ability to answer that same propositional question affirmatively.

Dummett (1973, pp. 316–317) sees his unilateral account of the relation between assertion and denial as having its origin in Frege's understanding of the relation between assertion, denial and negation. According to Frege, denying a sentence is logically equivalent to asserting its negation. The unilateralist endorses this equivalence and tries to explain it as a consequence of the fact that the circumstances where the denial conditions of a sentence are satisfied are all and only those where its assertion conditions could never be satisfied. Further ahead, we will discuss the unilateralist view of the relation between assertion and denial in considerable detail. For the time being, notice that the bilateralist distinguishes between circumstances where the assertion conditions of a sentence could never be satisfied and circumstances where its denial conditions are satisfied.

To continue our description of the disagreement between unilateralism and bilateralism, let CaS and CdS stand for, respectively, the assertion and denial conditions of S. If assertion and denial were entirely independent, the circumstances under which S can be asserted hold with complete independence from the circumstances under which S can be denied. We could thus distinguish four possibilities:

1. CaS can be satisfied while CdS cannot be satisfied.
2. CdS can be satisfied while CaS cannot be satisfied.
3. CaS and CdS can both be satisfied.
4. Neither CaS nor CdS can be satisfied.

In the first possibility we could assert S, in the second we could deny S, in the third we could neither assert nor deny S, and in fourth we could both assert and deny S.

As we have already mentioned, the unilateralist claims that assertion conditions have priority over denial conditions. More precisely, according to Dummett, CdS are satisfied if and only if CaS could never be satisfied. Consider a possibility where CaS can be satisfied and another where CaS could never be satisfied. By the unilateralist account of the dependence between denial and assertion, the denial conditions can only be satisfied when the assertion conditions could never be satisfied. Hence, the CdS cannot be satisfied in the first possibility. Also, since we could never assert S in the second possibility, it also follows from the unilateral account of assertion and denial that we should deny S in this possibility. Thus, we can assert or deny S but none of the above possibilities allows us to assert and deny S simultaneously, nor do they leave us in a position where we can neither assert nor deny S.

More generally, the assumption that the circumstances where the denial conditions of a sentence satisfied are all and only those where its assertion conditions could never be satisfied rules out possibilities where the assertion and denial conditions of a sentence can be simultaneously satisfied and possibilities where the assertion and the denial conditions of a sentence could never be satisfied. According to this assumption, if the assertion conditions of a sentence are satisfied, its denial conditions cannot be satisfied. So if the denial conditions of a sentence cannot be satisfied, its denial conditions are thereby satisfied. Therefore, the unilateralist allows possibilities 1 and 2 but it rules out 3 and 4.

Let us now consider the bilateralist approach. Rumfitt applied this approach in a characterization of the meaning of logical constants. According to this characterization, the meaning of a logical constant should be described in terms of its introduction and elimination rule and these rules should take into account the assertion and denial conditions of a formula. For example, (Rumfitt 2000, p. 802) argues that the negation operator should be governed by four rules:

$$\frac{-A}{+(\neg A)}\ [+\neg I] \qquad \frac{+(\neg A)}{-A}\ [+\neg E]$$

$$\frac{+A}{-(\neg A)}\ [-\neg I] \qquad \frac{-(\neg A)}{+A}\ [-\neg E]$$

Take the pair of rules [$+\neg$ I], [$+\neg$ E]. The introduction rule [$+\neg$ I] tells us that once we have established that the denial conditions of a sentence are satisfied, we can assert the negation of that sentence. The elimination rule [$+\neg$ E] tells us that once we have established that the assertion conditions of the negation of a sentence are satisfied, we can deny that sentence. The pair of rules [$-\neg$ I] and [$-\neg$ E] has a similar reading.

This characterization of the logical constants also employs two principles that coordinate the assertion and denial of a formula. Let Γ stand for a set of sentences that are either asserted or denied, S is an assertion/denial and S* is its denial/assertion. Rumfitt (2000: 804) argues that:

(C1) If $\Gamma \vdash S$ and $\Gamma \vdash S^*$ then $\Gamma \vdash \bot$,
(C2) If $\Gamma, S \vdash \bot$ then $\Gamma \vdash S^*$

Principle (C1) tells us that if S is provable from the set of sentences Γ and S* is provable from that same set of sentences, then Γ leads to a contradiction. Principle (C2) tells us that if a contradiction is provable given a sentence S and a set of sentences Γ, then S* is provable from Γ.

These principles are not compatible with the four possibilities previously distinguished. In particular, (C1) is incompatible with possibility 4. On the other hand, the coordination principles allow for the existence of sentences such that their assertion and denial conditions could never be satisfied.[2]

Notice that, independently of how the bilateralist might choose to formulate its coordination principles, their existence appears to be in tension with the claim that assertion and denial are independent.[3] We will see that this tension is not restricted to Rumffit's account, but it is instructive to illustrate it by considering principle (C2) once again.[4]

---

[2]It is worth noticing that a sentence might be presently undecided, without it being the case that its assertion and denial conditions could never be satisfied. For instance, S could be a mathematical claim that is presently undecided. This only means that its assertion and denial conditions are not presently satisfied. If someone came up with a proof or a refutation in the future, those conditions could be satisfied. Unilateralism is compatible with the existence of this kind of sentences. On the other hand, unilateralism rules out the existence of sentences such that its assertion and denial conditions could never be satisfied.

[3]It is known that these coordination principles raise difficulties for the bilateralist. Ferreira (2008) showed that assuming coordination for atomic formulae is insufficient to preserve (C2) at the molecular level. This result proves that coordination principles and the bilateral introduction and elimination rules for the logical connectives cannot rule out a failure of coordination for complex formulas, even when coordination of assertion and denial is assumed for atomic formulas. See Rumfitt (2008) for a reply.

[4]For a criticism of bilateralism aimed specifically at Rumfitt's proposal, see Dickie (2010).

As we mentioned, if the assertion and denial of S were completely independent, the satisfaction of CaS and CdS would also hold independently of one another. This complete independence would prevent us from drawing any conclusions about the satisfaction of CdS if we only had evidence about what is provable given the satisfaction of CaS. Nevertheless, according to (C2), if we know that a contradiction is derivable from the satisfaction of CdS, we can already infer the satisfaction of CaS. Therefore, by endorsing coordination principles like (C2), when the bilateralist argues that assertion and denial are independent, this cannot mean that they are entirely independent.

This tension between coordination and independence can even appear to be desirable. After all, it seems easy to find linguistic evidence contradicting the claim that assertion and denial are completely independent. As an illustration, let CaT and CdT be the assertion and denial conditions of a sentence T. If assertion and denial were completely independent, we could consider arbitrary combinations of assertion and denial conditions. For instance, we could consider the four following (unordered) pairs of assertion and denial conditions.

5. CaS and CdT.
6. CaT and CdS.
7. CaS and CaT.
8. CdS and CdT.

Notice that each of these pairs would allow two different sentences. For instance, 5 allows a sentence P that can be asserted when the assertion conditions of S are satisfied and denied when the denial conditions of T are satisfied. But it also allows a sentence Q that can be asserted when the denial conditions of T are satisfied and denied when the assertion conditions of S are satisfied.

If assertion and denial conditions were entirely independent, sentences like P and Q would be as legitimate as S and T. However, suppose that S stands for "Planet earth orbits the sun", and T is "Planet earth orbits the moon". It is hard to make sense of P and Q. Since planet earth orbits the sun, CaS are satisfied. Thus, P's assertion conditions and Q's denial conditions are satisfied. Since planet earth does not orbit the moon, CdT are satisfied. Thus, P's denial conditions are satisfied, and Q's assertion conditions are satisfied. Therefore, if assertion and denial were entirely independent, we could describe certain aspects of the solar system by asserting and denying P (or Q). However, that is not what we do. Instead, we describe those aspects of the solar system by asserting the conjunction of S with the negation of T (or a sentence that is logically equivalent to that conjunction).

Notice that, on their own, the assertion and denial conditions of both P and Q are legitimate (since they are the same as S and T's assertion and denial conditions and these are legitimate sentences). So, any problem that we might attribute to P and Q must be related to their combination of assertion and denial conditions. That is, we cannot make arbitrary combinations of assertion and denial conditions and expect that the resulting combination is a legitimate sentence. But then, if we cannot form a sentence by combining any two sets of legitimate assertion and denial conditions, it cannot be said that these conditions are entirely independent.

We saw that Rumfitt denies any priority in the relation between assertion and denial, claiming that these acts are on all fours. Nevertheless, that cannot mean that these speech acts are entirely independent. As we have seen, Rumfitt also argues that certain principles coordinate assertion and denial. It would appear that the validity of these principles is incompatible with these speech acts being completely independent. This gives rise to different questions. First, to which extent can the bilateralist maintain that assertion and denial are independent and to which extent are these speech acts dependent? Moreover, as a follow-up, since bilateralism rejects any priority between assertion and denial, something needs to be said about the source of this dependence. In other words, if the coordination principles (C1) and (C2) describe how assertion and denial depend on one another, how do these principles hold?

## 4.3 Restall on Truth-Value Gaps and Gluts

So far, we have been solely focused on Rumfitt's understanding of bilateralism and its ability to provide an account of the logical constants. However, the challenge that was just raised is not restricted to his approach. In this section, we argue that it applies to other proposals that endorse some of the assumptions of the bilateralist framework. In particular, I claim that the account of truth-value gaps and gluts provided by Restall (2013) suffers from a similar difficulty. Restall employs assertion and denial in his account of logical reasoning, while denying the existence of any priority between those speech acts.

To describe this account, recall that the unilateralist endorses the Fregean account of the relation between assertion, denial, and negation, claiming that the denial of S is logically equivalent to the assertion of its negation. Restall (2005, p. 109) denies this equivalence and distinguishes both acts.

> First, I will argue that the speech-act of denial is best not analyzed in terms of assertion and negation but rather, that denial is, in some sense, prior to negation

In particular, he argues that we can deny S without asserting its negation and that we can assert its negation without denying.[5] This distinction allows Restall (2013, p. 81) to provide the following account of truth-value gaps and gluts:

> Friends of truth-value GAPS and truth-value GLUTS both must distinguish the *assertion of a negation* (asserting $\neg p$) and *denial* (denying $p$). If you take there to be a truth-value *glut* at $p$ the appropriate claim to make (when asked) is to assert $\neg p$ without thereby denying $p$. If you take there to be a truth-value *gap* at $p$ the appropriate claim to make (when asked) is to deny $p$ without thereby asserting $\neg p$.

[5] For a related account of the relation between denial and negation see (Priest 1993, 1999).

Thus, according to Restall:

- S is a truth-value gap if we can deny S and its negation.

Given his distinction between denying S and asserting its negation, arguing that S is a truth-value gap does not imply the assertion of the negation of S nor the assertion of S. Similarly:

- S is a truth-value glut if we can assert S and its negation

By this definition, if S is truth-value glut, we are not committed to denying its negation or to denying its assertion.

A unilateralist would argue that no sentence satisfies these definitions. For instance, suppose that S is a truth-value glut. Then, in particular, we can assert the negation of S. By the unilateral equivalence between asserting the negation of S and denying S, we can deny S. By the definition of truth-value glut, we can assert and deny S. However, by the unilateral definition of denial, we can deny S if and only if its assertion conditions could never be satisfied. Therefore, according to the unilateral understanding of assertion and denial, there can be no truth-value gluts. A similar argument shows that the existence of truth-value gaps is incompatible with unilateralism.

The previous paragraph does not constitute an argument against the existence of truth-value gaps and gluts. After all, one might disagree with unilateralism in the first place. Still, it allows us to see this, given that the existence of gaps and gluts is incompatible with the existence of priority between assertion and denial. Thus, Restall must rely on a different understanding of the relation between those speech acts. We argue that this understanding faces questions similar to those raised at the end of the previous section. To do this, let us consider how Restall employs the notion of *state*.

Formally, a state is a pair of sets of statements, where the statements in one set are asserted, and the statements in the other set are denied. The intuitive idea behind this definition is that a state of affairs can be characterized by two sets of sentences. Namely, those that can be asserted (in that state of affairs) and those that can be denied (in that same state of affairs). Using the notation [S: T], we can describe the state consisting of the singleton {S} where S is asserted and the singleton {T} where T is denied.

Restall (2005, p. 82) then adds:

> With the notion of a state at hand, we may begin to consider how we might evaluate states [. . .] Not all states are on a par, for some states are self-defeating. In particular, if a state contains a statement in both the left set and the right set, then this state undermines itself [. . .] If the state represents the state of play in some dialogue or discourse, then some statement has both been asserted and denied. The state is undermined.

The notion of state can be employed in a new understanding of logical validity. According to the more traditional definition, when an argument is logically valid, asserting its premises implies asserting its conclusion. But according to Restall, our understanding of logical validity should say that asserting the premises of a logically valid argument also stands against denying its conclusion.

The idea behind this proposal can be illustrated by considering a state [S: S], where sentence S would be simultaneously asserted and denied. For Restall, this would be an incoherent state because asserting S stands against denying it. According to his understanding of logical validity, we can therefore say that S follows logically from S.

We have just seen how Restall describes his understanding of logical validity in terms of the notion of state and that some states are incoherent. However, we have not yet been told why there are some incoherent states.

Intuitively, it seems correct that asserting a sentence also stands against denying it. However, there are different ways of understanding this incompatibility. For instance, we have already pointed out that the unilateralist also agrees that asserting S stands against denying it. On the other hand, we have also seen that the unilateralist denies the existence of truth-value gaps and gluts. Since Restall claims that asserting S stands against denying it, while allowing the existence of truth-value gaps and gluts, it follows that merely saying that asserting S is incompatible with denying S is insufficient as a description of the relation between these speech acts.

Restall never puts forward a more detailed description of the incompatibility between asserting and denying S. We will now argue that, as with Rumfitt, the lack of a clear account of the relation between these speech acts raises a challenge. Our discussion will focus on the two following claims:

9. We can simultaneously assert S and its negation.
10. We cannot simultaneously assert and deny S.

Someone who thinks that there is no difference between denying S and asserting its negation does not accept the existence of a difference between 9 and 10. We have seen that Restall endorses both claims and that he rejects the Fregean view according to which, denying S is logically equivalent to asserting its negation. We claim that rejecting Frege's view cannot be the end of Restall's reply. We not only need to know what explains the difference between 9 and 10, but also why should someone endorse 10.

This need becomes apparent if we draw a contrast with unilateralism. Let us recall how Dummett motivates the Fregean view on the basis on his account of the relation between assertion and denial. Namely, asserting the negation of S is logically equivalent to denying S, because the satisfaction of CdS only means that CaS could never be satisfied. In other words, when we deny S, we are saying that S could not be asserted. Claim 10 is inbuilt into the unilateralist understanding of the relation between assertion and denial, so to speak. This view tells us that if we assert S, CaS can be satisfied and thus we cannot simultaneously deny S. And if we deny S, CaS could never be satisfied and thus we cannot deny S. Restall's proposal lacks an analogous justification for 10.

Notice that, by itself, the notion of incoherent state cannot identify acceptable combinations of assertion and denial conditions. As an illustration, let S stand for "1 < 2" and T for "All triangles have three sides". Let P be a sentence such that its assertion conditions are CaS and its denial conditions are CdT. We can assert P when $1 < 2$ and we can deny it when there is a triangle that has not three sides. Clearly, there is no priority between the definition of P's assertion and denial conditions.

Sentence P is such that [P: P] is an incoherent state. However, S and T are legitimate sentences while P is unintelligible. The problem with P has its source in the relation between CaS and CdT. Why does combining CaS with CdS (or CaT with CdT) give rise to an intelligible sentence, but combining CaS with CdT results in something unintelligible? Again, the unilateralist has an answer to these questions. A set of assertion conditions can only be combined with a specific set of denial conditions (and vice-versa). Since the denial conditions for S are defined as the impossibility to satisfy its assertion conditions, CdS is just an abbreviated way of saying that CaS could never be satisfied. This condition identifies every acceptable combination of assertion and denial conditions. Within the unilateralist framework, CdT refers to nothing other than the impossibility to satisfy CaT, and this set of assertion conditions has no relation with CaS. Hence, T is unintelligible.

## 4.4 Concluding Remarks

The bilateralist tries to explain the meaning of a sentence in terms of assertion and denial. However, following this route presupposes saying something about how assertion and denial are related to one another. The unilateralist, who follows the same route, claims that assertion enjoys priority over denial. How does the bilateralist understand this relation? On one hand, we know that she denies any priority between assertion and denial. On the other, both applications of bilateralism discussed above are also not saying that assertion and denial are completely independent.

Bilateralists must have in mind some middle ground, where assertion and denial are not entirely determined by one another but where these speech acts are also not completely independent. Even bilateralists should endorse the existence of some form of dependence between assertion and denial. The challenge that we wish to raise consists in providing a more detailed description of this dependence.

We believe that this is a worthy challenge, particularly given the inferentialist framework endorsed both by unilateralists and bilateralists. Within a unilateralist framework, the existence of dependence between assertion and denial follows analytically from the unilateral conception of denial. But this sort of explanation is unavailable to the bilateralist precisely because she rejects any priority between assertion and denial. Our challenge can then be formulated in the following way: what is the source of the bilateral dependence between assertion and denial and to what extent does it allow independence between these speech acts?

**Acknowledgements** This work was funded by the post-doctoral scholarship SFRH/BPD/117034/2016 of the Fundação para a Ciência e Tecnologia.

## References

Brandom, R. (2000). *Articulating reasons: An introduction to Inferentialism*. Cambridge: Harvard University Press.

Brandom, R. (1994). *Making it explicit: Reasoning, representing and discursive commitment*. Cambridge: Harvard University Press.

Dickie, I. (2010). Negation, anti-realism, and the denial defence. *Philosophical Studies, 150*, 161–185.

Dummett, M. (1973). *Frege: Philosophy of language*. London: Duckworth.

Dummett, M. (1977). *Elements of intuitionism*. Oxford: Clarendon Press.

Dummett, M. (1991). *The logical basis of metaphysics*. London: Harvard University Press.

Dummett, M. (2002). 'Yes' 'no' and 'Can't say'. *Mind, 111*(442), 289–296.

Ferreira, F. (2008). The co-ordination principles: A problem for bilateralism. *Mind, 468*(117), 1051–1057.

Kapsner, A. (2014). *Logics and falsifications: A new perspective on constructive semantics*. Cham: Springer.

Priest, G. (1993). Can contradictions be true? *Aristotelian Society Supplementary, 67*(1), 15–54.

Priest, G. (1999). What not? A defence of dialetheic theory of negation. In D. Gabbay & H. Wansing (Eds.), *What is negation*. London: Kluwer Academic Publishers.

Restall, G. (2013). Assertion, denial and non-classical theories. In E. Mares & K. T. F. Berto (Eds.), *Paraconsistency: Logic and applications* (pp. 46–71). Dordrecht: Springer.

Restall, G. (2005). Multiple conclusions. In P. Hajek, L. Valdes-Villanueva, & D. Westerstaahl (Eds.), *Logic, methodology and philosophy of science*. Amsterdam: College Publications.

Rumfitt, I. (2008). Co-ordination principles: A reply. *Mind, 117*(468), 1059–1063.

Rumfitt, I. (2002). Unilateralism disarmed: A reply to Dummett and Gibbard. *Mind, 442*(111), 305–321.

Rumfitt, I. (2000). 'Yes' and 'no'. *Mind, 436*(109), 781–823.

Santos, G. (2018). Bilateralism, independence and coordination. *Teorema, 37*(1), 23–27.

Smiley, T. (1996). Rejection. *Analysis, 56*(1), 1–9.

# Chapter 5
# Under the Talking-Tree: Proverbs as Reasons. The Dialogical Articulaton of Proverbs Within the Baule Tradition

**Adjoua Bernadette Dango and Shahid Rahman**

*Dedicated to Souleymane Bachir Diagne*

**Abstract** The *Talking-Tree* or *Palaver Tree* (*Arbre à palabres*) is a designated location (originally a large ancestral tree such as the baobab, but it can also be a grave) in many African traditions where the community comes together to discuss, in a peaceful and constructive manner, issues of common interest. It is conceived as an open gathering space of interactive communication led by the stance that finding a compromise or common solution is the best way to consolidate a community. At times, the interchange taking place at a Talking-Tree may also transform into conflict management. Conflict management unfolds into several specific patterns of argumentation including those that aim at deciding if some given accusation is justified or not. The main aim of this chapter is to study, within the Baule tradition of Talking-Tree debates involving accusations of wrongdoing, the meaning explanation underlying *proverbs* (*nyanndra*), which constitute the most fundamental elements of these debates. More precisely our study, based on a pragmatic approach to meaning, will focus on the distinction drawn by linguist Kouadio (2012) between *ascertainment*, (*epistemo*)*logical* and *moral Baule proverbs* by distinguishing their different role in a Talking-Tree debate. One of the main results of our approach is that it makes it patent that drawing a conclusion from a Talking-Tree debate is grounded on contentual functional links, rather than on the analysis of logical constants. This research should set the basis for a larger epistemological research on the structure of argumentation patterns born and developed in Africa, where meaning and knowledge are constituted during dialogical interaction. The dialogical system underlying

A. B. Dango
Département de Philosophie, Université Alassane Ouattara, Bouaké, Côte d'Ivoire
e-mail: bernafleure@yahoo.fr

S. Rahman (✉)
Département de Philosophie, CNRS, UMR 8163-STL, Université de Lille, Lille, France
e-mail: shahid.rahman@univ-lille.fr



T. Lopez-Soto (ed.), *Dialog Systems*, Logic, Argumentation & Reasoning 22,
https://doi.org/10.1007/978-3-030-61438-6_5

such form of argumentation, that we call *Dialogues of functional reasoning by proverbs*, we think provides a general instrument for the study of patterns of argumentation beyond the African tradition.

**Keywords** African Debates · Arbre à Palabres · Argumentation · Baule · Dialogue · Proverb · Palaver Tree · Talking-Tree

## 5.1 Introduction

The *Talking-Tree* or *Palaver Tree* (*Arbre à palabres*) is a designated location (originally a large ancestral tree such as the baobab, but it also can be a grave) in many African traditions where the community come together to discuss, in a peaceful and constructive manner, issues of common interest. It is conceived as an open gathering space of interactive communication led by the stance that finding a compromise or common solution is the best way to consolidate a community.

At times the interchange taking place at a Talking-Tree may also transform into conflict management. Conflict management unfolds into several specific patterns of argumentation, including those that aim at deciding if some given accusation is justified or not. Moreover, the dialogical process, the *Talking-Tree debate*, will usually be coupled with the task of determining what are the consequences of the outcome (e.g. the accusation is justified or not) of the debate. In the case of allegations of wrongdoing, the consequences can either involve some form of punishment to one of the parties or some kind of compensation to the other party or, more often than not, also both punishment to the wrongdoer and compensation to the complainant.

The main aim of this study is to analyse, within the Baule tradition of Talking-Tree debates involving accusations of wrongdoing,[1] the *meaning explanation*[2] underlying *proverbs* (*nyanndra*). *Nyanndra* are the elements of which these debates are made of.

In such a context the interaction between the two parts takes the form of a process in which a challenger (the complainant) deploys proverbs to attack the defender (the accused) on the facts which are reproached to him.

The defender, in turn, has the duty to defend himself by using proverbs too. The proverbs, as discussed in the next section, have the role of impartial "witnesses".

[1]The Baule-people inhabit mostly a region of Ivory Coast between the Comoé and Bandama rivers. The Baule are an Akan group, speaking a language of the Kwa branch. Nowadays the Baule people represent around 20% of the population of Ivory Coast. They came mostly from Ghana during the reign of queen Abla Pokou in the XVIIIth Century – see Kouadio (2007, pp. 21–27) and (2012, pp. 21–51).

[2]The notion of *meaning explanation* is the inferential counterpart of truth-functional semantics. The terminology is due to Martin-Löf and has a natural dialogical reading – see Rahman et al. (2018, chapters II and III). Namely, it amounts to setting the meaning of an expression by rules that establish how to challenge and defend it. These rules also indicate how to produce a local reason for a claim and how to analyse a reason.

Moreover, the proverbs brought forward during a debate on accusations of wrongdoing have the specificity of either bringing some justification for a claim or providing reasons for an action.

According to the linguist Kouadio (2012, pp. 131–284), whose book represents the most thorough study on Baule proverbs to date, Baule proverbs can be divided into *ascertainment proverbs* (*proverbes de constatation*), (*epistemo*)*logical proverbs* – Kouadio calls them *proverbes logiques* – and *moral proverbs* (*proverbes moraux*). While ascertainment and logical proverbs are brought forward as justifications in the sense just mentioned, moral proverbs occur as a conclusion of the argumentation. Actually, after the interchange between the contenders, the judge (or the elders) state a moral proverb conceived as a recapitulation of the whole argument.

In order to accomplish our task, we will deploy the recently developed pragmatic approach to meaning called *Immanent Reasoning* developed by Rahman et al. (2018), where the meaning explanation of an expression is established by fixing rules of challenge and defence of two players **X** and **Y**, that might change their roles (of challenger or defender) during the argumentation.

For short, we will distinguish ascertainment, epistemological and moral proverbs, by the ways they are challenged and defended within a Talking-Tree debate.

One of the main results of our approach is that it makes it patent that drawing a conclusion of a Talking-Tree debate is grounded on meaning dependence links, rather than on the analysis of logical constants.

This research should set the basis for a larger epistemological research on the structure of argumentation patterns born and developed in Africa, where meaning and knowledge are constituted during dialogical interaction, and that we call *Dialogues of functional reasoning by proverbs.*

## 5.2 Proverbs as Witnesses and Reasons

### *5.2.1 Etymology of the Baule Term for Proverb*

The Baule term for proverb is *nyanndra*. According to Kouadio (2012, pp. 58–60) its etymology indicates that it is constituted by

> the nominal phrase *y a, i.e. we*;
> and the verbal phrase *tra, i.e. caught you.*
> Putting both together we obtain: *We caught you.*

In order to grasp the sense underlying the etymology of the term *nyanndra* Kouadio Y. (2012, pp. 61–64) invites us to consider a debate in which a complainant accuses a second one of wrongdoing, in front of a third, an impartial *witness*, who has the role of deciding on the outcome of the debate. Notice that a crucial feature of the witness is that the third person is not called to give his personal opinion but to provide a justification rooted in the uses and traditions of the community. This is, what the *we* (*y a*) occurring in *nyanndra* brings to the fore. In other words, the justification is rooted in the collective understanding of the situation at stake. The conceptual content *catching* or *capturing you* indicates that the justification is contextually fixed to the alleged wrongdoing of one of the interlocutors.

Summing up, each *nyanndra* brought forward during a debate has the main role of an impartial witness, to which each of the contenders can apply as a *reason* that justify their claims.

More generally, a proverb encodes a meaning and knowledge rooted in the community tradition that in the context of a juridical debate determines the precise justification and content of the claims brought forward by the concrete interlocutors of that debate. Indeed, Kouadio (2012, p. 61) proposes to understand the role and constitution of the notion of *nyanndra* as deeply rooted in debates governed by traditional African Law. Classifying Baule proverbs.

## *5.2.2 Classifying Baule Proverbs*

As mentioned above, Kouadio (2012) provides a classification of Baule proverbs that proves to be useful for understanding their role as providing reasons within a debate. The classification distinguishes three main sets of proverbs:

- Ascertainment proverbs (*proverbes de constatation*)
- (Epistemo)logical proverbs (*proverbes logiques*)
- Moral proverbs (*proverbs moraux*)

**Ascertainment Proverbs**

These proverbs verify some specific links between facts, or kind of facts, that can be deployed as Kouadio (2012, pp. 147–205) reasons for justifying a claim. Most of them have a conditional structure, whereby the link of protasis and apodosis in the conditional has been established by experience.[3] They involve several topics, such as:

| | |
|---|---|
| **Endurance** | [Even if] *the chili-plant is struck by* [heavy] *rain, the fire of the chili remains.* |
| **Prudence and knowledge from experience** | [If] *a red buffalo killed your mother, you run when you see a termitary* [that from far has the shape and colour of a red buffalo]. |
| | *I am* [like] *the hut curtain, hanging in the door of a home:* |

[3]Notice that often the formulation of proverbs does not make explicit the particles "if" and "then" for binding antecedent and consequent of an implication – cf. Carteron (2018, p. 2). The implication is determined by the contentual dependence of the consequent upon the antecedent. Something similar happens with the propositional connectives "and" and "or".

| | |
|---|---|
| | *one side turned inwards and the other towards the outside.*[4] |
| **Happiness leads to success** | *Mushrooms sprout* [if the] *termitary is a happy one.* |
| **Taking time** | [When] *the woman takes her time in the kitchen, the sauce becomes succulent.* |

**Epistemo(Logical) Proverbs**

Kouadio (2012, pp. 209–250) calls these proverbs *logical*. We prefer to call them epistemological, since their main feature is that they encode general knowledge. In fact, what distinguishes them from the previous ones is that the link of protasis and apodosis is constituted by either meaning relations (rather than empirical,) or by general knowledge. Compare the epistemological proverbs:

> [If] *I come to say good evening, it does not follow that I ask to spend the night* [at your home].

with the ascertainment proverb:

> [When] *the woman takes her time in the kitchen, the sauce becomes succulent.*

If we rightly understood Kouadio's classification, the point is that in order to establish the relevance of the protasis for the apodosis of an epistemological proverb it requires more general knowledge than the one involved in the conditional expressed by an ascertainment proverb. Indeed, it seems that the content of the protasis of the second proverb, taking time for the cooking, is closely linked to the content of the apodosis, the quality of the result of the cooking. By contrast, linking the content of protasis and apodosis in the first proverb, requires a more a general epistemological perspective that goes beyond the meaning encoded by the protasis, *coming to say good evening*.

For sure, as pointed out by Kouadio (2012, p. 210) the borders of the classification are flexible, particularly so when the subject is rooted on general knowledge. In any case, both can be deployed as reasons for justifying a claim within a Talking-Tree debate.

Some of the topics involved in epistemological proverbs are:

| | |
|---|---|
| **Some acts do not entail self-interest** | [If] *I come to say good evening, it does not follow that I ask to spend the night* [at your home]. |
| **Acts entail/preclude other acts** | [If] *you see me with a broom, it means that there is dirt in the house.*<br>[If] *you do not sleep, you will not be able to dream.*<br>*One cannot look inside a gourd with both eyes at the same time.* |

[4]We owe this proverb to Carteron (2018, proverb 173, p. 57)

| | |
|---|---|
| **Death** | *Death wipes its sponge over every person.* [When] *men die, they do not come back,* [but when] *money dies* [is gone], *it comes back.*[5] |
| **Misfortune is unavoidable** | [If] *you did or did not take the egg of the nighthawk left on the cross-road you will experience misfortune anyway.* |

**Moral Proverbs**

Kouadio (2012, pp. 252–288) subclassifies moral proverbs into **advices**, **prescriptions** and **reproaches**. Within the context of a Talking-Tree debate, moral proverbs have the role of providing the justification for the conclusion of the whole debate and leads to a juridical decision towards resolving the initial conflict.

| | |
|---|---|
| **Advices** | [If] *you eat your* [own] *tongue, you are* [actually] *not* [feeding yourself by] *eating meat* [but hurting yourself].<br>*Even the bark of a tree can sometimes be useful when deployed* [as a pan] *for collecting rubbish.*<br>*Someone who has much travelled experiences many things without becoming old.*<br>*One backward step does not break the kidneys of the margouillat- lizard.*[6] |
| **Prescriptions** | *You should not water the new rice plants with old rainwater.* |
| **Reproaches** | [If] *you lost your teeth, do not harm* [blame] *the hunter* [who provides meat that you cannot eat].<br>[When] *the panther is absent, the grasscutter devours the rice.*<br>*The liar always claims that his witness is across the Comoé River.* |

As it is the case with ascertainment and (epistemo)logical proverbs, the content alone does not always furnish a clear criterium for distinguishing moral from other sorts of proverbs. Actually, it is the role of providing a justification for the conclusion of a debate, i.e. the *moral* of the argument, that characterises this kind of proverbs.

As discussed in the next section, the meaning of both claims and proverbs justifying them have in principle the structure of a functional dependence of claims upon proverbs. This functional structure becomes fixed to a contextually given debate, when the function takes it substitution instances form the concrete claims of that debate. One of the concrete examples we will study is the following:

**Claim**: There is no harm in admitting that leaving the village was a mistake. **Justification**: Recall the proverb: *one backward step does not break the kidneys of the margouillat-lizard.*

In the next section we turn to more general considerations on the role of proverbs.

[5]We owe this proverb to Carteron (2018, proverb 315, p. 105).

[6]We owe this proverb to Carteron (2018, p. 18), proverb 44.

## 5.3 The Open-Texture of *Nyanndra*

One of the most important general features of proverbs is its dynamics. A dynamic that eminent scholars in the field such as Mammoussé Diagne (2005) and Souleymane Bachir Diagne (2007) attach to the temporal dimension of language within oral traditions. Actually, those authors provide deep insights into the intertwining between the permanence of meaning and knowledge encoded by proverbs and their necessity to be contextually enriched, particularly so when deployed as vehicles of transmission and development of traditions.[7]

Yao and Koffi (2016), who studied this intertwining from the point of view of cognitive linguistics, suggest that the cognitive content of proverbs is neither *frozen in time* (*figeé dans le temps*) nor *arbitrarily free*.

Summing up, in relation to the meaning of proverbs occurring in a debate we could speak of their *open-texture*, that is, the possibility to extend the scope of application of a proverb, i.e. its "interpretation", to a new case (or claim), not already recorded by the tradition.[8]

Furthermore, one can see a proverb in principle as a kind of (universal) proposition that can be 'enriched' by the context, to yield another contextually given proposition.

Thus, enriching proverbs with contexts assumes:

(a) that the proverb at stake is already of the type proposition;
(b) that the (linguistic) meaning of a proverb can be extended by contextual "interpretation".

Let us work out these assumptions.

### 5.3.1 *Proverbs and the Two Sides of a Contextual "Interpretation"*

**The Two Sides of Contextual "Interpretation"**

Proverbs as such, are elements of a set. Now, in the context of a debate, they complete a claim or statement by providing the justification of the proposition involved in that claim. The statement, or claim itself, is here understood as an incomplete linguistic entity calling to be completed (or saturated) by a proverb. Thus, the abstract structure that articulates proverb and claim expresses the following dependence of the latter upon the former:

[7]See too Dadié (2003).

[8]We borrowed the term *open-texture* from Bartha (2010, p. 9).

| | |
|---|---|
| Given *Proverbs*: *set* | |
| *A*: *prop* (*x*: *Proverbs*) | *A* is a proposition, provided *x* is a proverb justifying the claim that *A* is the case. Or more loosely, ! *A* is a claim backed by a proverb. |

More precisely, justifying the claim is carried out by a function from proverbs to claims, so that we have:

$$\mathbf{X}b(x) : A(x : Proverbs) \ (x \text{ is some element of the set of proverbs})$$

In plain words, interlocutor's **X** justification for the claim that *A* is the case is a method *b*(*x*), that takes elements of some set of proverbs (assumed to be relevant for that claim) and yields a *reason*, for the claim that *A* is the case. For short, **X** uses the proverb as a reason for their claim. The execution of the method can be thought as an interpretation or proverb-decoding process. In other words, using a proverb as a good reason is providing an interpretation of the proverb in the context of a particular debate – though it might yield a different interpretation in a different one. One way to see the interpretation or decoding process triggered by the method *b*(*x*) is to understand it as the result of an analogical heuristic examination. This examination makes it apparent how the content of the claim at stake is dependent upon the conceptual content encoded by the proverb brought forward during the debate.

How the proverb-decoding process works is **certainly not a formal matter**, and requires linguistic, cultural, epistemological and argumentative skills.[9] Moreover, as we discuss in the final section of our paper, the interpretation process is crucially linked to *ekphrasis*, i.e.; the art of making a listener "see" in their imagination, through words alone, the concept to be conveyed – see Webb (2009). Our point is that the **visual imagination** attached to proverbs (see S. B. Diagne (2001), M. Diagne (2005), S. B. Diagne (2007) and Kouadio (2007)) – is triggered by the method *b*(*x*) that implements the contextual interpretation.

Hence, when an instance of *Proverbs*, e.g. a Baule proverb *c*, is enriched by associating it with statement *A* we obtain for example the following structure:

| | |
|---|---|
| Given, | |
| *c*: *Proverbs* | *One backward step does not break the kidneys of the margouillat-lizard* is an element of the set *Proverbs* |
| ! *A* | There is no harm in admitting that leaving the village was a mistake |
| We obtain | |
| **X** *b*(*c*): *A*[10] | There is no harm in admitting that leaving the village was a mistake. *Recall that one backward step does not break the kidneys of the margouillat-lizard* |

[9]As mentioned below this can be linked with Nzokou's (2016, pp. 336–339) operator "≈".

[10]For the dropping of the exclamation mark here see explanation of this use in the next section.

- Notice that contextual interpretation, in general and within a debate in particular, goes two ways, namely:

1. *Enriching* the proverb with a contextual proposition associated to the proverb – in our example enriching the proverb *c,* by associating it, by means of *b*(*c*), to the proposition *A*.
2. *Completing or saturating* the propositional function with a proverb – in our example saturating *A*: *prop* (*x*: *Proverbs*), with proverb *c* in order to yield *A: prop*

A way of conceptually precising the role of both sides of the interpretation process involved in the passage from *b*(*x*): *A* (*x*: *Proverbs*) to *b*(*c*): *A* is to recall Recanati's (2007) distinction between *saturation* and *enrichment.* Whereas *saturation* is the process by the means of which the free variable of a propositional function is bounded, *enrichment* is the process by the means of which the meaning of an expression is linked to another one. However, while in the first process the target is to complete an expression so that it provides a proposition, the target of enrichment is an expression that as such is linguistically complete.

Let us consider the following two examples:

1. Beethoven composed the 9th symphony with a chorus based on Schiller's *Ode to Joy*.
2. It is raining now.

While the second sentence seems to require from the hearer to complete it with contextual elements that fix the time of *now*, in contrast to some other moments, the first one does not seem in principle to require any additional information.

Indeed, it looks as if the second sentence invites the hearer to ask *when*? *where*? whereas the first sentence **can**, but does **not need**, to be completed with the date (and/or place) of composition.

The kind of completion required by the second sentence is called *saturation*, and the completion of the first sentence is called *enrichment*. Saturation is mandatory and enrichment is optional – see Recanati (2004, p. 7), Recanati (2010, p. 70), Recanati (2017, pp. 215–224).

Recanati (2007) himself thinks of the difference as being psychological rather than structural. According to our view, the distinction between dependent and independent types provides a new path for the study of Recanati's approach – see Rahman's (2020) contribution to the present volume. Moreover, in the context of our paper it opens the path to understanding Baule arguments as the intertwining of meaning dependences.

- To put it bluntly, our point is that a proverb can be enriched by associating it with a concrete proposition that *interprets* it in some contextual situation but, in order to grasp its general conceptual content, this is not necessary. For example, *One backward step does not break the kidneys of the margouillat-lizard,* can be understood as such in its literal meaning, it does not require to be interpreted as, for example, covering cases of persons making a U- turn in relation to some decisions. This not mandatory feature of enriching allows proverbs to be used in different Talking-Tree debates. Thus, we can say that when a claim is backed by a proverb, the justification of the claim is made dependent upon the chosen proverb.

So far so good, let us now work out this further on.

### 5.3.2 *Justifying Claims with Proverbs*

In the preceding sections "*A*" stands for claim, brought forward during a debate, and that requires being justified by a proverb. However, if the meaning explanation should be established by means of dialogical interaction we need to show how to articulate claims and proverbs during dialogical moves such as challenge (e.g. accusation) and defence. In order to distinguish challenges and defences a richer structure must be considered.

Within the framework of *Immanent Reasoning* (Rahman et al. 2018), the dialogical articulation of claims resulting in propositions and their justifications is spelled out by prescribing how to introduce reasons in order to justify a claim, and how to analyse a reason that justifies a claim.

If we implement this approach to our present study we obtain the following rules.

**Synthesis of Reasons**
This rule sets the moves that yield the choice of a proverb as reason.

**X** ! *A*
(player **X** brings forward some claim that *A* is the case. The exclamation mark indicated the assertion force. So, whereas "*A*" is the proposition claimed, "! *A*," indicates the claim that *A* is the case)
**Y** ?*A* (player **Y** asks for justification)
**X** *b*(*p*): *A* (player **X**, chooses some proverb *p* of the set *Proverbs*, and deploys it as reason *b*(*p*) for justifying *A*)

Notice that in the notation the exclamation mark occurring in "**X** ! *A*;" indicates that player **X** claims that they have *some reason* for backing their claim, but they did not bring it forward yet, the reason is still *implicit*. Once he had chosen the proverb, he has the element required for the constitution of the reason for their claim, and thus the reason is made explicit and submitted to public scrutiny. That is why the exclamation mark is dropped in the move **X** *b*(*p*): *A*.

The point of this notation is to stress that the process of enriching a proverb in the context of a debate is a dialogical one. The emerging meaning is the result of an argumentative interaction. Let us delve into this issue.

**Analysis of Reasons**

This rule sets the moves that question the choice of a proverb as reason. Or more precisely, it might be understood as the move where the defender must show that the analysis of the justification they bring forward yields a "canonical" interpretation of the proverb in relation to the claim. In other words, they must show that the justification, *d*, they bring forward for *A* can be defined (is equal) to an interpretation of the proverb the Elders **E**, the authority designated by the community has accepted or to one justification that the antagonist has already conceded.

**X** *d*: *A* (player **X** brings forward *d* as justification for the claim *A*)
**Y** ?*d* (player **Y** asks to decode the justification *d*)

$$\mathbf{X}\ d = b(p_i)^{\mathbf{E}}: A \qquad \mathbf{X}\ d = b(p_i)^{\mathbf{Y}}: A \qquad \mathbf{X}\ d = d^{\mathbf{Y}/\mathbf{E}}: A$$

Player **X** has three choices:

1. He can show that *d* is equal to an interpretation *b*( *p*i*)* accepted as canonical by the Elders **E** (the authority designated by the community)
2. He can show that *d* is equal to an interpretation *b*( *p*i*)* accepted as canonical by the antagonist **Y**
3. He can show that *d* is a justification already accepted by the antagonist **Y** or **E** for the same claim.

Of course, the use of a proverb can be contested and this in several manners. Not only by bringing forward another proverb (as in the example below) but also by refusing to accept that the proverb in question is relevant for the justification of the claim at stake. This points out to another crucial feature of the semantic constitution of proverbs. The set of proverbs put at work in an argumentation is presupposed to be relevant. Thus, we should **not assume one universal set of proverbs** but several specific ones to the context in question.

This suggests that the first two responses of the defender to the request to decode the reason *d*, presuppose some moves where the Elders or the antagonist accept *b*( *p*i*)* as a reason of *A*, even hypothetically. In other words, the first two equality responses presuppose that **E** and/or **Y** concede

*A*: *prop* (*x*: *Proverbs*)
*A* is a proposition under the **hypothesis** that the reasons backing this assertion stem from the set *Proverbs*

*b*(*x*): *A* (*x*: *Proverbs*)
*b*(*x*) is an interpretation of the proverb that yields a reason for *A* under the hypothesis that there is a suitable proverb to be chosen from the set *Proverbs*.

Moreover, the presupposition might involve a deeper structure where the concession is not directly a concession about the same claim, but the same *kind of claim*. This requires rules such as

**E** (or **Y**) $A = B$: *prop*    Under the presupposition *A*, *B*: *prop* (*x*: *Proverbs*).
**E** (or **Y**) $b(pi) = d$: *B*
⇓
**X** *d*: *A*

In other words, **X** has the right to deploy *d* as a justification for *A* if it has already been conceded (by **E** and or **Y**) that both *b(pi)* and *d* are both a suitable justification for *B* and it has also been conceded that $A = B$. Clearly, the third kind of response cannot be contested since it amounts to reflexive equality (the Elders or the antagonist has already brought forward such a justification for the same claim).

In the present paper, where we focus on articulating the link between proverbs and the claims they justify, we stop short before we come to this deeper sub-argumentation. So, we assume that once one of the two possible responses to the request of defining the justification brought forward has been chosen, the debate either stops (by the antagonist – or Elders – refusal to accept that the interpretation of the claim provides a suitable justification of the proverb) or continue (by the antagonist – or Elders – endorsement of the justification).

In the following example we will deploy both forms of moves; the one with an *implicit reason* and the one with an *explicit reason*. However, we will not include the moves contesting the explicit reason.

- Let us recall that the main of the present paper is to develop a pragmatist approach to the meaning of proverbs in their role as reasons within a Talking-Tree debate. We do not aim to furnish herewith a systematic study of the rules and development of such debates. This explains why the following examples, that should make the justifying role of proverbs apparent, only display fragments of a debate.

**Example 1**
Mr. **X**, accused of having stolen some good, says he was not in the village on the day of the robbery.

**Y's Challenge**:
I know that you were in my yard on the day of the robbery. Recall the proverb:

> *I am* [like] *the hut curtain, hanging in the door of a home: one side turned inwards and the other towards the outside.*

**X's Defence**:
On what grounds do you make such and accusation? I was not in the village on the day of the robbery, I was with my friend, who unfortunately, yesterday left the country. Recall the proverb:

> *One cannot look inside a gourd with both eyes at the same time.*

**E 's Conclusion**
The complainant **X** is right. Recall the proverb:

> *The liar always claims that his witness is across the Comoé River.*

Thus, **Y** must compensate **X**.

**Dependence of claims on proverbs in the first two moves:**

(a) Let "$p1$" stand for the proverb:

*I am* [like] *the hut curtain, hanging in the door of a home: one side turned inwards and the other towards the outside.*

Let "$A1$" stand for the sentence

I know that you were in my yard on the day of the robbery.

Thus, the justification has the following form:

$b(p1)$: $A1$, given $p1$: *Proverbs*

In plain words: the proverb $p1$ chosen by **Y** is one of the elements of the set of proverbs **Y** brings forward, in order to provide a reason for grounding their claim that **X'** has stolen of him some good.

(b) Let "$p2$" stand for the proverb:

*One cannot look inside a gourd with both eyes at the same time.*

Let "$A2$" stand for sentence

I was not in the village on the day of the robbery, I was with my friend, who unfortunately, yesterday left the country.

Thus, the justification has the following form:

$b(p2)$: $A2$, given $p2$: *Proverbs*

In plain words: the proverb $p1$ chosen by **X** is one of the elements of the set of proverbs, **X** brings forward in order to provide a reason for countering **Y**'s accusation

**Remarks**: for the sake of stressing our point and keeping things simple, we assumed in this example that the set *Proverbs* is the same for both contenders. This assumption is not in general necessary, so long as the different sets of proverbs are subsets of a set accepted by the community. Notice that, with the exception of the form of the conclusion (to be discussed in the next section) we refrain of integrating into the dependence structure the dependence of one move upon the others.

The dependence of the conclusion upon the other moves involves some deeper structural exploration. This takes us to the next section.

**Moral-Proverbs as Recapitulations**

The meaning explanation of *moral proverbs*, **when understood as a recapitulation of an argumentation**, requires a richer dependence structure. The point is that the form should display the fact that the justification of the conclusion is based on all of the claims and the proverbs brought forward as reasons during the whole debate.

In order to achieve this, we need to introduce devices of the higher-order type theory, which allows to express unities such as:

$$(x : Proverbs)A_i(x)$$

Which **represents both the sentence** $A$**i and its dependence upon a proverb** $x$, which justifies it. These unities, technically known as *function-types*,[11] constitute a claim, the justification of which is a function:

$$f : (x : Proverbs)A_i(x)$$

In our case, $f$ is an interpretation or proverb-decoding function that when applied to an element $p$i of *Proverbs*, yields the justification $f(p$i) of the statement $A$i:

$$\frac{f : (x : Proverbs)A_i(x) \quad p_i : Proverbs}{f(p_i) : A_i(p_i)}$$

The justification of a juridical decision, such as the one of example 1, grounded on, say; the proverb-decoding function $b1$, which justifies the statement $A1$; and - proverb-decoding function $b2$, which justifies the statement $A2$; and *moral*-proverb-decoding function $b3$, which justifies the statement $A3$ has a more complex form. Indeed, instead of unities of the form $f$: ($x$: *Proverbs*)$A$i($x$) that associate a sentence with a proverb by means of the proverb-decoding function $f$, we have unities such as:

$$g : (b_1 : (x : Proverbs_1)A_1(x), b_2 : (y : Proverbs_2)A_2(y), \ldots)A_n(b_1, b_2, \ldots)$$

that associate, by means of $g$, the conclusion with a whole sequence of claims justified by different sets of proverbs. More specifically, the conclusion of the Elder in our previous example has the form:

$$\mathbf{E}\, g: (b_1: (x: Proverbs_1)A_1(x), b_2: (y: Proverbs_3)A_2(y), b_3: (z: Moral\text{-}Proverbs)A_3(z))\ B(b_1, b_2, b_3)$$

Whereby $b3$, is dependent upon $b_2$, and $b_2$ upon $b_1$. Technically speaking, the sequence in brackets left of a sentence is called its *context.*[12] In plain words, the Elder's justification of the juridical decision $A4$ (**Y** must compensate **X**) is grounded on **X**'s justification $b1$, and **Y**'s justification $b2$ and their own justification $b3$. Whereas $b1$ justifies **X**'s claim that $A1$ is rooted in some proverb $x$, $b2$ justifies, with a fresh proverb $y$, their defence to the attack; and the Elders own choice of a moral proverb in order to justify $A3$ (that **Y** is guilty).

Technically speaking, the sequence in brackets left a sentence is called its *context*. If we wish to stress the dependence relations we can deploy the following simpler structure:

$$\mathbf{E}\, g: (x: Proverbs_1, y: Proverbs_2, z: Moral\text{-}Proverbs)\ B(x, y, z)$$

[11]See Ranta (1994, pp. 162–163).

[12]See Ranta (1994, pp. 126–137).

Summing up; the justification of a conclusion backed by a moral proverb, when conceived as a recapitulation of an argumentation developed in the context of a Talking-Tree debate, is a procedure that displays those claims, *backed* by the set of (relevant) proverbs *x*. The Elder establishes that some moral proverb can understood as the outcome or conclusion of the claims players **X** and **Y** brought forward during the argumentation.

**Example 2**

Assume a debate by the means of which it is disbelieved that a child, Koffi; has already the skills of a good farmer.

**X's Claim**.

Despite his young age Koffi is a skilled farmer (*A*1). Recall proverb *p*1:

*If a child manages to extract the flour of the fruit of the néré beans and the flour is succulent, the elders also eat of it.*

**Y's Objection**.

Koffi is too young. He needs to grow up in order to be a good farmer (*A*2). Recall proverb

*p*2:

*An old man sitting at the foot of a tree sees better than a child sitting on a high branch.*

**E's Conclusion**.

**X** is right (*A*3), Recall proverb:

*Wisdom follows wisdom.*

Koffi grew up in a family of wise men, he deserves the duly respect (*B*)

Thus, the simplified form of the justification of the conclusion has the following form E *g*: (*x*: *Proverbs*1, *y*: *Proverbs*2, *z*: *Moral-Proverbs*) *B*(*x, y, z*)

$$\begin{array}{l} b_1: Proverbs_1 \\ b_2: Proverbs_2 \\ b_3: Moral\text{-}Proverbs \end{array}$$

$$g(b_1, b_2, b_3): B(b_1/x, b_2/y, b_3/z)$$

- Notice that our reconstruction makes it patent that drawing a conclusion of a Talking-Tree debate is grounded on the meaning dependence of claims upon proverbs, rather than on the analysis of logical constants.

## 5.4 Conclusion and the Work Ahead

**Dialogues of Functional Reasoning by Proverbs**

As mentioned above, one of the main results of our study is that the inferential pattern that leads to the conclusion of a Talking-Tree debate, is an outcome of the quite complex meaning dependence that links claims and proverbs rather than an outcome grounded on the analysis of logical constants. In other words, concluding in such a debate is not connective-driven, but led by contentual functional links established during dialogical interaction.

Indeed, recall that $(x: Proverbs)A\text{i}(x)$ are functional types, the tokens of which are functions. More precisely, $f$: $(x: Proverbs)A\text{i}(x)$, indicates that the function $f$ is a decoding function that associates some proverb $x$ to the sentence $A\text{i}(x)$. Hence, the conclusion is grounded in nothing but a sequence of proverb-decoding functions.

*Dialogues of functional reasoning by proverbs*, as we call it, constitutes an argumentation framework based on sequences of proverb-decoding functions that features the kind of contentual reasoning involved in Talking-Tree debates. Notice that since this argumentation pattern is not led by the analysis of logical constants, incorrect arguments cannot be characterised by fallacies but by sophismata, i.e. by errors grounded on mistakes in grasping the meaning links required by a particular debate.

According to our view, such dialogues set the basis for a larger epistemological research on the structure of argumentation patterns born and developed in Africa, that could be extended to other forms of reasoning such as those involving allegories or metaphors.

The functional feature of this argumentation patterns also seems to fit nicely with our suggestion that proverbs have the *open-texture* of a *lekton* (in Recanati's sense) that can be contextually enriched by claims occurring in Talking-Tree debates. This deserves a deeper linguistic, philosophical and logical study, particularly so since the process of enriching a proverb involves analogy and thinking by images, which is not in principle grounded on logical connectives either. Let us mention these issues very briefly.

### *5.4.1 Analogy*

One challenging work ahead is to develop our study in the context of Gildas Nzokou's (2013, 2016) remarkable work on defeasible argumentation in the oral traditions.[13] Moreover, we think that a very good point to start joining both projects

[13]One important difference to our approach is that Nzokou's (2013, 2016) analysis is based on the idea that proverbs have the logical form of a universal quantified proposition. Thus, according to Nzokou's view, sentences and proverbs are related by universal elimination (plus analogy), whereas within the framework of *Dialogues of functional reasoning by proverbs,* decoding-functions do the

is to examine if our proposal of defining proverb-based justification of claims does in fact offer a way to push forward Nozkou's (2016, pp. 336–339) interpretation-operator "$\approx$" or even open to a new reading of it.

Indeed, according to Nzokou (2016, pp. 336–339), the crucial point of an argument in African oral tradition is to associate proverb and the claim by an analogical defeasible process. In our context, if we follow Kouadio's (2012) proposal to understand proverbs as constituting reasons, Nzokou's operator can be understood as associated to what we call the proverb-decoding function, that transforms the proverb into a justification of a claim.

The defeasible aspect of Nozkou's approach has some fruitful features that could be integrated into our framework. Indeed, if some justification has been brought forward by **X**, then they have to show that it is equal to a canonical one. If they do not, then the justification will be rejected as being not relevant for the claim: the interpretation of the proverb does not "match" with the claim, or it can be even overruled by another proverb more specific to the claim at stake. The important lesson to learn here is that what is overruled is not the proverb, but rather the application of a proverb when justifying a claim.

More generally, analogies constitute indeed one very important instrument of argumentation, not only in proverb-based argumentations (see Rahman and Iqbal, 2018, and Rahman et al. 2019). In a further paper we shall study the argumentative structure of analogies displayed in a Talking-Tree debate.

### 5.4.2 *Ekphrasis or Visual Imagination*

As mentioned above, the landmark works of Mammousé Diagne (2005) and Souleymane Bachir Diagne (2001, 2005) stress the crucial feature of the visual component of meaning associated to a proverb. In fact, decoding the meaning of a proverb in order to apply it to a concrete context (such as claim in a debate) involves the capacity of a proverb to trigger visual imagination.

Kouadio (2007) developed this view in his study of Baule proverbs based on cognitive linguistics. Now, it seems that a further fruitful step in the understanding of the *thinking with images* put at work in Talking-Tree debates is to confront it with *ekphrasis*, i.e. the art of making a listener "see" in their imagination, through words alone, the concept to be conveyed – see Webb (2009).

Our point is that the process of **visual imagination** attached to proverbs is triggered by the method $b(x)$ that implements the contextual interpretation. Webb's (2009) fascinating book, shows that restricting *ekphrasis* to the realm of the Arts is a late development which separated Arts and Sciences. Actually, the art of making of a

job of associating proverbs and sentences – whereby the latter constitute the contents of claims in a debate.

listener a *spectator* is part of the Ancient Greek tradition of the general theory of rhetoric and argumentation – see Webb (2009, p. 8).

Hence, confronting *ekphrasis* with the visual imagination required for Talking-Tree debates is a pressing pending challenge that needs to be dealt with. Particularly so, since the interlocutors of a Talking-Tree debate are engaged in exercising the collective task of creating new images rather than passive spectators. More generally, the thinking with images engaged by Talking-Tree debates does not only convey the meaning and knowledge of their own traditions, but it also enriches and renews it in a constant virtuous circle.

**Acknowledgments** Many thanks to Teresa Lopez-Soto (Seville) the editor of present inspiring volume and to Christian Plantin (Lyon), who suggested many improvements to an earlier version of the paper. We are also very grateful to Jérome Kouadio Yao (Univ. Alassane Ouattara, Bouaké) for his generous support and assistance in linguistic issues related to the subject of our paper. The first author would also like to thank Ayénon Ignace Yapi (Univ. Alassane Ouattara, Bouaké), for his fruitful advices and Kouakou Simplice (Univ. Alassane Ouattara, Bouaké) for his backing to our work. The second author would like to thank the Laboratory STL: UMR-CNRS 8163 and particularly Leone Gazziero (STL), Laurent Cesalli (Genève), and Tony Street (Cambridge) leaders of the ERC-Generator project "Logic in Reverse. Fallacies in the Latin and the Islamic traditions" and Claudio Majolino (STL), associated researcher to that project, for fostering the research leading to the present study and Gildas Nzokou (Libreville), who made S. Rahman aware of the exciting world of African Argumentation. Let us point out that the reflections on which this paper is based evolved under the influence of the responses of many audiences. We are profoundly grateful to all of them, particularly so to Yaovi Akakpo (Université de Lomé), Mouhamadou el Hady Ba (Université Cheikh Anta Diop de Dakar), Mawusse Kpakpo Akue Adotevi (Université de Lomé), Zacharie Bowao (Univ. Marien Ngouabi de Brazzaville, Congo), Christian Berner (Paris Nanterre), Michel Crubellier (Lille), Oumar Dia (Université Cheikh Anta Diop de Dakar), Souleymane Bachir Diagne (Columbia University), M. Iqbal (Université Lille, STL/Antassari I. State Univ, Banjarmassin), A. Klev (Academy of Sciences, Prague), Marcel Nguimbi (Univ. Marien Ngouabi de Brazzaville, Congo), to Auguste Nsonsissa (Univ. Marien Ngouabi de Brazzaville, Congo).

## References

Bartha, P. F. A. (2010). *By parallel reasoning. The construction and evaluation of analogical arguments*. Oxford: Oxford University Press.

Carteron, M. (2018). *Les proverbes baoulé pour entrer dans la Côte d'Ivoire profonde*. Bouaké: Mission Catholique.

Dadié, B. (2003). *Les légendes africaines*. Abidjan: Nouvelles Editions Ivoiriennes.

Diagne, S. B. (2001). *Reconstruire le sens. Textes et enjeux de prospectives africaines*. Dakar: Éditions Codesria.

Diagne, M. (2005). *Critique de la raison orale. Les pratiques discursives en Afrique noire*. Paris: Karthala.

Diagne, S. B. (2007). *Léopold Sédar Senghor: L'art africaine comme philosophie*. Paris: Riveneuve.

Kouadio, J. Y. (2007). *Autopsie du fonctionnement du proverbe*. Abidjan: Dagekof, 3ème édition.

Kouadio, J. Y. (2012). *Les proverbes baoulé (Côte d'Ivoire): types*. In *fonctions et actualité*. Abidjan: Dagekof.

Nzokou, G. (2013). *Logique de l'argumentation dans les traditions orales africaines*. London: Collegue Publications.

Nzokou, G. (2016). Defeasible argumentation in African oral traditions. A special case of dealing with the non-monotonic inference in a dialogical framework. In J. Redmond, O. Pombo, & A. Nepomuceno (Eds.), *Epistemology, knowledge and the impact of interaction* (pp. 322–341). Dordrecht: Springer.

Rahman, S. (2020). What the Weatherman Said. Enrichment, CTT and the dialogical approach to moderate contextualism. In T. López-Soto (Ed.), *Dialog systems. A perspective from language, logic and computation*. Cham: Springer.

Rahman, S., & Iqbal, M. (2018). Unfolding parallel reasoning in islamic jurisprudence. Epistemic and dialectical meaning within Abū Isḥāq al-Shīrāzī's system of co-relational inferences of the occasioning factor. *Cambridge Journal of Arabic Sciences and Philosophy, 28*, 67–132.

Rahman, S., McConaughey, Z., Klev, A., & Clerbout, N. (2018). *Immanent reasoning or equality in action*. Dordrecht: Springer.

Rahman, S., Iqbal, M., & Soufi, Y. (2019). *Inferences by parallel reasoning in Islamic jurisprudence*. Cham: Springer.

Ranta, A. (1994). *Type theoretical grammar*. Oxford: Clarendon Press.

Recanati, F. (2004). *Literal meaning*. Cambridge: CUP.

Recanati, F. (2007). *Perspectival thought*. Oxford: OUP.

Recanati, F. (2010). *Truth conditional pragmatics*. Oxford: OUP.

Recanati, F. (2017). About the *Lekton*. Response to Kölber. In I. Depraetere & R. Salkie (Eds.), *Semantica and pragmatics: Drawing a line* (pp. 215–224). Cham: Springer.

Webb, R. (2009). *Ekphrasis, imagination and persuasion in ancient rhetorical theory and practice*. Farnham-Surrey: Ashgate.

Yao, J. -M., & Koffi, J. (2016). Approche cognitive du figement dans les proverbes baoulé. *Paremia*, 149–160.

# Chapter 6
# What the Weatherman Said: Enrichment, CTT and the Dialogical Approach to Moderate Contextualism

**Shahid Rahman**

**Abstract** The main aim of the present paper is to show that the recently developed dialogical approach to Martin-Löf's Constructive Type Theory (CTT), called *Immanent Reasoning*, provides the means for distinguishing François Recanati's process of *free enrichment* and *saturation*, meets his own objections against perspectives based on unarticulated constituents and opens a new venue to pragmatic modulation, where the speaker-receiver interaction is integrated into the notion of enrichment. In such a setting enrichment operates on proof-objects that make fully articulated event-propositions true. The point is that distinguishing what makes a proposition true from the proposition made true offers a simple and clean way to avoid conflating the contextual elements that enrich a proposition with the proposition itself. Such a framework abounds in means for expressing reference structures such as anaphora, including time and/or location reference. Furthermore, the notion of *dependent types* of CTT (absent in Montague-style semantics) and the associated formation rules allow for a straightforward analysis of composition of meaning at work in Recanati's cases concerning occasion meaning as determined by context. The brand of dialogical contextualism, grounded on the play-level (where propositional content is not necessarily truth-conditional), advocated herewith is not a form of *propositional syncretism*. The framework offers a straightforward response to the failure of third excluded in some instances of *faultless disagreement* without giving up the notion of propositional content. More generally, this suggests an alternative way to tackle the interface pragmatics semantics underlying the notion of pragmatic modulation by integrating into the interface the dialogical game of asking and giving reasons.

**Keywords** Contextualism · Dialogical logic · Enrichment · Lekta · Pragmatic modulation · Temporal reference

---

S. Rahman (✉)
Département de Philosophie, CNRS, UMR 8163-STL, Université de Lille, Lille, France
e-mail: shahid.rahman@univ-lille.fr



T. Lopez-Soto (ed.), *Dialog Systems*, Logic, Argumentation & Reasoning 22,
https://doi.org/10.1007/978-3-030-61438-6_6

## 6.1 Introduction

In his work *Perspectival Thought* François Recanati (2007a), one of the most highly estimated representatives of contemporary Contextualism, distinguishes three semantic levels:

(i) the "Fregean" context-independent meaning of a sentence (associated with the unrelativized proposition expressed by the sentence),
(ii) the *lekton*, a term that Recanati borrows from Stoic Logic,[1] the content of a sentence with respect to context, which falls short before constituting a proposition since some determinants of truth-conditions (i.e. circumstances of evaluation) are left unarticulated (do not correspond to any element in the sentence) and are provided by the situation,
(iii) the Austinian proposition that comes out by associating the *lekton* with a situation serving as circumstance of evaluation.

Recanati's point is to introduce the intermediate level (ii) for sentences such as *it is raining* where the contextual circumstance of utterance (place or time) is tacit in the *lekton,* despite the fact that the utterance of the sentence, e.g. *It is raining*, is false in some circumstance and false in others – cf. Recanati (2007a, pp. 50–51).[2] In contrast, to a sentence where a location and/or time indexical makes of the circumstance of evaluation an articulated part of the *lekton*, such as *it is raining here; it is raining now.*

More generally, Contextualists argue that the influence of context, or pragmatic factors, is necessary in the determination of *semantic* content – understood as truth-conditional propositional content. According to this view, the compositional elements of a sentence rarely, if ever, deliver propositional content. It is the *utterance* or *speech act* that is the proper unit of linguistic analysis according to contextualists, for it is only at the point of use that propositional content is expressed.[3]

Recanati uses the example of the sentence *I am French* to distinguish *formal meaning*, *what is said* and *implicatures*. The *formal* meaning of the first level of meaning, or the literal sentence meaning in this example, is the context-independent idea that *the speaker of this sentence is French*. This literal sentence meaning does not vary from context to context; it always expresses the notion that whoever utters the sentence is French. Formal meaning is opposed to the *context-dependent*

[1]In a fascinating paper that displays skills proper of a detective, Gabriel et al. (2009) suggest that there are strong indications that Frege's notion of *Gedanke* (*thought*) has been directly inspired if not borrowed from the Stoic notion of *lekton.*

[2]The process by the means of which the *lekton* is linked to the circumstance of evaluation should not be thought as providing unarticulated constituents to some incomplete but, in the case of enrichment, the process should be thought as pragmatic top-down modulation procedure by the means of which the contextual meaning of some lexical item is rendered more specific [cf. Recanati (2017, pp. 219–220)].

[3]Cf. Grant (2019), who develops a helpful general discussion on Recanati's Contextualism.

proposition that gets expressed by the *lekton* within particular contexts of use. For example, if Recanati utters the sentence it expresses the proposition that he is French, but if I were to say it, it would be a different proposition, namely, that I am French. Finally, there is the distinction between *what is said* –the *lekton*- and the *implicature*. Recanati supposes a context in which he is asked whether or not he is a good cook. He responds: "I am French". Clearly in this case, his utterance expresses not only that he is from France, but it also *implicates* that he is indeed a good cook. Now, implicatures assume that the *lekton* has been already grasped, this is where, according to Contextualists, the Gricean approach gets it wrong: the latter perspective goes from the context independent proposition to the implicature.

The point of Recanati's approach is that propositional content cannot be grasped without a pragmatic process of *fleshing out the meaning of the sentence so as to make it propositional*" – Recanati (2004, p. 25). In order to show this, he describes three further pragmatic processes*: free enrichment*, *loosening*, and *transfer*. Each of which is defined by the fact that they are top-down, or optional context-driven processes that are involved in the primary interpretation of linguistic utterances and yield truth-conditional content.

*Free-enrichment* essentially consists of *making the interpretation of some expression in the sentence contextually more specific*" – Recanati (2004, p. 24). Take the example *Mary took out her key and opened the door*. The idea here is that (under normal circumstances) the receiver of the utterance of the sentence would assume that the expression means that Mary opened the door *with* her key. Yet, there is no constituent in the sentence itself that articulates this fact. On strict literal reading the sentence expresses a conjunction *punkt*.

*Loosening,* the converse of enrichment, relaxes the conditions of application as opposed to tightening them. Take the sentence *The ATM swallowed my credit card*. By loosening the criteria of use for the term "swallowing" one can easily understand the truth-conditions for this sentence. Also, there is, again, nothing in the sentence itself that explicitly permits this loosening to occur; it is top-down.

The third primary pragmatic process is known as *semantic transfer*. An example of transfer is found in the utterance *The ham sandwich left without paying* – Recanati (2004, p. 26). It seems that the meaning of *Ham sandwich order* is transferred on to "ham sandwich customer" though there is no linguistic mandate to do so.[4]

Thus, despite the fact that the *lekton* of the intermediate level, a *relativized proposition* (true at some situations and false at others) or *a quasi-proposition*, falls short of determining its absolute truth-conditions, a pragmatic modulation process of *free enrichment* **can**, but *must not* be brought to the fore a situation of evaluation relevant for determining its truth-value. This view contrasts with other

[4]Notice that the kind of moderate Contextualism professed by Recanati does not commit him to the claim that every process of completing incomplete proposition must fall in one of the three categories. There are cases that are not result of enrichment, such as completing *Everyone loves Sally* to *Everyone loves Sally and his mother*. However, identifying those cases contribute to the task of identifying the class of linguistic phenomena captured by modulation – Elbourne (2008), Recanati (2010, pp. 10–12).

contextualist approaches that assume that the content of sentences like *it is raining* require a mandatory tacit variable for location (for instance, city, country, etc.). Such approaches, launched by John Perry's (1986) famous paper "Thought without Representation", conceive in fact the *content* of *It is raining* as a propositional function with a variable for location that ***needs*** to be *saturated*, despite the fact that they acknowledge that syntactically nothing is missing in sentences such as *It is raining*:

> [. . .]. *Thus though:*
> *(7) It is raining*
> *is missing no syntactically mandatory sentential constituent, nonetheless it is semantically incomplete. The semantic incompleteness is manifest to us as a felt inability to evaluate the truth value of an utterance of (7) in the absence of a contextually provided location (or range of locations). This felt need for a contextually provided location has its source, I claim, in our tacit cognition of the syntactically argument place of the verb 'to rain'.* Taylor (2001, p. 53).

For short, saturation is *a pragmatic process of contextual value-assignment that is triggered (and made obligatory) by something in the sentence itself, namely the linguistic expression* [such as an indexical] *to which a value is contextually assigned*" – Recanati (2010, p. 4). Recanati's main objections to the saturation approach as a *general approach* to contextuality in a nutshell are three. The third main objection carries most of the weight of Recanati's plaidoyer for contextualism:

- The first main objection can perhaps be declined in two parts. The first part recalls John L. Austin's warning not to conflate content and circumstance of evaluation.[5] The second part joins Michael Dummett's criticism of those approaches that take tenses as constitutive arguments of the content of adjectives. As pointed out by Recanati (2004, pp. 118–19) while commenting Dummett's observation, if we choose the relational view on tenses as mandatory constituents of adjectives, adjectives such as *warm* and *yellow* can no longer be considered as expressing properties but as a relation between the object having the property and the time it entertains that property. Such a relational view departures significantly from our habitual way of learning the use of an adjective. Dummett's point is that to [. . .] *understand 'warm' or 'will be warm' we apply to our prior understanding of what is meant by saying that something is warm our general comprehension of what is to speak of how things were or will be in another time*. Dummett (1997).

[5]In such a setting enrichment operates on proof-objects that make fully articulated event-propositions true. The point is that by distinguishing what makes a proposition true from the proposition made true offers a simple and clean way to avoid conflating the contextual elements that enrich a proposition with the proposition itself. Such a framework abounds in means for expressing reference structures such as anaphora, including time and/or location reference. *As Austin once put it, 'it takes two to make a truth'. The circumstance of evaluation is not an aspect of the content to be evaluated, but an entity with respect to which that content is evaluated. Still, according to the theory of situations to be introduced in this chapter, the circumstance of evaluation is an aspect of content in a broader sense of 'content'. And that aspect of content is irreducibly contextual.* Recanati (2004, p. 115).

- The second main objection parallels the saturation approach to the incorporation of unarticulated constituents with the traditional *argument analysis* of adverbs. The traditional analysis of adverbs as values of propositional functions overlooks the fact that is not possible to specify in general the exact number and kind of adverbial arguments that a predicate might hold.[6] In a similar way as adverbs and modifiers can be multiplied in several dimensions, the content of the verb *to rain* in *It is raining* can always be *further specified* in different degrees (even if we only consider the locative dimension) – e.g. (i) *It is raining in Lille* (given some evidence of a rain-event taking place in that location), or (ii) *It is raining somewhere on earth* (given some evidence of a rain-event taking place at least one location on earth), (iii) *It is raining over earth* (given some evidence of rain-events taking place at most locations on earth): *optionality is the hallmark of enrichment*. However, this does not preclude acknowledging that some verbs such as *arrive* do require a slot for a location argument. Recanati's (2007b, pp. 143–145) point is that while *John has arrived* commits to saturation, *It is raining* patterns with *John has danced* in the sense that their logical form of both do not include a slot for location. This contrasts with the followers of the saturation approach, who acknowledge that *to dance* does not require a variable for location but refuse to pattern *to rain* with *to dance*. Thus, according to the saturation perspective a sentence either expresses a complete proposition, such as *John has danced*, or it does not, such as *John has arrived*:[7] there is no intermediate case. Recanati's all point is that there is such an intermediate level, and this is why enrichment must be added to the process that account for communicative success. This takes us to his third objection.
- The third main objection constitutes the core of *Recanati's moderate contextualism*. According to the saturation view; whereas the answer *Have not a clue*! is an acceptable answer to the question *Where did John dance*? (given the assertion *John has danced*), the same answer is patently unacceptable if the question is *Where did John arrive*? (given the assertion *John has arrived*).[8]

---

[6]*The view I have sketched escapes the difficulties that beset the traditional 'argument analysis' of adverbs. The problem with treating what adverbs contribute as further arguments of the relation expressed by the verb is that this assumes something patently untrue* [. . .]. *As adverbs and modifiers can always be multiplied, and new dimensions of modification can always emerge, the standard argument analysis is clearly hopeless. But the view I have sketched meets both objections: the number and identity of adverbial arguments do not have to be specified in advance, and whatever information they convey does not have to be regarded as implicit when they are not provided (whether linguistically or contextually).* Recanati (2002, footnote 18, pp. 322–323).

[7]Notice that Recanati's analysis of *John has arrived* also applies to the examples brought forward by Tomohiro Sakai (2014). such as *I like very much.* Sakai (2014) joins Stanley (2005) in casting doubts about the (grammatical) force of Recanati's arguments for enrichment. Perhaps, the reconstruction of enrichment within a framework of type-theoretical grammar developed in the next sections will help to dissipate some doubts.

[8]Kent Bach (2004, 2005, 2006), who labels himself as a *radical minimalist*, shares with Recanati the view that there are sentences that are semantically incomplete, such as *John arrived*, though he calls them *propositional radicals* rather than *Lekta*. However, different to Recanati's contextualism

Similarly, under this perspective the speaker of *It is raining*, cannot avoid answering *Where*? Now, if the saturation perspective is right there is no possible context where an expression with a tacit constituent (e.g. a location indication) yields a truth-evaluable statement unless that constituent has been provided.[9] However, Recanati's (2002, p. 316) invites us to consider the following case where the fact that an evaluation circumstance is tacit – namely, location – neither prevents from distinguishing a fully articulated content nor does it frustrate the constitution of a complete proposition – the latter is the result of the free pragmatic modulation process of enrichment:

> *I can imagine a situation in which rain has become extremely rare and important, and rain detectors have been disposed all over the territory (whatever the territory—possibly the whole Earth). In the imagined scenario, each detector triggers an alarm bell in the Monitoring Room when it detects rain. There is a single bell; the location of the triggering detector is indicated by a light on a board in the Monitoring Room. After weeks of total drought, the bell eventually rings in the Monitoring Room. Hearing it, the weatherman on duty in the adjacent room shouts: 'It's raining!' His utterance is true, iff it is raining (at the time of utterance) in some place or other.* Recanati (2002, p. 317).

Indeed, in this example the bare ringing of the bell makes the answer *I have not a clue!* a plausible response to the question *Where?* directed at the weatherman's assertion *It is raining*. The weatherman conveyed an information that can be used to draw some further inferences or decisions – such as reducing the restrictions on the consumption of water.

Another important criticism of Recanati, relevant to our paper, concerns what Jason Stanley (2005) calls *propositional Syncretism* as represented by Soames (2002, 2005), Borg (2004), and Cappelen and Lepore (2005). In fact Recanati's rejection of *propositional Syncretism* constitutes an important motivation of promoting *Lekta*, or *quasi-propositions*, as the inputs of enrichment processes. *Lekta* are neither propositional functions waiting to be saturated nor minimal propositions acting as *common denominators* of whatever assertions might result from pragmatic modulation processes:

---

Bach (2006) strongly contests the view that semantically incomplete sentences can be completed by context. Completion is a semantic and not a pragmatic process. Expansion is a pragmatic process but on Bach's view it applies to already semantic complete sentences.

[9]*I conclude that what characterizes genuine unarticulated constituents is the fact that their contextual provision is not mandatory - it is not required in virtue of a linguistic convention governing the use of a particular construction (or class of constructions). In context, it may be that the unarticulated constituent is 'required'; but then it is required in virtue of features of the context, not in virtue of linguistic properties of the expression-type. A constituent is mandatory in the relevant sense only if in every context such a constituent has to be provided (precisely because the need for completion is not a contextual matter, but a context-independent property of the expression-type). This, then, is the criterion we must use when testing for (genuine) inarticulateness: Can we imagine a context in which the same words are used normally, and a truth-evaluable statement is made, yet no such constituent is provided? If we can imagine such a context, then the relevant constituent is indeed unarticulated (in the strong sense); if we cannot, it is articulated, at some level of linguistic analysis.* Recanati (2002, 316).

- According to *propositional Syncretism*, also called (propositional) *Minimalism*, semantic contents of sentences in contexts are always propositions, but not usually the propositions the users of those sentences intend primarily to assert. Rather, semantic contents are generally "minimal propositions" [as in the work of Cappelen and Lepore (2005)]. Stanley (2005), based on Recanati's (2004, pp. 51–67) objections, provides the following example that stresses some of the main points of Recanati against *propositional Syncretism*. If we assume that the minimal content expressed by *Every bottle is in the fridge*, in any context, is the false proposition *that every bottle in the entire universe is in the fridge*, adherents of *propositional Syncretism* must endorse the view that this content, that in fact it is *never* asserted or conveyed by an utterance is the input of the process that yields the content of the uttered sentence. Similarly, the speaker who assertively utters *The ham sandwich left without paying*, does not assert the minimal proposition *that the sandwich left without paying*! – Recanati (2004, pp. 60–61). Thus, in this case, contrary to the principles of Propositional Syncretism, the minimal proposition is not part of the content of what is asserted. In fact the kind of minimalism advocated by *propositional Syncretism* only works when *the asserted content is richer than the alleged semantic content* (Recanati (2004, p. 60)). This is related to the availability constraint of genuine content. The point is that the pragmatically enriched proposition is the only one that the interlocutors are consciously *aware of* within a speaker- receiver interaction. In other words, the non-enriched proposition, such as the one claimed by propositional Minimalists, is not available to the interlocutors involving sentences such as *Every student passed the logic exam*.

Now, Recanati (2010, p.120) points out that one way to implement enrichment, the modulation process we will focus on, is to build an account that takes the locationless reading as basic and the location--specific reading as pragmatically derived, while appealing to the notion of *variadic* shift to account for the pragmatic derivation of the latter from the former. Variadic shifts are the result of what Recanati (2002, pp. 318–323) calls a *variadic function,* that increases or decreases the arity of the relation it applies to. A useful way to grasp the notion of variadic function is to contrast those variadic functions that implement enrichment by *expansion*, to Quine's (1960) *recessive* de- relativization operator DER.[10] Indeed whereas Quine's recessive-DER suppresses an argument of an n-adic relation (e.g. DER transforms the dyadic relation *John-kisses-Mary* into the monadic *Mary-is-kissed(by John)*), the variadic function that implements enrichment is an expansive function that *adds* an argument. Now, given that according to Recanati's approach the *lekton* of *It is raining* is fully articulated, and it thus has the logical form of a zero-adic predicate,

[10]In fact, also Quine's DER-operator can do both increase or decrease the arity of a relation.

the enrichment process as implemented by an expansive variadic function, transforms the 0-adic predicate into monadic one, namely one where there is an argument for location (leaving the temporal dimension aside). More precisely: *The variadic functions that increase the valence of the input relation through the addition of a* circumstance *to the set of its argument-roles can be represented by means of an operator (or rather, a family of operators)* ***Circ****. When applied to an n-place predicate P,* ***Circ*** *produces an n + 1 place predicate (****Circ P****). There will be as many* ***Circ****- operators as there are argument-roles which can be added to the set of argument-roles of the input relation. There will be a temporal* ***Circ****-operator, a locational Circoperator, etc., depending on the nature of the extra argument-role. Which Circ-operator is at issue will be indicated by means of a subscript. For example, the operator _Circlocation 'contributed by locative modifiers (such as the prepositional phrase _in Paris') will map the [0-adic* ***rain****][11] *into the monadic predicate* ***rain_in*** *relation by adding a Location argument-role.* Recanati (2002, p. 321). Thus, enriching *It is raining*, into *It is raining (in Paris)* is carried out by the variadic function

- Circlocation: Paris(*It is raining*) = *It is raining_in* (*Paris*)

Thus the result of an expansive variadic function such as Cirlocation or simply *Loc*, takes us from the set of those events *e* that are raining events

$$\lambda e[\text{RAINING}(e)] \quad \text{given}\, e \in \textit{Events}$$

to the set of those events that are raining-events and have an assigned location

$$\lambda(l)\lambda(e)\ [\text{RAINING}(e)\&\text{LOCATION}(l, e)] \qquad \text{given}\, l \in \textit{Locations}, e \in \textit{Events}$$

However, this is not yet enrichment. According to Recanati (2010), who follows here McConnell-Ginet (1982) account of adverbials, enrichment is implemented when the expansive variadic function accomplishes two roles at the same time: namely (i) adding a dimension, by integrating an argument role (in our case a locative dimension); (ii) filling the argument with a specific value (say, *Lille*). Enriching *raining* with a locative dimension, when implemented by an expansive variadic function yields

$$\lambda(e)\ [\text{RAINING}(e)\&\text{LOCATION}(\textit{Lille}, e)]\ \text{given}\, \textit{Lille} \in \textit{Locations}, e \in \textit{Events}.$$

[11]The original text maps *Eat* relation to the *Eat-in* relation.

Or in the more usual notation of Montague-Grammars:

$$\lambda(e)\ [\text{RAINING}(e)\&\text{LOCATION}(l,e)(\textit{Lille})] \qquad \text{given}\,\textit{Lille} \in \textit{Locations},$$
$$e \in \textit{Events}.$$

The enriched predicate can be now deployed to build a Davidsonian event-proposition of the form

$$\exists(e)\ [\text{RAINING}(e)\&\text{LOCATION}(\textit{Lille},e)]$$

Thus, in this version, the result of enrichment is represented as the contextual provision of a conjunct. This conjunction is a dyadic relation between events and locations. If we make time explicit, we have the following conjunction:[12]

$$\exists(e)\exists(t)\ [\text{RAINING}(e)\&\text{PRESENT}(t)\&\text{TIME}(t,e)\&\text{LOCATION}(\textit{Lille},e)]$$
$$\text{given}\,\textit{Lille} \in \textit{Locations}, e \in \textit{Events}, t :\in \textit{Time} - \textit{Scale}$$

Now, while representing LOCATION as a relation linking events and places seems to be in principle plausible, a TIME relation defined over a quantification domain of time moments is less appealing – even if the quantification is of the substitutional brand - as the one favoured by Recanati (2007a, pp. 58–59). In fact, as we will discuss below it is quite straightforward to define timing functions that take events as input and yield names of time moments instead. In any case, we do not need to assume that all contextual provisions have the same structure.

Be that as it may, there are four main criticisms to Recanati's moderate pragmatism that are relevant for our present paper. The first is in principle in sympathy to Recanati's proposal. The other two include different readings of the weatherman example congenial with saturation rather than with enrichment. The latter three criticisms can be understood as receiving support from Stanley's (2005) binding-argument. According to Stanley's viewpoint, there cannot be binding without a variable ready to be bound, hence that an argument-role can be bound shows that the contextually provided constituent filling that role is articulated by a free variable occurring in the logical form, for short the logical form is that of a (tacit) propositional function. Furthermore, saturation, so the argument goes, not only explains how to unify unarticulated constituents with propositional content, it explains also in recursive way that preserves syntactic and semantic compositionality.

[12] Cf. Recanati (2007b, p. 133).

- Max Kölbel (2017, pp. 208-210), who shares important views with the ones of Recanati's moderate contextualism, points out that if the notion of *lekton* is equated with the notion of *what is said – lekton* is the Greek word for *what is said* after all, then it looks as if some tension might arise between the concept of *lekton* deployed in Recanati's books *Literal Meaning* and *Perspectival Thought.* According to this worry, one hand Recanati's (2007a, 2007b) *lekton* of the intermediate level is *fully articulated* in the sense that nothing is in the *lekton* that does not correspond to some element in the sentence; on the other, in his earlier work seems to argue that *what is said* tacitly involves unarticulated constituents provided by *free enrichment.* In his response to Max Kölbel (2017) Recanati (2017, pp. 219–220) indicates that enrichment should not be conceived as a process of adding contextual constituents to a some underlying tacitly assumed Austinian proposition from which these constituents have been supressed, but as top- down optional aggregative *specification* process of adding adjunctive time or locative adverbials to a fully articulated content, the *lekton*, that does not contain the contextual parameters required for its evaluation. In other words, we do not have first a fully complete Austinian proposition from which one extracts the *lekton*, but enrichment can produce one or other Austinian proposition.[13]
- The second criticism, which follows from Perry's (1986) analysis of meteorological sentences, insists that *It is raining* does include a tacit slot for a *specific* location, and this also applies to the weatherman example. The specific location tacit in the weatherman's assertion is *On Earth* – cf. Luisa Marti (2006, pp. 153–154). However, as pointed by Recanati (2007b, pp. 137–138) this proposal owes a linguistic-driven explanation on why the specific location Earth should be understood in a *broad* sense (in at least one location on Earth) rather than in a *narrow* sense (*Over Earth*, i.e. in most of the locations on Earth). Moreover, even if it is conceded that the location specific to weatherman is Earth in the broad sense this shows that *rain* patterns with *dance* not with *arrive.* Indeed, whereas *John has arrived* cannot be understood as *John arrived somewhere* on Earth (if we consider the answer *I do not have a clue!* to the question *Where?* to be inappropriate), both *John has danced somewhere on Earth* and *It is*

[13] *I deny that there is any such tension. I agree with Kölbel that the lekton should be equated to what is said for all the reasons he gives. Indeed their being identical is one of the reasons why I use that term 'lekton' which means 'what is said' (and additionally conveys the suggestion of semantic incompleteness, due to the use of the term by Stoic logicians in connection with tensed propositions).* [...]. *Is not free enrichment, the paradigmatic modulation process, the provision of unarticulated constituents? No it is not. In free enrichment some aspect of meaning is contributed in a top down manner by the context. This is often interpreted as the provision of 'unarticulated constituents', but that is not my interpretation. Free enrichment typically corresponds to a process of specifization* [sic], *through which we make the contextual meaning of a lexical item more specific than its literal (conventional) meaning. Is this a matter of providing unarticulated constituents? No. The contextual meaning, resulting from free enrichment, is not unarticulated, because it corresponds to something in the sentence, namely the lexical item whose meaning has been made contextually more specific.* Recanati (2017, pp. 219–220).

*raining somewhere on Earth* are compatible with the answer *I do not have a clue!* to the question *Where?* – cf. Recanati (2007b, pp. 144–145).[14] This might suggest that there is a tacit variable, for a specific location but that sometimes it should be understood in the broad sense and sometimes in the narrow sense. This form of response is close to the following form of criticism that appeals to *optional variables*.

- According to an alternative reading, weatherman meteorological predicates like *rain* carry an argument slot for location. However, so the alternative proposal goes, the argument slot needs not to be filled with a specific location (in the narrow sense); it may be bound by a covert existential quantifier. Moreover, *existential closure should be assumed by default*. Thus, *It is raining*, can be understood as both, *It is raining (in Lille)* or if specific location is not available – as in the weatherman example – then it should be understood as the closed sentence *It is raining (somewhere on Earth)*. This position, a follow-up from Partee's (1989) work on indexicals, faces the problem of providing a lexical driven explanation on how to choose between a narrow and broad scope of the existential quantifier in relation to negation when a negative variant of the weatherman is at stake – whereby instead of detecting rain the device detects absence of rain. Indeed, if existential closure is the default binding procedure, why is it that in the case of a negative variant the weatherman's assertion *It is not raining* should be read as *It is not the case that at some location there is rain*, rather than *There is a location, where there is no rain*? In fact, according to this approach *It is not raining* should be read as *It is not raining on Earth*, but this should be read as *There is no raining spot* – cf. Recanati (2010, pp.104).
- Perhaps the toughest general objection against Recanati's takes on contextualism is the complain that the notion of context-dependence makes it difficult if not impossible to deal with systematic, recursive and computationally tractable aspects of language.[15] The worry is that contextualism is committed to semantic flexibility (i.e. that the meaning of a word may vary from occurrence to occurrence, and, it may vary, in particular, as a function of the words it combines with). This amounts to acknowledging that the meaning of an expression may well not only depend upon the meaning of the complex in which it occurs, but it also may depend upon the meaning of the other words that occur in the same complex – e.g. the meaning of *big* in *big mouse*. Thus, from this perspective it follows that contextualism undermines compositionality. Recanati's (2010, chap. 1) solution,

[14] John Collins (2019), who in his online-paper "On Saturation in Weather Reports" pushes towards a radical pragmatism is not convinced of Recanati's formulation of the weatherman example and offers another variant involving detectors all over the universe and including the assumption that the weatherman does not know if he is or not on Earth. Now, it seems to me that Recanati's answer to the proposal to fill up (by default) the argument slot with *on Earth* still applies to Collins' variant of raining *on the Universe*. Independently of the possible weatherman-variants, at the end of the paper I will come back to the dialogical view on radicalizing contextualism.

[15] See Fodor (2001, 2003) and Bach (2012), who also casts doubts on the of notion of context-dependence deployed by contextualists.

is to make the adjective dependent upon a context, that may be made explicit by linguistic means. For example, the contribution of *big* in *big mouse*, is rendered by the contribution of *big* in relation to the class of mice. Now, as discussed in the next section of the present paper, the introduction of CTT-notion of dependent-types seem to offer a straightforward approach to Recanati's *intersective* understanding of the contextual dependence of complex adjectives. Questions on compositionality are also involved in the availability constraint mentioned above, since the minimal proposition of propositional Minimalists is not computed at all in the modulation process. The very first available proposition understood form an utterance of a sentence is, on Recanati's view; one which is already composed by modulation.

The main aim of the present paper is to show that the recently developed dialogical approach to Martin-Löf's Constructive Type Theory (CTT), called *Immanent Reasoning*,

- provides, the means for distinguishing François Recanati's process of *free enrichment* and *saturation*;
- offers a straightforward approach to context-dependence that responds to compositionality worries. For short, Recanati's account of context dependent *occasion meaning* amounts to the introduction of *dependent types* (absent in Montague-style semantics);
- meets his own objections against perspectives based on unarticulated constituents;
- gives a straightforward response to the failure of third excluded in some important instances of *faultless disagreement* without giving up the notion of propositional content;
- opens a new venue to pragmatic modulation, where the dialogical speaker-receiver interaction is integrated into the notion of enrichment.

The proposed setting understands enrichment as operating on (contextually) proof-objects that make fully articulated event-propositions true. The point is that by distinguishing what makes a proposition true from the proposition made true offers a simple and clean way to avoid conflating the contextual elements that enrich a proposition with the proposition itself.

Such a framework abounds in means for expressing reference structures such as anaphora, including time and/or location reference. Indeed, a fundamental part of our proposal is to implement enrichment by the use of Arne Ranta's (1994, pp. 106–111) *timing*- and/or *locative*- functions, that associate proof-objects to contextual elements (e.g. time moments or locations) – instead Recanati's *variadic functions* – and which can be object of reference. In such a framework, neither before enrichment nor after enrichment does *It is raining* carry a free variable for events, or location and/or time, nor does timing assume quantifying over time moments.

According to this proposal, enrichment is a process of dialogical interaction by the means of which the relativization of a proposition is carried out by responding to questions on specifying the proof-object for that proposition *epistemically assumed to* be true.

More generally, the present paper suggests an alternative way to tackle the interface pragmatics semantics underlying the notion of pragmatic modulation by integrating into the interface the dialogical game of asking and giving reasons. This leads to the following points:

- Top-down processes in general and enrichment in particular are *rights* conferred by speaker to the receiver concerning an assertion of the former. They are meaning setting processes carried out from the *receiver's point of view* concerning the speaker's assertion.
- Bottom-up processes in general and saturation in particular are *obligations* contracted by the speaker concerning their own assertion. They are meaning setting processes carried out from the *speaker's point of view* concerning their own assertion.

The dialogical approach to contextualism, shares the view with Recanati's contextualism the rejection of propositional *Syncretism*. However, from the dialogical point of view the most basic form of propositional content, the proposition at the play-level, is not (necessarily) truth-conditional. Moreover, the dialogical framework includes both a layer dealing with the context sensitivity of language, namely the play level, were meaning formation games intertwine with material games of asking and providing for (local) reasons, and a layer, namely the strategy level, that captures the logical and recursive aspects of language.

## 6.2 Insights of Constructive Type Theory on Free Enrichment

The most important source of resistance to the idea of pragmatic modulation is the fear that, if pragmatic modulation is allowed as a determinant of semantic content, the project of constructing a systematic, truth-conditional semantics for natural language, due to the instability or never-ending feature of the process, will be doomed to failure – see Fodor (2001 and 2003) and Cappelen and Lepore (2005). Recanati (2012, p. 76) summarizes the arguments of his opponents in the following way:

> In contrast to the contextual assignment of values to indexicals, modulation is not driven by the linguistic meaning of words. Nothing in the linguistic meaning of the words whose sense is modulated tells us that modulation ought to take place. Modulation takes place purely as a matter of context, of 'pragmatics'; what drives it is the urge to make sense of what the speaker is saying. So modulation is unsystematic. If we allow it as a determinant of semantic content, we make it impossible to construct a systematic theory of semantic content.

Recanati (2010, Chapter 1; 2012, pp.76–77) proposes to tackle this issue with the help of *truth-conditional pragmatics* based in the tenet that not only it is the case that pragmatics processes such as modulation are constitutive of meaning, but it also holds that their contribution to meaning can be shaped as a systematic compositional procedure. The idea is to defend the claim that compositionality holds at least in the minimal sense that *the modulated meaning of the complex is a function of the modulated meanings of their parts (and the way they are put together) plus in addition, the context which determines how the content of the whole itself is modulated* – Recanati (2010, p. 46).

In his response to the objection of *instability* Recanati (2010, pp. 32–39) develops a procedure by the means of which, what the *standing meaning* – the meaning fixed by the semantic conventions of language, is *contextually enriched* to its *occasion meaning* – determined by the standing meaning and the context of utterance. More precisely, the occasion meaning of a word is the meaning which an occurrence of the word takes on in a *particular context*, **not** only in a *particular* ***linguistic*** *context.*[16] On his view, this sharply contrasts with *saturation* that requires providing values to explicit or implicit variables. The point of Recanati's truth-conditional pragmatics is that the standing meaning of say, *big*, may contribute – in some compositional way – to *big mouse*, given that the occasion where the meaning of *big* is to be apprehended is the context of a relevant comparison class, namely the set of mice. However, the occasion meaning of *big* as ingredient of *big mouse* might be the context of a class of small living beings. In other words, according to the contextual theory underlying truth-conditional pragmatics the occasion meaning is understood as the context-dependent content of the expression, determined by (i) the standing meaning of the expression and (ii) the context of utterance – Recanati (2010, p. 39).

More generally, Recanati's (2010) *truth-conditional pragmatics* aims to show that pragmatic accounts of meaning do not lack *per se* the systematic means of formal model-theoretic semantics, despite the flexibility of meaning underlying modularity. Moreover, according to this account, at the end of a modularity process the proposition obtains a truth-conditional evaluation.

Thus, in such a framework, while the object of an enrichment process, the *lekton*, is said to fall short before determining absolute truth-conditions, in the sense that no truth-values can be assigned to it yet, the contextually enriched *lekton* does determine those conditions. Thus, though Recanati (2012) clearly recognizes that, in contrast to the standard approach to *implicature*, pragmatic modulation is not a *post-semantic* communicative addendum to the utterance of a sentence, it seems that Recanati endorses after all that a systematic account of compositionality of pragmatic modulation must be rendered compatible with model-theoretic semantics in the style of Montague grammar. However, this is not the only option to respond to the charge of being unsystematic.

In this context, it might be worth exploring an approach that furnishes a systematic and compositional way to constitute instances of the type proposition before and after the enrichment and explain their formation during speaker-receiver interaction.

[16] Recanati (2010, pp. 38–39).

Moreover the point is that we do not need to assume that truth-conditions are constitutive of meaning after all, but rather **truth- making conditions.**[17]

We will develop our proposal in two main sections, in the present section, section **2**, I will show how the CTT-notions of:

- canonical and non-canonical proof-object of a proposition avoid conflating the evaluation circumstance and the proposition, while respecting the type-token internal relation between proof-object and proposition;
- type-formation rules, and particularly the formation of dependent-types, show how the meaning of the parts of complex expressions are put together, and render the dependent proof-bjects (i.e. functions), that make the whole complex expressions true;
- complementary and adjunctive adverbials allow to shape the processes of saturation and enrichment;
- assertions with tacit proof objects render the idea of tacit evaluation-circumstances.

In sect. **3** of the present paper I will propose a dialogical setting for the relevant CTT distinctions that yields a dynamic perspective of Recanati's availability constraint. In such a dialogical setting, literal meaning is not processed first, as assumed by Minimalists, but is dialogically processed in parallel with the occasioning meaning determined by the formation rules of the play-level proposition at work.

## *6.2.1 Dependency, Independency and their Objects*

### 6.2.1.1 Hypothetical and Categorical

One of the general philosophical tenets of CTT is linked to the task of avoid *keeping content and form apart* – Martin-Löf's and Sambin (1984, p.2).[18] More precisely, within Per Martin-Löf's constructive type theory (for short CTT), both, logical and non-logical constants are interpreted through the Curry-Howard correspondence between propositions and sets. A proposition is interpreted as a set whose elements represent the proofs of the proposition. It is also possible to view a set as a problem description in a way similar to Kolmogorov's explanation of the intuitionistic propositional calculus. In particular, a set can be seen as a specification of a programming problem, the elements of the set are then the programs that satisfy

[17]In fact, *truth-making theory* and CTT are quite different frameworks, but, in the present paper, in order to give a flavour of what a proof-object is, we will deploy *evidence*, *truth-maker* and *proof-object* as synonym. The main point of difference is that within CTT proof-object and proposition are conceived as enjoying a type-token relation: no token without type.

[18]Cf. Sundholm (1997, 2001).

the specification – Martin-Löf and Sambin (1984, p. 7). Furthermore, in CTT sets are understood also as types so that propositions can be seen as data (or proof-)-types.[19]

Additionally, in the CTT framework it is possible to express at the object-language level

$$A\ \boldsymbol{true} \text{ or or } \vdash A\ or$$

which, when asserted by some individual **g**, conveys the information that this individual is in possession of some proof-object *a* for *A*, a proof-object that *makes* *A* true. Moreover, it can be rendered explicit by means of the **categorical judgement**

$$a : A,$$

which reads, *there is a proof-object a of A* – or the individual **g** can bring forward the proof- object *a* in support of their claim that *A* is ***true.***[20]

Summing up, within CTT a proposition is interpreted as a set the elements of which represent the proofs of the proposition, the solution to a problem, the fulfilments of an expectation.

Accordingly,

| **Explicit** | **Tacit** |
|---|---|
| ***a*: *A*** | ***A true*** or $\vdash$***A*** |

can be read as

| | |
|---|---|
| *a* is an element of the set *A* | *A* has an element |
| *a* is a proof of the proposition *A* | *A* is true, there is a truth-maker for *A* |
| *a* is a solution to the problem *A* | *A* has a solution |
| *a* fulfils the expectation *A* | *A* is fulfilled |

One of the characteristic features of CTT is that it also allows, at the object-language level, expression of **hypothetical judgements** as a form of statement distinguishable from the assertion of the truth of an implicational proposition. Hypothetical judgements give rise to dependency structures in CTT, such as

$$B(x) : prop\ (x : A)$$

This is a formation rule for the hypothetical. More generally, formation rules, a distinctive feature of CTT, by the means of which semantic and syntactic features are processed together, establish well-typing rules.

The proof-object of an hypothetical judgment is a function:

---

[19]Cf. Nordström et al. (1990).

[20]See Martin-Löf (1984, pp. 9–10). For a short introductory survey see Rahman et al. (2018, chapter II).

$$b(x) : B(x)\ (x : A),$$

which reads:

*b*(*x*) is a (dependent) proof-object of *B*(*x*), provided *x* is a proof-object of the. proposition *A*;

whereby the function *b* takes elements from the set *A*, and yields proof-objects for.

*B*(*x*). In other words, in this frame the dependence of the truth of *B* upon the truth of *A* amounts to the dependence of the proof-object of *B* upon the proof-object of *A*. And the dependence of the proof-object of *B* upon the proof-object of *A* is expressed by means of the function *b*(*x*) (from *A* to *B*), where *x* is a proof-object of *A* and where the function *b*(*x*) itself constitutes the dependent proof- object of *B*.

Thus, if we have $b(x) : B(x)\ (x : A)$ as a premise, and we have as a second premise the fact that indeed that there is some evidence *a* for the proposition *A* (i.e. if we have as premise *a*: *A*), then we can infer that $b(a) : B(a)$.

In plain words, from the premises
some *x* is a *B*, provided it is of the type *A*;

and
*a* is indeed of the type *A* (a : *A*);

we can infer:
performance a is a B (b(a): B(a)).

$$\frac{a : A \qquad b(x) : B(x)\ (x : A)}{b(a) : B(a)}$$

- Notice that the assertion *b*(*a*) : *B*(*a*), **presupposes** the formation *b*(*x*): *B*(*x*) (*x: A*),.

In other words, the assertion *b*(*a*) : *B*(*a*) or even the tacit formulation ⊢*B*(*a*), presupposes a suitable set *A* that provides the element a occurring in the function that makes *B*(*a*) true. It is the context of the assertion that determines what the suitable set is.

Let us apply these notions to some of Recanati's examples.

#### 6.2.1.2 Recanati's Contextualism Meets Type Theoretical Grammar

The original work of Martin-Löf had as main aim to reconstruct (in the best possible way) informal mathematical reasoning. But, as already mentioned, Ranta (1994) applies CTT as a general theory on meaning and extended its use for the study of natural languages. Ranta (1994) shows in *Type-Theoretical Grammar* (TTG) how the original CTT- language for mathematical content can be extended to cover natural language phenomena such as pronouns, indexicality, anaphora, text-discourse analysis and temporal reference.

TTG seems to have the means to furnish a systematic framework for the delving into the inner structure of pragmatic modulation in general and of free-enrichment in particular. In the present paper we will focus on distinguishing free-enrichment from saturation, however let us very briefly discuss some of the salient examples involving compositionality.

#### 6.2.1.3 Occasion Meaning

**On Big and Small-Mouses** As already mentioned, Recanati's take on the meaning of adjective constructions such as *big mouse* and *small mouse* is that their contextually enriched propositional content – resulting from applying a variadic function – is grounded, on intersective constructions such as the following

The set of all those $x$ that are both *mice* and *big mice*
The set of all those $x$ that are both *mice* and *small mammals*

Recanati's point is that the choice of underlying domain, that set the comparative standards, is optional and contextually dependent. In the TTG framework this is rendered by the following formation rule, which render the dependency structure for the intersective *big mouse*

$$Big(x) : prop(x : Mice);$$

which renders the predicate *Big Mouse* occurring in propositions such as

*Some mice are big (mice)*

$$\vdash (\exists x : Mouse)Big(x)$$

We can even add some more dependencies

*Big mice are slow*

$\vdash(\forall z : (\exists x : Mouse)\ Big(x))\ Slow(left(z)$, or using the subset separation notation

$$\vdash (\forall z : \{x : Mouse | Big(x)\}) Slow(left(z),$$

*All those (elements of the set of) mice that are big, those are slow*

> In this notation, *left* is a projection function which extracts the left-side element of every *z* that is both *mouse* **and** *big* (*mouse*): it selects a *big mouse*. This construction is in fact a Σ-type and in the propositional interpretation it renders existential. Similarly, *right* can be defined as the projection function which extracts the right-side element of every *z*.[21]
>
> So if *z*, any of the big mice, is a *compositum* of the form <*x* , *b*(*x*)> in which *x* is an element of *Mice* and *b*(*x*) is a method evidencing that *x* can be described as being *big mouse*. Thus, *left* (*z*)= *left*(<*x* , *b*(*x*)>)= *x*: *Mice* and *right*(*z*)= *right*(<*x* , *b*(*x*)>)= *b*(*x*): *Big*(*x*) (*x: Mice*).
>
> The above construction can also be seen as involving an anaphora the head of which is one of those animals described as being a mouse. The tail of the anaphora is constituted by the projection function *left*(*z*) which picks out those animals that are described as big mice in the grammatical subject and of which it is said that they are slow

Alternatively, if we wish to consider *Mouse*(*x*) as separating a subset from some domain, say, *Rodents,* we have the predicate.

*Big for those rodents that are mice*

which can be deployed to build the proposition

*Some of those rodents that are mice are big ((mice-)rodents)*

$$\vdash (\exists z : \{x : Rodents \mid Mouse(x)\}) Big(left(z))$$

whereby, the projection *left*(*z*) selects one of those rodents that are mice.

This seems to be close to what Recanati (2010, p. 35) has in mind when he deploys *Mouse* both as a predicate and as the underlying set over which *Big for a Mouse* is defined.

If the context provides a different set for comparing the size of our mice, say *Mammals*, then we can build the assertion.

*All those mammals that are mice are small ((mice_)mammals)*

[21]In fact, within TTG intersectivity of adjectives is a consequence of applying projection-rules to the pair that constitutes a proof-object of a Σ-type.

$$\vdash (\forall z : \{x : Mammals \mid Mouse(x)\})Small(left(z)).$$

We can certainly add more layers, to produce *All those mammals that are big mice are nevertheless small (mammals)*, without generating, to use Recanati's (2007a, pp. 87–94, and 2017, pp. 220–24) terminology, *genuine disagreement* between interlocutors – at the end of the paper I will come back to Recanati's take on *disagreement*. Similar holds for cases such as *x likes y*, whereby interlocutors might define *like* over quite different sets, e.g. *the set of either human beings* or *the set of those human beings considered as suitable food* (among cannibals), and so on – cf. Recanati's (2010, p. 36).

I will, however, leave it here and turn to the issue on how to systematize the difference between saturation and enrichment within TTG.

## 6.2.2 Adjunctive and Complementary Time Adverbials

### 6.2.2.1 Timing and Locative Functions

Instead of starting with Recanati's (2007a, b) contrast between *It is raining* and *It is raining now*,[22] let us for the moment consider first the following two examples of Ranta (1994):[23]

1. *Napoleon invaded Spain*
2. *The sun was shining*

Let us, for the sake of the comparison, take it that whereas the second sentence *seems* to require from the hearer to complete it with contextual elements that fix the time of that *sun-shining*, in contrast to some other moments; the first one does not seem in principle to require any additional information. Indeed, it looks as if the second sentence *requires* of the hearer to ask *when*?, *where*? in order to be grasp what is said, whereas the first sentence *can*, but does *not need* to be completed with the date of the invasion. This is the analysis followed by Ranta (1994) according to whom:

- The time adverbial that the sentence is endowed with in the first example is *optional.* In fact, such a kind of time adverbial is called in traditional grammar an *adjunct*. According to Ranta's TTG, the logical view on an adjunct is that of an operator turning a proposition into another proposition.
- The time adverbial that the sentence is endowed with in the second example is *necessary*. Within TTG, such adverbials constitute *complements*. As pointed out by Ranta (1994, p. 107) this may well not be the sense of complement in

[22]In fact, as we will discuss further on, Recanati (2007a, b) would contest that the examples below are structurally different.

[23]In fact, the presentation of adjuncts and complements in TTG in the present section stems from Ranta (1994, pp. 106–109).

traditional grammar, but it is a complement in logical sense: it completes the expression with a time variable into a propositional expression.

Thus, within Ranta's TTG the logical formation of an expression involving temporal reference declines in two main cases, namely:

1. Those cases where the expression is understood as a propositional function on a time scale of the form $A[t]$. The complement itself is the explicit or implicit time variable **required** in order to turn the propositional function into a proposition:

$$A(t) : prop(t : time) \quad The\ sun\ was\ shining(t) : prop(t : time)$$
$$\vdash The\ sun\ was\ shining(11hs)$$

which is an implicit way to express that there is some kind of empirical method that renders the proposition *The sun was shining(11hs)* true, i.e. a function *b(tk)*, that brings evidence for the proposition, that he sun was shining at some specific hour *tk*:

$$b(11\text{hs}) : It\ is\ raining(11hs).$$

- Notice that the variable *must* occur in order to make of the expression *The sun was shining*, a proposition.[24] The **dependence of a proposition upon a variable** (in this case a temporal one) is what makes of the time adverbial a **complement**.

2. Those cases where the expression is understood as a full-fledged proposition of the form *A* (with no variable occurring in it, neither explicitly nor implicitly), that **can** but **must not** be endowed with an adjunct. The adjunct itself is constructed as a propositional function that times proof-objects (e.g. events) of *A* by means of a *timing function*

$A$: *prop Napoleon invaded Spain*: *prop*
$\tau(x) : time\ (x : A)\ \tau\ (x) : time\ (x : Napoleon\ invaded\ Spain)$
$\tau(a) : time$, given that $a$, is the evidence of Napoleon's invasion of Spain.

thus, the timing function takes the content of the proposition, the event, and times it. In our case $\tau = (a)$ evaluates to the year *1808*.

More generally expressions of the second kind constitute propositions the formation of which does not require time components. However, they can be

[24]Below, following Recanati (2002) we will distinguish between *It is raining* and *It is raining (here)*.

temporally modified by means of adjuncts defined in terms of timing functions and equality – see Ranta (1994, p. 108). Thus, a temporally modified sentence, like

*Napoleon invaded Spain in 1808*

can then be analysed as the assertion constituted by the **progressive conjunction** of the event proposition that Napoleon invaded Spain **and** the identity-proposition (the adjunct) that the year of that event is indeed *1808:*

$\vdash(\exists x : \textit{Napoleon invaded Spain})\ \tau(x) = \textit{year1808})$

$$(a, b) : (\exists x\text{: } \textit{Napoleon invaded Spain})\ \tau(x) = \textit{year1808})$$

whereby, *a*, is the evidence of Napoleon's invasion of Spain, and *b* transforms this evidence into a proof that the timing of the invasion at stake is the year 1808.

- Notice, that *Napoleon invaded Spain* expresses an independent proposition **not dependent** upon any variable

**Keys to Notation** Recall that within CTT the formation of an existential is a kind of a anaphoric conjunction, such that the second element of the conjunction is dependent upon the first one. In our example, the pair that makes the existential true is composed by (i) the event that brings evidence of Napoleon's invasion of Spain and (ii) evidence that the timing of that event is 1808. The notation $\tau(x) = \textit{year1808}$, stands for the identity relation $I(\textit{year}, \tau(x), \textit{1808})$: *prop* (*x: Napoleon invaded Spain)*, defined within the set *year* – cf. Ranta (1994, p. 52).

#### 6.2.2.2 Enrichment and Saturation within TGG Enrichment

The reader has certainly already guessed that our proposal is to link the **optional process** of adding an adjunct to Recanati's *free-enrichment* and to link the **mandatory process** of *constituting* a proposition out of a propositional function (with time and/or location variables) to Recanati's *saturation*.

Furthermore, the TTG-analysis supports Recanati's claim that the *lekton* involved in free-enrichment is fully articulated: contextual adjunctives are added to complete expressions not to propositional functions. Moreover, it also supports the claim that the enriched proposition can be made true in a context but false in another.

Indeed, Recanati (2007a, b) contests that the logical form of expressions such as *It is raining*, implicitly assume some index that needs to be saturated. *It is raining* **concerns** some indefinite context, in contrast the indexed *It is raining here* is **about** a particular context, namely the contextual value that saturates the variable constituting the indexical.

*It is raining*, conveys just that it is raining: it is raining **punkt** – Recanati (2007b, p. 132). However, *It is raining*, if further accuracy is required by the communicative context, might be enriched by locative and/or temporal indications deploying the same procedure we described for adding a temporal adjunctive to *Napoleon invaded Spain*. This explains how the enriched proposition can be true at some contexts and false at others.

For example, the logical form that results from enriching *It is raining* with *It is raining in Lille at 12*, s, as a response to when? and where? is the following:

$$\vdash (\exists x : \textit{It is raining})k(x){=}_{City}\textit{Lille} \wedge \tau(x){=}_{Hour}12$$

whereby instead of deploying only a timing function defined on the set *Hour*, we also have the locative function $\kappa(x)$ defined over the set *City* – as mentioned below *Hour* and *City*, will be introduced respectively as *Time-Scales* and *Location-Scales* defined over the locative and temporal dimensions *Time* and *Location*.

Thus, *It is raining*, says that there is some raining event, and it allows this assertion to be contextually understood as saying that this event takes place in Lille at 12 o'clock (or somewhere else) – in other words this assertion allows to understand the event as informing about the kind of change undergoing some place and time. Or to put it openly into Aristotelian terminology, the locative and timing functions turn raining-events into a specific kind of change that places at some time undergo – cf. Recanati (2002).[25]

This presupposes that the resulting enriched proposition is built upon the full-fledged proposition *It is raining*

$$\kappa(x){=}_{Location}z \wedge \tau(x){=}_{Time}w : prop(x : \textit{It is raining})$$

given that rain-events $x$ are changes taking place at some location $z$ and time $w$: So we need to define the *dimensions:*

*Time*: *set Location*: *set*

Following Ranta (1994, p. 102) we shall display the sets *Time* and *Location* as involving several *time scales* and *location scales*, such as:

| | |
|---|---|
| ***Time: Set*** | ***Location: Set*** |
| *year*: *set* | *Continent: Set* |
| *month*: *set* | *country*: Set |
| *week*: *set* | *Region: Set* |
| *day*: *set* | *city*: *set* |
| *hour*: *set* | *town*: *set* |
| *minute*: *set* | *village*: *set* |

The canonical elements of the set *year* are numbers. One can define dependencies such as the day *6 of December of 1960*: (*1917, December 6*): *day* – see Ranta (1994, pp. 102–103), and the village *Coutiches in Nord-Pas-de-Calais in France* (*France, Nord-Pas-de-Calais, Coutiches*): *village.*

[25] Indeed the dependence of time upon events expressed by $\tau(x)$: *time* ($x$: $A$) comes close to the Aristotelian thesis that time is not something that can exist independently of (essential) change. Indeed, according to Aristotle's influential dictum *time is the number of change in respect of before and after* (*Physics*, IV, 219b 1–5) it makes no sense to speak of time during which there is no change at all.

Thus, enrichment as implemented by the timing and the locative functions, indeed achieve two tasks at the same time they add a new contextual parameter, such as *Hour* and *City*, and they add the corresponding dimension of those parameters, namely *Time* and *Location*, as envisaged by Recanati (2007b, pp. 133–134). This is made clear if we write down the proof-objects that support the assertion:

$$(r, b) : (\exists x : \textit{It is raining})\kappa(x){=}_{City}\textit{Lille} \wedge \tau(x){=}_{Hour}12$$

Indeed, that what provides the elements for the evaluation is a pair, constituted by *r*, and evidence *r* for a raining-event and *b* a function, a method, that does both adds a locative and temporal dimension and locates and times the raining event in a *City* at some precise *Hour*.

#### 6.2.2.3 Saturation

In contrast to *It is raining*, the sentence

*It is raining here, now,*

once *here* and *now* are evaluated yields the following assertion, where the indexicals *here*
and *now* have been saturated:

*It is raining* in-Lille at-12 ***true***

whereby the formation indicates that we are in presence of a propositional function:

*It is raining* **here**(*c*) **now**(*h*): *prop* (*c*: *City*, *h*: *Hour*), given *here*(ci) = ci: *City*, and *now*(*h*i) = *h*i: *Hour.*[26]

In this case the evaluation of *here*(*c*) and *now*(*h*) turn the *unsaturated* propositional function *It is raining here*(*c*) *now*(*h*) into a proposition.

[26]The idea underlying the TTG approach to indexical expressions such a *here*, is that some location *c*i has been fixed, so that *here* stands for the function *here*(*c*), so that if the variable *c* is substituted by some fixed location *c*i, the function *here*(*c*/*c*i) evaluates as *c*i. In our example, the location has been fixed as Lille, so that *here* in *It is raining here*, evaluates as *It is raining in Lille* – in the terminology of computer linguistics it is said that the sugaring of the function *here*(*c*) yields the natural language indexical expression *here*. Similar holds for the sugaring of *now*(*h*) – cf. Ranta (1994, pp. 98–99 and p. 119).

#### 6.2.2.4 Conclusion

According to Recanati's analysis the truth-making-conditions for both, *It is raining* and *It is raining somewhere* are the same (letting the time parameter aside). This might be one of the reasons behind Kölbel's (and others) worry that the *lekton* involved in enrichment and the one involved in saturation amount both to an Austinian proposition after all.

Recanati's response involves the claim that the success of a communicative function of an assertion can be achieved without assuming that the asserted sentence (either explicitly or implicitly) articulates by some linguistic means the relative truth conditions imposed by a context for its truth-conditional evaluation. In our framework this comes up by the setting of the formation rules. Only the context can provide the suitable sets for building meaning dependencies.

Let us take, the sentence *Everyone went to Lille:* It is the context that indicates the formation rule should look like. Should it look like:

*went-to-Lille*(*x*) : *prop* (*x* : *Human Being*) or?
*went-to-Lille*(*x, y*) : *prop* (*x* : *Human Being*, *y* : *Student of Kuno Lorenz* (*x*)), or?
*went-to-Lille*(*x, z*) : *prop* (*x* : *Human Being*, *z* : *Red-Hair*(*x*)) or?
*went-to-Lille*(*v, w*) : *prop* (*v* : *Elephant, w* : *White*(*v*))

What is for sure is that the assertion

⊢*Every Student of Kuno Lorenz went to Lille,*

involving the specification

*went-to-Lille*(*x, y*) : *prop* (*x*: *Human Being*, *y* : *Student of Kuno Lorenz*(*x*))

is **NOT** an outcome of the assertion:

⊢*Every Human-Being went to Lille,*
Even, if the formation of being a *Student of Kuno Lorenz,* presupposes that the predicate applies to *Human Being.*

The formation that enriches *Human-Being to Human Being who is a Student of Kuno Lorenz,* leading to the assertion *Every Student of Kuno Lorenz went to Lille* does not assume the preposterous detour of asserting *Every Human-Being went to Lille.*

So, though according to the TTG enrichment takes propositions as input it is not a form of.

*Propositional Minimalism* as promoted by Herman Cappelen, Ernie Lepore and Emma Borg.

## 6.3 Enrichment and *Immanent Reasoning*: An Interactive Stance

Recanati's variadic functions deploy the Davidsonian approach to event-sentences. More precisely, notice that

- the sentence *∃e* [*RAINING* (*e*)]
- is the result of *saturating* the propositional function
- *RAINING*(*e*): *prop* (*e*: *EVENTS*).

In contrast, according to the TTG analysis, a variable of the event type does not occur in the proposition itself, but in the assertion of the truth of it, as a proof-object.

In fact,

- according to the proposed TTG-analysis, the assertion expressed by the sentence *It is raining* operates on a full proposition not as a quasi-proposition in the waiting for contextual truth-condition.

In the case of the weatherman, what makes the proposition *It is raining* true is indeed an event. Some rain-event is a truth-maker of the event-proposition *It is raining*: the rain event does not saturate the propositional function *RAINING*(*e*).

Moreover, the point of the weatherman scenario is that there is no *direct evidence* of a rain event, but an indirect one, namely a non-canonical proof-object for rain-events, the *ringing of the bell*. In CTT the execution of a non-canonical proof-object delivers a canonical one, in our case, executing the *ringing of the bell*, amounts to the process of verifying which detector triggered the ringing. However, the bare ringing of the bell allows the receiver to trigger an enrichment process that yields the assertion *It is raining somewhere*.

Notice that the particular enrichment processed by the receiver is totally dependent upon the specific proof-object brought forward by the speaker in the context of the weatherman-scenario. Certainly, as in Recanati's own framework, other contexts might involve different proof-objects that assume different formation rules.

Recall that the standard way of recognizing if we are or not in presence of an assertion involving a saturated propositional function is the *mandatory* feature of saturation as implemented by its proof-object – namely, a function that encodes the dependency structure at work. If the propositional function has not been saturated and the uttered sentence involves an *incomplete* proposition, then, from the communicative point of view, saturating the indexical is the speaker's duty.

However, in the current forms of Contextualism it looks as if the dialogical roles of speaker and receiver are not constitutive of the pragmatic modulation processes engaged in communicative interaction. If pragmatics should be constitutive of meaning this must be integrated into the framework.

To put it bluntly, from a dialogical point of view *saturation* obliges the speaker to fulfil *hic et nunc*, since it is the speaker who undertook such a commitment by making it explicit that the content of their assertion is made dependent upon filling up the slots imposed by their use of the indexicals *here* and *now*. Dually, the receiver has the right to ask the speaker to fulfil those slots in order the communicative interaction to succeed. Alternatively, the receiver, might be able to fulfil them by himself. However, in this case the receiver cannot choose a context at will and must adopt the speaker perspective.

Enrichment goes the other way round; it is the receiver who will add or not a new temporal and or locative dimension. It is the receiver's perspective that prevails here. In fact, it is the very notion of propositional content that requires to the thought from a dialogical point of view, particularly so if the framework should be able to integrate cases where truth-conditionality seems to fail – see Recanati (2017, pp. 222–224), Bach (2004, 2005, 2006).

More generally we need a framework for the notion enrichment where the notion of proposition, does not only integrate the dialogical interaction but it is not restricted to laying down absolute truth-making conditions – a restriction underlying the proof-theoretical framework of CTT. So what we would like is to have our cake, the TTG analysis of enrichment, and eat it, namely

- a notion of proposition not restricted to validity – be it by proof-theoretical or truth-conditional means, (2) a differentiated approach to the meaning explanations of adjunctive and complementary temporal reference. It is our claim that *Immanent Reasoning* delivers such and undertaking where enrichment involves a fully articulated proposition, defined at the play level, and clear dialogical meaning explanation for distinguishing enrichment from saturation in temporal contexts.

### 6.3.1 The Dialogical Framework: A Pragmatist Approach to the Constitution of Meaning

*Dialogic logic* was conceived as a pragmatist approach to meaning in logic that resorts to concepts of game theory such as *winning a play* and that of the *existence of a winning strategy*. Nowadays it has been extended to a general framework for the study of meaning, knowledge and inference constituted during interaction. The new developments include cooperative dialogues and dialogues deploying a fully interpreted language (*dialogues with content*).[27]

According to the dialogical perspective, knowledge, meaning and truth are conceived as a result of social interaction, where, as recently pointed out by Martin-Löf (2017a, b), normativity is not understood as a type of pragmatic operator acting on a propositional nucleus destined to express knowledge and meaning, but on the contrary: the type of normativity that emerges from the social interaction

[27] It was the philosopher and mathematician Paul Lorenzen who in the late 1950s was the first to introduce a game- theoretical approach to meaning in logic. Lorenzen (1958) called this semantics *Dialogische Logik*. Later, it was further developed by him and Kuno Lorenz – see Lorenzen and Lorenz (1978).

associated with knowledge and meaning is constitutive of these notions. In other words, according to the conception of the dialogical framework, the intertwining of the right to ask for reasons, on the one hand, and the obligation to give them, on the other, provides the roots of knowledge, meaning and truth.[28]

#### 6.3.1.1 Local, Global Meaning and Strategies

As hinted by its name, this framework studies dialogues, but it also takes the form of dialogues. In a dialogue, two parties (players) argue on a thesis (a certain statement that is the subject of the whole argument) and follow certain fixed rules in their argument. The player who states the thesis is the Proponent (for short **P**), and the rival, the player who challenges the thesis, is the Opponent (**O**). In challenging the Proponent's thesis, the Opponent is requiring of the Proponent that s(he) defends their statement.

The interaction between the two players is spelled out by challenges and defences. Actions in a dialogue are called moves; they are often understood as speech-acts involving declarative utterances (*assertions*) and interrogative utterances (*requests*). The rules for dialogues thus never deal with expressions isolated from the act of uttering them.

The rules in the dialogical framework are divided into two kinds of rules: *particle rules* and *structural rules*. Whereas the first determine *local meaning*, the second rules determine *global meaning'*.

Local meaning explains the meaning of an expression independently of the rules setting the development of a dialogue. Global meaning set the meaning of an expression in the context of some specific form of developing a dialogue.

More precisely:

Particle rules (*Partikelregeln*') determine the legal moves in a play and regulate interaction by establishing the relevant moves constituting "challenges". More precisely, a challenge is a move prescribed as being an appropriate attack to a previous move (a statement) and thus require that the challenged player play a moved indicates as the appropriate defence to that attack. If the challenged player defends their statement, s(he) has answered the challenge.

Structural rules (*Rahmenregeln*) on the other hand determine the general course of a dialogue game, such as how a game is initiated, how to play it, how it ends, and so on. The point of these rules is not so much to spell out the meaning of the logical constants by specifying how to act in an appropriate way—this is the role of the particle rules—; it is rather to specify according to what structure interactions will take place. It is one thing to determine the meaning of the logical constants as a set of

[28]This formulation aims to link the perspective of Robert Brandom with that of the logic of dialogue. See Mathieu Marion (2009, 2010). For a discussion about what they have in common and what distinguishes both approaches, see Rahman et al. (2018, pp. 10-12).

appropriate challenges and defences, it is another to define whose turn it is to play and when a player is allowed to play a move.

According to the structural rules a play ends when it is a player's turn to make a move but that player has no available move left. That player loses, the other player wins.

Now, inferences and validity are defined in relation to a winning strategy for **P**. However, notice the following point

- winning a dialogue (a play) is not enough for defining validity. Indeed, wining a play does not ensure validity. Dually losing, a play does not mean that the thesis is not valid.

What we need now is to define strategies.

#### 6.3.1.2 Winning Strategy

- A player **X** has a winning strategy if for every move made by the other player **Y**, player **X** can make another move, such that each resulting play is eventually won by **X**.

In dialogical logic validity is defined in relation to winning strategies for the proponent **P** .

- A *winning strategy for* **P** *for* a thesis *A* is a tree ***S*** the branches of which are plays won by **P**, where the nodes are those moves, such that

(i) S has the move **P** *A* as root node (with depth 0),
(ii) if the node is an **O**- move (i.e. if the depth of a node is odd), then it has exactly one successor node (which is a **P**-move),
(iii) if the node is a **P**-move (i.e. if the depth of a node is even), then it has as many successor nodes as there are possible moves for **O** at this position.

- One crucial point is that, different to proof-theory, the notion of proposition is not defined top-down, from validity (a **P**-winning strategy) but bottom-up from the play-level. Thus, the notion of proposition is not defined at the strategy level. In other words it is neither the proof-theoretical level nor the distribution of truth values that yields the dialogical notion of proposition but winning and losing a single finite play.

#### 6.3.1.3 Dialogue-Definiteness and Propositions

As already mentioned, the dialogical approach to meaning is structured in three levels, (i) that of the local meaning (determined by the particle rules for the logical constants), (ii) that of the global meaning (determined by the structural rules), and (iii) that of the strategic level of meaning (determined by what is required for having a winning strategy). A characteristic of the local meaning is that the rules are player independent: the meaning is thus defined in the same fashion for each player; they are bound by the same sets of duties and rights when they start a dialogue. This normative aspect is thus constitutive of the play level (which encompasses both the local meaning and the global meaning): it is even what allows one to judge that a dialogue is taking place. In this regard, meaning is immanent to the dialogue: what constitutes the meaning of the statements in a particular dialogue solely rests on rules determining interaction (the local and the global levels of meaning). The strategy level on the other hand is built on the play level, and the notion of demonstration operates on the strategy level (it amounts to having a winning strategy).

Two main tenets of the dialogical theory of meaning can be traced back to Wittgenstein, and ground in particular the pivotal notion of dialogue-definiteness:

1. the internal feature of meaning (the *Unhintergehbarkeit der Sprache*,[29]) and
2. the meaning as mediated by language-games.

If we relate the notion of internalization of meaning with both language-games and fully- interpreted languages of CTT, then a salient feature of the dialogical approach to meaning can come to fore: the expressive power of CTT allows all these actions involved in the dialogical constitution of meaning to be incorporated as an explicit part of the object-language of the dialogical framework.

In relation to the second tenet, the inceptors of the dialogical framework observed that if language-games are to be conceived as mediators of meaning carried out by social interaction, these language-games must be games actually playable by human beings: it must be the case that *we can actually perform them*,[30] which is captured in the notion of dialogue-definiteness.[31] Dialogue-definiteness is essential for dialogues to be mediators of meaning, but it is also constitutive of what propositions are, as Lorenz clearly puts it:

> [...] *for an entity to be a proposition there must exist an individual play, such that this entity occupies the initial position, and the play reaches a final position with either win or loss after a finite number of moves according to definite rules.* Lorenz (2001, p. 258).

A proposition is thus defined as a dialogue-*definite expression*, that is, an expression *A* such that there is an individual play about *A*, that can be said to be lost or won after a finite number of steps, following given rules of dialogical interaction.

The notion of *dialogue-definiteness* is in this sense the backbone of the dialogical theory of meaning: it provides the basis for implementing the human-playability requirement and the notion of proposition.

Furthermore, dialogue-definiteness sets apart rather decisively the level of strategies from the level of plays, as Lorenz's notion of dialogue-definite proposition does not amount to a set of winning strategies, but rather to an individual play.

---

[29]See *Tractatus Logico-Philosophicus,* 5.6.

[30]Cf. Marion (2006, p. 245).

[31]The fact that these language-games must be finite does not rule out the possibility of a (potentially) infinite number of them.

Within the framework of *Immanent Reasoning* – Rahman et al. (2018), *dialogue-definiteness* is further worked out by integrating the dialogical articulation of propositions and their justifications. More precisely, the articulation of propositions and their justifications is spelled out by prescribing how to introduce reasons in order to justify a challenged claim, and how to analyse a reason that justifies a claim.

## *6.3.2 Immanent Reasoning*

### 6.3.2.1 Some Relevant Notions

**Local Reasons** Dialogues are games of giving and asking for reasons; yet in the standard dialogical framework, the reasons for each statement are left implicit and do not appear in the notation of the statement: we have statements of the form! *AA* for instance where *AA* is an elementary proposition. The framework of dialogues for immanent reasoning allows to make explicit the reason for making a statement, statements then have the form XX *aa* : *AA*, where *aa* is the (local) reason XX has for stating the proposition *AA*. But even in dialogues for immanent reasoning, all reasons are not always provided, and sometimes statements have only implicit reasons for bringing the proposition forward, taking then the same form as in the standard dialogical framework:! *AA*. Notice that when (local) reasons are not explicit, an exclamation mark is added before the proposition: the statement then has an implicit reason for being made.

The most basic contribution of a local reason is its contribution to a dialogue involving an elementary proposition. Informally, we can say that if the Proponent **P** states the elementary proposition *AA*, it is because **P** claims that s(he) can bring forward a reason in defence of their statement, it is this reason that provides content to the propositional expression.

**Local-Meaning – Analysis and Synthesis** The local meaning of such statements results from the rules describing how to compose (synthesis) within a play the suitable local reasons for the proposition *A* and how to separate (analysis) a complex local reason into the elements required by the composition rules for *A*. The synthesis and analysis processes of *A* are built on the formation rules for *A*.

**Formation** It is presupposed in standard dialogical systems that the players use well-formed formulas (*wff*). The well formation can be checked at will, but only with the usual meta reasoning by which one checks that the formula does indeed observe the definition of a *wff*. We want to enrich our CTT-based dialogical framework by allowing players themselves to enquire on the formation of the components of a statement within a play.

For a condensed overview on how to develop this framework for logic and beyond logic see Rahman (2019). In the next section, we launch a first exploration on how to provide meaning explanations for enrichment and saturation within *Immanent Reasoning*.

#### 6.3.2.2 Dialogical Meaning Explanations for Enrichment and Saturation

Since, as shown below, the dialogical interaction leading to enrichment is cooperative rather than competitive it seems better to think of **X** and **Y** as **Speaker** and **Receiver**, rather than Proponent and Opponent.

By the same token it is the case that during such a form of cooperative interaction, some responses to previous moves, are neither challenges nor defences but moves aimed at specifying the propositional content involved in the claim, we speak of **response** and **request**.

#### 6.3.2.3 Enrichment

The canonical dialogical meaning explanation of enrichment is based on the idea that **adjoining a suitable context is a choice** (in general by the **Receiver**). This also entails that the original claim is understood as a full-fledged proposition on the grounds of which other assertions can be grounded (even if the temporal and/or locative contextual parameters of the original claim are left unspecified). In such a setting the meaning explanation of enrichment has the following features:

1. The moves of the **Receiver** are **Responses,** whereby the evidence that is brought forward as evidence for rain is **specified** by means of adding a context.
2. It is the **Receiver who can choose** to specify the context. The **Receiver** might propose one location and, possibly, if requested by the **Speaker**, a temporal indication might be added – by default the temporal reference of the **Speaker**'s utterance.
3. The **Receiver** might ground some of their further assertions in the original, not enriched claim of the **Speaker**. More precisely the **Receiver** might ground their own assertion *We should stop using up the water of the reservoirs* on the Speaker's assertion *It is raining*. Here the **Receiver** relies on the **Speaker's** Authority. This kind of move has been called by Sundholm (1997) called an *Epistemic Assumption*. Martin-Löf (2015) suggested to endow it with a dialogical reading. See Martin-Löf (2015), and Rahman et al. (2018, pp. vii–xii).

This yields the following rules of local meaning.

| Enrichment claim | Enrichment response |
|---|---|
| | **(1)**<br>**Y?** Reason<br>(on what grounds?) |
| | **X** *r*: *It is raining* |
| | **Y!** $(\exists x$: *It is raining*$)$ $(\exists c$: *City*$)$ $\kappa(x) =_{City} c$<br>(this response assumes that *r* is the non-canonical proof- object *ringing of the bell*) |
| | **Or**<br>**Y!** $(\exists x$: *It is raining*$)$$)$ $\kappa(x) =_{City}$ *Lille*<br>(this response assumes that *r* provides enough information for identifying the location specific to the rain event at stake) |
| **X!** *It is raining* | **Or** |
| | **(2)**<br>**Y**!. *We should stop using up the water of the reservoirs* (this response assumes that the receiver takes the weatherman's at face value. The receiver makes an *epistemic assumption*). |

Notice too that **no winning-strategy is required**. A play is sufficient. In fact, every play, might be built on a different choice of the **Receiver** for enriching or not the original claim, such as, Paris, Bahía Blanca, Sevilla. Moreover, the specification is defeasible, and might thus be revised in the further development of the dialogical interaction, triggering different plays. This is not a problem at all for the dialogical approach: a full and sound notion of proposition requires dialogue- definiteness not truth-conditionality.

#### 6.3.2.4 Saturation

The canonical dialogical meaning explanation of saturation is based on the idea that **the choice of completing the claim with a context is enforced by the indexical**. This also entails that the original claim can only by understood as a full-fledged proposition iff the variable constituting the indexical has been evaluated with the suitable contextual parameters. Thus the canonical meaning explanation of saturation in a dialogical setting has the following features:

1. The moves of the **Receiver** are **Requests,** whereby the evidence that is brought forward as evidence for rain is **specified** by means of making explicit the time and place of utterance.
2. Neither **Receiver** nor **Speaker** can choose a context other than place or time of utterance of the **Speaker**'s assertion.
3. **Requests** indicate that such a move is necessary in order the **Receiver** to draw further inferences.

This yields the following rules of local meaning

| Indexical claim | Saturation request | Saturation response |
|---|---|---|
| **X!** *It is raining here* | **Y?** ***here***(*Lille*), given *Lille: City* (we were talking about Lille, so here must be Lille) | **X!** *It is raining* ***here***(*Lille*) |

Notice that also in this case **no winning-strategy is required**. A play is sufficient.

However, what the formation presupposes is the following:

- *It is raining here*(*c*): *prop* (*c: City*)

Notice too that the salient feature of saturation is that the **Receiver must request** the evaluation in order to continue the interaction. He cannot simply respond, he must before have the saturation of the indexical. Expressions with implicit free variables require formation moves even before starting:

| Claim | Request | Response |
|---|---|---|
| **X!** *John finished* | **Y?** *Formation* | **X!** *John finished* (*x*): *prop* (*x: writing*). |

## 6.3.3 Brief Remarks on Faultless Disagreement

### 6.3.3.1 Propositional Content without Third-Excluded

Recanati's (2017, pp. 220–224) response to some objections raised by Kölbel (2017, pp. 210–220) on the analysis of *faultless disagreement* suggested in *Perspectival Thought* provides an excellent opportunity to illustrate one of the main points of the present paper. More precisely, it shows how to handle within *Immanent Reasoning* instances where although third-excluded (at the strategic level) fails, genuine propositional content is still present and governs dialogical interaction.[32]

By the way, the whole issue seems to be closely related to the rich and large debates on relativism in Ancient Greece. More precisely, Recanati's and Kölbel's discussion on faultless disagreement recalls some of the debates of Protagoras's Relativism in several parts of Plato's *Theaetetus.*[33] I will not develop herewith a

[32]Other interesting instances of such kind of phenomena are being discussed in Chakraborty and Lion (2020) in their contribution to the present volume.

[33]I had the chance to be reminded of these debates during the inspiring session of the seminar on the *Theaetetus* held at the laboratory STL: UMR 8163, Univ. Lille on the 14th of November 2019. The meeting of that date was held by Philippe Rousseau and Thomas Bénatouïl and focused on the *Theaetetus*. (170a-171d and 171e-174a). The seminar is organized by Thomas Bénatouïl and Claire Louget.

study of the ancient sources, although I think this is a crucial pending task to which I hope to come back in the near future.

#### 6.3.3.2 Sustained Disagreement as Prescriptions

In *Perspectival Thought,* Recanati (2007a, pp. 87–94) proposes to study agreement and disagreement as involving *complete* content (involving the *lekton and* the situation of evaluation). The point is that if two people entertain the same *lekton* but evaluate it with respect to distinct situations, no genuine disagreement takes place. However, faultless disagreement seems to pose a problem to Recanati's approach. Moreover, Kölbel (2017) brings forward the case of *sustained disagreement*, where neither of the interlocutors are prepared to change their minds, though no misunderstanding takes place. Recanati's (2017) response is to understand cases of sustained disagreement as *prescriptions* to adopt some common evaluation standards. Since prescriptions do not, in the standard view, satisfy truth-conditions, third-excluded fails:

> *Faultless disagreement seems to be a counterexample: people who disagree about e.g. matters of taste seem to evaluate the same lekton (e.g. the relativized proposition that Vegemite is tasty) with respect to their respective standards of taste and end up with distinct truth-values when the standards are sufficiently different. Thus Vegemite is tasty to you, but not to me. You say, 'Vegemite is tasty'; I respond: 'No, it is disgusting'. The disagreement here seems genuine, but there is no complete content which the discussants share and over which they disagree. They only share the lekton (that Vegemite is tasty) but evaluate it with respect to their respective standards. The complete contents of their respective thoughts are therefore different: subject A evaluates the lekton with respect to A's standards of taste (and ends up with the value 'true'), while B evaluates the same lekton with respect to B's different standards (and ends up with the value 'false'). So what is going on? What explains the difference between the 'it's raining' case, in which there is no genuine disagreement, and the Vegemite case, in which it seems that there is?*
>
> *[...] 'Vegemite is tasty' has an objective flavour (in many contexts at least) while 'Vegemite is tasty to me' or 'I find it tasty' are more subjective. According to Perspectival Thought, what accounts for the objective flavour of 'Vegemite is tasty' is the fact that the relevant judge is the community to which both the speaker and the hearer belong. [...].*
>
> *This leaves many possible options for analysing alleged cases of faultless disagreement. First, when A says, 'Vegemite is tasty' and B responds, 'it is not', A may be wrong in presupposing that her standard of state regarding Vegemite is shared by the community. B's dissenting voice suggests that the standard may actually not be shared. If that is so, then A is at fault (and must retreat to the subjective statement 'I find it tasty'). Second, A is free to maintain his statement regardless of B's dissension, by suitably adjusting 'the community' and excluding B from it. For example, A may judge that B departs, by his bad taste, from the standards of the community. If this is true, then, from A's point of view, B is at fault. However we interpret the case, the disagreement is not faultless.*
>
> *I agree with Kölbel that there are also cases of a third type: cases of 'faultless disagreement' such that no failure whatsoever is involved on the part of either speaker or hearer. The protagonists may enter an episode of sustained disagreement in which both parties (re)affirm diverging views without ever retreating to a weaker, subjective statement of their taste*
>
> *[...] I propose that, in sustained disagreement about matters of taste, the interlocutors' moves and countermoves ('Vegemite is tasty', 'no, it is disgusting') are (i) neither true nor*

*false, yet (ii) perfectly felicitous (involving no 'failure'). [...]. In sustained disagreement the interlocutors negotiate the standards for the local community they form. I propose that their utterances (e.g. 'Vegemite is tasty') are not assertions but prescriptions, inviting the hearer to adopt standards with respect to which the lekton is true. The speaker offers her own standards as the coordinative standard for the community.*

[...]

*When the utterance is a prescription the content of the speech act is a relativized proposition (lekton): that Vegemite is tasty. The speaker tries to get the hearer (and the local community more generally) to adopt standards which make that lekton true. The lekton has truth-at conditions (it is true at certain standards and false at others) but it carries no absolute truth-conditions in these circumstances, for lack of a communal standard accepted by all parties. The conversation aims at establishing such a standard. Until it is settled, no determinate, stable situation of evaluation is provided to turn the lekton into a full Austinian proposition. The speech act is nondefective, however. It has a determinate force and a determinate content (the lekton) but, like orders, it does not allow for truth-evaluation.* Recanati *(*2017, *pp. 220-223).*

#### 6.3.3.3 Dialogical Perspectives on Sustained Disagreement

As mentioned above, according to the dialogical perspective, knowledge, meaning and truth are conceived as a result of an interaction that is gouverned by communicative prescriptions. Interesting is that this prescriptive feature does not prevent the framework to shape both a logic with and without third-excluded. In the case of disagreement, third-excluded holds iff one of the interlocutors withdraws from their initial claim and adopts the position of the other and the disagreement is solved. But certainly, this cannot be granted in general, and does not count as an instance of sustained disagreement.

Let us start with our general approach to enrichment. Assume there are two incompatible standards for evaluating the beauty of a painting, and that for each of these standards there is a function that provides some evaluation supporting the initial assertion – I will not here introduce a measurement order. The evaluation functions are the ones that implement the enrichment of the initial assertion in a similar way as in the case of *It is raining*.

$\varepsilon 1(x) : S1$ ($x$ : *This Painting is beautiful*), given *This Painting is beautiful*: *prop.*
$\varepsilon 2(x) : S2$ ($x$ : *This Painting is ugly*), given *This Painting is ugly*: *prop*

Let us assume too that *ugly* and *beautiful* are incompatible

So, we might have the following dialogue, where for the sake of simplicity I ignore the anaphoric reference "*It is ugly*" and simply assume that the anaphora reference is present in *This Painting is ugly*.

Speaker: *This Painting is beautiful*!

Audience: No: *This Painting is ugly*!
! ($\exists x$ : *This Painting is ugly*) ($\exists z : S2$) $\varepsilon 2(x) = S2\ z$

Now, there are three possibilities:

1. The Speaker adopts the standards of the Audience and accepts the proposed enrichment.

In dialogical logic such kind of move amounts to coming back or withdrawing – a move that differentiates classical logic from intuitionistic logic, whereby in the latter withdrawing is not allowed. Thus, in classical setting third-excluded amounts to adopting the challenger's view.

2. The Speaker rejects the Audience's proposal and proposes the enrichment

! ($\exists y$ : *This Painting is beautiful*) ($\exists w$: $S1$) $\varepsilon 1(y) = S1\ w$

This might continue until some end has been achieved without any of both giving up their minds.

3. After a while a new standard is agreed upon which a decision can be taken. Notice that in our framework the input of an enrichment is a proposition, the further development does not prevent the initial claim of having propositional content.

Now, the most interesting case is the intermediate one. Recall that crucial to the notion of propositional meaning in dialogical logic is that each play must be finite, though there might be an infinite number of those plays. So, in any of these infinite plays, one of the interlocutors wins. However, this does not mean that there is a winning strategy since, it might well be that he loses in others. Moreover, each of the plays might engage different standards that might have different outcomes.

We can certainly adopt a global look, from the outside and formulate that whole as an hypothetical, where it is not granted that either of the sides of the disjunction can be made true, and whereby the two sides are incompatible. Let "*PB*" stand for "*This Painting is beautiful*" and "*PU*" for "T*his Painting is ugly*", "$=_{\{H\}}$" for identical within the hypothesis, that is within the disjunction; and let "$first^{\vee}(y)$" stand for the injection that selects an element of PB and renders the disjunction true by providing a proof object for its left side. Similar holds for $second^{\vee}(z)$:

$$b(x) : (\forall y : PB)\ \left[first^{\vee}(y) =_{\{H\}} x \supset (\exists w : S_1)\varepsilon_1(y) =_{S_1} w\right]$$
$$\wedge(\forall z : PU)\ \left[second^{\vee}(z) =_{\{H\}} x \supset (\exists z : S_2)\varepsilon_2(x) =_{S_2} z\right]\ (x : PB \vee PU)$$

Which admits the gloss: Under the hypothesis that the painting is either beautiful or ugly, if some evidence can be brought forward in favour for the claim that the painting is beautiful, then there is some suitable evaluation-method against which the claim is backed. Similar holds if the evidence backs the ugliness of the painting at stake. Propositional content is granted, since we can lay down the assertion-conditions for each claim, however third-excluded is not granted.

The global view is proof-theoretic and does not require the play-level. In either way, locally or globally, this case of faultless disagreement does not seem to require incomplete Austinian propositions.

## 6.4 Conclusions and Work Ahead

From the perspective of dialogical logic Recanati's (2007b) point on the un-shiftability of the contextual saturation of indexical expressions amounts to the fact that players do not have the choice for evaluating indexicals. Moreover, the saturation process must be completed before further assertions grounded on claims involving indexical expressions can be brought forward. This strongly contrasts with enrichment, where the specification process can take place or not, even for making further assertions.

This is linked to the point that from the dialogical point of view, the proposition occurring in a claim that can be enriched is a full-fledged one, even at the play-level where no absolute truth-making conditions are laid down. Another way to put it is that whereas the formation of an anaphoric construction at work in a process of enrichment has a proposition (*It is raining*) as head of the anaphora. In a process of saturation *It is raining here* constitutes the tail of an anaphoric construction with a head from which *here* gets its value, namely *It is raining here(x): prop* (*x: Location*).

More generally, under this perspective enrichment and other modulation processes are the outcome of identifying and establishing meaning dependencies. What syncretic propositionalism gets it wrong is that it assumes that contextualisation processes take as input the proposition asserted in the utterance. But enrichment starts at the deeper level of meaning constitution as set by both the formation rules and by identifying the local reasons for each type (or proof-objects at the strategy level). Modulating *Everyone went to Lille,* starts by laying down the type-formation presupposed by the quantified expression, namely *went to Lille*(*x*): *prop* (*x: Student in this Seminar*). This assumes a framework that includes hypothetical assertions, assertions involving dependent types. In short, enrichment affects the formation rules for the constitution of meaning.

As already mentioned, the present paper is only a first exploration. There are many issues that need to be further studied, including a large study of the different forms the anaphoric constructions can take, time-aspects, and exploring further the case of faultless disagreement.

Historic studies constitute a further important pending research task, particularly so in relation to the notion of *lekton* Bronowski (2019).

All of these pending research tasks should contribute to further explore the main idea underlying our approach: a genuine pragmatist approach to meaning can be developed from the dialogical stance on communicative interaction.

**Acknowledgments** Many thanks to Teresa Lopez-Soto (Sevilla) the editor of present inspiring volume and to the Laboratory STL: UMR-CNRS 8163 and particularly so to Leone Gazziero (STL), Laurent Cesalli (Genève), leaders of the ANR Project *SEMAINO* (STL) and Claudio Majolino (STL), associated researcher to that project, for fostering the research leading to the present study. The pluri-disciplinary STL-seminar on Plato's *Theaetetus* lead by Thomas Bénatouïl (U. Lille) and Claire Louget (U. Lille) offered a forum for rich and inspired discussions on subjects relevant to Contextualism, particularly so on the challenges of Protagoras relativism. I am very thankful to all the participants who helped me to reflect on the philosophical and historical roots of Contextualism. Many thanks too to Zoe McConaughey, Clément Lion, and Vincent Wistrand, doctorates at the Department of Philosophy at University of Lille and members of the laboratory UMR: 8163, STL who contributed to my many fruitful discussions and specially to Bert Cappelle (STL) for his helpful remarks to an earlier version of the paper.

## References

Bach, K. (2004). Minding the gap. In C. Bianchi (Ed.), *The semantics/pragmatics distinction* (pp. 27–43). Stanford: CSLI Publications.

Bach, K. (2005). Context *ex Machina*. In Z. G. Szabó (Ed.), *Semantics versus pragmatics* (pp. 15–44). Oxford: Clarendon Press.

Bach, K. (2006). The excluded middle: Semantic minimalism without minimal propositions. *Philosophy and Phenomenological Research, 73*(2), 435–442.

Bach, K. (2012). Context-dependence (as it is). In M. García Carpintero & M. Kölbel (Eds.), *The continuum companion to the philosophy of language* (pp. 153–184). London: Continuum International Publishing Group.

Borg, E. (2004). *Minimal Semantics*. Oxford: Oxford University Press.

Bronowski, A. (2019). What is wrong with *lekta*? Ancient critics of Stoic logic and language. In L. Gazziero (Ed.), *Methodos*, vol. 19. Special number *Dire et vouloir dire dans les arts du langage anciens et tardo-antiques,* https://journals.openedition.org/methodos/5276.

Cappelen, H., & Lepore, E. (2005). *Insensitive semantics. A defense of semantic. Minimalism and speech act pluralism*. Oxford: Blackwell.

Chakraborty, R. & Lion, C. (2020). *Two convergences to dynamic formalism: Bakhtin's dialogism and brouwer's creating subject*. In the present volume.

Collins, J. (2019). "On saturation in weather reports". Online https://www.academia.edu/6566639/Chapter_3_On_Saturation_in_Weather_Reports

Recanati, F. (2017). About the *Lekton*. Response to Kölbel. In I. Depraetere & R. Salkie (Eds.), *Semantics and pragmatics: Drawing a line* (pp. 215–224). Cham: Springer.

Dummett, M. (1997). "Existence, possibility and time". In G. Meggle (Ed.), *Analyomen*, Berlin: De Gruyter, vol. 2/1, pp. 43–67.

Elbourne, P. (2008). The argument from binding. *Philosophical Perspectives, 22*, 89–110.

Fodor, J. (2001). Language, thought and compositionality. *Mind and Language, 16*, 1–15.

Fodor, J. (2003). *Hume variations*. Oxford: Oxford University Press.

Gabriel, G., Hülser, K., & Schlotter, S. (2009). Zur Miete bei Frege - Rudolf Hirzel und die Rezeption der stoischen Logik und Semantik in Jena. *History and Philosophy of Logic, 30*(4), 369–388.

Grant, R (2019). "Contextualism: What it gets wrong". Online https://www.academia.edu/20122529/Contextualism_What_it_Gets_Wrong

Kölbel, M. (2017). About concerns. In I. Depraetere & R. Salkie (Eds.), *Semantics and pragmatics: Drawing a line* (pp. 197–214). Cham: Springer.

Lorenz, K. (2001). Basic objectives of dialogue logic in historical perspective. *Synthese, 127*(1–2), 225–263.

Lorenzen, P. (1958). "Logik und Agon". *Arti del XII Congresso Internationale de Filosofia*, pp. 187–194.
Lorenzen, P., & Lorenz, K. (1978). *Dialogische Logik*. Darmstadt: Wissenschaftliche Buchgesellschaft.
Marion, M. (2006). Hintikka on Wittgenstein: From language games to game semantics. In T. Aho & A.-V. Pietarinen (Eds.), *Truth and Games: Essays in Honour of Gabriel Sandu X* (pp. 237–256). Helsinki: Acta Philosophica Fennica.
Marion, M. (2009). Why play logical games? In O. Majer, A. V. Pietarinen, & T. Tulenheimo (Eds.), *Logic and games: Unifying logic* (pp. 3–26). Dordrecht: Springer.
Marion, M. (2010). Between saying and doing: From Lorenzen to Brandom and Back. In P. E. Bour, M. Rebuschi, & L. Rollet (Eds.), *Constructions: Essays in honour of Gerhard Heinzmann* (pp. 489–497). London: College Publications.
Marti, L. (2006). Unarticulated constituents revisited. *Linguistics and Philosophy, 29*, 135–166.
Martin-Löf, P. (2015). "Is logic part of normative ethics?" Lecture Held at the research Unity Sciences, *Normes, Décisions* (FRE 3593), Paris, May 2015. Transcription by Ansten Klev.
Martin-Löf, P. (2017a). "Assertion and Request". *Lecture held at Oslo, 2017*. Transcription by Ansten Klev.
Martin-Löf, P. (2017b). "Assertion and Request". *Lecture held at Stockholm*. Transcription by Ansten Klev.
Martin-Löf, P., & Sambin, G. (1984). *Intuitionistic type theory* (Vol. 9).
McConnell-Ginet, S. (1982). Adverbs and logical form. *Language, 58*, 144–184.
Nordström, G., Peterson, K., & Smith, J. (1990). An Introduction to Martin-Löf's Theory of Types.
Partee, B. (1989). Binding implicit variables in quantified contexts. *Proceedings of the Chicago Linguistic Society (CSL), 25*, 342–365.
Perry, J. (1986). Thought without representation. *Supplementary Proceedings of the Aristotelian Society, 60*, 263–283.
Quine, W. v. O. (1960). Variables explained away. In W. V. O. Quine (Ed.), *Selected logic papers* (Vol. 1995, pp. 227–235). Cambridge Mass: Harvard University Press.
Rahman, S. (2019). Dialogues, reasons and endorsement. In C. Weiss (Ed.), *Constructive semantics* (pp. 15–84). Cham: Springer.
Rahman, S., McConaughey, Z., Klev, A., & Clerbout, N. (2018). *Immanent reasoning or equality in action*. Dordrecht: Springer.
Ranta, A. (1994). *Type Theoretical Grammar. Oxford*. Oxford: Clarendon Press.
Recanati, F. (2002). Unarticulated constituents. *Linguistics and Philosophy, 25*, 299–345.
Recanati, F. (2004). *Literal meaning*. Cambridge: CUP.
Recanati, F. (2007a). *Perspectival thought*. Oxford: OUP.
Recanati, F. (2007b). It's raining (somewhere). *Linguistics and Philosophy, 30*, 123–146.
Recanati, F. (2010). *Truth conditional pragmatics*. Oxford: OUP.
.Recanati, F (2012)
Sakai, T. (2014). [Review] "*Truth-conditional pragmatics*. By François Recanati. Oxford University Press, 2010, vii+324pp.". *English linguistics* (edited by the English Linguistic Society of Japan), vol. 31, pp. 365–375.
Soames, S. (2002). *Beyond rigidity*. Oxford: Oxford University Press.
Soames, S. (2005). Naming and asserting. In Z. Szabo (Ed.), *Semantics versus pragmatics* (pp. 356–382). Oxford: Oxford University Press.
Stanley, J. (2005). "Review of François Recanati's *Literal Meaning*," *Notre-Dame Philosophical Reviews*, online at http://ndpr.nd.edu/news/24857/?id=3841.
Sundholm, G. (1997). Implicit epistemic aspects of constructive logic. *Journal of Logic, Language and Information, 6*(2), 191–212.
Sundholm, G. (2001). A Plea for logical atavism. In O. Majer (Ed.), *The Logica yearbook 2000* (pp. 151–162). Prague: Filosofía.
Taylor, K. (2001). Sex, breakfast and Descriptus interruptus. *Synthese, 128*, 45–61.

# Chapter 7
# How Surprising! Mirativity, Evidentiality and Abductive Inference

**Cristina Barés Gómez and Matthieu Fontaine**

**Abstract** Mirativity is a grammatical category or a linguistic strategy that makes explicit the surprising aspect of a piece of information. Different mirativity strategies appear in different languages. Evidentiality is a grammatical category that explicitly expresses the source of information, i.e. if something has been seen, heard or inferred. Whether mirativity forms part of evidentiality is an open question. An agent makes use of a mirativity marker when she or he expresses something about a surprising fact with respect to her or his background knowledge. But there are different kinds of mirativity markers. Some of them are simple and direct and others, more complex, involve inferential processes. Here, we focus on complex mirativity and we compare it with inferred evidentials and deferred realizations. Our proposal goes beyond the purely linguistic analysis, since we try to interpret mirativity, and its role in interaction, as forming part of or involving a particular kind of inference, namely abduction. Mirativity can be used to express the surprising state that triggers an abductive reasoning but it can also encapsulate its result in such a way that it can be understood in relation to evidentiality. Thus, at least in some cases of complex mirativity, mirativity may convey indication about the source of information. Interesting for studies on dialogue is that they also indicate the degree of commitment of the speakers with the content of their own utterances.

**Keywords** Abduction · Evidentiality · Inference · Information · Mirativity

## Abbreviations

| | |
|---|---|
| 1,2,3 | first, second, third person |
| A | transitive subject function |
| ABL | ablative |

C. Barés Gómez (✉)
Departamento de Filosofía, Lógica y Filosofía de la Ciencia, Universidad de Sevilla, Sevilla, Spain

M. Fontaine
Departamento de Filosofía, Lógica y Estética. Universidad de Salamanca, Salamanca, Spain



T. Lopez-Soto (ed.), *Dialog Systems*, Logic, Argumentation & Reasoning 22,
https://doi.org/10.1007/978-3-030-61438-6_7

| | |
|---|---|
| ASP | aspect |
| ATTR | attributive |
| CONT | continuous |
| DECL | declarative |
| DU | dual |
| F | feminine |
| GEN | genitive |
| IMM | immediate |
| IMPF | imperfective |
| INFR | inferred |
| INTR | intransitive |
| MIR | mirative |
| N | neutral gender |
| NF | non-feminine |
| NMLZ | nominalization |
| NONFIRSTH | non-firsthand |
| NONVIS | non-visual |
| PASS.PRESS.NOM | present participle nominative |
| PFV | perfective |
| PL | plural |
| PST | past |
| REC | recent |
| REP | reported |
| S | (intransitive) subject function |
| SG | singular |
| SIN | singular action, intransitive |
| TOP.NON.A/S | topical non-subject case |
| VCLASS | verb class |

## 7.1 Introduction

It is sometimes argued that mirativity is a separate linguistic category, different from evidentiality. Unlike evidentiality, mirativity does not express anything about the source of information and is confined to the expression of surprise, as in the example from Turkish *Kemal gel – miş* ("Kemal come") where *–miş* is a mirative marker expressing the surprise.[1] In this study, we object that although mirativity is concerned with surprise, it sometimes refers back to a speaker's inference triggered by the occurrence of a surprising fact. As such, it provides an indication of the source of information. In the same vein, inferred evidentials indicate that the source of

[1]See e.g. Aikhenvald (2004, 2006, 2012), DeLancey (1997, 2012), Watters (2002), who also put forward other arguments we will not deal with in this paper (e.g. morphologic...).

information is an inference. They may even involve a similar inferential process encapsulating such a surprising element, albeit not explicitly. Our point is that in several cases, such an inferential process cannot be dissociated from the surprising element, as it is the case when the underlying reasoning is abductive. Then, the expression of surprise and the source of information are not clear-cut criteria to distinguish between mirativity and evidentiality. Given that the notion of inference is explicitly invoked in linguistic studies,[2] a philosophical analysis of these concepts based on theory of argumentation turns out to be relevant in order to understand the manifestation of surprise in mirativity and evidentiality. In this way, we do not intend to definitely answer the debate concerning the definition of evidentiality and mirativity as separate linguistic categories.

Let us begin by distinguishing between simple mirativity and complex mirativity. In both cases, surprise occurs when something contrary to the speaker's expectation happens. The former expresses a direct evidence with surprise. The latter refers back to an inference with a surprising overtone. This is of a peculiar interest for us, since surprise and inferential aspects are encapsulated in one mirativity sentence, as if there were indissociable. Mirativity has sometimes been studied in relation to evidentiality, which expresses the source of the speakers' knowledge (visual, heard, inferred. . .). Although she considers that mirativity is a separate category, Aikhenvald (2004, 2012) recognizes that evidentials have sometimes mirativity overtones, as it happens for example with inferred evidentiality. In what follows, we highlight, in number of interesting examples, how these features can be related. Beyond evidentiality, mirativity and inferred evidentiality, we also have a look at deferred realization. Though it does not constitute by itself a separate linguistic category, it is according to Aikhenvald (2004, p. 202) "a post-factum inference made on the basis of something that the speaker had previously witnessed but only later could realize what it had meant", which connects non-first-hand evidentials with mirativity.

Thus, a closer look at the links between the so-called source of information and surprise sheds light on the similarities between evidentials and mirative statements, at least in some significative cases. Indeed, authors like Aikhenvald (2012) and DeLancey (2012) emphasize that mirativity is not about the source of information, but the lack of evidence. Yet, complex mirativity, for example, is also concerned with the source of information, albeit an inferred one. From the perspective of dialogical interactions, complex miratives convey information with respect to the speaker's degree of commitment. That is, the speaker conjectures a hypothesis drawn in the course of an inference triggered by a surprising fact, she or he is not asserting something as being true. This is characteristic of abductive inference. Surprise is fundamental in abduction. It triggers the process. Simple miratives only express a surprising fact by means of which abductions could be triggered. Complex miratives sometimes encapsulate surprising facts and abductive responses, making of a particular inference a new source of information. This may also happen with

[2] Aikhenvald (2004, 2006).

inferred evidentials. Deferred realizations also involve such surprising elements, as we will see later on. Anyway, we do not completely reject that all of them are different categories. We only reject the argument previously mentioned, according to which they are distinct because miratives express surprise and evidentials the source of information. On the one hand, mirative can refer back to the source of information, albeit an inferred one. On the other hand, evidential can involve surprise, albeit more implicitly.

After having introduced various relevant examples, taken from linguistic studies, we will define abduction more precisely from the perspective of Gabbay and Woods' (2005) and Woods' (2013) model of abduction (GWm). As stressed by Gabbay and Woods, abduction is an inference (neither deductive nor inductive) in which the surprising element is fundamental.[3] A surprising element triggers an inference in the course of which a hypothesis is introduced as a basis for new actions despite a persisting state of ignorance. So that the conclusion of an abduction is not an assertion, but a conjecture. In this context, simple mirativity is nothing more but the expression of a surprising fact, without inference, while complex mirativity involves a surprising fact and the result of an abductive inference. The category of inferred evidentials also subsumes different categories depending on the underlying inference. One is called assumed inference by Aikhenvald (2004), the other is what we could call "abductive inferred evidence". Deferred realizations can sometimes be understood in terms of inferred evidentials with mirative overtones, too; that is why we will also introduce them in this paper.

In what follows, we begin with mirativity from a linguistic perspective (Sect. 7.2). We illustrate these linguistic concepts by means of various examples. Then, we introduce inferred evidentials (Sect. 7.3) and deferred realization (Sect. 7.4) in view of spotting similarities with mirativity after we will have presented the GWm of abduction (Sect. 7.5). Finally, we concretely explain how we understand mirativity in the context of abductive reasoning (Sect. 7.6) before concluding on some remarks about the interface between linguistic and philosophical studies (Sect. 7.7).[4]

## 7.2 Mirativity

The question of what mirativity is has first been approached in relation to evidentiality. Evidentiality is a linguistic category by means of which sources of our knowledge are made explicit. Although it might share linguistic similarities with evidentiality, mirativity is rather concerned with the status of information and its

---

[3]As it was actually the case in Peirce's (1931–1958, 5.189) of abduction, see Sect. 7.5 below.

[4]It is worth noting that we will focus on languages with explicit mirativity markers. Indeed, surprise may be expressed by means of other linguistic devices in languages without mirativity marker; e.g. exclamation marks or expressions like oh my God! in English. We are thankful to an anonymous reviewer for this remark.

surprising character. According to DeLancey (1997, p. 33) mirative meanings reflect "the status of the proposition with respect to the speaker's overall knowledge structure". That is, mirativity expresses the surprise that comes along with the unexpectedness of a fact. Whereas evidentiality expresses the source of information, mirativity conveys the speaker's surprise. Therefore it seems that mirativity does not say anything about the source of information and is subsequently a separate linguistic category.[5] The importance of these structures in natural linguistic dialogues is that they are made to be communicated. They are a way to transmit the evidence, or lack of evidence, or surprise, to a hearer or an audience. Their complete meaning is rooted at a pragmatic level, not only semantic. Indeed, they convey information that goes beyond the apparent content of an utterance, in particular with respect to the source of information or the surprising status of this information. From a linguistic point of view mirativity meaning subsumes the concept of a sudden discovery, surprise and expresses an unprepared mind of the speaker (Aikhenvald 2012), but also the unexpectation of the audience. It expresses the counter expectation of a new information.

Several languages have different mirativity markers. According to Aikhenvald (2012, p. 437), different kinds of mirativity markers subsume the following values:

1. "Sudden discovery, sudden revelation or realization (a) by the speaker, (b) by the audience (or addressee), or (c) by the main character;
2. surprise (a) of the speaker, (b) of the audience (or addressee), or (c) of the main character;
3. unprepared mind (a) of the speaker, (b) of the audience (or addressee), or (c) of the main character;
4. counterexpectation (a) to the speaker, (b) to the addressee, or (c) to the main character;
5. information new (a) to the speaker, (b) to the addressee, or (c) to the main character."

In the following example, mirativity expresses nothing more but the surprise of a first-hand fact:

**Example 1. Example from Turkish[6]**
*Kemal gel – di.* "Kemal come" –PST (without MIR).
*Kemal gel – miş.* "Kemal come" –MIR.

Actually, DeLancey (2012) lists several contexts for Example 1:

(a) Inference: the speaker sees Kemal's coat in the front hall but has not yet seen Kemal.

[5]See also Aikhenvald (2012) and DeLancey (1997, 2012).

[6]Turkish is a member of the Oghuz group of languages, a subgroup of the Turkic language family. It is spoken mostly in Western Asia, Anatolia. These examples come from DeLancey (2012, p. 37), who takes them from Slobin and Aksu (1982).

(b) Hearsay: the speaker has been told that Kemal has arrived but has not yet seen Kemal.
(c) Surprise: The speaker hears someone approach, opens the door, and sees Kemal -a totally unexpected visitor.

The last of these contexts has a mirativity extension, but not the two first ones. This is something we will discuss later in this paper when we will compare these examples from a philosophical and inferential perspective.

Another example of simple mirativity is the following:

**Example 2. Example from Kham[7]**
*juhpurya u – hũ : u – wo o – le – o*: Jhupurya 3SG -come -PFV.NMLZ 3SG-be-NMLZ.
"Jhupurya has arrived!"

This happens when the speaker has invited some people at home and Jhupurya arrived, uninvited and unexpected. Surprise is characteristic of these two examples of mirativity (with context c for Example 1). This is what we call simple mirativity. They express the surprising status of the information that is transmitted.

Below, we introduce complex mirativity, which is more difficult to figure out. Indeed, these examples mix surprise with inferential source of information, the limit of which are sometimes unclear:

**Example 3. Example from Kham[8]**
*kãhbul u – ri : h – zya – o o – le – o* : blanket 3SG -waeve-CONT-NMLZ 3SG-be-NMLZ.
"She's weaving a blanket!"

This sentence is uttered by an agent when she or he says that Maya is weaving a blanket, on the basis of her or his finding a partially completed blanket attached to the loom in Maya's room. Following Delancey (2012), *oleo* marks the absence of evidence. The only evidence the speaker has is that there is an unfinished blanket, not that Maya was weaving it.

**Example 4. Example from Athabaskan language Hare[9]**
*júhye sa k'ínayeda lõ*: here about bear walk.around.IMPF MIR.
"There was a bear walking around here!" (Inferred from discovery of bear tracks).

[7]Kham is a complex of Sino-Tibetan Magaric languages spoken natively in the highlands of the Rolpa and Rukum districts of Rapti and the westernmost part of Baglung district in Dhawalagiri Zone and Karnali region. The examples are from Aikhenvald (2012, p. 442).

[8]See Aikhenvald (2012, p. 443).

[9]Athabaskan is a large family of indigenous languages of North America, located in western North America in three groups of contiguous languages: Northern, Pacific Coast and Southern (or Apachean).The example is taken from Delancey (2012, p. 539), who says that this language represents the touchstone of his concept of mirativity.

Complex mirativity expresses a surprising fact, new and unexpected to the speaker, which in some cases triggers an inference. What is expressed with a tone of surprise is the result of this inference. In some sense, the inferential source of the information is transmitted with an emphasis on surprise. Later, we will clarify this connection between surprise and inferential source in terms of abduction.

## 7.3 Inferred Evidentiality and Mirativity

Mirativity and evidentiality maintain a strong and conflictive relationship. A connection can be found at the inferential level, in comparison with inferred evidentials. Inferred evidentials cover inferences based on visual evidence, assumptions and various kinds of reasonings.[10] Evidentiality is about the source of knowledge. There are languages in which the speaker must say how she or he has learnt what she or he is communicating. It is worth noting that evidentiality has nothing to do with evaluation of sources. It only communicates the sources of pieces of information or evidence. Evidentiality can be expressed differently in different languages. Even within a language, there can be different kinds of evidentiality. Aikhenvald (2004, xxv) distinguishes between various evidential systems. First are the systems with two choices, e.g. in which evidentials can be (A1) first-hand or non-firsthand, (A2) non-firsthand or 'everything else, (A3) reported ('hearsay') or 'everything else, etc. Second are the systems with three choices, (B1) namely direct (visual), inferred, reported, (B2) visual, non-visual sensory, inferred, etc. There are also systems with four choices, e.g. (C2) direct (or visual), inferred, assumed, reported, etc., and five choices. Depending on the underlying system, inferred evidentials are usually expressed by means of non-firsthand evidentials or inferred evidentials markers.

Inferred evidentials can be used for various purposes. For example, they can be used to talk about someone else's psychological and physical states, to which the speaker has no direct access. Inferred evidentials may or may not be based on firsthand evidences. Assumed evidentials also involve an inferential source, but they are generally based on non-firsthand evidence. The fact that different kinds of inferences and assumptions can be involved will have consequences in terms of the commitment carried by such utterances. Indeed, a speaker who is communicating the result of an inference, whether it be based on firsthand or non-firsthand evidence, is only committed with a conjecture and need not assent to its truth as if she or he was asserting it. According to Aikhenvald (2004, p. 187), "[d]ue to its links with inference based on conjecture, the inferred evidential may acquire epistemic overtones of doubt and non-committal in some systems [...], especially if the sentence already contains some formal marking of doubt". But, as she stresses it, it is not in the nature of inferred evidential to express doubt [Aikhenvald (2004, p. 165)],

[10]See Aikhenvald (2004, 2006) for a deeper survey of inferred evidentials.

although an epistemic overtone can be expressed by means of extensions involving probability, uncertainty, lack of personal responsibility, or with adverbs like 'surely', 'maybe', or 'very likely'. They can also have the force of a query or challenge as an answer, sometimes with rhetorical overtones. Various degrees of commitment can be explained by the underlying kind of inference, as well.

The following examples offer us an overview of inferred evidentials:[11]

**Example 5. Example from Bora**[12]

ó áxṭʰɯ *m*⍰ – ʔ *ts*ʰà – *há* – ʔ*ha*ᴴ – *a*ᴸ *h*à: aíɁ–: ɓ̥ɛ̀ – *h*à: I see -(t) that -(shelter)-INFR -remote.PST shelter burn -SIN -(shelter).
"I saw a burned house." (One that had burned before I saw it).

The inferred evidential expresses the fact that the speaker has no direct evidence of the process of burning, she or he only saw the result. On the basis of the visual evidence of a burned house, she or he infers that it had burned before.

**Example 6. Example from Tucano**[13]

*dĩ͡ayɨ wa'* ĩ – *re yaha* – *ápĩ*: dog fish -TOP.NON.A/S steal -REC.PST.NONVIS. 3SGNF.
"The dog stole the fish". (I inferred it).

Aikhenvald affirms that this evidential might be used when someone comes into the kitchen and sees that the fish is gone, there are bones and there is a dog which looks happy and satisfied. Again, the speaker has a visual evidence of what she or he actually sees, i.e. the bones and the dog seemingly happy and satisfied, but not that the dog ate the fish. What is expressed is the result of an inference based upon this visual evidence.

Another kind of evidence is what has been called "assumed evidential" by linguists.[14] Whereas Example 7 expresses the result of an inference based on a visual evidence, Example 8 is an assumed evidential which expresses something inferred on the basis of background assumptions. Both of them convey some kind of doubt or a non-commitment (or a lower degree of commitment) with what is expressed.

**Example 7. Example from Tsafiki**[15]

*Manuel ano fi – nu – e*: Manuel food eat -INFER-DECL.
"Manuel ate". (The speaker sees the dirty dishes).

---

[11]See Aikhenvald (2004) for a complete analysis of these evidentials and more examples.

[12]Bora is an indigenous language of South America spoken in the western region of Amazon rainforest. See the example in Aikhenvald (2004, p. 164), who takes it from Weber and Thiesen.

[13]Tucano, also Tukano or Tucana, endonym Dahseyé (Dasea), is a Tucanoan language spoken in Amazonas, Brazil and Colombia. See the example in Aikhenvald (2004, p. 52).

[14]See Aikhenvald (2004) in evidentials with 4 or 5 choices.

[15]Tsafiki, also known as Tsachila or Colorado, is a Barbacoan language spoken in Ecuador by c. 2000 ethnic Tsáchila people. See example in Aikhenvald (2004, p. 54).

Indeed, what is expressed is the result of an inference based on a physical evidence, the dirty dishes. The lower degree of commitment can be explained by the fact that someone else might have eaten in these dirty dishes.

**Example 8. Example from Tsafiki**[16]
*Manuel ano fi – n – ki – e*: Manuel food eat -NMLZ -VCLASS: do-DECL.
"Manuel ate". (He always eats at eight o'clock and it's now nine o'clock.)

This inference based on a general knowledge is called "assumed evidential" by Aikhenvald. There is no direct evidence of anything. Given that Manuel always eats at eight o'clock, it is inferred that today he will have eaten at eight o'clock as well. Inferred evidentials express a non-commitment of the speaker with the source. The source is indirect and inferential. Not all inferred evidentials have a mirativity overtone. This last example has not. As we will see later on, this might be linked to the inference underlying the inferred evidential.

## 7.4 Deferred Realization

'Deferred realization' does not properly refer to a category – i.e. mirativity or Evidentiality – but a feature of several distinct categories, a semantic nuance that appears in various systems of inferred evidentials. Deferred realization is usually connected with non-firsthand evidential and conveys information obtained post factum. For example, it can be used to report something a speaker saw, but she or he only interpreted later. It can be expressed by means of different markers, e.g. non-firsthand evidentials or inferred evidentials, depending on the evidential system. They often have a mirative overtone, in particular when the post factum interpretation gives rise to unexpected results. In systems in which mirativity is associated with inference, deferred realization is an integral part of mirative meanings but whether they must or must not have this mirative overtone remains an open question according to Aikhenvald (2004, p. 204 and 209). It is also unclear whether or not they should always involve an inferential dimension.

Let us now illustrate the notion of deferred realization by means of the following examples:

**Example 9. Example from Yukaghir**[17]
*ataq – un kun′ il – get ningo : i : die – l′ el – d′ i : l′ i*: two-ATTR ten -ABL lots.of catch-NONFIRSTH -INTR:1PL.
"It turned out (later) that we had caught more than twenty (fish)".

[16]See example in Aikhenvald (2004, p. 54).

[17]The Yukaghir languages are a small family of two closely related languages Tundra and Kolyma Yukaghir spoken by the Yukaghir in the Russian Far East living in the basin of the Kolyma River. See Aikhenvald (2004, p. 102). She takes it from Maslova (2003, pp. 223–224).

It seems that the speaker takes part in fishing, but the fishes were counted after the event. The action is described with a non-firsthand evidential. Deferred realization may be expressed as an inferential which can be used to signal that the speaker did not witness the event as it was going on, even if she or he has firsthand eyewitness evidence of that event by the time of speech.

**Example 10. Example from Jarawara**[18]
*o – hano – hani o – ke*: 1SG.S-be.drunk-IMM.PST.NONFIRSTH.F 1SG-DECL.F.
"I got drunk (and I don't recall it)". Non-firsthand.

It happens if the speaker woke up drunk, with a hangover and no memory of what she or he had done.

**Example 11. Example from Western Apache**[19]
*Yáhwąhyú nashāā lę̂k' eh*: store + at 1SG.IMPF.ASP.be.around REP/deferred realization.
"I was at the store". (But was not aware of it at the time).

This morpheme is a mark of the story tellers that in non-narrative genres acquire an overtone of past deferred realization. The speaker was not aware of the event when it occurred, but she or he realized later. The speaker has no personal recognition that she or he was on a store, she or he may be unconscious, or temporary lost her or his memory. She or he realized later because she or he could have been told about it or inferred it.

**Example 12. Example from Lithuanian**[20]
*Mano serga – ma* ! ?*:* I.GEN sick-PASS.PRES.NOM.N.
"Evidently I am sick!?"

This is a passive form used as evidentiality strategy with inferential meaning which acquires mirative reading in the context of first person. The speaker has just realized by surprise that she or he was sick. This strategy means a lack of control.

Deferred realization is a semantic feature that appears in numerous inferred evidentials and even in evidentiality strategies through other grammatical forms. Most of the time it seems to also have a mirativity overtone. Properly said, it is the expression of an inference post-factum which usually has a surprise tone. Nevertheless, is there always a link between deferred realization and inferential evidentiality and mirativity? Or are there forms of deferred realization or postfactum inferences

[18] Madí – also known as Jamamadí after one of its dialects, and also Kapaná or Kanamanti (Canamanti) – is an Arawan language spoken by about 1000 Jamamadi, Banawá, and Jarawara people scattered over Amazonas, Brazil. See Aikhenvald (2004, p. 221) and Aikhenvald (2003).

[19] The Western Apache language is a Southern Athabaskan language spoken among the 14,000 Western Apaches in east central Arizona. There are approximately 6000 speakers living on the San Carlos Reservation and 7000 living on the Ft. Apache Reservation. See Aikhenvald (2004, p. 203), who takes it from Reuse (2003, p. 86).

[20] Lithuanian (Lithuanian: lietuviu kalba) is an Eastern Baltic language spoken in the Baltic region. See Aikhenvald (2004, p. 205), who takes it from Gronemeyer (1997, p. 107).

without surprise? Aikhenvald lets the question open, but she always mentions the work of authors as Maslova when talking about deferred realization without surprise. Actually, Maslova does not say that "there is no surprise", she does not mention this subject at all.[21] In fact, the examples that Maslova offers are examples of deferred realization that do not mean the source of the information but just the post-factum feature. The source may be an event of which the speaker has visual evidence or another type non-witness evidence. According to Maslova, the source is not important. In what follows, we will explain why the source is also important.

Up to now, we have seen how the surprise in mirative constructions appears in different languages. The link with the unprepared mind in a complex mirativity structure has a narrow link with what is called inferential evidential, and at least in some cases they are also linked by a semantic nuance called "deferred realization".

## 7.5 Abduction: From Surprise to Hypothesis

Most of the time, "inference" is used to mean deductive inference. Deductive validity characterizes a relation between the premises and the conclusion of an argument such that if the formers are true, the latter is necessarily true. Deduction is thus defined in terms of necessary truth-preservation. Deductive inference is analytic; that is, no new information is added when passing from premises to conclusions. For example, the following schema represents a deductively valid inference, from the premises 1 and 2 to the conclusion 3:

1. *If* $\alpha$ *then* $\beta$
2. $\alpha$
3. $\beta$

This schema represents a deductively valid argument well-known as modus ponens, where the arrow is a conditional whose intended meaning is "if $\alpha$, then $\beta$". Indeed, if the premises 1 and 2 are true, then the conclusion necessarily follows. Nevertheless, correct reasoning cannot be restricted to deduction. Other kinds of inference can also be correct, even if the truth of the premises does not necessarily entail the truth of the conclusion. This is the case in abductive reasoning, in which different concurrent (and sometimes incompatible) conclusions can be drawn [Gabbay and Woods (2005), Woods (2013), Barés and Fontaine (2017) and Magnani (2001, 2009)]. The canonical definition of abductive reasoning is due to Peirce (Peirce 1931–1958, 5.189):

[21] Several examples of deferred realizations are given by E. Maslova (2003, p. 224), in the chapter "Evidentiality in Yukaghir". But the question of the link with mirativity or surprise is not addressed. Moreover, Maslova says that the deferred evidence is used when the event cannot be accounted for in terms of inference. What is expressed is something like "It turned out that we had caught more than twenty" when the speaker participated in fishing, yet the fish was counted only afterwards. As we will see later for us this is also an inference, but a non-deductive inference.

The surprising fact C is observed.
But if A were true, C would be a matter of course.
Hence there is reason to suspect that A is true.

At first sight, abduction might have the following propositional form:[22]

1. *If $\alpha$ then $\beta$*
2. $\beta$
3. $\alpha$

This schema represents a deductively invalid inference, usually condemned by theoreticians of argumentation of being the fallacious scheme of affirming the consequent. Indeed, although it might look like a *modus ponens*, it is not, given the consequent is affirmed in order to derive the antecedent. But the truth of β does not warrant the truth of α. Nonetheless, deductive reasoning needs not be the good standard to judge the correctness of such an inference. In fact, it may display a cognitive virtue from another perspective; in particular, from the perspective of cognitive economy. This means that if we take into account the agent's cognitive resources (memory, computational skills, information, time) and her or his goals, a form of reasoning can be apt with respect to a given situation without providing accurate results. Indeed, it is sometimes better to set a hypothesis as a basis for new actions, and possibly to retract it later in the light of other information, than refraining from inferring anything. This is the case of abduction, a pragmatic reasoning, which obeys neither to deductive standards nor inductive ones.

These cognitive economic insights relate to Woods's (2013) naturalized logic and leads us to consider more concretely abduction from the perspective of the GW model [following Gabbay and Woods (2005)]. First of all, Peircean abduction begins with surprise, as it is explicitly expressed in the first premise of the scheme above. Defining what makes an event surprising is not an easy task. For example, according to Peirce (1931–1958, 7.189) irregularity would not do the job, since "[n]obody is surprised that the trees in a forest do not form a regular pattern", and that it is rather regularity that would call for an explanation. According to Woods (2013, p. 367), surprise can be understood in terms of ignorance-problem, which acts as a cognitive irritant and triggers a cognitive response of the agent. If there is a question Q and some proposition α that would answer it, an agent who has not α in her or his present knowledge-base has an ignorance-problem with respect to Q. In front of an ignorance-problem, three attitudes are possible:

- Subduance: new knowledge removes ignorance (e.g. by the discovery of an empirical explanation),
- Surrender: the agent gives up and does not look for an answer,
- Abduction: a hypothesis is set as a basis for new actions.

[22]It is worth noting that in Peirce's original account, inferences were defined with respect to different kinds of syllogism. Here we express them in a propositional language.

To put it in Woods's terms (2013, p. 368): "With subduance, the agent overcomes her or his ignorance. With surrender, her or his ignorance overcomes them. With abduction, her or his ignorance remains, but they are not overcome by it". It is worth noting that abduction is ignorance-preserving; that is, its conclusion is only hypothetical and should not be considered as being true until it has not been investigated. In an unpublished letter written by Peirce to Lady Welby, and quoted by Bellucci and Pietarinen (2016), abductive conclusion can thus be referred to as an "investigand", and abduction called "Reasoning from Surprise to Inquiry". But inquiry lies beyond abduction, which does not involve verification. With respect to the scheme above, the agent introduces a hypothesis $\alpha$ such that if α were true, $\beta$ would be a matter of course. But this does not mean that α must be the case, given that α is only a correct abductive solution among others and that it might be revised in the light of new information. In abduction, surprise and hypotheses are gathered together in a "scant resource adjustment strategy" according to Woods (2013, p. 371) as in the following GW scheme of abduction (Gabbay and Woods 2005; Woods 2013):

1. $T\,!\,Q(\alpha)$
   Abduction begins with surprise; i.e. a cognitively irritant problem relative, in response to which an agent sets T as her or his epistemic target at a given time, with respect to an unanswered question Q to which α would be the answer.
2. $\sim(R(K, T))$ [*Fact*]
   There is no attainment relation R between the agent's knowledge-base K and the target T; i.e. the agent does not know the answer of the question Q.
3. $\sim(R(K*; T))$ [*Fact*]
   There is no attainment relation R between an immediate successor K* of K and T; i.e. the agent is not able to produce an answer in a timely way.
4. $H \notin K$ [*Fact*]
   The hypothesis H does not pertain to K.
5. $H \notin K*$ [*Fact*]
   The hypothesis H does not pertain to K*.
6. $\sim R(H, T)$ [*Fact*]
   There is no attainment relation R between H and T.
7. $\sim R(K(H); T)$ [*Fact*]
   There is no attainment relation between K enriched by H and T either.
8. $H \rightsquigarrow R(K(H), T$ [*Fact*]
   If H *were* true, there would be an attainment relation between K enriched by H and T; $\rightsquigarrow$ being a subjunctive conditional.
9. *H* satisfies conditions $S1, \ldots, Sn$ [*Fact*]
   We might require that the hypothesis satisfies additional conditions; e.g. consistency, minimality, plausibility, etc.[23]

[23]Providing such conditions is problematic, given that although various filters are applied in the selection of hypotheses, they are never sufficient or necessary. This is the notorious cut-down problem, with respect to the selection of hypotheses. See Gabbay and Woods (2005) for a critical

10. *Therefore*, $C(H)[Sub - conclusion, 1 - 7]$
    The agent conjectures a hypothesis H.
11. *Then*, $H^c$ [*Conclusion* 1 – 8]
    The hypothesis is released in an ignorance preserving way.

Although the abductive process thus described is a warrant for the hypothesis set by the agent in response to an ignorance-problem, abduction is an ignorance preserving relation. It is not a warrant of the truth of the conclusion. In other words, the abductive process does not provide any reason to believe the hypothesis. As previously explained, it is an invitation to investigate (investigand) in relation to a surprising element. In this context, we should emphasize the distinction between partial and full abduction, reflected by the sub-conclusion 10 and the conclusion 11, respectively. Indeed, step 10, a hypothesis is introduced. This provides us with three possibilities. First, the hypothesis can be (empirically) confirmed, and it loses its hypothetical status. Second, it is not confirmed, and we are let with the initial ignorance-problem again and the three possibilities (subduence, surrender, abduction). Third, in a full abduction, step 11, the hypothesis is released as a basis for further action (and reasoning) as if it were true, and despite a persisting state of ignorance.

## 7.6 Abductive Source of Information

The GW model of abduction offers a tool to point at some similarities between complex mirative and (inferred) evidentials. Abduction is an inference that processes from surprise to hypotheses. At least in some of its manifestations in natural language, complex mirativity refers back to an abductive inference, triggered by a surprising information. Mirativity thus specifies the source of information, an abductive inference indissociable from a surprising element. In fact, whereas simple mirativity is usually confined to the expression of a surprising fact, complex mirativity expresses a conjectured set in response to such a surprise.

Let us come back to concrete examples of mirativity, inferred evidentials and deferred realizations, and analyse them in parallel with the supposed underlying inferential processes. Examples 1 ("Kemal comes" (with context c)) and 2 ("Jhupurya arrived!") are cases of simple mirativity. They do not seem to be related to any inferential process. The speaker only expresses his surprise with respect to an unexpected fact. Simple mirative is the mark of an unprepared mind and its function in natural language dialogical interaction is to convey that surprise to the hearer. In these examples, Kemal and Jhupurya have appeared, we saw them, but their venue was not expected.

discussion of such conditions. See also Magnani (2001, 2009) for the fill-up problem when abduction is not selective but creative.

According to Aikhenvald (2012, p. 436), mirativity is a separate linguistic category, different from evidentiality. She advances various reasons: they are different in their semantics, uses and occurrences with other categories and the surprising reaction might be from any source. But there is another argument, which is precisely the one we are concerned with in this paper. In line with DeLancey (1997, p. 33), who considers that mirative meanings reflect "the status of the proposition with respect to the speaker's overall knowledge structure", and Watters (2002, p. 436) who thinks that mirativity "makes no claim about the source of information", Aikhenvald (2012) claims that mirativity does not deal with evidence, but with no evidence.

However, without claiming that mirativity is a sub-category of evidentiality, we find cases of complex miratives in which the surprising overtone is itself an indication of the inferential source of information. Examples 3 ("She's weaving a blanket!") and 4 ("There was a bear walking around here!") are cases of complex mirative in which the source of information is an abductive inference. It is therefore difficult to (and even impossible) delineate clearly when the surprise ends and when the source of information starts. Indeed, "Maya is weaving a blanket" is uttered by the speaker who sees an unfinished blanket in the loom of her room. "There was a bear" is uttered by a speaker who sees footprints on the floor. Thus, the source of the information conveyed by these utterances is not a direct perception, but an inference triggered by a direct perception of another fact (the blanket in the loom, the footprints on the floor). "She's weaving a blanket" in Example 3 is a hypothesis, defeasibly inferred by an abduction triggered by a surprising fact. It is defeasible, since although the abductive process is itself a warrant of the hypothesis, it might be revised in the light of new information. Indeed, given the perception of an incomplete blanket near the loom, the speaker rightly infer that Maya may have been weaving a blanket. But it might be the case, and the speakers knows that, that the blanket is there for other reasons. Perhaps Maya's father has left the blanket in Maya's room. The same holds for the Example 4, in which the footprints might have been left by someone disguised as a bear. It is true that there is no direct evidence of what is expressed by the statement, and that what comes first is a state of ignorance, but this does not mean that it is not concerned with the source of information.

In parallel with the GW model of abduction, the surprising situation arises from an ignorance-problem: there is a question Q, "why is there an unfinished blanket in the loom of Maya's room?", to which some proposition $\alpha$ might be the answer. The target T of the agent-speaker is to find such an $\alpha$ (step 1 in the GW scheme above). If she or he has no immediate answer, there is no attainment relation R between her or his knowledge-base K and the cognitive target T (step 2). It is worth noting that this perfectly matches with DeLancey's claim that mirativity is primarily concerned with the epistemic status of the proposition. Then, there is no direct successor K* such that there would be an attainment relation R between K* and T (step 3). That is, the speaker remains in a state of ignorance, otherwise there would be subduence and perhaps another kind of evidential construction would have been employed. Instead, the speaker may perform an inference by means of which she or he will introduce a new hypothesis H. Such a hypothesis H does not pertain to K (step 4) or K* (step 5).

There is no attainment relation between H and T (step 6) or between the union of K and H and T (step 7). Indeed, if it is nothing but a hypothesis, it does not solve the ignorance-problem. The hypothesis H can be conjectured thanks to a subjunctive relation $\rightsquigarrow$; that is, if H were true, then there would be an attainment relation between K enriched by H and T (step 8). In other words, if H were true, together with the knowledge-base of the agent, it would solve the ignorance-problem. However, since it is still a hypothesis, ignorance is preserved. Nevertheless, the agent can rightly conjecture that hypothesis H (step 10), and even make use of it independently of its confirmation (step 11). Complex mirativity expresses that a hypothesis, defeasibly warranted by an abductive inference triggered by a surprising fact, is conjectured.

If an abduction is the source of information, as it seems to be the case in these examples, then it cannot be dissociated from its intrinsic surprising element. Therefore, complex mirativity may also concerned with the source of information, as well as inferred evidentials. And this has pragmatic implications from the perspective of natural language dialogues. Indeed, mirativity conveys information concerning the speaker's degree of commitment with the truth of what she or he is uttering. Her or his statement is nothing more but a conjecture based upon an abductive inference triggered by a surprising fact. Subsequently, mirativity indicates a lower degree of commitment than with standard evidentials. The speaker is only committed with a defeasible conjecture stated despite a persisting state of ignorance. In Examples 3 or 4, the speaker does not know why the blanket or the footprints are there, but she or he affirms what it could be on the basis of an inference, not what it is. Such a hypothesis can even be released as a basis for new action, for example if despite a persisting state of ignorance the speaker or a hearer decide to buy a book on weaving in order to make a present to Maya, or to run away in the Example 4. Complex mirativity may play a particular role in a dialogue, if the speaker, or even an interlocutor, pursues by saying something like "she has used her brother's preferred color", "perhaps she will give him the blanket as a present". In both cases, correctness of inference has nothing to do with the truth of the conclusion. The correctness of the inference is warranted by the fact that in response to a surprise, a hypothesis has been set in accordance with the different step of the scheme described above. Since there is no abduction without surprise, surprise thus forms part of the mirative statement and cannot be excluded from the expression of the source of information. Although mirativity is concerned with a lack of knowledge or pieces of evidence, it may provide indications about the source of information. Even if what is uttered is a hypothesis inferred in an ignorance-preserving way, it makes sense to say that mirativity is concerned with the source of information.[24] In fact, complex mirativity comprises something similar to non-firsthand evidentials, in the sense that both are involved in cases of non-direct evidence. Of course, this depends on the language and the evidential-mirativity

[24] Notice that other authors consider that is not exactly about ignorance, but about enhanced knowledge see (Magnani 2001; Bertolotti et al. 2016).

system. We do not say that mirativity and non-firsthand evidentials are the same, but they are different ways to express an indirect source of information.

For the sake of comparison, Examples 5 ("I saw a burned house" – one that had burned before I saw it) and 6 ("The dog stole the fish" – I inferred it) are cases of inferred evidentials. They are used to express an indirect source of information, in particular that it proceeds from an inference. In these examples, the underlying inference is also an abduction. Indeed, someone sees a burnt house in Example 5 or that the fish has disappeared and a dog happy near the place where the fish was in Example 6. These are nothing but hypotheses, uttered in response to an ignorance-problem set by a surprising fact, of which the speaker has evidence. Whereas complex mirativity may be the mark of an underlying abductive inference, abductively inferred evidentials involve a surprising element, due to the nature of abduction itself. Although it is concerned with the absence of direct evidence of what is explicitly uttered, it is concerned with the inferential source of information and the resulting commitment towards a hypothesis it carries. Eventually, it shares a structure similar to complex mirativity, which was excluded from evidentiality. It is true that mirativity appears to be more explicit with respect to the surprise conveyed by the utterance, but if inferred evidentiality can also be in some cases explained in terms of abductive inference, then it must be recognized that it also involves an indissociable initial surprise. On the one hand, mirativity can be concerned with the source of information, as it is the case in complex mirativity. On the other hand, surprise characteristic of mirativity can also be involved in inferred evidentiality. This does not preclude that they could be distinct linguistic categories, but this should not be done on the basis of the fact that mirativity expresses surprise and not the source of information.

It is worth noting that inferred evidentiality can be based upon different kinds of inferences, as it can be illustrated by Examples 7 ("Manuel ate" – the speaker sees the dirty dishes) and 8 ("Manuel ate" – he always eats at eight o'clock and it's now nine o'clock). Although it is uttered that "Manuel ate" in the two examples above, they are based upon different inferences. In the first case, the speaker sees the dirty dishes and conjectures the hypothesis that Manuel ate. It is an abductive inference. In the second case, the inference is based on induction. That is, if Manuel had always eaten at eight o'clock in the past, he has eaten at eight o'clock tonight. Actually, it might also be the result of a deduction if it is inferred that Manuel ate at eight o'clock from the general law "Manuel always eats at eight". According to Aikhenvald (2004, p. 54), Example 8 is an assumed evidential, i.e. it is an inference based on assumptions pertaining to the speaker's background knowledge, not firsthand pieces of evidence. So, in the case of abduction, what is uttered is a hypothesis. In the case of induction, it is a prediction based on past events. In the case of deduction, a conclusion necessarily follows from what is assumed. These examples do not explicitly display any kind of surprise. Nonetheless, if the source of information is an abductive inference, then surprise intrinsically forms part of this source of information.

According to Aikhenvald, when mirativity is associated with inference, deferred realizations have a mirative overtone. Roughly, deferred realizations are used when a speaker later realizes that something was the case, possibly on the basis of fact she or he already knew. They are sometimes defined in terms of post factum inference. But deferred realizations do not necessarily involve inference. In the following example, a non-firsthand evidential is used to express that something unexpected has been discovered, and thus acquires a mirative extension:

**Example 13. Example from Northern Khanty**[25]
*śi x ∩ t − Ən wer − lƏ−ɳƏn pa x⍰ti ul − lƏn.*
so house-3DU make-PRES-3DU and so pole-3DU
*kurte − t ul − m − el*
iron-PL be-NONFIRSTH.PST -3SG
"So they are making the house, and the poles turned out to be iron".

In this example, a non-firsthand evidential is used to express the speaker's surprise. This would be appropriate in a context in which the speaker knew they would have built a hose, but only later she or he realized that the poles would be made of iron. But this example does not seem to involve any inference at all, at least in the sense we have previously defined it, since the speaker saw later that the poles turned out to be iron. So, although mirative overtones of inferred evidentials are usually expressed by deferred realizations, deferred realizations need not involve inference.[26] Other examples of deferred realization previously mentioned display a closer link between inferred evidentiality and mirativity. This seems to be the case with Example 11 ("I got drunk" – and I don't recall it) which is uttered with a non-firsthand evidential, or Example 12 ("I was at the store" – but I was not aware of it at the time), and Example 13 ("Evidently I am sick !?"). A lower degree of commitment can be related to the underlying inference, when its result is nothing more but a conjecture.

## 7.7 Meaning: Dynamic and Dialogic

Mirativity may be expressed by different linguistic resources as aspect, tense, gender or evidentiality.[27] It has a semantic value and we may talk about "mirative strategies". As it has already been emphasized, for authors like Aikhenvald (2012), we cannot say that mirativity is an evidential. But, some evidentials have mirative aspects, and conversely. In this paper, we have analysed complex mirativity and inferred evidentials by focusing on the inferences they involve. Complex miratives, with their surprising tone, refer back to abductive inferences. Inferred evidentials may also involve abductive inferences. In that sense, it must be recognized that mirativity, at least in the cases we have analysed, is also concerned with the source of information. Even though mirativity deals with non-evidence, it can also be

[25] See Aikhenvald (2004, p. 196).
[26] This might be in line with Maslova (2003).
[27] See DeLancey (1997, 2012) and Aikhenvald (2012).

concerned with the source of information. And this is precisely the case when the source is an abductive inference, which has been defined as an ignorance-preserving inference.[28] It may have an instrumental value with respect to management of ignorance or enhancing knowledge.[29] So, from this point of view, inferred evidentiality and complex mirativity share common features, at least in some of their manifestations.

Mirativity refers back to the expression of different kinds of surprises. A fact of which we have evidence, whether it be firsthand or not, can be contrary to the speaker's expectation. This characterizes what we have called simple mirativity. But this surprising fact can also trigger an inference which gives rise to a new hypothesis uttered with a mirative extension. This is complex mirativity. If it involves an abductive inference, it intrinsically relates to a surprising element. Inferred evidential may also involve abductive inference, in which case they also intrinsically relate to surprise, albeit not explicitly. Inferred evidentials are non-firsthand evidentials, they are concerned with the source of information even if it is an indirect one. Our proposal is that complex mirativity may also be concerned with the source of information. Indeed, it indicates that the speaker is only committed with a conjecture set as a response to a surprising fact, whereby it expresses that the source of information is an abductive inference.

Evidentiality is the mark of the source of information. Mirativity may be seen as the mark that the speaker needs not assent to the truth of what she or he is uttering, although she or he might have reasons to conjecture it. In formal language, this can be expressed explicitly by means of dynamic operators. For example, Barés et al. (2019) interpret evidentiality in a dynamic epistemic logic with public announcement operator. Evidentiality is understood in terms of a dynamic process between an initial epistemic state and another one resulting from the transmission of a piece of information. If complex mirativity is to be understood in relation to abductive inference, we may also follow Soler et al. (2012), Velázquez-Quesada et al. (2013) and Nepomuceno-Fernández et al. (2013) who describe abductive processes in terms of epistemic dynamics. This would provide a formal semantics in a model-theoretical approach.

Nonetheless, if we are thinking of the specificity of these categories in terms of inference, a study from the perspective of argumentative dialogues turns out to be relevant. Mirativity is the mark that the speaker is committed to give reason of what she or he is uttering only in specific language games; those in which something can be conjectures in response to an ignorance-problem. In dialogical logic, this can be modelled by means of games whose rules are different from the rules of standard deductive dialogical logic. In dialogical logic, deductive validity is approached within a game between the proponent of a thesis and an opponent. The proponent's thesis is deductively valid if she or he has a winning strategy; that is, if she or he is able to defend himself against every criticism of the opponent. In abductive

[28]See Bertolotti et al. (2016) for different types of ignorance.

[29]See Magnani (2009) and Woods (2013).

dialogues, the proponent is allowed to introduce hypotheses as a basis for hypothetical plays. This yields a less strong justification of the thesis, since hypotheses are defeasible. As we have understood it, simple mirativity is the expression of an abductive problem, whose meaning can be given in the context of specific plays, i.e. a sequence of challenges and defences. In the dialogical approach of Barés and Fontaine (2017), an abductive game may be triggered after the Proponent has justified the fact that she or he were facing an abductive problem. Then, a hypothesis may be introduced. Nonetheless, the utterance of such a hypothesis is not an assertion of standard deductive dialogical logic. In abduction, conclusions are drawn defeasibly. And the conjecture is made by an agent who is aware that it might be defeated in the light of new information. This is what might be expressed by complex miratives, at least as we understood them in relation to abduction. Non-monotonic dialogues for abduction have been defined by Fontaine and Barés (2019) and Barés and Fontaine (2020).[30]

## 7.8 Conclusion

It has been argued by a number of authors that evidentiality and mirativity are distinct categories. Whereas the former is concerned with the speaker's source of information, the other expresses the speaker's surprise. However, when we pay attention to more sophisticated forms of evidentials and miratives, things are not always so clear. Complex mirativity may be the mark of an abductive inference, and its constitutive triggering surprise. As such, mirativity is an indication of the source of information, i.e. an abductive inference-and of the subsequent lower degree of commitment from the part of the speaker. From this perspective, the expression of surprise is itself an indication of the source of information, and we cannot thus distinguish between an evidential and a mirative extension within complex mirativity. Therefore, although we recognize different kinds of miratives and evidentials with different functions in natural languages, it sometimes appears that mirativity and evidentiality-respectively defined in terms of surprise and source of information-cannot be so clearly distinguished.

A lot of questions remain unanswered, and the question of knowing whether "deferred realizations" form part of mirativity is left open. Aikhenvald says it is quite similar to complex mirativity but she leaves open the question about the possibility of "deferred realization" without surprise. From our point of view, the answer might depend on the underlying inference. If it relies on a kind of abductive inference, then it will involve a surprising element as well. In this case, like complex mirativity, it will be a mirative with indication of the source of information. But as we have seen it

[30]Another way to approach mirativity in dialogues would be in the context of the Constructive Type Theories, as in Rahman et al. (2018), where they would get their full meaning in the context of hypothetical dialogues.

in the previous sections, the fact that they are based upon abduction is not clear at all. Their more salient feature seems to be the connection between temporality and surprise.

We do not claim to have definitely defined or ordered the concepts of mirativity and evidentiality. Nonetheless, given that the notion of inference is fundamental in the linguist's studies-that explicitly refer to the notion of inference-the inferences at stake must be relevant to answer open questions. This was the point of this paper, i.e., we have clarified what a complex mirative is in comparison to the so-called inferred evidentials. On this basis, we have recognized that, when they are ground on abduction, complex mirative markers may be concerned with the source of information, like inferred evidentials.

**Acknowledgement** We are particularly thankful to the editor of this volume Teresa Lopez-Soto and two anonymous reviewer for their helpful comments. We also thank Angel Nepomuceno, Olga Pombo and Shahid Rahman for their support and their advice. Matthieu Fontaine acknowledges the postdoctoral program of the FCT-Portugal (Gran Number SFRH/BDP/116494/2016) and the financial support of FCT CFCUL UID/FIL/0067872019. Cristina Barés Gómez acknowledges the support of VPPI-US (Contrato de acceso al Sistema Español de Ciencia, Tecnología e Innovación para el desarrollo del programa propio I + D + I de la Universidad de Sevilla).

## References

Aikhenvald, A. Y. (2004). *Evidentiality*. Oxford University Press.

Aikhenvald, A. Y. (2006). *Evidentiality in grammar*. Elsevier.

Aikhenvald, A. Y. (2012). The essence of mirativity. *Linguistic Typology, 16*(3), 435–485.

Barés Gómez, C. & Fontaine, M. (2017). Argumentation and abduction in dialogical logic. In *Springer handbook of model-based science* (pp. 295–314). Cham: Springer.

Barés Gómez, C., & Fontaine, M. (2019). Between sentential and model-based abductions: A dialogical approach. *Logic Journal of the IGPL.*

Barés Gómez, C., Fontaine, M., & Nepomuceno, A. (2019). Knowledge in action: Logico-philosophical approach to linguistic evidentiality. *Logic Journal of the IGPL.*

Bellucci, F., & Pietarinen, A. V. (2016). Charles Sanders Peirce: Logic. In *International Encyclopedia of Philosophy.*

Bertolotti, T., Arfini, S., & Magnani, L. (2016). Abduction: From the ignorance problem to the ignorance virtue. *FLAP, 3*(1), 153–173.

DeLancey, S. (1997). Mirativity: The grammatical marking of unexpected information. *Linguistic Typology, 1*(1), 33–52.

DeLancey, S. (2012). Still mirative after all these years. *Linguistic Typology, 16*(3), 529–564.

Fontaine, M., & Barés Gómez, C. (2019). Conjecturing hypotheses in a dialogical logic for abduction. In D. Gabbay (Ed.), *Natural arguments – A tribute to John Woods*. London: College Publications.

Gabbay, D., & Woods, J. (2005). The reach of abduction: Insight and trial.

Gronemeyer, C. (1997). Evidentiality in Lithuanian. *Working Papers-Lund University Department of Linguistics*, 93–112.

Magnani, L. (2001). *Abduction, reason and science: Processes of discovery and explanation.* Springer.

Magnani, L. (2009). *Abductive cognition: The epistemological and eco-cognitive dimensions of hypothetical reasoning* (Vol. 3). Springer.

Maslova, E. (2003). Evidentiality in Yukaghir. In A. Y. Aikhenvald & R. M. W. Dixon (Eds.), *Studies in evidentiality* (pp. 219–235). Amsterdam/Philadelphia: John Benjamins Publishing Company.

Nepomuceno-Fernández, Á., Soler-Toscano, F., & Velázaquez-Quesada, F. R. (2013). An epistemic and dynamic approach to abductive reasoning: Selecting the best explanation. *Logic Journal of the IGPL, 21*(6), 943–961.

Peirce, C. S. (1931–1958). *Collected Papers of Charles Sanders Peirce*. Cambridge: Harvard University Press.

Rahman, S., McConaughey, Z., Klev, A., & Clerbout, N. (2018). *Immanent reasoning or equality in action: A plaidoyer for the play level* (Vol. 18). Springer.

Reuse, W. J. (2003). Evidentiality in Western Apache (Athabaskan). In A. Y. Aikhenvald & R. M. W. Dixon (Eds.), *Studies in evidentiality* (pp. 79–101). Amsteram/Philadelphia: John Benjamins Publishing Company.

Slobin, D. I., & Aksu, A. A. (1982). Tense, aspect and modality in the use of the Turkish evidential. *Tense-Aspect: Between Semantics and Pragmatics*, 185–200.

Soler-Toscano, F., Fernández, D., & Nepomuceno-Fernández, Á. (2012). A modal framework for modelling abductive reasoning. *Logic Journal of the IGPL, 20*(2), 438444.

Velázquez-Quesada, F. R., Soler-Toscano, F., & Nepomuceno-Fernández, Á. (2013). An epistemic and dynamic approach to abductive reasoning: Abductive problem and abductive solution. *Journal of Applied Logic, 11*(4), 505–522.

Watters, D. E. (2002). *A grammar of Kham*. Cambridge University Press.

Woods, J. (2013). *Errors of reasoning – Naturalizing the logic of inference*. London: College Publications.

# Chapter 8
# Two Convergences to Dynamic Formalism: Bakhtin's Dialogism and Brouwer's Creating Subject

**Ravi Chakraborty and Clément Lion**

**Abstract** We argue that the recent developments of the dialogical framework towards the incorporation of materiality within dialogues certainly enables one to extend its possible applications beyond the domain of logic. We ask the question of linking Bakhtin's criticism of literary formalism, based on advocating dialogical features within novels, and the dialogical sight on formalism, in order to assess the program of constituting a dynamical formalism as a means towards literary analysis, enabling to speak of subjectivity without falling into psychologism. By the way, we propose a dialogical reading of the alleged non constructivity of Kripke's schema in (Sundholm Constructivity and computability in historical and philosophical perspective, logic, epistemology, and the unity of science. Springer, Dordrecht, 2015) and we indicate a new path towards another understanding of its constructive content.

**Keywords** Intuitionism · Dynamic formalism · Creating subject · Philosophy of mathematics · Intersubjectivity

## 8.1 Introduction

If logic is conceived of as dealing exclusively with truth preservation through inferential moves, there is no question in using logical devices in order to clarify the meaning of literary texts: their essential equivocality makes their own fields of objects located beyond any binary opposition between truth and falsehood. We can thus wonder whether literary texts properly aim at fixing global utterances, the

---

R. Chakraborty
IIT, Delhi, India
e-mail: huz158130@hss.iitd.ac.in

C. Lion (✉)
UMR 8163 CNRS, Université de Lille, Savoirs, Textes, Langage (STL), Lille, France
e-mail: clement.lion@univ-lille.fr



T. Lopez-Soto (ed.), *Dialog Systems*, Logic, Argumentation & Reasoning 22,
https://doi.org/10.1007/978-3-030-61438-6_8

meaning of which would depend on their being usable in inferences. It is further more than a novel aim at demonstrating anything. From a Fregean point of view, it might be argued that literature depends on something that is beyond the scope of logic, because it is based on shades that are propositionally irrelevant, especially when dealing with style and composition.

If one admits that the process of formalizing mathematical reasonings helps overcrossing fuzziness that can remain within mathematics, it is accordingly not natural to consider it goes the same way when one formalizes a literary text: if one fixes the meaning of literary texts by reducing them to sets of (implicit) utterances, then it is equivalent to neutralize something that is essential to their literary being, namely a certain plasticity, such that their meaning does not preclude their being transferred into unpredictable contexts of uses, through a reading which intends to be accurate to their genuinely literary content.

We will ask here however whether a notion of formality could eventually guide a correct formalization of literary texts, while not neglecting their equivocality. We must accordingly decide to which extent there can be a formality which is not reducible to a "structure of validity", that always seems to presuppose a full definiteness of meaning. Does the notion of a formal rule, that is to be found in the dialogical framework, suit for such a purpose? Can we put it in league with Bakhtin's view on formalism, given that he promotes a dialogical view on novels, in order to get rid of a certain rigidity in the formalist approach? Can both traditions be brought closer as they presently are, due to their belonging to separated academic fields?

## 8.2 Formalization as a Device Towards Literary Analysis

As deployed by the Russian School, the formalistic reading of pieces of literature was intended to replace "causerie" by a rigorously scientific approach of literary texts, based on separating formal features of the language that is specific to them from prosaic use. The aim was thus to identify objective strokes within literary texts, such that a well-defined domain of objectivity may arise, enabling literary critic to establish facts, depending on the adoption of an adequate perspective on literariness, which is distinguished by specific devices of linguistic construction. Instead of making sense of a poem or a novel by referring to biographical, historical or sociological elements surrounding its production, the formal method focuses on its internal compounds without assuming an external pre-existing material that would be transcribed from a stylistically neutral ground: the material is rather thought of as being immanent to the formal elaboration of the literary language itself, which corresponds to a specific regime of the construction of meaning. Formalism promotes construction – rather than representation – as being the kernel of literary activity, because what essentially matters is the process according to which a certain type of object is specified rather than its external horizon. The process of isolating formal strokes of literary texts – or equivalently the process of formalizing them –

does not belong accordingly to the creating act in which they originate (this act being so to stay pushed away from the domain of literary analysis), but it is rather the outcome of a critical sight on the literary object, taken as being achieved and completed in an irremovable totality, taking part of the universe of facts.

## 8.3 Bakhtin's Take on the Formalist Project

In the first instance, Bakhtin's thought appears to be antagonistic to the spirit of formalization. The insistence on the materiality of language means that Bakhtin is fundamentally averse to the reduction of language to sets of syntactic rules which is the typical mode adopted by any formalism. However, Bakhtin describes the process of the generation of meaning to be essentially dialogical. Besides, Bakhtin also insists that the fundamental unit of meaning is the word or the utterance and not the abstract sentence.

These two observations constitute what could be called a description of the form of a process. This is the process of the generation of meaning. In this essay, we will highlight this formal aspect of Bakhtin's dialogism by throwing it in relief against the more unreservedly formalist approaches to literature. If this is a formalism, then we argue that it aspires to capture the dynamic nature of literary meaning which gets suppressed in what is traditionally identified as the formalist approach.

The materiality of language entails a recognition of the constituent speech events of language occurring in actual space and time. As such, language is a process that happens through various speech events. Any endeavour to explain the process of meaning generation is then an attempt to model a process occurring in space and time. Linguistic and thereby, literary meaning cannot be reduced to the play of relations within a formal system.

This revised appreciation of the materiality of language means that the consequent theory cannot afford to invoke a formalism that is reduced to the logical syntax of a reductionist view. The significance of this view is further established when we compare the phenomenon of language and literature to natural phenomenon. Just as mathematical formalisms acknowledge the unique ontologies of specific kinds of phenomena, any theory must recognize the phenomenon of language and literature as such. Instead of the wager that a logical syntax with axiomatic foundations could be somehow invented to model how literary meaning is produced, Bakhtin is more receptive to the actual specificities of language and literature.

However, avowedly formalist approaches are sceptical of any view that reifies the specific and the particular. The particular is to be produced as the result of a generative framework that is constructed.

## 8.4 Bakhtin's Reflections on Formalism in Science and Mathematics

Bakhtin seeks to invert this approach towards scientific explanation by valuing the particular which also happens to be the contingent. In a remarkable observation, Bakhtin (2014) asserts that the mathematization of sciences is a reality. But these mathematical techniques are specific to the phenomena being captured. The emphasis on the specificity of these techniques echoes Brouwer's aversion towards the totalizing ambitions of formalism. But even prior to such a resonance, Bakhtin is invested in the philosophical grounding of the human sciences which demands a certain effort to resist a relatively unreflective imitation of natural science including the fact of its formalization through mathematics.

Bakhtin himself admits to the influence of the German philosopher Wihelm Dilthey's distinction between explanation and understanding.[1] Here, it is useful to revisit Dilthey's philosophical efforts in clearly establishing the grounds on which human sciences are different from natural sciences. Firstly, Dilthey was absolutely clear that human activity and its organizational structures must be studied rigorously in all their empirical reality.

Following Kant, Dilthey (1988) first agrees that natural science cannot account for what is called the inner experience, but outer experience cannot also be explained fully insofar as it is a fact of consciousness. This offers Dilthey the opportunity to question the primacy of the natural sciences over the human sciences. If everything is a fact of consciousness, Dilthey may slip into a Kantian primacy of transcendental philosophy. Not only would such a move preclude the radical ascendancy of human sciences as being primary to the natural sciences, it would also ensure that the notion of the subject would be a given rather than it being a problem. Dilthey refuses to go down this path and proposes the framework of 'life'. His philosophy of life is turned against any idea of a transcendental self-explanation of consciousness, to track the emergence of concepts from the basis of life itself. For Bakhtin and for our purposes, this dynamism in the constitution of subjectivity will serve as an argument for the proposition of dialogism.

Dilthey says that the abstractions which constitute the physical laws are only a part of external reality. The law-like relations between these abstractions may be expressed through the language of mathematical formalisms. These attempts at formulating causal laws is how the mode of explanation works in the natural

[1]It is important to underline that this distinction between explanation and understanding is not a repetition of the canonical debates in philosophy of science. This is because, within philosophy of science, both explanation and understanding employ the power of intuition without explicitly locating the contours of the subject. Hence,this contribution from Dilthey is useful because it makes the case for the role of the subject in the human sciences. By invoking the subject in this manner, we are able to introduce inner experience (which Brouwer also invokes in his view of mathematical intuition) as a factor in the understanding involved in human sciences.

sciences. Natural sciences proceed through explanation while human sciences emphasize on understanding.

The task of causal explanation in natural sciences involves starting from some axiomatic givens, say, for example, atoms. However, Dilthey says that in human sciences, we cannot take the human subject as an equivalently readymade monad. One may locate an incipient notion of Bakhtin-ian dialogism in this observation. The incompleteness of the subject is to be inferred from its constructed-ness and then one can further ask if the construction of the subject is a process and indeed a process that always involves the other entity which forms the dialogic framework.

The primary criticism levelled at the Formalists was that it was not grounded in a philosophy but rather imitates the formalist aesthetics of the Futurist movement. Either the Formalists were ideologically motivated or were adopting a certain aesthetics to their theorizing gestures. As far as the provision of a sound epistemological basis for formalism is concerned, it is unclear whether the Formalists are philosophically grounded enough. Getting involved in such philosophical questions was inimical to the advancement of a possible literary science.

## 8.5 The Philosophical Case for the Primacy of the Subject in Bakhtin and Brouwer

It is this regard that Bakhtin's departure from Formalism is apparently a more substantial shift. For Bakhtin, the literary study had to be grounded in philosophy. If such is the case, then the divergence from the Formalist movement does not deter one to carefully underline the formal aspects of Bakhtin's thought. Beginning from the emphasis upon dialogue over dialectic to the rejection of the notion of the system, we strive to emphasize these formal aspects of Bakhtin's thought and show them to echo the concerns raised by the critique of another formalist movement: the one in philosophy of mathematics. We aim to establish a resonance between the thought of Bakhtin and that of the intuitionists like Brouwer and Heyting.

We note here that Formalists aspired to construct the totality of a 'literary system". This 'closed' conception of the system bounds in literature in two ways: it attempts to either bound off literature as an autonomous system which can be studied independent of events external to it. Peter Steiner (2014) notes carefully the philosophical implications of thinking in terms of the 'system' in the work of the later Russian Formalist, Yuri Tynyanov. Even in Tynyanov, there is an acknowledgement of the multiplicity of literary facts that make up literature, but Tynyanov also proposes a Hegelian alternation between automatization and defamiliarization to force a harmony between the co-evolution of these literary facts to form a literary system. The element of contingency in the creation and evolution of literature is ignored for the sake of preserving the conception of a 'system'. As opposed to this notion of the system, Bakhtin's dialogism (as opposed to dialectic resolution) seeks to emphasize the processual character of the phenomenon of literature which is essentially open-ended and hence contingent. In fact, Bakhtin does not even properly consider the problem of what is literature in isolation from reference to particular literary phenomena.

Ultimately, the formal aspect of literature that Bakhtin wished to capture was not a system that could explain all literature, or even parts of literature as a whole, subsumed within a system. Rather Bakhtin aspired to comprehend a specific literary phenomenon in all its particularity. It is in this regard that Bakhtin's approach to literature mirrors that of Brouwer. Brouwer, like Bakhtin, wishes to take into account, within some (controversial) demonstrations, how the creating subject constructs, in a temporal process, a specific mathematical entity. However, in his radical gesture of recovering the primacy of the subject, he insists that these constructions are purely mental and hence independent of language. This is where Bakhtin would seemingly diverge from Brouwer because the very notion of the subject is not prior to language or linguistic activity for that matter.

When we explore Brouwer's thought later in this essay, we will examine how Brouwer's position on the language-independence of mental constructions is untenable. This will prepare us for Heyting's (implicit) advocacy of dialogism which we argue is both a formal and a philosophical commitment that does adequate justice to capturing the complexity of the respective discourses of mathematics and literature.

Returning to Bakhtin, a dialogism without an explicit transcendental subjectivism means that the subjects constituting the dialogic framework have been abstracted into poles of the dialogic framework. This abstraction may be short of the kind of simplification observed in other dialogical frameworks which have been formalized (as in game-theoretic models) and yet one may see this as a fundamentally formal approach. Within the philosophy of mathematics, the initial Kantian turn in Brouwer's intuitionism first gave way, in Heyting's thought, to an understanding of the subject that was informed more by Husserlian phenomenology (see Heyting 1930). But Heyting's (1956) specific intervention invokes pragmatically the dialogic form to *perform* the mental construction of mathematical entities.

A subjectivism is invoked but it is highly formalized, consistent with Bakhtin's anti-phenomenological stance. Such a subjectivism devoid of psychologism is a manner of formally constituting the dialogical process. If one calls this a formal approach, it would seem, understandably, much impoverished when compared to the generative promise of axiomatic formalisms. It is possible that one can design axiomatic formalisms where the initial axiom can be an initial concession in a dialogic process. But the ensuing dialogic process cannot be accorded any amount of redundancy relative to the axiom/initial concession. The Bakhtinian dialogism is context-sensitive and cannot be reduced to the initial conditions of possibility that led to it. This is what is meant by the non-generative nature of the formalism. Even within mathematics, the privileged nature of axiomatic generativism is premised on the minimal number of axioms relative to the theorems they generate. Axioms are an initial set of irreducible statements to begin with. However, as a mathematician like Gregory Chaitin (1998) has pointed out, the number of logically and computationally irreducible statements can be potentially infinite.

## 8.6 The Intuitionist Program as Opposed to Formalism

Hilbert's programme was intended to reduce mathematics – as it has been clarified through Cantor's actual infinite sets – to strings of symbols, submitted to syntactical rules, such that, starting from axioms, one can derive theorems without having to ask what they refer to. In von Neumann's words, mathematics is reduced to a "combinatory play with symbols" (Heyting 1962, p. 194). Locating the generative essence of mathematics in this play of symbols anticipates the Russian Formalists in their reification of the internal dynamics of the literary text as the source of literariness. Such an internalism is synonymous with formalism as a movement in literature. This essay seeks to critically examine this driving assumption and retrieve formality from formalism within philosophy of mathematics itself. Deriving such a parallel between both the discourses of mathematics and literature will show that the philosophical critique is not incidental to one domain or the other.

The essential point against formalism, as Brouwer (1912) formulates it, is that, by putting aside any notion of subjectivity (which is accordingly thought of as a specific task for the psychologist), no explanation can ever be supplied for choosing determined syntactic relations rather than other as true. When truth is being defined through consistency, mathematics are spinning in the void, as long as no modelling is provided of what lays apart of the syntactic system that has been chosen. By the way, one may see, in metaphorical terms, as Girard (2016) suggests, such a semantic modelling of axiomatics as being ultimately nothing else as a "selfie" of syntax. In Brouwer's (1912, p. 129) words:

> The formalist wishes to leave to the psychologist the task of selecting the "truly mathematical" language amongst the many symbolic languages that may be consistently developed. Inasmuch as psychology has not yet begun on this task, formalism is compelled to mark off, at least temporarily, the domain that it wishes to consider as "true mathematics and to lay down for that purpose a definite system of axioms and laws of reasoning, if it does not wish to see its work doomed to sterility. The various ways in which this attempt has actually been made all follow the same leading idea, viz. The presupposition of the existence of a world of mathematical objects, a world independent of the thinking individual, obeying the laws of classical logic and whose objects may possess with respect to each other the "relation of a set to its elements". With reference to this relation various axioms are postulated, suggested by the practice, suggested by the practice with natural finite sets.

The intuitionist view enables one to give an account of the choices that are made while one is propositionally referring to a mathematical object, through a particular syntactic system, by grounding them on a pure intuition whose content backs up the additional choice of the symbolic system that is intended to supply mathematical expressions. In the formalist view, the choice of the symbolic system has no place within the mathematical framework itself, but it belongs to another field of knowledge, namely *psychology*; in the intuitionist one, the symbolic system should not represent an essential part of mathematical activity, but one should recognize its choice as based on the essential source from which stems the mathematical objects that are to be expressed.

In other words, there should be no independent and purely syntactic constitution of an empty form, such that it could come, in a second step, to be fulfilled by the finding of a corresponding model. It should rather be the case that the syntax which is needed in order to express constructions evolves according to the construction itself, and that it is actually *a secondary part of it*: a sufficient expression may reveal itself as *vague* provided that a certain degree of specification of the object be overpassed. There should accordingly be an internal relation between symbolic expressions and mathematical constructions, such that, contrary to the formalist way, the accuracy of a symbolism should depend on the mathematical experience itself, as it mirrors the growth of developing entities.

Nevertheless, Brouwer clearly insists, from the beginning to the end of his philosophical work, on the secondarity of language in regard to mathematical experience. To him, "mathematics is a languageless activity" (1949). Furthermore, logic itself is no way prior to mathematics. Sundholm (1983) points out that "nowadays constructive mathematics in general, and intuitionism in particular, are often presented as axiomatic extensions of Heyting's basic axiom system for first order logic, very much in the style of classical first-order theories with the primitive vocabularies and non-logical axioms". Following Bakhtin, one may argue that any logical opposition that is underlying literature may be seen as a consequence of a more primary dialogism. This is not unlike Brouwer's insistence on the primacy of mathematics which means that logic is a spin-off from mathematical thought and has no special apriority.

Heyting's own take on constructivism aims however at guaranteeing the very possibility of a dialogue between the intuitionist and classical mathematicians, by supplying a framework within which it becomes possible to assess the validity of mathematical results, without entering into psychological considerations about the mental content to which mathematical expressions refers.

According to Heyting, the most important thing in communicating the content of mathematical intuitionism is not to express *which* subject lays beneath constructions, but rather the mathematical construction itself. One should accordingly "formalize the way in which [the intuitionists] make their constructions, without reference to the subject" (Kreisel, 1967, p. 173). Now, one should say that, by promoting the objectivity of constructions, one tacitly presupposes a transcendental subjectivity, which is to be understood as the unity function that is to be postulated whenever the constitution of an object is *a priori* submitted to logical (universal) norms. When no reference is made to the constructive subject at stake in mathematical constructions, it does not mean that no such subject has been tacitly postulated: it just means that a *separation* is been fixed between the field of mathematical activity and philosophical enquiries about the principle of its constitution as an objective field.

However, as Dummett (1993) insists on, no one can make abstraction of the *linguistic turn*, that has been carried out along the last century, such that no rigorous philosophical take can economize the burdensome take of analysing how meaning is constituted, and, in particular, the meaning of subjectivity expressions. It seems clear that no such burden has been undertaken by Brouwer when philosophizing about mathematics. It is not certain that Van Atten's (2004) proposal to base a right understanding of Brouwer's creating subject on a Husserlian sight, in league with a non-Kantian understanding of the transcendental subject, escapes to Dummett's objection against any claim of having a direct access to the intentional life without a theory of meaning, that yields a clear view of the ways words are to be articulated with things. Fink (1933) explicitly talks of the "dialogical situation" which is necessary to end up the case that "no adequate linguistic presentation of the phenomenological analysis of the deep layers of transcendental subjectivity is possible", given that the "phenomenological proposition harbours, by an eidetic necessity, an internal contradiction between the mundane meaning of a word and the transcendental meaning that it points to".[2]

In a similar way, Brouwerian emphasis on the subjective feature of mathematical constructions might be made sense of in a broadened analytic framework, in which a naive representational understanding of meaning be dialogically grounded, while the irreducibility of mathematical activity to its axiomatized form be safeguarded. We will see later in this essay to which extent the dialogical framework might supply technical bases towards a full account of the subjective compound that come into play at the margins of constructive mathematics.

The Kantian notion of a subject, whose paternity Brouwer (1912, p. 127) explicitly acknowledges, cannot be strictly taken over within Brouwerian intuitionism, because it depends essentially on the claim that logical laws represent a *rigid* framework for any sort of mathematical argument. The Kantian subject supplies an accurate sight on what is to be thought behind finite arithmetic systems or geometrical analysis, but it is not accurate anymore when one wants to encode analysis by arithmetizing it. The disconnection between Brouwerian intuitionism and Kantian constructivism, beyond the abandonment of space as an *a priori* intuition, has already been pointed out by Popper (1967). According to Popper, the strict separation between discursive and intuitive thought, that lays at the basis of Kant's *Critique*, is contradictory with the promotion of construction as representing the only reliable basis for mathematical truth.

Brouwer's solution to the difficulty that stems from this separation consists in radically distinguishing the realm of mathematical construction and the realm of its linguistic expression, that is only dealing with communication. The consequence is

---

[2]Let us note here that in his Marburg lessons, Heidegger (1925) already carries out such a *linguistic turn*, because of the critic of consciousness. See Gethmann (1991). By reparametrizing the concept of truth, Heidegger retrieves it from idealism of validity, which is behind Husserl's notion of the transcendental, by coming back to the concrete human, who lives amongst multiplicity, change and isolation. Beneath the transcendental subject, stands the layer of time, whose flowing is denied by *Scholastic Logic*, which is a form of sloth tailor-made for instructors (Heidegger 1925, p. 10). Such a critic threatens any formalist reduction. By contrast, "speaking is [...] the way that humans direct and guide all their other kinds of behavior. It is in and through speaking that the modes and the objects of human action are disclosed, explained, and determined." Logic investigates language in order to fix the conditions of its truth, which is not to reduce to validity, given that there are further conditions beneath the institution of a notion of what validity is. These conditions, we claim, are essentially dialogical, speaking being always "speaking to each other" for the sake of interacting and working with each other" (p. 2).

that Brouwer cannot take over Kant's concept of transcendental subjectivity, because there is no way to think of such a subject without identifying it with unity functions, enjoining to submit any mathematical argument to objective norms, irrespective of which material content is being constructed within the normative framework that makes mathematics universally communicable. In Brouwer's view, there cannot be such an *a priori* normative framework, because, as said before, logic is essentially a description of regularities within the language that people make use makes use of in communicating, eventually to themselves, their own mathematical constructions, on the basis of the so called *primordial intuition*. If there is to be a basis for mathematics being universal (and they are asserted as such by Brouwer), it must be the intuition of time, whose prediscursive structure should not be relative to any *particular* subjective stance. Such a concept of a temporal prediscursive constructive subject, to be distinguished from the Kantian transcendental subject, has found a mathematical use through the so called "theory" of the *creating subject*, as it expresses itself along Brouwer's reasonings.

It is this lack of an a priori normative framework which Mikhail Bakhtin rejects in his recovery of a non-Kantian notion of the subject. Bakhtin will go so far as to implicate language in the very construction of the subject but such a gesture does not relapse into loosely defined paradigm of linguistic constructionism. Bakhtin looks at the indexicality of any discourse as the residue of a primary dialogism and it is this dialogism that is the engine of meaning and not language as such. We must remember that the shift away from formalism in the domain of mathematics was not as popularly received by the discipline. The question of metaphysical debate was frowned upon because it was unnecessarily philosophical at a time when it seemed that the most appropriate philosophy of mathematics was itself supposed to be mathematical.

## 8.7 The Objection that a Metaphysical Stance Lays Behind the Theory of the Creating Subject

If we try to go a little further into a correct understanding of what can precisely be the *creating subject* according to Brouwer, we must begin by observing that when he invokes it [see Brouwer (1948), but also tacitly in Brouwer (1929)], Brouwer's aim is exclusively at arguing against a reduced constructive notion of the continuum, and to model the full classical continuum, without admitting a pre-existing infinite sets of rationales. The structure of this *subject* is definitely to be inferred from what can be mathematically accomplished by admitting it, namely, for instance, an actual construction of real numbers not being apart one from another while nevertheless not being equal. There is no explicit formulation of a proper theory of it. Let us consider the first occurrence of its expression in Brouwer's writing. As we see, it plays a role, while not being defined or associated to any sort of rule.

Brouwer (1948) defines a particular infinitely proceeding sequence of rational numbers in the following way. Let A be a mathematical assertion that cannot be tested, i.e. for which no method is known to prove either its absurdity or the absurdity of its absurdity. Then the Creating Subject can, in connection with the assertion A create a sequence $\boldsymbol{a_1}, \boldsymbol{a_2}, \boldsymbol{a_3}, \ldots$ according to the following rule:

$$\alpha(\boldsymbol{n}) =_{def} \begin{cases} \mathbf{0} \;\; \textbf{\textit{if CS has experienced neither the truth nor the absurdity of A}} \\ \mathbf{2^{-n}} \textbf{\textit{if CS has experienced the truth of A}} \\ \mathbf{2^{-n}} \textbf{\textit{if CS has experienced the absurdity of A}} \end{cases}$$

This sequence is positively convergent and thus defines a real number $\boldsymbol{\rho}$ for which one can demonstrate that none of these relations holds: $\boldsymbol{\rho} > \mathbf{0}$; $\boldsymbol{\rho} < 0$; $\boldsymbol{\rho} = \mathbf{0}$.

Once it has been axiomatized by Kreisel (and then shown reducible to Kripke's schema, namely $\exists\alpha(A \leftrightarrow \exists x. \alpha(x) \neq 0)$ the mathematical content of this creating subject gets a rather clear mathematical content. Kreisel's axioms have been furthermore shown conservative over Kripke's schema + intuionistic analysis (see van Dalen, 1982, p. 75). However, it has been argued that it misses sufficient constructive bases. Sundholm (2015) makes clear the lack of a constructive path towards a genuine derivation of Kripke's schema within the framework of Constructive Type Theory, which is nowadays the leading approach in mathematical constructivism.

Firstly, in a general way, he insists on "intuitionism [as defining Brouwer's own specific position, to be distinguished from constructivism] [sharing] a realist stance with Platonism", both being forms of an "ontological descriptivism" (2008, p. 15). Infinitely proceeding free choice sequences, even though they are thought of as "mental constructions" are nevertheless objects whose reality depends on the metaphysical assumption that a (dynamical) subjective principle lays behind the structure of the continuum.

Secondly, Sundholm convincingly argues that when one attempts to axiomatizing the Brouwerian concept of a creating subject, as Kreisel did, one is actually obliged to go out of a straight constructive sight. From a very general point of view, it seems rather obvious that axiomatizing creation is equivalent to denying its proper *creative* compound. Now, when things are analysed from a closer sight, it must appear that the problem stems from the very concept of a function, whose meaning explanation presupposes to dig into the materiality of propositions, i.e. to their extra-logical compounds. It is to be noted, that every mathematical result based on the *creating subject* has been shown depending on the admittance of a function (expressed through Kripke's schema), which says that for every proposition P, there is a value $n$, such that $P(n) = 1$ or for all $n$ $P(n) = 0$. Such a function cannot be constructive, unless one admits a proof of the excluded-middle, i.e. no indeterminacy for truth values. It is of necessity to overpass a purely formal definition of it, on the basis of an "undecided separation of cases". The point is that it seems hardly possible to supply *meaning explanations* – i.e. to explicate the meaning of the expression of such a function by making its operative bedrock explicit – without assuming a non-constructive proof of the principle of the excluded-middle. In order to fully understand the technical aspects of Sundholm's proposal towards a derivation of Kripke's schema (and of Kreisel's axioms), we refer the interested reader to (Sundholm 2015), where the creating subject is rejected as being not constructible otherwise than through a switch into a classical notion of validity, by starting from the point that Kripke's schema represents the very material kernel of the creating subject theory.

Sundholm's criticism is certainly important, to the extent that it forces to admit that an extremely subjective stance such as Brouwer's one tends to turn into a mentalist ontology, seemingly contradicting the intuitionist claim for constructivity of any mathematical assertion. The way Brouwer claims being able to regain as much of the continuum as one can refer to, when admitting infinite sets into its ontology, imposes admitting instead, potentially infinite strings of choices, indexed on epistemic events whose definiteness presupposes that truth values be definite in themselves, while being beyond the reach of any epistemic subject. However, the point appears when Brouwer's notion of a creating subject comes to be axiomatized, which contradicts Brouwer's own rejection of axiomatization in general. In Heyting's (1962) own view, axiomatic devices are not to be rejected, as they are useful on the way towards the constitution of an agreement between the *formalist view*, that tends to make the communicative content of a mathematical theory fully explicit and the *intuitionist one*, that tends to reduce the (implicit) metaphysical needs that lay behind mathematical theorems.

As a matter of fact, any mathematician would prefer purely constructive proofs, but the field of the whole mathematics is still beyond the reach of purely constructive methods. If one sticks to Brouwer's emphasis on what stands beyond any axiomatic system, there is also a *residuum* of not objectified mathematical creative activity that resists to its being axiomatized because of its being essentially irreducible to a logical framework it would be forever submitted to. Thus, the question is not whether one would ever be able to determine the logic that lays behind Brouwer's controversial takes on the continuum; it is rather whether one must ascribe any sort of mathematical argument to a logical framework whose structure anticipates, from the outset, any constructive path that may be sketched within it. It means that the *creating subject* should not be located amongst the things that are to be axiomatized [as Heyting (Kreisel 1967, p. 173) claims it should be in order to assess his mathematical relevance], but that it would rather represent the still remaining distance between what can be fixed through axioms and what represents the concrete constructive activity beneath it, as it is anchored in singular effective paths. In other words, the *creating subject* could be axiomatized when objectified (i.e. denied as a *creating* subject), but not when taken as what stands at the source of any axiomatization process, considered as a means to promote a possible universal agreement based on taking an initial stance towards construction through a symbolic system of mutual understanding, ultimately based on choices.

The question is to know to which extent such a non-axiomatizable *residuum* might find an eventual *formal* expression, if one considers that no genuine meaning can be given to an expression – such as the expression of a *creating subject* – if no indication is furnished about the way it works within a regulated frame of discursive interactions. It forces us to dissociate ourselves from Brouwer's radical *solipsistic* take on the matter, while taking over the aforementioned *linguistic turn*, according to which, in order to understand the meaning of an expression, one must necessarily look at the role it plays within its own whole contexts of use. Accordingly, we will be able again to gain a broadened understanding of what formality can be that will not reduce it to the mere structure of validity while enabling us to make explicit the meaning of mathematical expressions contributing to material truth beyond purely logical one. We will show in the next section how the dialogical framework enables us to ensure a certain constructivity to the creating subject. Then we will try to sketch a possible extension of this model towards a broadened device through which literary meaning, in its dynamic feature, might be formalized through a not-so formalistic device.

## 8.8 The Dialogical Solution to the Problem of the Non Constructivity of Kripke's Schema

Technically speaking, in the derivation of Kripke's schema, there is a step that is not constructive. In order to translate Sundholm's proposal into a dialogical setting, we have here to follow Rahman et al. (2018), whose theoretical setup cannot be explained exhaustively in the limits of the present essay. We will just give an account of its essential tenets by assuming that Martin-Löf's Constructive Type Theory be known [see Martin-Löf (1984)].

Let us start with a few words about the standard dialogic, as developed from Lorenzen and Lorenzen's seminal works. The kernel of the dialogical view on semantics consists in the idea that the meaning of an utterance is given by the way a justification process can be supplied through the execution of a *finite* dialogue starting from it according to determined *interaction rules*. No basis for justification has to be looked for outside the dialogue itself. No matter which *private* content one locates behind an assertion, the only relevant point is that, by making the assertion, they entitle their interlocutor to tackle it according to the rules (which are at least of two sorts: *particle rules*, which are *player-dependent* and *structural rules*, which takes the nature of the player into account). The defender of the assertion is called the Proponent (**P**); the challenger is the Opponent (**O**).

Within the standard dialogical framework, *formality* is given account of in dialogical terms. A dialog is not formal in the sense that the content of propositional account would not be taken into account: it is not a feature of a dialogue in which propositional forms are empty, in such a way that a content could fulfil it in a secondary step. It is rather the case that there exists a certain way of playing in which the Proponent accept to defend their initial assertion only by backing it up with elementary statement that have been epistemically assumed by its Opponent. A proposition is formally valid if a player has a winning strategy no matter which private content is located by the Opponent beneath its linguistic expression, that is associated with the mood of assertion ("force"). A formal play is nothing else than a play in which a *formal rule* (called in Rahman et al. (2018) "*Socratic rule*") is applied to a dialogical interaction. By cutting it off, dialogues are not formal anymore.

In Rahman et al. (2018), following a proposal by Sundholm, a link has been built between Martin-Löf's CTT, with one of his main features being that it holds as a "meaningful formalism", i.e. there is no need to associate *models* with the *language*: the way the language is to be interpreted is made explicit within the language itself. Accordingly, instead of having, as basic elements, *proposition* such as A, we have statements, whose expression is a: A. The latter expression can be equivalently read as: "a is an element of the set A", or "a is a proof of the proposition A". A proposition "A" is constructively *true* if there is an element "a", having a canonical form or being translatable into a canonical form, that proves it. We will see later how the notion of *formation rules* enables to work on a certain notion of *form*, which is irreducible to any *formalism*, to the extent that it is accorded to a dynamical process of *formation*, that belongs to an ante-predicative layer.

In the dialogical set up, things are a little more complex than in Constructive Type Theory because of the distinction between several levels, namely the *play level* and the *strategic level*.

The former corresponds to the way players can concretely interact according to the rules; to this extent, a play can be correct even though a player loses by badly defending an assertion he could have won by playing better.

The latter level rather corresponds to the level of a universal normativity: for a proposition to be true it is not enough that a player wins a play, but it must be established that there is a way to win every possible play, no matter how the other player plays. In other words, an expression such as "a: A" is ascribed different uses according to the level at which a play is read.

Martin-Löf's "proof-objects" correspond to "strategic reasons", in which (potentially infinite) sets of strategy are to be encoded. Now, if one locates oneself at the play level, a player is able to back up a statement by using a reason, which has no equivalent in Constructive Type Theory, namely a *local reason*. Our claim is that this sort of reason admits an incidental psychological reading: it might be seen as corresponding to the concrete private mental state through which a player backs up a statement and that are, so to say, indexed on its symbolic expression. According to the *Socratic rule*, there is *formality* when a bridge is built between these private mental states, in such a way that, by entering into the dialogue, each player admits the possibility to go along the bridge, i.e. to understand each other and to push away any solipsistic temptation. We will see that the dialogical layer that corresponds to subjective life enables one to overpass this psychological notion of private contents, by replacing it through a special kind of interactions, namely those that are regulated by what will be called *material rules*.

To the reader who would like to go through the details of the rules at stake in the dialogical translation of Sundholm's derivation of Kripke's schema that we propose here, we ask to refer to (Rahman et al. 2018). Let us point out that, amongst the technical devices that are deployed in this handbook, we shall mention the following points.

*Firstly*, the *particle rules*, according to which players proceed to challenge and defend themselves by referring to the logical complexity of the propositions at stake, are specified as being of several types: a) *synthesis rules* are the ones according to which one is allowed to produce a local reason; b) *analysis rules* are the ones that indicate how to parse a complex local reason associated with a complex statement. When a player claims she actually possesses a construction, that backs up an assertion she is ready to defend, the other player is allowed to require that she *implements an instruction*. It means, for instance, that if X claims that a: A and B, Y can ask her to implement the instruction "take the left part of A and B". In a second step, X can also require that X *resolves* this instruction, i.e. that she backs up A with a *local reason* a', that is equal to Left(a). The general meaning of such a distinction between *implementation* and *resolution* is that, when asked to play according to the rules, a player has to engage into a concrete execution which is equivalent to say that the dialogue is, at least at the *play level*, always to be thought of as being *materially* anchored in flesh and blood players, with concrete (though unexpressed) epistemic state laying beneath what they utter. It leads us to the following point.

*Secondly*, the content of a material statement is itself to be conceived in a dialogical way. Referring to an object, such as a number for instance, implies specific rules of interactions, i.e. rules that are specific to the interactions that are dealing with this object. In other words, each elementary statement on which the reductive process of a formal dialogue has to stop, in order to be finite, triggers implicitly a material dialogue, whose rules hold for the very material content of this elementary statement. For instance, if I assert that 3 is a natural number, an Opponent is entitled to ask me to express it through the (canonical) form "s(n)" and to require that I assume that 0 is a natural number. These are the types of rules that make out the very meaning of any elementary statement. Such a device enables the dialogician to supply an entirely inferentialist take on meaning. Now, we shall consider that such rules are not rigidly fixed but are submitted to playful variations.

We claim that subjectivity, in its essential wandering towards truth, is to be explained through the intertwining of these material rules at the play level.

Our specific contribution consists in providing specific material rules for playing with an infinitely proceeding choice sequence, which is indexed on the truth of a certain proposition A, as seen in Table 8.1:

**Table 8.1** Specific Socratic rules for $\alpha_A$

| | Move | Challenge | Defence |
|---|---|---|---|
| Specific Socratic rules for $\alpha_A$ | $\boldsymbol{a}: \boldsymbol{A}_{(\alpha_A:\mathbb{N}\to \boldsymbol{bool})}$ | $?{=}_{\mathbb{N}}\ \boldsymbol{a}$ | $\boldsymbol{a} =_{\mathbb{N}} n$ |
| | | $?{=}_{\boldsymbol{Bool}}\ \boldsymbol{\alpha_A}(n)\ [n: \mathbb{N}]$ | $\boldsymbol{\alpha_A}(n) =_{\boldsymbol{Bool}} \text{yes!}$ |
| | $\boldsymbol{b}: \boldsymbol{A} \to \bot_{(\alpha_A:\mathbb{N}\to \boldsymbol{bool})}$ | $?{=}_{\mathbb{N}}\ \boldsymbol{b}$ | $\boldsymbol{b} =_{\mathbb{N}}\ \boldsymbol{m}$ |
| | | $?{=}_{\boldsymbol{Bool}}\ \boldsymbol{\alpha_A}(m)\ [m: \mathbb{N}]$ | $\boldsymbol{\alpha_A}(m) =_{\boldsymbol{Bool}} \text{no!}$ |
| | $\boldsymbol{\alpha_A}(n) =_{\boldsymbol{Bool}} \text{yes!}[n: \mathbb{N}]$ | $?{=}_{\boldsymbol{reason}}\ \boldsymbol{yes}$ | $\boldsymbol{A}!_{(\boldsymbol{n})}$ |
| | $\boldsymbol{\alpha_A}(m) =_{\boldsymbol{Bool}} \text{no!}[m: \mathbb{N}]$ | $?{=}_{\boldsymbol{reason}}\ \boldsymbol{no}$ | $(\boldsymbol{A} \to \bot)!_{(\boldsymbol{m})}$ |

The general meaning of these rules is that if a player claims having a construction that enables them to back up the assertion that A (under the presupposition that a function $\alpha_A$ is definable, associating a boolean value to certain steps in a search history, tacitly associated with the proposition A), then their challenger is allowed to ask them to fix a date $n$ to this statement *and* to concede, once this date has been fixed, that the value for $\alpha_A(n)$ is **yes** (N.B. **yes** is the dialogical form that take the Boolean value **true**).

Conversely, if a player claims that the aforementioned function yields the value **yes** for a step $n$ in the search history, then the other player is entitled to require that the proposition A, to which the function is associated, be asserted by them (eventually without any other reason than the simple fact that he has actually stated that they knew the value of the function for $n$. We will see that this is the essential point in the claim that the derivation of Kripke's schema is not constructive.

The following translation enables us to get now the same result as in Sundholm (2015) (see Table 8.2 below):

**Step by Step Explanation of the Play Reported in Table 8.2:**

Step 0: **P** asserts the thesis (under the conditional of the concession of the function $\alpha_A$).

Step 0.1: **O** concedes it.

Step 1 and 2: each player choses a repetition rank, that fixes how many time a player can attack the same move (NB: this rank cannot be fixed in advance but must be looked for by throwing through the game).

Step 3: **O** challenges the implication by conceding the antecedent and backing it up with a local reason $\boldsymbol{c_1}$.

Step 4: **P** defends herself by assuming she has a local reason that backs up her assertion of the consequent, which is here an existential.

Step 5: **O** asks **P** to implement the "left" instruction to $\boldsymbol{c_2}$.

Step 6: **P** implements the "left" instruction to $\boldsymbol{c_2}$.

Step 7: **O** asks **P** to execute the "left" instruction by applying it to $\boldsymbol{c_2}$

**Table 8.2** $A \supset (\exists x : \mathbb{N})(\alpha(x) =_{bool} yes)$

| O | | | P | | |
|---|---|---|---|---|---|
| 0.1 | $\alpha_A : \mathbb{N} \to \boldsymbol{bool}$ | | | $\boldsymbol{A \supset (\exists x : \mathbb{N})(\alpha(x) =_{bool} yes)}$ $[\alpha_A : \mathbb{N} \to \boldsymbol{bool}]$ | 0 |
| 1 | $m = 2$ | | | $n = 3$ | 2 |
| 3 | $\boldsymbol{c_1 : A_{(\alpha_A)}}$ | 0 | | $\boldsymbol{c_2 : (\exists x : \mathbb{N})(\alpha(x) =_{bool} yes)}$ | 4 |
| 5 | $?\, \boldsymbol{L^{\exists}}$ | 4 | | $\boldsymbol{L^{\exists}(c_2)}: \mathbb{N}$ | 6 |
| 7 | $?.../\, \boldsymbol{L^{\exists}(c_2)}$ | 6 | | $\boldsymbol{0}: \mathbb{N}$ | 10 |
| 9 | $\boldsymbol{c_1} =_{\mathbb{N}} \boldsymbol{0}$ | | 3 | $? =_{\mathbb{N}} \boldsymbol{c_1}$ | 8 |
| 11 | $? = 0$ | 10 | | $\boldsymbol{c_1} =_{\mathbb{N}} \boldsymbol{0}$ | 12 |
| 13 | $?\, \boldsymbol{R^{\exists}}$ | 4 | | $\boldsymbol{R^{\exists}(c_2): \alpha(0) =_{bool} yes)}$ | 14 |
| 15 | $?.../\, \boldsymbol{R^{\exists}(c_2)}$ | 14 | | $\boldsymbol{\alpha_A}(0) =_{\boldsymbol{Bool}} \text{yes!}$ | 18 |
| 17 | $\boldsymbol{\alpha_A}(0) =_{\boldsymbol{Bool}} \text{yes!}$ | | 3 | $? =_{\boldsymbol{Bool}} \boldsymbol{\alpha_A}(0)$ | 16 |

Step 8: **P** has to wait for **O**'s own execution of an equal local reason, because of the Socratic rule. He rather solicit such an execution by applying the first specific rule for $\alpha_A$.
Step 9: **O**, being obliged to assume that A is true *now*, choses the value 0, which means that from now = step 0 in the search history, he considers A as being true.
Step 10: **P** is now in position to defend herself against the challenge that was launched at step 7.
Step 11: **O** asks to what this value is equal to.
Step 12: **P** defends herself by copycatting **O**'s move at step 9.
Step 13: **O** asks **P** to implement the "right" instruction to $\boldsymbol{c_2}$.
Step 14: **P** implements the "right" instruction to $\boldsymbol{c_2}$.
Step 15: **O** asks **P** to execute the "right" instruction by applying it to $\boldsymbol{c_2}$.
Step 16: **P** has to wait for **O**'s own execution of an equal local reason, because of the Socratic rule. She rather solicits such an execution by applying the second specific rule for $\alpha_A$.
Step 17: **O** is obliged to concede that $\alpha_A$ yields the value **yes** for (0).
Step 18: **P** is now in position to defend herself against the challenge that was launched at step 15.

Let us proceed with further analysis summarised in Table 8.3 below:

**Step by Step Explanation of the Play Reported in Table 8.3:**
Step 0: **P** asserts the thesis (under the conditional of the concession of the function $\alpha_A$).
Step 0.1: **O** concedes it.
Step 1 and 2: each player choses a repetition rank, that fixes how many time a player can attack the same move.
Step 3: **O** challenges the implication by conceding the antecedent, which is now an existential, and backing it up with a local reason $\boldsymbol{d_1}$.
Step 4: **P** defends herself by assuming she has a local reason $\boldsymbol{d_2}$ that backs up her assertion of the consequent, which is here the elementary statement $\boldsymbol{A}$.

**Table 8.3** $(\exists x : \mathcal{N})(\alpha(x){=_{bool}}\, yes) \supset A$

| O | | | P | | |
|---|---|---|---|---|---|
| 0.1 | $\alpha_A : \mathcal{N} \to \boldsymbol{bool}$ | | | $(\exists \boldsymbol{x} : \mathcal{N})(\boldsymbol{\alpha}(\boldsymbol{x}){=_{bool}}\, \boldsymbol{yes}) \supset \boldsymbol{A}$ $[\alpha_A : \mathcal{N} \to \boldsymbol{bool}]$ | 0 |
| 1 | $m = 1$ | | | $n = 2$ | 2 |
| 3 | $\boldsymbol{d_1} : (\exists \boldsymbol{x} : \mathcal{N})(\boldsymbol{\alpha_A}(\boldsymbol{x}) =_{bool} \boldsymbol{yes})$ | 0 | | $\boldsymbol{d_2} : \boldsymbol{A}$ | 4 |
| 5 | $? = \boldsymbol{d_2}$ | 4 | | $\boldsymbol{A}!$ | 16 |
| 7 | $\boldsymbol{L}^{\exists}(\boldsymbol{d_1}) : \mathcal{N}$ | | 3 | $?\, \boldsymbol{L}^{\exists}$ | 6 |
| 9 | $\boldsymbol{k} : \mathcal{N}$ | | 7 | $?\ldots/\boldsymbol{L}^{\exists}(\boldsymbol{d_1})$ | 8 |
| 11 | $\boldsymbol{R}^{\exists}(\boldsymbol{d_1})\!:\ \boldsymbol{\alpha_A}(\boldsymbol{k}) =_{bool} \boldsymbol{yes}$ | | 3 | $?\, \boldsymbol{R}^{\exists}$ | 10 |
| 13 | $\boldsymbol{\alpha_A}(\boldsymbol{k}) =_{bool} \boldsymbol{yes}!$ | | 11 | $?\ldots/\boldsymbol{R}^{\exists}(\boldsymbol{d_1})$ | 12 |
| 15 | $\boldsymbol{A}!$ | | 13 | $? =_{reason}\, \boldsymbol{yes}!$ | 14 |

Step 5: **O** asks **P** to what the local reason $\boldsymbol{d_2}$ is equal (application of the socratic rule: **P** can justify an elementary statement only if **O** has stated it before).
Step 6: **P** is not in position to defend herself; she asks **O** for implementing the "left" instruction to $d_1$.
Step 7: **O** implement the "left" instruction to $d_1$.
Step 8: **P** asks **O** to execute the "left" instruction by applying it to $d_1$.
Step 9: **O** execute it by choosing a value *k*, for which she must tacitly assume that the function will yield the value **yes**. It is to be noted that this choice is done according to the rules of the game: even though O has assumed the existential in order to be able to challenge the implication, there is no particular reason that she knows what this value $\boldsymbol{k}$ is. It is an empty choice. This precise move corresponds to a dialogical reading of the *undecided separation of cases* Sundholm's started his derivation from. Here we have a notion of formality which is to be distinguished from the one which is at stake when playing according to the formal rule. We have here a step beneath which no proper constructive content is given.
Step 10: **P** asks now to implement the "right" instruction to $\boldsymbol{d_1}$.
Step 11: **O** implements the "right" instruction to $\boldsymbol{d_1}$.
Step 12: **P** asks to execute the "right" instruction by applying it to $\boldsymbol{d_1}$.
Step 13: **O** executes the "right" instruction by applying it to $\boldsymbol{k}$.
Step 14: **P** asks for the reason of the claim that $(\boldsymbol{k})$ ***yes***!
Step 15: **O** cannot supply another reason to this claim than the fact that he assumes that $\boldsymbol{A}$ is true.
Step 16: **P** is now entitled to defend herself against **O**'s challenge that was launched at step 5, by asserting that $\boldsymbol{A}$ is true, even though no construction has been given during the play, *except the execution of the play itself!*

We can see that the constructivity problem is mainly concerned with the reverse direction of the equivalence, i.e. when one goes from the existential statement of the Boolean function to the assertion of the elementary statement $A$. The dialogical translation reveals that when the Opponent epistemically assumes the antecedent of the implication, they commits themselves to assert a proposition that they will not be actually able to back up through an effective construction. A distinction is to be made between what one undertakes by playing a game and what one is actually able to do. There is here a notion of formality that deals with the consistency between taking part into a dialogue, according to definite rules, and having a mental construct that actually corresponds to what is at stake in the dialogue. We have here an instance of an axiomatic reasoning which reveals itself as being void because of a span between what the Opponent is committed to state, given the initial concession she made, and the material content of her own commitment. If the very axiomatic content that lays beneath the theory of the creating subject corresponds to Kripke's schema, then we understand very well to which extent the admittance of it is ultimately *knowledge transcendent*, and therefore *non-constructive*.

In order to overpass the difficulty, let us point out that Kreisel's axiomatic rendering of what the creating subject is does not correspond exactly to his essential dynamical features. One must acknowledge an essential unpredictable compound in it. One point we have deliberately omitted until now is the question of *formation rules*. These are the rules which fix the way of using *types*, either understood as sets or propositions. Beneath *operators*, corresponding to the aforementioned *particle* and *structural rules*, there are *material Socratic rules*, defining *functions*, that can be either rigidly defined or associated with *future choices* (in that case, functions cannot hold as standard objects in Constructive Type Theory). Brouwerian infinitely proceeding sequences, we claim, correspond to a definite way of playing a dialogue, no sense can be made of within CTT alone). Let us assume that such a function $\boldsymbol{\alpha_A}$ (depends on a proposition A. If one asserts the truth of the latter, without having fixed a *bar* to the corresponding spread of constructions that are attempting to reach the better possible way to fix it, then it means that one is considering the proposition A in itself, i.e. in its iconic features, as part of a diagram.

If we semiotically extend our reading of what a sign is, following Peirce's insights, it must appear that any sign is also able to operate as an index, that fixes extensionally through a potentially infinite process, the different paths that are to be chosen towards a dialogical finiteness of play. In the play reported on the Table 8.3, the initial admittance of a function associated to the proposition A is not intuitively equivalent to its full determination. Thus, the formation rule aims at defining this function throughout each play; it is a move that enables a player to make the request of further constructive determinations. The indefiniteness of the equality to zero for the choice sequence ρ, in Brouwer's (1948) demonstration, stems from the indefiniteness of the truth of A that corresponds to the whole field of a *search history* regarding *A*, which is not necessarily closed. The formation rule entitles the challenger to ask for an effective *formation* of a content for A throughout the function $\boldsymbol{\alpha_A}$, that indexes concrete acts of construction emerging from the very basis of time which is the *dyad*. These acts of construction can be dialogically thought of as a spread of potential answers to questions, that work ultimately like wagers towards *mutual understanding*. In Becker's (1927) reading of what free choice sequences are, they are to be thought of as being transcendent to themselves, in the sense that their own history is not closed. Accordingly, the accurate equality is empirically never achieved, but it is (ideally) possible. If a player is entitled to ask for the formation of a function, it means that both players are invited to define it through a continuous process of common searching. By the following rule as seen in Table 8.4 below:

One gets the possibility to "formally" express what formalization itself is, namely an indexical process associated with an icon that is being associated with the whole pragmatic situation of its being used as a key-device towards definiteness of truth. Any axiom has however the implicit form of an act of closure, that cannot ultimately

**Table 8.4** Specific formation rule for $\alpha_A(k)$

| | Move | Challenge | Defence |
|---|---|---|---|
| ***Formation rule for*** $\boldsymbol{\alpha_A(k)}$ | $\boldsymbol{\alpha_A(k)} =_{\boldsymbol{Bool}}$yes! | ***form*** $\boldsymbol{\alpha_A(k)}$? | $\alpha_A =_{ext.\ def}\ \alpha_1, \alpha_2, \ldots, \alpha_k$, [*i*] |

enclose the creating process that it triggers, by defining an implicit rule towards the constitution of a space of play that ascribes to each player logical duties and forces him accordingly to close the possibility of an *assertion* still being neither confirmed, nor quashed. In this in-between, Brouwer identifies a genuine constructive source that liberates possible future elements still to be defined and lacking a definite relation to any axiom that would aim at drying up the source by functionally closing the possibility of any fuzzy residual interaction with external constructive material that is yet naturally being indexed on any undecidable question. However, any concrete dialogue has to be finite and a player cannot invoke an undecidable question that makes impossible any agreement about its propositional corollaries.

The formation rule digs, so to say, into the semiotic layer that stands beneath the layer of validity, which is dialogically definable only by projecting oneself into the (ideal) situation of enclosing a potentially infinite spread of possible – and unpredictable – strategies, stemming from the processing otherness of the other: a dialogue is ultimately a(n ideal) form of mutual understanding, that presupposes refusing the invocation of any solipsistic take within a properly called dialogical play (see Table 8.5 below).

Let us describe the changes this rule brings to the game.

Step 14: **P** asks **O** to bring forward an effective search history numerically indexed until the value for $k$ that has been chosen, by applying the formation rule for $\boldsymbol{\alpha_A(k)}$.
Step 15: **O** brings forward this search history that takes the form of an explicit list of tasks beyond which there remain future possibilities of defining new tasks.
Step 16: By applying the specific Socratic rule for $\boldsymbol{\alpha_A}$, **P** is now in position to get from **O** a particular effective construction whose content corresponds to not algorithmically defined task that would be defined from the outset.
Step 17: **O** supplies such a particular effective construction under the index $k$.
Step 18: **P** can without a danger state that A is true by copycatting the aforementioned construction which is backed up by **O**'own authority.

**Table 8.5** $(\exists x : \mathbb{N})(\alpha(x){=_{bool}}\, yes) \supset A$; indexically constructive dialogue

| O | | | P | | |
|---|---|---|---|---|---|
| 0.1 | $\alpha_A : \mathbb{N} \to \boldsymbol{bool}$ | | | $(\exists \boldsymbol{x} : \mathbb{N})(\boldsymbol{\alpha(x)}{=_{bool}}\, \boldsymbol{yes}) \supset \boldsymbol{A}$ $[\alpha_A : \mathbb{N} \to \boldsymbol{bool}]$ | 0 |
| 1 | $m = 1$ | | | $n = 2$ | 2 |
| 3 | $d_1 : (\exists \boldsymbol{x} : \mathbb{N})(\boldsymbol{\alpha_A(x)} =_{bool} \boldsymbol{yes})$ | 0 | | $\boldsymbol{d_2} : \boldsymbol{A}_{(\alpha_A)}$ | 4 |
| 5 | $? = \boldsymbol{d_2}$ | 4 | | $\boldsymbol{a_k : A}$ | 18 |
| 7 | $\boldsymbol{L^{\exists}(d_1)} : \mathbb{N}$ | | 3 | $?\, \boldsymbol{L^{\exists}}$ | 6 |
| 9 | $\boldsymbol{k} : \mathbb{N}$ | | 7 | $? \ldots / \boldsymbol{L^{\exists}(d_1)}$ | 8 |
| 11 | $\boldsymbol{R^{\exists}(d_1)}$: $\boldsymbol{\alpha_A}(k) =_{bool} \boldsymbol{yes}$ | | 3 | $?\, \boldsymbol{R^{\exists}}$ | 10 |
| 13 | $\boldsymbol{\alpha_A(k)} =_{bool} \boldsymbol{yes}$ | | | $? \ldots / \boldsymbol{R^{\exists}}$ | 12 |
| 15 | $\boldsymbol{\alpha_A = a_1, a_2, \ldots, a_k}, [i]$ | | F13 | $\boldsymbol{form(\alpha_A(k))}$? | 14 |
| 17 | $\boldsymbol{a_k : A}$ | | 13 | $? =_{reason} \boldsymbol{yes}!$ | 16 |
| 19 | $? =_{reason} \boldsymbol{a_k}$ | | | $\boldsymbol{a_k} =_{reason} \boldsymbol{L^{\exists}(d_1)}$ | 20 |

Step 19: **O** asks for the equality of $\boldsymbol{\alpha_k}$.

Step 20: **P** defends herself by advocating the equality of the construction it stands for with the execution needed towards the resolution of the instruction that had been implemented at step 7.

The whole point is that, in this play, the possibility is still open that, if an effective numerical value is given to *k*, then the concrete process of construction of a proof of A may abort; in this case, the play itself shall abort. The correctness of the move carried out at step 15 is beyond any possible formalization or any mechanic verification process: it must be thought of as incorporating epistemic events, that are out of the dialogic diagram, though eventually related to it, as defining the main shape of future plays. It means that the initial concession of the existence of the function $\alpha_A$ is rather to be seen as an active wager than as the description of an effective list of tasks whose possibility would be finitely encapsulated in an axiom, at least as long as the search history is not frozen into an early dropout. What stands ultimately, out of reach, beyond any axiomatic formalization, is the potentially infinite repetition of the same initial concession through every possible variation that stems from unpredictably new paths of indexation, that are the proper dialogical accomplishment of potentially infinitely proceeding free *choice sequences*. If the (allegedly mental)-object that is initially claimed to be a proof of A ends up being an effective proof, then **O** was right in making this proposal towards a way to validate the truth of A; if it does not, then the play goes on unless an artificial principle of closure be defined, ending up each play. If so, the play reported on Table 8.4 is (*iconically*, and in a determined sense: *formally*) well defined; however, it still remains *indexically* undefined.

There is accordingly a gap between the diagrammatic closure of the expression of the dialogue, on the one hand, and, on the other hand, its essential openness depending on the actual initial assertion supporting A throughout a particular token of the dialogue, which is itself dialogically interacting with requests that are pragmatically addressed to it from evolving situations of play. In case the wager is neither won nor lost, there is a mathematical opening of a path within the continuum, that is essentially defined as being on the way to be fully defined.

## 8.9 What is the Creating Subject?

The creating subject is thus definable as the dynamical layer of every implicit dialogical interactions through which the whole field of mutual understanding is (ideally) looking for itself. It must be dialogical, even if the continuous experimenting of mental outcomes, allegedly stemming from a private intuition, easily leads to the (false) inference that a unified set of predefined faculties (or functions) is operating behind them. Subjectivity, as yielded by the intertwining of material dialogues at the play level, syntactically consists in the indefinite repetition of the same game, in a circular shape, along a rectilinear sequence of free choices, whose freedom corresponds to the triggering of undefined different future dialogues of the same shape, located one next to another in the flux of time through wandering steps that never go further than *now*, still separated by a gap, from the otherness of what still remains to come.

The non constructivity of the strategy reported on Table 8.3 came definitely from the fact that in the previous version of the play the notion of a function was not dialogically defined, but frozen into a predetermined (metaphysical) path. As soon as the dialogical layer that lays beneath the effective process of definition, the function gets a fully constructive meaning: the undecided separation of cases is to be taken as a corollary of a rough pragmatic requirement, namely that *a concession is to be effectively backed up by constructions, that aim at fixing its proper scope amongst the continuous space of search*.

By thus dialogically thinking the concept of a function, in such a way that whenever a player puts forward the existence of a function f($x$), then the other player is responsible for choosing any $x$ he pleases, committing the former to choose a value for f($x$), which is accordingly not fixed in advance. One cannot consider that a function be necessarily determined in advance for all its course of value. Making sense of it implies actually choosing it, i.e. instantiating it through a token, beyond its being a type. No mathematical entity is fully carried out, but every real point must be pursued beyond any explicit description of it. This being incomplete is such that in order to understand a function, one must specify its course of value by constructing it further on. No axiom can render creativity, because any function whose expression is present within an axiom is still to be specified by a constructive act which is not fully determined by the expression itself. This is the very thing that corresponds to Bakhtin's conception of the particular as irreducible to any generative framework.

If one defines in a Kantian way the subject as a set of ready-made functions, then the place where Brouwer locates subjectivity is beyond such a set of function, in the concrete instantiations of it, through acts of choices, that get their own norms of using by playing a role in effective dialogical plays. Any *subject* must be thought of as likely to be an *object* only by being projected into the strategic level, that hypostasiates in a transcendental layer what is ultimately an impossible totalization of the potentially infinite spread of every possible indexical paths. It is possible only by shortcoming the openness of the indexical compounds of meaning, by sticking to a purely iconic sight on dialogical diagrams.

The processual overpassing of the semantical closure of any given system of functions, which comes to be indexed on a search history, is deeply analogue to the way a novel should be modelled along the line of Bakhtin's own dialogical take against literary formalism. We would like to show now that it does not exclude the use of a determined formal device to encode the processual content of the dynamic of reading, understood in the sense of taking a concrete path into a novel. Due to the polyphonic structure of novels, no rigid formalism ascribing a function to several interacting character can ever hold as revealing the genuine structure of their accorded world: there must be figures whose role consists, amongst other functional role, in digging into their own side of the story as it reshapes entirely the fields of parameters that are to be taken into account while formalizing the structural relations defining a world.

Maybe no formalization of a literary text could ever encode it into a complete generative form, because an irreducibly contingent compound stems from a kind of indexical parameter of the text in relation to the context in which it is read. But one can read this indexical parameter itself to be only the residue of an active dialogism that is operating at an implicit level. Unlike the case of Kreisel, who freezes the subject by axiomatizing the act of mental construction of a specific mathematical entity, Bakhtin's dialogism operates unceasingly at several levels both within and without the literary text .It is this unceasing dialogism that lends, especially in the case of the novel, an essential indeterminacy to the genre. In fact, it seems the dialogism is prior to the explicit construction of the subject itself.

Bakhtin is also not concerned with an axiomatic formalization of literature. This is because Bakhtin (1981) does not invoke the theoretical lens where literature is supposed to begin but those categories where literary theory is inadequate such as the novel. To put it in terms of the philosophy of mathematics, Bakhtin is not concerned with the foundational problem of literature. It is the specific character of the most modern literary form, which is the novel, which presents itself as a problem to Bakhtin. However, the dialogism of the novel also presents an occasion to think of the dialogic as a principle of formality that underlies the creation of all meaning, not just specific kinds of literary meaning. Such a generalization of the dialogic principle is also suggested when Heyting indicates that Formalism itself is part of the larger dialogue happening in the history of mathematics.

As an instance of an application of this dialogic principle, inspired by Bakhtin, Lockyer (1991) analyses Faulkner's novel *As I lay Dying* by shaping the explicitly polyphonic structure of the novel through the dialogical investigation of the general reliability of language, recognizing, beyond any rigid monological formalization, the dynamism of re-indexation of iconic structures that work as material elements of the novel and get in a flow through reading. "The very structure of *As I Lay Dying* indicates Faulkner's interest in articulating consciousness; the number of narrators provides him the means to explore how language connects these otherwise isolated narrators. [...] To paraphrase Bakhtin, it presents perspectives and opposing evaluations to provide the interaction that will allow Faulkner to move freely among the worlds of his narrators" (p. 75) For example, "while Addie is the novel's strongest proponent of the frailty of language, Darl Bundren embodies the conviction that the word can create reality and connect isolated consciousness" (p. 74). "Between the dead and the mad, Faulkner establishes a range of possibilities for language" (ibid.). Free choice sequences, working in a dialogical frame as a dynamic reshaping of a given function, deliver the accurate way to formalize the unpredictable paths of meaning through its clash with opposing figures that cannot be located in any generative axiomatic framework.

By broadening this kind of analysis, we suggest using dialogical constructivism as a framework for the analysis of literariness in novels, but also in the sciences. While Formalism is based on the idea that a whole field of meaning can be enclosed in a generative form, Constructive Dialogism is a formal method that tends to go beyond formalisms in order to make sense of them. Because every rule is not fixed from the outset, but rather depends on the way subjects are using them to grasp an open domain of *actions*, their being concretely used continuously reshapes them into new prisms of *interactions*. Formalism depends on a functional treatment of literary texts, whereas Constructive Dialogism puts the emphasis on the open process of indexation, through which the icon signs work as a material of construction aiming at something which is beyond them. It promotes a reading of novel as *living dialogues* encapsulated within material diagrams.

## References

Bakhtin, M. (1981). *The dialogical imagination four essays*. (Holquist, M., tr). Austin: University of Texas Press.

Bakhtin, M. M. (2014). *Speech genres and other late essays*. (Holquist, M., McGee, V.W., tr) (p. 145). University of Texas Press.

Becker, O. (1927). Mathematische Existenz. Untersuchungen zur Logik und Ontologie mathematischer Phänomene. *Jahrbuch für Philosophie und phänomenologische Forschung, 8*, 439–809.

Brouwer, L. E. J. (1912). 'Intuitionism and formalism', inaugural address at the University of Amsterdam. *English translation in* Brouwer (1975), 123–138.

Brouwer, L. E. J. (1929). Mathematik, Wissenschaft und Sprache. *Monatshefte für Mathematik und Physik, 36*, 153–164. English translation in Mancosu 1998, pp. 45–53.

Brouwer, L. E. J. (1948). Essentieel negatieve eigenschappen. *Indagationes Mathematicae, 10*, 322–323. English translation in Brouwer, 1975, pp. 478–479.

Brouwer, L. E. J. (1949). Consciousness, philosophy and mathematics. *Proceedings of the 10th International Congress of Philosophy, Amsterdam, 1948*(3), 1235–1249.

Brouwer, L. E. J. (1975). In A. Heyting (Ed.), *Collected works 1. Philosophy and foundations of mathematics*. Amsterdam: North-Holland.

Chaitin, G. J. (1998). *The limits of mathematics*. Singapore: Springer.

Dilthey, W. (1988). *Introduction to the human sciences, by (Betanzos, R. tr.)* (pp. 56–72). Wayne State University Press.

Dummett, M. (1993). *The origins of analytical philosophy*. Cambridge, MA: Harvard University Press.

Fink, E. (1933) [2000]. The phenomenological philosophy of Edmund Husserl and contemporary criticism. In (Translated and edited by Elveton, R.), *The phenomenology of Husserl. selected critical and contemporary readings* (pp. 70–139). Seattle: Noesis Press.

Gethmann, C. F. (1991). Phänomenologie, Lebensphilosophie und Konstruktive Wissenschafttheorie. In *Lebenswelt und Wissenschaft. Studien zum Verhältnis von Phänomenologie und Wissenschaftstheorie*. Bonn: Bouvier Verlag.

Girard, J.-Y. (2016). *Le fantôme de la transparence*. Paris: Éditions Allia.

Heidegger, M. (1925) [2010]. *Logic: the question of truth.* (Sheehan T. tr) Indiana University Press.

Heyting, A. (1930). Die formalen Regeln der intuitionistischen Logik. In *Sitzungsberichte der Preussischen Akademie von Wissenschaften.* Physikalisch-mathematische Klasse (pp. 42–56).

Heyting, A. (1956). *Intuitionism, an introduction*. Amsterdam: North-Holland.

Heyting, A. (1962). *After thirty years. Logic, Methodology and Philosophy of Science (Proc. 1960 Internat. Congr.)* (pp. 194–197). Stanford: Stanford Univ. Press.

Holquist, M., et al. (1981). Epic and novel. In M. Bakhtin (Ed.), *Dialogic imagination: Four essays* (pp. 1–40). Austin: University of Texas Press.

Kreisel, G. (1967). Informal rigour and completeness proof. In I. Lakatos (Ed.), *Problems in the philosophy of mathematics* (pp. 138–186). Amsterdam: North-Holland.

Lockyer, J. (1991). *Ordered by words. Language and narration in the novels of William Faulkner*. Carbondale: Southern Illinois University Press.

Mancosu, P. (Ed.). (1998). *From Hilbert to Brouwer. The debate on the foundations of mathematics in the 1920s*. Oxford: Oxford University Press.

Martin-Löf, P. (1984). *Intuitionistic type theory: Notes by Giovanni Sambin of a series of lectures given in Padua, June 1980*. Napoli: Bibliopolis.

Popper, K. (1967) [1972]. Epistemology without a knowing subject. In *Objective knowledge: An evolutionary approach*. Oxford: Clarendon Press.

Rahman, S., McConaughey, Z., Klev, A., & Clerbout, N. (2018). *Immanent reasoning or equality in action. A Plaidoyer for the play level*. Dordrecht: Springer.

Steiner, P. (2014). The system. In *Russian formalism: a metapoetics* (pp. 99–138).

Sundholm, B. G. (1983). Brouwer's anticipation of the principle of charity. *Proceedings of the Aristotelian Society, 84*, 145.

Sundholm, B. G. (2015). Constructive recursive functions, Church's thesis, and Brouwer's theory of the creating subject: afterthoughts on a Paris joint session. In J. Dubucs & M. Bordeau (Eds.), *Constructivity and Computability in Historical and Philosophical Perspective* (Logic, Epistemology, and the Unity of Science no. 34) (pp. 1–35). Dordrecht: Springer.

Van Atten, M. (2004). *On Brouwer*. Belmont: Wadsworth.

Van Dalen, D. (1982). Braucht die konstruktive Mathematics Grundlegung. In *Jahresbericht der Deutschen Mathematiker-Vereinigung, Band 84, Heft 2*. Stuttgart: Teubner.

# Chapter 9
# Parallel Reasoning by *Ratio Legis* in Contemporary Jurisprudence. Elements for a Dialogical Approach

**M. Dolors Martínez-Cazalla, Tania Menéndez-Martín, and Shahid Rahman**

**Abstract** Nowadays, there is a quite considerable amount of literature on the use of analogy or more generally of inferences by parallel reasoning in contemporary legal reasoning and particularly so within Common Law. These studies are often motivated by research in artificial intelligence seeking to develop suitable software-support for legal reasoning. Recently, Rahman et al. (Inferences by Parallel Reasoning in Islamic Jurisprudence. Al-Shīrāzī's Insights into the Dialectical Constitution of Meaning and Knowledge. Springer, Dordrecht, 2019) developed a dialogical approach in the framework of Constructive Type Theory to what in Islamic Jurisprudence was called *qiyās* or *correlational inferences*. In their last chapter the authors suggested that such an approach contributes to the study of patterns of reasoning by precedent cases within contemporary Common Law. In the present paper we will further motivate the deployment of the dialogical framework developed in Rahman et al. (2019) within Civil and Common Law. After a presentation of Scott Brewer's take on analogy within Common Law, that has striking structural similarities to reasoning by precedent case rooted in *ratio legis* (known in Islamic Jurisprudence as *qiyās al-'illa* or correlational inference by the *occasioning factor*), we will illustrate the implementation of the framework with a brief discussion of some cases of legal reasoning based on Spanish Civil Law but where the accent is put in the emerging ruling rather than in the existing of a case in Common Law. Moreover, quite surprisingly, the case under study suggests that even cases of Law interpretation fit the argumentation pattern of *qiyās al-'illa*. A caveat: in the present paper we will focus mainly in discussing the dynamics of the meaning constitution

M. D. Martínez-Cazalla (✉)
GILLIUS, HUM690, Universidad de Sevilla, Seville, Spain

CNRS, UMR 8163-STL, Université de Lille, Lille, France

T. Menéndez-Martín
Independent researcher in Law, Madrid, Spain

S. Rahman
Département de Philosophie, CNRS, UMR 8163-STL, Université de Lille, Lille, France
e-mail: shahid.rahman@univ-lille.fr



T. Lopez-Soto (ed.), *Dialog Systems*, Logic, Argumentation & Reasoning 22,
https://doi.org/10.1007/978-3-030-61438-6_9

involved rather than in setting the rules of the underlying dialogical framework, the latter is the subject of a follow-up paper.

**Keywords** Legal reasoning · Common Law · Civil Law · Analogy · Disanalogy · Argumentation · Dialogical Logic

## 9.1 Introduction

Nowadays, there is a considerable amount of literature on the use of analogy or, more generally, of *inferences by parallel reasoning*[1] in contemporary legal reasoning, and particularly so within Common Law. These studies, many of them based on argumentation-based frameworks, are often motivated by research in artificial intelligence seeking to develop suitable software-support for legal reasoning.[2]

Recently, Rahman et al. (2019) developed a dialogical approach in the framework of Constructive Type Theory to what in Islamic Jurisprudence was called *qiyās* or *correlational inferences*.[3] In their last chapter, inspired by Wael B. Hallaq's (1985) seminal article "The Logic of Legal Reasoning in Religious and Non-Religious Cultures: The Case of Islamic Law and Common Law", the authors suggest that such an approach contributes to the study of patterns of reasoning by precedent cases within contemporary Common Law.

Indeed, the aim of correlational inferences within Islamic Law is to provide a rational ground for the application of a juridical ruling to a given case not yet considered by the original juridical sources. It proceeds by combining heuristic (and/or hermeneutic) moves with logical inferences.[4] The simplest form follows the following pattern:

- In order to establish if a given juridical ruling applies or not to a given case, called the *branch-case, al-farʿ*, we look for a case we already know from the sources that falls under that ruling – the so-called *root-case, al-aṣl*. Then we search for the property or set of properties upon which the application of the ruling to the root-case is grounded (the *ratio legis* or *legal cause* for that juridical decision).

[1]The term *inference by parallel reasoning* stemms from Paul Bartha (2010).

[2]Cf. Rissland & Ashley (1987, 1989), Posner (1995), Hage et al. (1994), Prakken (1995), Prakken & Sartor (1996), Brewer (1996), Kloosterhuis (2000). Some reject logical approaches such as Weinreb (2005) and Woods (2015) – despite the fact that the latter, as pointed out by Rahman et al. (2019, pp. 240–246), is closer as expected to the logical approach of Brewer.

[3]Cf. Young (2017).

[4]The theory of *qiyās* was mainly developped by the Shāfiʿī-school of jurisprudence (*uṣūl al-fiqh*), and particularly so by Abū Isḥāq al-Shīrāzī (393H/1003-476H/1083CE), who rendered one of the most influential systems of legal reasoning – see Al-Shīrāzī (1987, 2003, 2016). For a comprehensive study, see Young (2017).

If that grounding property (or set of them) is known, it is examined whether that property can also be asserted of the new case. In the case of an affirmative answer, it is inferred that the new case also falls under the juridical ruling at stake, and so the range of its application is extended. When the legal cause is explicitly known (by the sources) or made explicit by specifying a relevant set of properties, we are in presence of an inference by *qiyās al-'illa* or correlational inference by the *occasioning factor*.

When the grounds behind a given juridical ruling are neither explicit nor can they be made explicit, we are in presence of correlational inferences by indication (*qiyās al-dalāla*) or by resemblance (*qiyās al-shabah*). Whereas the former are based on pinpointing at specific relevant parallelisms between rulings (*qiyās al-dalāla*) shared by both the root-case and the branch-case, the latter are based on asserting the resemblance of root-case and branch-case in relation to a set of (relevant) properties (*qiyās al-shabah*).

Thus, *qiyās al-dalāla* and *qiyās al-shabah*, sometimes broadly referred as arguments by analogy (or better by the Latin denomination, arguments *a pari*) are put into action when there is absence of knowledge of the occasioning factor grounding the application of a given ruling. The plausibility of a conclusion attained by **parallelism between rulings** (*qiyās al-dalāla*) is considered to be of a higher epistemic degree than the conclusion obtained by **resemblance of the branch-case and the root-case in relation to some set of (relevant) properties** (*qiyās al-shabah*). Conclusions obtained by either *qiyās al-dalāla* or *qiyās al-shabah*, have a lower degree of epistemic plausibility as conclusions inferred by the deployment of *qiyās al-'illa*, where the **occasioning factor** can be pinpointed.[5]

Not unlike to present rejections of logical approaches to legal reasoning[6], during Classical Islam there was a long and deep controversy concerning the pertinence of logic and epistemology within Law. The main objections can perhaps be summarized as follows[7]:

1. Within the legal sources one very rarely finds attempts to deduce a general rule from the specific rule for each legal act. What we actually find in the legal writings, more often than not, are **specific rules.**[8]
2. Finding out the general rules by abduction or induction and **setting them as fixed norms** leads to ground legal normativity on uncertainty. This casts doubt on even *qiyās al-'illa*, purported to provide the most certain conclusion attained by legal reasoning.

[5]Cf. Young (2017, pp. 108–128).

[6]Cf. Weinreb (2005) and Woods (2015).

[7]For a thorough discussion on these points, see Zysow (2013, pp. 160–191).

[8]Like in contemporary Common Law.

3. Understanding the general norm behind a specific juridical ruling requires the deployment of an **interpretative** process rather than of a dubious epistemological argument purported to identify a relevant property featuring the cause of the Law.

One cardinal feature of the most mature form of *qiyās al-'illa* that emerged from such a controversy is the inception of the test of efficiency or *ta'thīr* that provides the means to verify whether the property P purported to be relevant for the juridical sanction at stake is indeed so. The test declines into two complementary procedures:

> testing *co-extensiveness* or *ṭard* (if the property is present then the sanction too), and testing *co-exclusiveness* or *'aks* (if the property is absent then so is the juridical sanction. While *co-extensiveness* examines whether sanction H follows from the verification of the presence of the property P, *co-exclusiveness* examines whether exemption from the sanction H follows from the verification of the absence of P[9]

As pointed out by Zysow (2013, p. 215), the doctrine of efficiency represents an impressive attempt to answer the cardinal questions of those that opposed the deployment of *qiyās*. Notice that the method of efficiency not only tests the relevance but also responds to the point on the legal foundation of the general rules. The fact is that the general schema is both grounded and extracted from specific rulings found in the legal sources. Moreover, by means of *ta'thīr* the occasioning factor is identified as the application of a schema that yields a ruling grounded in the sources.

By way of an illustration, let us recall the classical example of *qiyās al-'illa*. Date liquor intoxicates, just as (grape) wine does, so that it is prohibited like wine. The canonical analysis identifies four elements in such an argument: the branch-case or case under consideration, date liquor; the root-case or case verified by the sources, wine; the character they have in common their power to intoxicate; and their common, legal qualification, prohibition (inferred in the case of date liquor, verified by the sources in the case of wine). The crucial step that underlies this form of argumentation is the identification of the occasioning factor, the *'illa*, that lies behind its prohibition by means of the test of efficiency. The point here is that applying the general schema that *drinks that have the power to induce intoxication should be forbidden* to the case of date liquor *occasions* its interdiction, since the presence of intoxication-power of a drink leads to the interdiction of consuming it and the absence of such a power leads to the conclusion that the consumption of that drink is not forbidden.

In the present paper, we will further motivate the deployment within contemporary Civil and Common Law of the dialogical framework developed in Rahman et al. (2019). More precisely, after a presentation of Scott Brewer's take on analogy within Common Law, that has striking structural similarities to reasoning by precedent case rooted in *ratio legis* (known in Islamic Jurisprudence as *qiyās al-'illa* or correlational inference by the *occasioning factor*). We will illustrate the implementation of the framework with a brief discussion of some cases of legal reasoning based in Spanish

---

[9]See Rahman et al. (2019, Preface).

Civil Law but where the accent is put in the emerging ruling rather than in the existing of a case as in Common Law.[10]

Moreover, quite surprisingly, the cases under study suggest that even cases of Law-interpretation fit the argumentation pattern of *qiyās al-'illa*. This seems to open a new path for the study of argumentation by parallel reasoning.

A final caveat: in the present paper we will focus mainly in discussing the dynamics of the meaning constitution involved rather than in setting the rules of the underlying dialogical framework, the latter is the subject of a follow-up paper.

## 9.2 Scott Brewer on Parallel Reasoning

Scott Brewer (1996, pp. 1003–1017) developed an approach to parallel reasoning based on extracting a general reasoning schema for parallel reasoning from some specific rules. Brewer (1996, p. 1004) speaks of schemas of *exemplary reasoning* (ERS).[11]

The legal context of both Brewer is *reasoning by precedent*, one of the hallmarks of Common Law. So the specific rules ERS generalize are precedent cases recorded by the legal sources.

In fact, the main aim of Brewer's is to describe the emergence of a legal ruling as the result of generalizing an inferential schema that unifies the cases under consideration. According to Brewer (1996, p. 1004) such a generalization is carried out by means of a specific inference rule called *analogy-warranting rule* (AWR), which makes of the whole argument an instance of the general schema at work (that is why the whole pattern is called *exemplary reasoning schema* – ERS). This deductivist approach, as acknowledged by Brewer (1996, p. 1006) himself, should in principle have problems in dealing with *defeasibility*.

One of Brewer's (1996, pp. 1003–1004) main example is the following:

> [ ... ] *valuables were stolen from a passenger's rented steamboat cabin. The issue in that case was whether the steamboat owner was strictly liable to the passenger for the loss (it has been decided below that neither the steamboat owner nor the passenger was negligent). Apparently, only a couple of cases were directly on point: one held that an innkeeper was strictly liable for the theft of boarders' valuables, while another held that a railroad company was not strictly liable to passengers for the theft of their valuables from*

[10] A landmark in the contemporary studies of analogy in legal reasoning is Alchourrón's (1961) paper *Los argumentos jurídicos a fortiori y a pari*, which as pointed out by Alchourrón himself was a reaction to Perelmann's mistrust of the use of formal logic within legal reasoning. Alchourron's proposal seems to be closer to patterns of reasoning based on the **resemblance of the branch-case and the root-case in relation to some set of (relevant) properties** (*qiyās al-shabah*), rather than on identifying an occasioning factor. We will not discuss here Alchourron's paper.

[11] We will focus here in Brewer's approach, though as discussed in the last chapter of Rahman et al. (2019), Brewer's proposal can be seen to be quite close to the one of John Woods (2015, pp. 273–281), despite the fact that Woods (2015, pp. 275–277) criticizes 'logical' studies such as that of Brewer.

*open-berth sleeping-car trains. One might say that the legal issue was put to Judge O'Brien thus: in the "eyes of the law," was the steamboat sufficiently like an inn, on the one hand, or sufficiently like a railroad, on the other, to receive the same legal treatment?*

*Reconstructed in accord with the schema presented above, the argument is as follows:*
***Target*** *(y) = the steamboat owner.*
***Source*** *(x) = the innkeeper.*

***Shared characteristics:***
*F: has a client who procures a room for specified reasons R (privacy, etc.).*
*G: has a tempting opportunity for fraud and plundering client.*

***Inferred characteristic:***
*H: is strictly liable.*

***Argument:***

1. *y has F and G (target premise);*
2. *x has F and G (source premise);*
3. *x also has H (source premise)*
4. *AWR: if anything has F and G also has H, then everything that has F and G also has H;*
5. *Therefore, y has H.*

In the formulation of an ERS, Brewer deploys the terminology: *shared characteristics*. This might suggest that what is at stake here is the similarity between the target and the source case, as in typical arguments by analogy [such as Al-Shīrāzī (2003) *qiyās al-shabah*). However, notice that the argument in the quote above does **not** deploy substitution of identicals.

The logical structure of Brewer's (1996) argument in the ERS quoted is based on the open assumptions *x and y have F*, *x and y have G*, and the propositional function *x also has H*. The cardinal step is to trigger an inference without assuming an identity relation. In order to do so, Brewer introduces AWR which accomplishes the task of embedding the step *if anything has F and G also has H* into a standard deductive framework, where *any* becomes *every*, that is, a universal quantifier that binds the variables of the open assumptions. Thus, AWR produces logically valid inferences. After all, the ERS do not rely on similarity of cases but in subsuming target- and source-case into a general universal rule.

Let us provide two different reconstructions of

*If anything has F and G also has H,*

(1) *H* and *G* are understood as being linked by a conjunction within an open assumption

$H(x)true(x : F \wedge G)$,
that can be glossed as:
*x is liable if it instantiates both having a client who rents a room and having a tempting opportunity for fraud and plundering of client.*

(2) *H* and *G* are understood as being linked by a dependence relation. *Having a tempting opportunity for fraud and plundering of client* is restricted to *having a client who rents a room*

$H(x, y)true(x : F, y : G(x))$,

that can be glossed as: *Those x of whom G can be predicated (G(x)) are liable, provided they instantiate F.*

If we wish to have more an expressive structure we can go deeper into the structure:

$H(u, v)true(u : Individuals, v : F(u) \wedge G(u))$

*x is liable if it instantiates an individual that is also an instance of those individuals having both F and G.*

$H(x, y, z)true(x : Individuals, y : F(y), z : G(x, y))$

*x is liable if it instantiates an individual that is also an instance of those individuals having G, provided they instantiate F* (first).

Notice that even in the simpler version our analysis makes the liability dependent upon *F* and *G*. It is not liability in general, but that liability that is *inferentially* dependent upon *F* and *G*, and thus specific to having these properties.

How does this inferential structure produce actual inferences? Well, by instantiating. The instrument of inference is a method that for any individual that instantiates the premises *F* and *G* takes us to the liability of this individual. The method is obviously a function; i.e., the dependent object that provides instances from open assumptions.

Let us now assume that *a* is an instantiation, then we obtain the following variants of the inference rules within an ERS underlying Brewer's example quoted above.

$$\frac{a : F \wedge G \qquad \begin{matrix}(x : F \wedge G)\\ b(x) : H(x)\end{matrix}}{b(a) : H(a)} \qquad \frac{a : F, c : G(a) \qquad \begin{matrix}(x : F, y : G(x))\\ d(x, y) : H(x, y)\end{matrix}}{d(a, c) : H(a, c)}$$

It is important to keep in mind that if ERS is to be considered an instantiation schema supporting inferences, the inferential structure must be based on open assumptions of the form *x*: *A* upon which propositional functions are defined. In our case the functions at stakes are:

$$b(x) : H(x)\ (x : F \wedge G) \qquad \text{or} \qquad d(x, y) : H(x)true(x : F, y : G(x))$$

Let us deploy the terminology of *qiyās al-ʿilla* in the inference rule, which stresses the *occasioning* or causative force of the function. In other words, let the functions *b* (*x*) and *d*(*x,y*) stand for the functions that render the *occasioning factor* or *ratio legis* for the rulings *H*(*x*) and *H*(*x,y*). Accordingly let us deploy the notation *ʿilla*(*x*) and *ʿilla*(*x,y*):

$$\text{'}illa(x)\text{: } H(x)\ (x\text{: } F \wedge G) \qquad \text{or} \qquad \text{'}illa(x, y)\text{: } H(x)\ (x\text{: } F\text{, } y\text{: } G(x))$$

The idea is that when the judge delves into the content behind one specific rule that has been acknowledged by the legal sources as setting a precedent, the judge grasps the meaning as constituted by a schema that tightens inferential legal ruling and conditions. In other words, the judge presupposes that the propositional functions *unify* some set of cases that constituted a precedent:

$$H(x) : prop(x : F \wedge G) \qquad \text{or} \qquad H(x) : prop(x : F, y : G(x))$$

Notice that so far we have kept silent on Brewer's deductivist *analogy-warranting rule* (AWR). Non-deductivists as John Woods (2015) will certainly take exception to AWR, and if we follow the inferential schema described above we do not seem to need AWR at all.

However, one way to understand the role of this rule is to link it with *taʾthīr*, the possibility of testing if the applied instantiation schema does indeed manage to unify the relevant set of precedent cases put into action. In order to do so, we need to display the inferential structure behind AWR.

Inferentially speaking, the passage from the general schema to the universal quantification is only a step away

$$\frac{\begin{array}{l}(x : F \wedge G) \\ b(x) : H(x)\end{array}}{\lambda x.b(x) : (\forall x : F \wedge G)H(x)}$$

This is, in our view, the way to formulate Brewer's (1996, p. 1004) *analogy-warranting rule* (AWR) as emerging from an instantiation schema.

Nevertheless, this is only half of the story. As observed by Brewer (1996, pp. 1006–1016), AWR should be linked with the possibility of objecting to the relevance of the properties by means of a disanalogy.

Here again, Al-Shīrāzī's (1987, 2003, 2016) insights help. As discussed in our introduction, the idea is that *taʾthīr*, the test of efficiency, provides the means to test whether the property, or set of them, purported to be relevant for the juridical sanction at stake is indeed so.

The test declines into two complementary procedures: testing *co-extensiveness* or *ṭard* (if the property is present then the sanction too) and *co-exclusiveness* or *ʿaks* (if the property is absent then so is the juridical sanction – the consumption of vinegar is in principle not forbidden).

While *co-extensiveness* examines whether the legal qualification *H* follows from the verification of the presence of the property or set of properties, *co-exclusiveness* examines whether exemption from the legal qualification follows from the verification of the absence.

If we formulate AWR as such a kind of testing procedure, we need to have the following expansion of AWR:

For every $x$, if it instantiates the property $F$ (or set of them), then the legal qualification follows, if it does not instantiate $F$ then the legal qualification does not apply:

$$\lambda x.c : (\forall x : F \vee \neg F)\{\ [(\forall y : F) thickmathspaceleft^{\vee}(y) =_{\{F\vee\neg F\}} x \supset H(y)] \wedge$$
$$[(\forall z : \neg F) thickmathspaceright^{\vee}(z) =_{\{F\vee\neg F\}} x \supset \neg H(z)]\ \}$$

Recall that the point of Brewer (1996, p. 1006) of introducing AWR is to unify some set of precedents specific to a giving ruling $H$. This is also the point of al-Shīrāzī's *taʾthīr*, where the testing amounts to unifying cases *recorded in the legal sources*. This was al-Shīrāzī's way of answering to the antianalogists, a response that Brewer (1996, p. 1006) brings to the context of contemporary legal reasoning.

Accordingly, a disanalogy, that is, a counterexample to the claim that the presence of a property triggers the juridical ruling and its absence the failing of that ruling, can then defeat the use of some specific AWR.

It is here that the dialogical approach comes on the scene: criticism amounts to a game of giving and asking for reasons during a fixed argumentative context though this does not mean that during the procedure the proposed cannot be contested. In our view this is related to the distinction between play level and strategy level. The latter, as claimed in Rahman et al. (2019, chapter 2.4), should be understood as a *recapitulation* that settles the matter.

Let us finish this section with the remark that in our framework, instantiating a general schema is the way to *justify* it. Indeed, justifications are, in our framework, instances or tokens of a type. Moreover, *local reasons* or reasons brought forward during a play should be distinguished from *strategic reasons*, or reasons that constitute (the justification of) a winning strategy either by establishing validity or by establishing the truth of material inferences). Thus, despite the scepticism towards justification of Woods (2015, pp. 263–272 ) and other approaches, the instantiations at work are, after all, either (local) reasons or justifications, that is, strategic reasons encoding a recapitulation of the process leading to the resulting legal ruling.

Perhaps the problem comes from overseeing both:

1. the difference between assertions brought forward to justify other assertions and justifying objects, i.e., truth-makers or proof-objects, and
2. ignoring the distinction of reasons brought forward in the context of a play (with all its material and temporal restrictions) and strategic reasons yielding logical validity.

Be that as it may, interesting is that some cases of interpretation of Law fit quite well with our reconstruction of inferences by occasioning factor. This is quite of a surprising result, since in the hermeneutics of Law is not, in principle, assumed to follow the pattern of arguments by precedent cases.

## 9.3 Parallel Reasoning and the Hermeneutics of Law. Elements for a Case Study

Actually, there are three main cases. However, all of them can be conceived as different plays on deciding about the interpretation of the Law concerning who must pay some particular tax specific to loans linked to a mortgage (either a mortgage loan or a credit warranted with a mortgage) included in the taxes called *Tax on Documented Legal Acts* (Impuesto sobre Actos Jurídicos Documentados – IAJD). More crucially, they can be seen as different plays concerning the meaning of the concepts of *Mortgage Loan*, *Right* (to acquire a Mortgage Loan) and *Beneficiary of a Mortgage Loan*.

### *9.3.1 Three Cases and the Dynamics of Meaning*

In the first case, Supreme Court Judgment 9012/2001 – see our appendix, the appellant party, the borrower *Inmobiliaria Manuel Asín, S.A.* (IMA), submits a cassation appeal (an appeal to overturn the previous decision) against the decision that it is, themselves, the borrower; who is in charge of paying the IAJD tax involving the mortgage loan granted by the *Caja de Ahorros y Monte Piedad de Zaragoza, Aragón y Rioja* (Ibercaja). The argument of the appellant is based on the idea that though a mortgage loan is a loan, one should distinguish the two components. In other words, the point of the appellant is that mortgage loans should be understood in the divided sense – in Islamic Jurisprudence such a move is called ***kasr*** or breaking apart. The point is that the IAJD tax is linked to the mortgage component, not to the loan as such. In other words, according to the appellant, the property of being a loan is not the occasioning factor for determining who is in charge of the taxes at stake. The Supreme Court dismissed the appeal based on denying the divided reading of the notion of mortgage loans and stressing the fact that this unity also leads to the unity of beneficiary, namely the borrower:

> [...] *it is true that the traditional interpretation of this Chamber [3$^{rd}$ Chamber of the Supreme Court of Spain] has always accepted the premise that the taxable event, mortgage loan, was and is unique, and therefore, the conclusion of this subjection to AJD is, nowadays, coherent, whatever the legislative tendencies that, may be in the near future, could consecrate mortgage loan exemption in this particular tax—*. (p. 3, para. 2)
>
> *In any case, the unity of the taxable event related to the loan, produces the consequence that the only possible beneficiary is the borrower, in accordance with the provision in art. 8°. d)—*. (p. 3, para. 3). Supreme Court Judgment 9012/2001 – see our appendix –

One way to put the issue of the interpretative contention concerning this case is to focus on the different ways the contenders build the meaning dependence between loan, mortgage and IAJD-duty.

Indeed, whereas the argument of IMA, the appellant party, is based on the following meaning formations, which *break apart* the notions of Mortgage, Loan and the Mortgage-dependent tax duty IAJD:

- *Mortgage*: *prop* *Loan*: *prop* *Bearer-of*-IAJD-*duty*(*x*): *prop* (*x*: *Mortgage*).
  In words, the tax duty IAJD is dependent upon the notion of Mortgage. Accordingly, this duty is independent of the notion of Loan.

The argument of the Supreme Court in favour of Ibercaja is based on the following meaning constitution:

- *Loan*: *prop* *Mortgage*(*x*): *prop* (*x*: *Loan*)
  *Beneficiary*(*x*,*y*): *prop* (*x*: *Loan*, *y*: *Mortgage*(*x*))
- *Bearer-of*-IAJD-*duty*(*x*,*y*,*z*): *prop* (*x*: *Loan*, *y*: *Mortgage*(*x*), *z*: *Beneficiary*(*x*,*y*)).
  In words, *Mortgage Loan* is a complex concept, namely it concerns those mortgages dependent upon a loan. Accordingly, the tax duty IAJD is dependent upon the complex concept Mortgage Loan, they are inseparable of the notion of Loan. Moreover, the notion of Beneficiary is made dependent upon the notion of the acquirer of the Mortgage Loan. Thus, strictly speaking, the tax duty IAJD is understood as dependent upon the *Mortgage-Loan-Beneficiary*.
- Notice that the beneficiary is defined as the one that benefited of the mortgage loan. It defines the *Borrower* as the beneficiary.

The second case, Supreme Court Judgment 7141/2006 – see our appendix, also involving mortgage and loan, yields the same juridical decision as the precedent case. However, it is interesting that the reason brought forward by the Court stresses, as relevant for the decision, an aspect of the legal feature of the transaction different to the one occasioning the decision 9012/2001. Indeed, the argument does not contest the unicity of the tax event, the credit opened by the *Caixa d'Estalvis i Pensions de Barcelona* (La Caixa) in favour of *Establecimientos Industriales y Servicios, S.A.* (EISSA, S.A.) and linked with a *mortgage warrant*, nevertheless, it stresses the point that the passive subject of the purchase of the *right*, namely the credit, is the beneficiary, i.e., the borrower. Thus, according to this argument of the Court, the uniqueness of the beneficiary of this kind of transaction is the relevant feature occasioning the decision that it is the borrower's duty rather than the lender's duty to pay the taxes involving the mortgage. The point is that, according to the Supreme Court, the beneficiary is the beneficiary of the main business or of the purchase of the right. The main business is the loan, the mortgage being a subject of the loan; the beneficiary of the loan is the borrower, namely EISSA; therefore, it is EISSA who has the duty to pay the due taxes:

> [. . .] *"the beneficiary is the purchaser of the good or of the right and, failing that, the persons who request notarial documents, or those in whose interest the documents are issued"*—. (Quoted in the STS 7141/2006, p. 3, para. 3)

> [. . .] *The purchaser of the good or of the right can only be the borrower, not because of an argument such as the unity of the taxable event related to the loan,* [. . .], *but because the* ***right*** *referred to in the precept is the loan reflected in the notarial document, even if it is*

> *guaranteed with a mortgage and its registration in the Property Registry is the constituent element of guarantee—*. (Cf. *Reasoning for the dismissal of appeals* and Supreme Court Judgment 7141/2006, p. 3, para. 3 – see our appendix)

From the meaning constitution point of view, the Supreme Court adds more complexity by squeezing the notion of *right (to acquire a loan)*, between the compound *Mortgage-Loan-Beneficiary* and the IAJD-*duty*:

- *Bearer-of-*IAJD-*duty(x,y,z,w)*: *prop* (*x*: *Loan*, *y*: *Mortgage*(*x*), *z*: *Right*(*x,y*), *w*: *Beneficiary*(*x,y,z*)).

  Under this perspective; the notion of *acquired right* is dependent upon the compound *Mortgage-Loan-Beneficiary*. In other words, the right is *the right acquired by being the Beneficiary of the Loan in any way attached to a Mortgage*, and the duty to the pay the IAJD is then made dependent upon this right.
- Hence, this alternative interpretation, that defines the right as the one acquired by the beneficiary of the loan attached to a mortgage, also leads to identifying the *Borrower* as the one who has to carry the burden of the IAJD.

The last case of our study, Supreme Court Judgment 3422/2018 – see our appendix, also involving mortgage and loan, overturns the juridical decisions of the precedent cases concerning who carries the duty of paying the taxes induced by the mortgage loan. Indeed, the decision 3422/2018 establishes that it is the lender, not the borrower, who has to pay the due taxes. Moreover, it explicitly overturns juridical decisions as the ones established by Judgments 9012/2001 and 7141/2006. The argument behind the overturning indicates that if, as argued in 7141/2006, it is the case that the main business is the loan, i.e., the purchasing of a right, this right is not a *real one*, in the sense that, for example, it does induce change of ownership. A real right is the one linked to the mortgage, but this is accessory to the right acquired by the beneficiary and in fact the beneficiary of that real right is the lender, not the borrower. Hence, the due taxes must be paid by the direct beneficiary of the mortgage, namely the lender.

> *The Supreme Court held that loans are not registrable,* [. . .], *as they are obviously not a* ***real*** *right, nor does the right have the typical real significance mentioned in the second of these precepts (since they do not modify, now or in the future, several of the rights of ownership over real estate or inherent to real rights). The mortgage, on the other hand, is not only registrable, but it is also the mortgage is a real right—.*
>
> *The fact that the mortgage is a real right of registry constitution makes it clearly the main business for tax purposes in public deeds in which mortgage loans or loans with mortgage guarantee are documented—.*
>
> *If we still consider the loan as the main business it does not make much sense to submit to the tax a non-registrable legal business only because there is an accessory real right constituted as a guarantee of compliance with the main one.*

> *The Supreme Court held also that:*
>
> [. . .] *there is no doubt that the beneficiary of the document in question is no other than the creditor, because they (and only they) are qualified to exercise the (privileged) actions that the code offers to the holders of the registered rights. They are the only party interested in the registration of the mortgage (the determining element subject to the tax analysed here), since the mortgage is ineffective if it is not registered in the Property Registry—*. (STS 3422/2018, p.11, para 9)

> *Thus, the conclusions were:*
> 1. *Based on the previous reasoning, we can now answer the question that we have considered preferential, out of the two questions raised by the First Section (Civil Chamber) of this Chamber (Supreme Court). The beneficiary of a mortgage (by loan over itself or as guarantee of a loan) is the money-lender and not the borrower. Therefore, the tax on Documented Legal Acts –when the document subject to the tax is a public deed of a mortgage (by loan over itself or as guarantee of a loan)– should be paid by the lender and not by the borrower.*
> 2. *In order to comply with the decree of admission, the above statement needs to be completed making it explicit that such a decision involves adoption of a guideline opposite to that supported by the jurisprudence of this Chamber (Third Camber – Contentious-Administrative Chamber – of the Supreme Court) until now, as presented in the judgments (STS 9012/2001 and STS 7141/2006) among others, and therefore modifying the previous jurisprudential doctrine.*
>
> Supreme Court Judgment 3422/2018, see our appendix.

In fact, Supreme Court Judgment 3422/2018 concerns the request of the *Empresa Municipal de la Vivienda de Rivas-Vaciamadrid, S.A.* (EMVRivas, S.A.) to be exempted of the taxes required by the *Public Administration* linked to the mortgage that warranted a loan credited to EMVRivas by a bank entity. Nevertheless, as mentioned above, the decision involves a general judgment on who is the beneficiary of the mortgage linked to a mortgage loan. The argument can again here be put as concerning meaning constitution.

The main point of the Supreme Court's argument is related to distinguishing *real rights* from those acquired by taking a *loan*, and more crucially, to set as beneficiary, the beneficiary of a real right. There are several ways to implement these distinctions, but for keeping our framework as simple as possible let us compose *Loan* and *Mortgage* by a conjunction. However, the notion of *Real Right* will be made dependent upon *Mortgage*, furthermore, *Beneficiary* will be defined as those who acquire a *Real Right* by registering the *Mortgage* (brought forward as a warrant by the borrower). Accordingly, the IAJD-*duty* will be defined as the duty of the *R-Beneficiary*, i.e., the *Beneficiary* of the *Real Right.*

- *Loan*: *prop*
  *Bearer-of*-IAJD-*duty*(*x*,*y*,*z*): *prop* (*x*: *Mortgage*, *y*: *Real Right*(*x*), *z*: *R-Beneficiary*(*x*,*y*)).

In order to stress the accessory feature of the Mortgage and the dependence of the notion of *R-Beneficiary* upon the concept or *Real Right,* and the dependence of IAJD-*duty* upon the former, we can express all this as the conjunction of *Loan* with the sigma-type (the existential) expressing those dependences:

- *Loan*$\wedge\exists v$: [(*x*: *Mortgage*, *y*: *Real Right*(*x*), *z*: *R-Beneficiary*(*x*,*y*)) *Bearer-of*-IAJD-*duty*(*v*)].[12]

## 9.3.2 Three Plays on the Same Theme

All these cases are in fact cassation appeals and, as mentioned above, they all amount to say it bluntly to decide who of both, borrower or money-lender, is the beneficiary of either a mortgage loan or a credit warranted with a mortgage, if we are prepared (or not) to distinguish the (real) right linked to the mortgage from the right acquired with the loan.

Thus, we can see the three plays as sub-plays of a whole argument. However, for the sake of oversight in the present reconstruction, we will present each play by its own, and we will leave for a follow-up paper the tasks of integrating all the plays in a whole dialogue, where each relevant step is associated to a dialogical move. Moreover, instead of describing each play we will provide the ERS constituting the argumentative core of each play.

In order to keep stress, for the general structure of each argument, we adopt as starting point (the target or branch-case) the point of view of the Supreme Court. In the second and third play the source or root-case refers to the precedent plays. Different to Brewer's schema we do not start by setting the target and source-case with a free variable, that will be bounded with the information of the concrete cases, but we bind them directly. This saves some steps, though admittedly it does not make so manifest that what is at stake is conceptual schema rather than a concrete case. However, it is closer, we think, to the actual legal practice. In any case, transforming one into the other is only one inference step away.

**First Play- Supreme Court Judgment 9012/2001: IMA versus Ibercaja**

***Target or Branch-Case.*** IMA, the borrower of the Mortgage Loan granted by Ibercaja, must pay the IAJD-duty.

***Source or Root-Case.*** Precedent-Cases *u*, decided in favour of the creditor concerning the payment of IAJD tax induced by a mortgage loan granted to *u*.

***Shared characteristic claimed by the Supreme Court:***

Unity of the Mortgage Loan

*Loan*: *prop* *Mortgage*(*x*): *prop* (*x*: *Loan*).

***Un-Shared characteristic claimed by the* IMA*:***

IMA claims that the notion of *Bearer-of*-IAJD-*duty* applies to *Mortgage* not to the compound *Mortgage-Loan*.

***Inferred characteristic:***

*Bearer-of*-IAJD-*duty*(*x*,*y*,*z*): *prop* (*x*: *Loan*, *y*: *Mortgage*(*x*), *z*: *Beneficiary*(*x*,*y*)).

[12]We simplified the notation here. In fact, it should not be "*v*" but the *second proof object* of *v*, i.e., the function *second*(*v*). Since in CTT, the proof-object of a sigma-type is a pair. In this case the pair is <(*x*,*y*), *z*> such that the *first* element is also a pair.

***Argument of the Supreme Court:***

$b^{IMA}$: *Beneficiary*($l_i$,$m_i$); (IMA is the beneficiary *b* of a mortgage loan granted by Ibercaja. Thus, '$b^{IMA}$' stands for IMA in its quality as beneficiary);

$b^{u}$: *Beneficiary*($l_j$,$m_j$); (precedent cases were *u* was the beneficiary *b* of a mortgage loan granted by a credit entity. Thus, '$b^{u}$' stands for some juridical person of precedent case in its quality as beneficiary of a mortgage loan);

*u*: *Bearer-of-*IAJD*-duty*($l_j$,$m_j$,$b_j$); (the tax duty IAJD concerning the mortgage loan credited to *u*, has been set as a payment duty for *u*);

*AWR*: if the tax duty IAJD has to be paid by whoever is the beneficiary a mortgage loan (i.e., the borrower), then every such a borrower does;

Therefore, IMA has to pay the IAJD-duty.

## Second Play- Supreme Court Judgment 7141/2006: EISSA versus La Caixa

***Target or Branch-Case.*** The borrower, namely EISSA must pay the IAJD-duty, induced by the Loan (warranted by a Mortgage) granted by La Caixa.

***Source or Root-Case.*** Case $s_1$ involving the Supreme Court Judgment 9012/2001.

***Shared characteristic claimed by the Supreme Court:***

Unity of the Mortgage Loan

*Loan*: *prop* *Mortgage*(*x*): *prop* (*x*: *Loan*).

***Shared inferred characteristic:***

The borrower is the one who has to pay the IAJD-duty.

***Un-Shared characteristic:***

*Bearer-of-*IAJD*-duty*(*x*,*y*,*z*,*w*): *prop* (*x*: *Loan*, *y*: *Mortgage*(*x*), *z*: *Right*(*x*,*y*), *w*: *Beneficiary*(*x*,*y*,*z*)).

The borrower is the one who acquired the **right** associated with being the beneficiary of a loan warranted by a mortgage.

In fact, this is the crucial property behind the Supreme Court Judgment 7141/2006, instead of the simpler structure deployed for the decision involved in the Supreme Court Judgment 9012/2001. So, what happens is that the meaning constitution of *Bearer-of-*IAJD-*duty* underlying 9012/2001:

*Bearer-of-*IAJD*-duty*(*x*,*y*,*z*): *prop* (*x*: *Loan*, *y*: *Mortgage*(*x*), *z*: *Beneficiary*(*x*,*y*)).

is extended with one component yielding

*Bearer-of-*IAJD*-duty*(*x*,*y*,*z*,*w*): *prop* (*x*: *Loan*, *y*: *Mortgage*(*x*), *z*: *Right*(*x*,*y*), *w*: *Beneficiary* (*x*,*y*,*z*)).

***Argument of the Supreme Court:***

*EISSA*: *Beneficiary*($l_i$,$m_i$,$r_i$); (EISSA, becomes the beneficiary by acquiring the right associated with the loan (warranted by a mortgage) granted by La Caixa);

As established by the source case 9012/2001, the tax duty IAJD has to be paid by the borrower;

*AWR*: If the tax duty IAJD has to be paid by the borrower, whoever this borrower is (this borrower being the one who acquired the right associated with being the beneficiary of the loan (warranted by a mortgage) granted by the creditor), then every such a borrower does;

Therefore, EISSA has to pay the IAJD-duty.

### Third Play- Supreme Court Judgment 3422/2018: EMVRivas versus Unnamed Credit Entity

***Target or Branch-Case.*** The money-lender must pay the IAJD-duty, induced by the registration of the Mortgage Loan granted to EMVRivas.

***Source or Root-Case.*** Case $s_1$ involving the Supreme Court Judgment 9012/2001.

***Shared characteristic:***

Both of the appellant parties in the target-case and in the source-case were granted a mortgage loan.

***Un-Shared characteristic:***

*Bearer-of-*IAJD*-duty(x,y,z)*: *prop* (*x*: *Mortgage*, *y*: *Real Right*(*x*), *z*: *R-Beneficiary*(*x*,*y*)).

According to the Supreme Court, it is the money-lender, the creditor, who is the beneficiary of the real right acquired by registering the mortgage that warrants the loan.

This is the crucial property that overturns the arguments brought forward by precedent cases, among others the Supreme Court Judgments 9012/2001 and 7141/2006.

***Argument of the Supreme Court:***

*Credit-entity*: *Bearer-of-*IAJD*-duty*(*x*,*y*,*z*,*money-lender*); (EMVRivas is the beneficiary of a mortgage loan granted by unnamed credit entity);

As established by the source case 9012/2001, the tax duty IAJD has to be paid by the borrower;

*AWR*: If the tax duty IAJD has to be paid by the money-lender, whoever this creditor is (this creditor being the one who acquired the real right associated with being the (real) beneficiary of the registration of the mortgage linked to the loan granted by this creditor), then every such a creditor does;

Therefore, EMVRivas is exempted to pay to the Public Administration the IAJD-duty linked to the registration of the mortgage that warrants the credit granted by the money-lender. The Credit-entity that granted the mortgage loan to EMVRivas is in charge of paying the IAJD.

## 9.4 Conclusions

Wael B. Hallaq's (1985) seminal article "The Logic of Legal Reasoning in Religious and Non-Religious Cultures: The Case of Islamic Law and Common Law" suggested comparing contemporary legal reasoning within Common Law with the main concepts of argumentation of Islamic Jurisprudence developed during the Era of Classical Islam. Inspired by this provocative insight of Hallaq and the thorough study of Islamic Jurisprudence by Walter Young (2017), Rahman et al. (2019) developed a contremporary formal analysis that should facilitate and extend the comparison tasks.

The present paper presents a further step in that direction, comparing not only Scott Brewer's (1996) ERS-schema for the analysis of arguments by precedent cases within Common Law, but we extend it to Civil Law, and quite surprisingly to arguments involving the *interpretation* of legal terms. The advantage of the argumentative stance is that it naturally expresses the dynamics of an argument, and more precisely when disanalogy comes to the fore.

According to our study, whereas from the perspective of Civil Law the point is to settle the emerging Law (who is the one who has to pay the taxes induced by either a mortgage loan or a credit warranted with a mortgage, borrower or creditor?), within Common Law, as stressed by Woods (2015, p. 279), establishing a general Law is not the aim of an argument by precedent cases, despite the fact that the argument as such requires its formulation.

Thus, whereas in the context of Civil Law the concrete specific precedent cases are instrumental to grasp the general Law behind, in the context of Common Law it is the general Schema that is instrumental. Thus, in this respect, the conceptual background underlying some specific argumentation patterns crucial in Civil Law might be closer to the perspective of Islamic Jurisprudence than to the one of Common Law. Perhaps this is not that surprising. After all, Islamic Jurisprudence of the Classical Era seems to have shared many insights of Stoic Logic, Roman Law, and their interaction.

**Acknowledgments** Many thanks to Teresa Lopez-Soto (Sevilla) the editor of present inspiring volume and to Leone Gazziero (STL), Laurent Cesalli (Genève) and Tony Street (Cambridge) leaders of the ERC-Generator project "Logic in Reverse. Fallacies in the Latin and the Islamic traditions", and to Claudio Majolino (STL), associated researcher to that project, for fostering the research leading to the present study.

Many thanks, too, to Matthias Armgardt (Univ. Konstanz), Hans Christian Nordtveit Kvernenes (UMR: 8163, STL), Walter Young (McGill), John Woods (British Columbia) and to Farid Zidani (Alger II), who contributed with many fruitful discussions and insights on the matter.

A special word of gratitude to the private library's Bar Association of Madrid which allowed the first author the access to specialized works on legal terminology in Spanish/English.

## Appendix

### *Summary of the Supreme Court Judgment 9012/2001 (Sentencia del Tribunal Supremo –STS– 9012/2001) dated 19 November 2001. Full text is available on: http://www.poderjudicial.es/search/TS/openDocument/3a301e6cd9d857da/20031030*

The cassation appeal number 2196/1996 filed before the Supreme Court challenged the dismissed judgment issued by the Second Section of the Contentious-Administrative Chamber of the National Court, dated 23 January 1996, on the contentious-administrative appeal brought by *Inmobiliaria Manuel Asín, S.A.* against the April 23, 1992, judgment of the Central Economic-Administrative Court (Tribunal Económico-Administrativo Central –TEAC), which, at the time, had dismissed the appeal lodged against the judgment of the Regional Court of Aragon, not giving rise to a claim filed against the settlement of 14,901,015 pesetas for the concept of Tax on Documented Legal Acts (Impuesto de Actos Jurídicos Documentados –IAJD). This amount was ordered on the occasion of a mortgage loan of 1,702,000,000 pesetas that had been granted by the *Caja de Ahorros y Monte de Piedad de Zaragoza, Aragón y Rioja* (Ibercaja) which had been implemented by a public deed on May 4, 1989.

The appellant party submits its cassation appeal and articulates its reasons from the common point that in a mortgage loan there are two independent legal conventions or businesses (the loan and the mortgage), which require differentiated tax treatment, but which demand a joint exam.

The first instance judgment emphasises the inapplicability to this case of the tax exemption recognized in art. 48.I.B.19 of the Consolidated Text of the Law of Tax on Property Transfer and Documented Legal Acts (texto refundido de la Ley del Impuesto sobre Transmisiones Patrimoniales y Actos Jurídicos Documentados – LITPAJD, in short, ITPAJD) enacted on December 30, 1980. This judgment also omits any reference to the analysis of the problem of the duality of conventions, which the appellant party claimed as a fundamental argument of its contestation, and of the need, which was also argued, of a differentiated treatment of that situation for tax purposes. In fact, the judgment of the first instance is limited to an appointment of the judgments of this Chamber that reflected the doctrine of the inapplicability of the above mentioned exemption, although without transcribing, even briefly, its argumentation for inapplicability and therefore, it maintained the affirmation that the taxpayer, in a deed of a mortgage loan, is the beneficiary of the main legal business, that is, the borrower.

The Supreme Court Judgment 9012/2001 (STS 9012/2001) maintains that:

> (. . .) it is true that the traditional interpretation of this Chamber [3rd Chamber of the Supreme Court of Spain] has always accepted the premise that the taxable event, mortgage loan, was and is unique, and therefore, the conclusion of its subjection to AJD is, nowadays, coherent, whatever the legislative tendencies that, may be in the near future, could consecrate mortgage loan exemption in this particular tax—. (p. 3, para. 2)[13]

and that:

> In any case, the unity of the taxable event related to the loan produces the consequence that the only possible beneficiary is the borrower, in accordance with the provision in art. 8°.d) in relation to 15.1 of the 1980 and 1993 ITPAJD Consolidated Text, and also in relation to art. 18 of its 1981 Regulations, now art. 25 of the current Regulations (enacted on May 29, 1995) which refers already to the constitution of, among others, mortgage rights as guarantee of its loan and not to that of loans guaranteed by a mortgage. (p. 3, para. 3)[14]

The Supreme Court Judgment, therefore, **dismissed the appeal.**

---

[13]Our translation for: *(. . .) es lo cierto que la interpretación tradicional de esta Sala ha aceptado siempre la premisa de que el hecho imponible, préstamo hipotecario, era y es único, y que, por tanto, la conclusión de su sujeción a AJD, hoy por hoy, es coherente, cualesquiera sean las tendencias legislativas que, en un futuro próximo, pudieran consagrar su exención en esta última modalidad impositiva–.*

[14]Our translation for: *En cualquier caso, la unidad del hecho imponible en torno al préstamo, produce la consecuencia de que el único sujeto pasivo posible es el prestatario, de conformidad con lo establecido en el art. 8°.d), en relación con el 15.1 del Texto Refundido ITP y AJD, y en relación, asimismo, con el art. 18 del Reglamento de 1981, hoy art. 25 del vigente de 29 de Mayo de 1995, que, por cierto, ya se refiere a la constitución de, entre otros, derechos de hipoteca en garantía de un préstamo y no a la de préstamos garantizados con hipoteca.*

## *Summary of the Supreme Court Judgment 7141/2006 (Sentencia del Tribunal Supremo –STS– 7141/2006) dated 31 October 2006. Full Text is Available on: http://www.poderjudicial.es/search/AN/openDocument/12ebfb21e3676207/20061214*

Cassation appeal number 4593/2001 brought by *Establecimientos Industriales y Servicios, S.A.* (*EISSA, S.A.*), against the judgment of the Contentious-Administrative Chamber of the National Court issued in the appeal of the aforesaid jurisdictional order brought by the forenamed commercial entity against the decision of the Central Economic-Administrative Court dated 21 October 1998, which dismissed the appeal raised against the decision of the Regional Court of Catalonia on April 9, 1997, that denied the request for the return of undue income of 49,500,000 pesetas as Documented Legal Acts.

On June 12, 1992, the *Caixa d'Estalvis i Pensions de Barcelona* (*La Caixa*) opened a credit account in favour of *EISSA, S.A.*, up to a maximum amount of 5,500,000,000 pesetas. This credit account was guaranteed by a mortgage over an estate owned by company *INMA, S.A.* to warrant the resulting balance of the account that *La Caixa* accredited, up to 5,500,000,000 pesetas, of the amounts exceeding the limit granted as a result of interest debts, of late payment interest, as well as a sum for expenses and costs, for a total amount of 9,900,000,000 pesetas. As the estate was valued at 1,169,050,000 pesetas in case of auction, *EISSA, S.A.* was asked to establish a joint liability clause as guarantee of the credit by Mr Enrique, Mr Jon, Mr Sebastián and the commercial entities *INMA, S.A.*, *HIDRODATA, S.A.* and *Molinos Hidráulicos, S.A.* This deed was accompanied by a self-settlement for Documented Legal Acts on a tax base of 9,900,000,000 pesetas. At a rate of 0.50 percent, the debt deposited was 49,500,000 pesetas.

In 1993, *EISSA, S.A.* impugned the self-settlement and requested the return of the amount deposited, considering the exemption provided in art. 48.I.B.19 of the Consolidated Text of the Law of Tax on Property Transfer and Documented Legal Acts (ITPAJD) enacted on December 30, 1980. This claim was denied by agreement, notified on July 27, 1995.

On July 31, 1995, an economic-administrative claim was filed against the previous agreement, claiming the provenance of the exemption invoked in the process, reason why the refund of the amount deposited was requested; besides, it was pointed out that the tax base taken into consideration was not correct, as it should only be either the value of the mortgaged property, or that of the credit. The Regional Court of Catalonia issued a judgment on April 9, 1997, dismissing the claim because the alleged exemption was considered not applicable, and the tax base set by the financial entity for the self-settlement was considered right.

*EISSA, S.A.* filed an appeal against the aforementioned judgment of the Economic-Administrative Regional Court of Catalonia (Tribunal Económico-Administrativo Regional –TEAR– de Cataluña), insisting on the allegations made in the first instance, and on the contravention of the Sixth Directive (Sixth European Economic Community Council Directive of 17 May 1977) by requiring another tax, in addition to VAT, for the same operation. The Central Economic Administrative Court (TEAC), in a judgment dated 21 October 1998, agreed to dismiss this appeal and confirm the contested judgement.

The Chamber of this Jurisdiction (contentious-administrative) of the National Court issued a judgment dismissing the appeal and confirming the judgment of the TEAC for complying with the legal system on February 27, 2001.

The juridical representation of *EISSA, S.A.* brought a cassation appeal to the Supreme Court, requesting for a judgment to quash the one previous one –declaring it null and void–, a declaration of the inadmissibility of taxation for Documented Legal Acts of the deed of credit opening with mortgage guarantee, in recognition of a particular legal situation, and to agree to the return of the unduly deposited for such concept, plus the delay interests, or otherwise, at least a declaration that the maximum taxable base cannot exceed the value of the mortgaged that guarantees the credit.

The Supreme Court **dismissed this cassation appeal** for considering this operation as a dual business: a loan (main business) and a mortgage (subsidiary business). As a loan it has to be fully taxed, and as a mortgage it has to be taxed as a mortgage loan, considering in this case that the mortgage is subject to the loan. Being the loan the main business, the tax base for all concepts (both loan and mortgage taxes) is that of the loan and *not* that of the good that guarantees the loan. The judgment also pointed out that the taxpayer is always the beneficiary of the main legal business, that is, the borrower.

## Reasoning Behind the Dismissal of Appeals

As mentioned in the analysis of the Judgment 9012/2001, the rationale for the dismissal of the appeals is that:

> (. . .) the traditional interpretation of this Chamber [3rd Chamber of the Supreme Court of Spain] has always accepted the premise that the taxable event, mortgage loan, was and is unique, and therefore, the conclusion of its subjection to AJD is, nowadays, coherent, whatever the legislative tendencies that, may be in the near future, could consecrate mortgage loan exemption in this particular tax—. (p. 3, para. 2. See footnote 13 for the original text)

and therefore, "(. . .) the unity of the taxable event related to the loan produces the consequence that the only possible beneficiary [taxpayer] is the borrower—" (p. 3, para. 3. See footnote 14 for the original text).

The jurisprudence of this Chamber [3rd Chamber of the Supreme Court of Spain] has repeatedly understood that article 29 (art. 30 in the ITPAJD of 1980) of the 1993 ITPAJD Consolidated Text and article 68 of its 1995 Regulations indicates that, for notarial documents affected by IAJD, "(. . .) "the beneficiary is the purchaser of the good or of the right and, failing that, the persons who request notarial documents, or those in whose interest the documents are issued"—"[15] (quoted in the STS 7141/2006, p. 3, para. 3). The purchaser of the good or of the right can only be the borrower, *not* because of an argument such as the unity of the taxable event related to the loan, as occurs in the modality of onerous transfers –art. 8°.d) in relation with art. 15.1 of the 1980 and 1993 ITPAJD Consolidated Text, and also in relation with art. 25 of the 1995 Regulations (art. 18 in the Regulations of 1981), but because the *right* referred to in the precept is the loan reflected in the notarial document, even if it is guaranteed with a mortgage and its registration in the Property Registry is the constituent element of guarantee. In conclusion, art. 31 of the 1980 and 1993 ITPAJD Consolidated Text demands, among others, the requirement that the deeds or notarial acts which contain acts or contracts inscribable in the Property Registry they pay inseparably for both, the loan and the mortgage.

## *Summary of the Supreme Court Judgment 3422/2018 (Sentencia del Tribunal Supremo –STS– 3422/2018) dated 16 October 2018. Full text is available on: http://www.poderjudicial.es/search/openDocument/979d8e2ccabb7187*

Cassation appeal number 5350/2017 brought by the *Empresa Municipal de la Vivienda de Rivas-Vaciamadrid, S.A.* (the Municipal Housing Company of Rivas-Vaciamadrid), against the judgment of the Contentious-Administrative Chamber (Fourth Section) of the Supreme Court of Justice of the Community of Madrid on June 19, 2017, issued in an ordinary procedure no. 501/2016, on the settlement of the tax on Documented Legal Acts of a public deed of formalization of a mortgage loan on several dwellings.

The *Empresa Municipal de la Vivienda de Rivas-Vaciamadrid, S.A.* (EMVRivas, S.A.) filed a tax exempt self-settlement for Documented Legal Acts regarding the public deed of constitution of a mortgage loan. As basis for the exemption, it invoked to article 45.I.B.12 of the 1993 ITPAJD Consolidated Text.

Once the Technical Office for Tax Inspection of the Community of Madrid confirmed that the useful size of the dwellings for which the loan was formalized was less than 90 square meters, the settlement of the taxes for the concept of Documented Legal Acts regarding the mortgage liability of the aforementioned dwellings was charged.

A contentious-administrative appeal was brought by the same party before the Madrid Chamber, in which, in addition to the tax exemption, the quashing of the charged settlement was requested. This appeal was founded on the fact that the borrower is considered *not* liable for the tax on Documented Legal Acts because they

[15]Our translation for: *"será sujeto pasivo el adquirente del bien o derecho y, en su defecto, las personas que insten o soliciten documentos notariales, o aquellos en cuyo interés se expidan".*

are *not* the beneficiary of this business. The Economic-Administrative Regional Court (TEAR) of Madrid rejected the economic-administrative appeal brought by the interested party (in which only the origin of the exemption was defended).

The procedural representation of the plaintiff prepared a cassation appeal in which infringed norms were identified in article 45.I.B.12 of the 1993 ITPAJD Consolidated Text. In their formal claim document, they also claimed the illegality of article 68, paragraph 2, of the 1995 ITPAJD Regulations.

Regarding the issue of the beneficiary, they stated that requiring for the mortgage debtor to pay for the tax is against the protectionist regulations toward mortgage debtors that exist in the European Union. For this purpose, they recalled that the judgment of the Civil Chamber (First Section) of the Supreme Court (STS 5618/2015)[16], dated 23 December 2015 (fallen on appeal 2658/2013), considered that the money-lender is *not* excluded from the taxes that may be accrued due to the commercial operation, but "(. . .) "at least in regard of the tax on Documented Legal Acts, the lender is the beneficiary for matters referring to the constitution of the right and, in any case, of the issuance of copies, records and appropriate testimonies"—" (quoted in the STS 3422/2018, p. 3, point 2)[17]; so, a clause in which the tax is transferred to the other party –the borrower– is abusive.

On this occasion the Supreme Court understood that the person obligated to pay the tax in such cases was the creditor, subject in whose interest the granted loan and the mortgage established as refund guarantee are publicly documented.

The Supreme Court held that loans are *not* registrable, according to article 2 of the Mortgage Law (Ley Hipotecaria) and article 7 of its Regulations, as they are obviously *not* a real right, *nor* does the right have the typical real significance mentioned in the second of these precepts (since they do not modify, now or in the future, several of the rights of ownership over real estate or inherent to real rights). The mortgage, on the other hand, is *not* only registrable, but it is also the mortgage is a real right. So much so, that article 1875 of the Civil Code strongly states that "(. . .) it is indispensable, for the mortgage to be validly constituted, that its concluding document be registered in the Property Registry"[18]; article 1280 of the Civil Code corroborates that and the Mortgage Law, in its article 130, specifies that statement when affirming that the procedure for direct execution against mortgaged goods "(. . .) can only be exercised as realization of a registered mortgage, on the basis of points that are contained in the title and included in its entry"[19].

[16]Cf. full judgment 5618/2015 on: http://www.poderjudicial.es/search/documento/TS/7580921/Clausulas%20abusivas/20160122

[17]Our translation for: *"al menos en lo que respecta al impuesto sobre actos jurídicos documentados, será sujeto pasivo en lo que se refiere a la constitución del derecho y, en todo caso, la expedición de las copias, actas y testimonios que interese".*

[18]Our translation for art. 1875 of the Civil Code: *(. . .) es indispensable, para que la hipoteca quede válidamente constituida, que el documento en que se constituya sea inscrito en el Registro de la Propiedad.*

[19]Our translation for art. 130 of Mortgage Law: *(. . .) sólo podrá ejercitarse como realización de una hipoteca inscrita, sobre la base de aquellos extremos contenidos en el título que se hayan recogido en el asiento respectivo.*

The fact that *the mortgage is a real right of registry constitution* makes it clearly *the main business for tax purposes in public deeds in which mortgage loans or loans with mortgage guarantee are documented*, since the only reason that makes such complex legal act be submitted to the tax on Documented Legal Acts is that it is registrable; in fact, of the two businesses that make up that act, only the mortgage is registrable.

If we still consider the loan as the main business it does *not* make much sense to submit to the tax a non-registrable legal business only because there is an accessory real right constituted as a guarantee of compliance with the main one.

The Supreme Court held also that:

> (...) there is *no* doubt that the beneficiary of the document in question is *no* other than the creditor, because they (and only they) are qualified to exercise the (privileged) actions that the code offers to the holders of the registered rights. They are the only party interested in the registration of the mortgage (the determining element subject to the tax analysed here), since the mortgage is ineffective if it is *not* registered in the Property Registry [emphasis added]. (STS 3422/2018, p. 11, para. 9)[20]

and that:

> Therefore, article 68.2 of the Regulations [ITPAJD Regulations of 1995] does *not* have the interpretative or explanatory quality granted by the jurisprudence that we are now modifying [emphasis added]; on the contrary, it constitutes an obvious regulatory excess that makes the provision contained therein illegal. Such illegality must be declared in the judgment hereby as provided in article 27.3 of the Law of this Jurisdiction [Contentious-Administrative Jurisdiction Law]. (STS 3422/2018, p. 12, para. 1)[21]

Thus, the conclusions were:

1. Based on the previous reasoning, we can now answer the question that we have considered preferential, out of the two questions raised by the First Section (Civil Chamber) of this Chamber (Supreme Court). The beneficiary of a mortgage (by loan over itself or as guarantee of a loan) is the money-lender and *not* the borrower. Therefore, the tax on Documented Legal Acts –when the document subject to the tax is a public deed of a mortgage (by loan over itself or as guarantee of a loan)– should be paid by the lender and *not* by the borrower.
2. In order to comply with the decree of admission, the above statement needs to be completed making it explicit that such a decision involves adoption of a guideline

[20]Our translation for: *(...) no nos cabe la menor duda de que el beneficiario del documento que nos ocupa no es otro que el acreedor hipotecario, pues él (y solo él) está legitimado para ejercitar las acciones (privilegiadas) que el ordenamiento ofrece a los titulares de los derechos inscritos. Solo a él le interesa la inscripción de la hipoteca (el elemento determinante de la sujeción al impuesto que analizamos), pues ésta carece de eficacia alguna sin la incorporación del título al Registro de la Propiedad.*

[21]Our translation for: *El artículo 68.2 del reglamento, por tanto, no tiene el carácter interpretativo o aclaratorio que le otorga la jurisprudencia que ahora modificamos, sino que constituye un evidente exceso reglamentario que hace ilegal la previsión contenida en el mismo, ilegalidad que debemos declarar en la presente sentencia conforme dispone el artículo 27.3 de la Ley de esta Jurisdicción.*

opposite to that supported by the jurisprudence of this Chamber (Third Camber – Contentious-Administrative Chamber– of the Supreme Court) until now, as presented in the judgments (STS 9012/2001 and STS 7141/2006) among others, and therefore modifying the previous jurisprudential doctrine.

Thus, in this case, the Supreme Court understood that the settlement was charged to those who do *not* have the quality of beneficiary, reason why they were *not* the taxable person for this tax. Therefore, **the cassation appeal was deemed** in favour of the *Empresa Municipal de la Vivienda de Rivas-Vaciamadrid, S.A.* **This judgment modified all the previous jurisprudence.**

## References


Alchourrón, C. E. (1961). Los argumentos jurídicos *a fortiori* y *a pari*. *Revista Jurídica de Buenos Aires, IV*, 177–199.

Al-Shīrāzī, A. I. (1987). In ʻAlī b. ʻAbd al-ʻAzīz al-ʻUmayrīnī. Al-[illegible]afāh (Ed.), *Al-Maʻūna fī al-Jadal*. Kuwait: Manshūrāt Markaz al-Makhṭūṭāt wa-al-Turāth.

Al-Shīrāzī, A. I. (2003). *Al-Lumaʻ fī Uṣūl al-Fiqh*. Beirut: Dār al-Kutub al-ʻIlmiyah.

Al-Shīrāzī, Abū Isḥāq. (2016, February 1). *Mulakhkhaṣ fī al-Jadal*. Retrieved from https://upload.wikimedia.org/wikisource/ar/e/ea/[illegible].pdf

Bartha, P. F. A. (2010). *By Parallel Reasoning. The Construction and Evaluation of Analogical Arguments*. Oxford: Oxford University Press.

Brewer, S. (1996, March). Exemplary reasoning: semantics, pragmatics, and the rational force of legal argument by analogy. *Harvard Law Review, 109*(5), 923–1028.

Hage, J. C., Leenes, R., & Lodder, A. R. (1994). Hard cases: A procedural approach. *Artificial Intelligence and Law, 2*, 113–166.

Hallaq, W. B. (1985). The logic of legal reasoning in religious and non-religious cultures: The case of Islamic law and common law. *Cleveland State Law Review, 34*, 79–96.

Kloosterhuis, H. (2000). Analogy argumentation in law: A dialectical perspective. *Artificial Intelligence and Law, 8*, 173–187. https://doi.org/10.1023/A:1008385531494.

Posner, R. A. (1995). *Overcoming law*. Cambridge, Massachusetts/London: Harvard University Press.

Prakken, H. (1995). From logic to dialectics in legal argument. In *Proceedings of the Fifth International Conference on artificial intelligence and law* (pp. 165–174). College Park: ACM Press.

Prakken, H., & Sartor, G. (1996). A dialectical model of assessing conflicting arguments in legal reasoning. *Artificial Intelligence and Law, 4*, 331–368.

Rahman, S., Iqbal, M., & Soufi, Y. (2019). *Inferences by parallel reasoning in Islamic jurisprudence. Al-Shīrāzī's insights into the dialectical constitution of meaning and knowledge*. Dordrecht: Springer.

Rissland, E. L., & Ashley, K. D. (1987). A case-based system for trade secrets law. In *Proceedings of the First International Conference on artificial intelligence and law* (pp. 60–66). New York: ACM Press.

Rissland, E. L., & Ashley, K. D. (1989). HYPO: A precedent-based legal reasoner. In G. P. V. Vandenberghe (Ed.), *Advanced topics in law and information technology*. Deventer: Kluwer.

Weinreb, Ll. L. (2005). *Legal reason: The use of analogy in legal argument*. Cambridge: Cambridge University Press.

Woods, J. (2015). *Is legal reasoning irrational? An introduction to the epistemology of law*. London: College Publications.
Young, W. E. (2017). *The dialectical forge. Juridical disputation and the evolution of Islamic law*. Dordrecht: Springer.
Zysow, A. (2013). *The economy of certainty. An introduction to the typology of Islamic legal theory*. Atlanta: Lockwood Press.

## References for Appendix

Civil Code enacted on July 24, 1889 (August 4, 2018 version). Retrieved from https://www.boe.es/eli/es/rd/1889/07/24/(1)
Consolidated Text of the Law of Tax on Property Transfer and Documented Legal Acts (Texto refundido de la Ley del Impuesto sobre Transmisiones Patrimoniales y Actos Jurídicos Documentados) enacted on December 30, 1980. Retrieved from https://www.boe.es/eli/es/rdlg/1980/12/30/3050
Consolidated Text of the Law of Tax on Property Transfer and Documented Legal Acts (Texto refundido de la Ley del Impuesto sobre Transmisiones Patrimoniales y Actos Jurídicos Documentados) enacted on September 24, 1993. Retrieved from https://www.boe.es/eli/es/rdlg/1993/09/24/1
Contentious-Administrative Jurisdiction Law (Ley de la Jurisdicción Contencioso-Administrativa) enacted on July 13, 1998 (July 19, 2017 version). Retrieved from https://www.boe.es/eli/es/l/1998/07/13/29/con/20170719
Mortgage Law (Ley Hipotecaria) enacted on February 8, 1946 (October 6, 2015 version). Retrieved from https://www.boe.es/eli/es/d/1946/02/08/(1)/con/20151006
Mortgage Law Regulations enacted on February 14, 1947 (March 4, 2017 version). Retrieved from https://www.boe.es/eli/es/d/1947/02/14/(1)/con
Regulations enacted on December 29, 1981, of the Consolidated Text of the Law of Tax on Property Transfer and Documented Legal Acts enacted on December 30, 1980. Retrieved from https://www.boe.es/eli/es/rd/1981/12/29/3494
Regulations enacted on May 29, 1995, of the Consolidated Text of the Law of Tax on Property Transfer and Documented Legal Acts enacted on September 24, 1993. Retrieved from https://www.boe.es/eli/es/rd/1995/05/29/828
Sixth European Economic Community Council Directive of 17 May 1977. Retrieved from https://eur-lex.europa.eu/eli/dir/1977/388/oj
Supreme Court Judgment 9012/2001 (Sentencia del Tribunal Supremo 9012/2001) dated 19 November 2001. Retrieved from http://www.poderjudicial.es/search/TS/openDocument/3a301e6cd9d857da/20031030
Supreme Court Judgment 7141/2006 (Sentencia del Tribunal Supremo 7141/2006) dated 31 October 2006. Retrieved from http://www.poderjudicial.es/search/AN/openDocument/12ebfb21e3676207/20061214
Supreme Court Judgment 3422/2018 (Sentencia del Tribunal Supremo 3422/2018) dated 16 October 2018. Retrieved from http://www.poderjudicial.es/search/openDocument/979d8e2ccabb7187

# Chapter 10
# Communication in Tourism: Information Technologies, the Human User, Visual Culture and the Location

**Alcina Pereira de Sousa and Gonçalo Ferreira de Gouveia**

**Abstract** This chapter intends to reflect upon and discuss the discursive materiality and its impact on the (de)construction of the identity of destinations – location, people and cultural artefacts as represented in multimodal texts (verbal and non-verbal language in interplay) among the wide array of communicative events in tourism. The analysis of meaning production and reception in this dialogic encounter is believed to benefit from a multidisciplinary analysis of some discursive practices across domains in tourism. They comprise some instances (i) of speakers' interaction in local accommodation facilities mediated by digital media, for example booking.com. Guesthouse – Message: Guest – SMS, cross-culturally, (ii) together with cultural traits of multimodal kind (Kress G, Van Leeuwen T, Multimodal discourse: the modes and media of contemporary communication. Routledge, London, 2001) in destinations. It also aims to promote some necessary reflection on the nature of representations and the impact of multimodal communication in users' interaction evidenced in communicative practices in the realm of immersive tourism, among other alternative types. In the scope of the approach foreshadowed in the title, this chapter also draws on online visitors' comments to one of the cafés displayed on TripAdvisor's webpages about a destination (pages 1 to 10; entries: March to September 2019, Portuguese version), all of which of cross-cultural kind. It is argued that committed citizenship is fostered by the necessary dialogue in urban areas between visitors and locals/residents about and with the location, facilitated by information technologies, the human user, and visual culture. As such, the dialogue should involve multidisciplinary research fields and practitioners to foster effective communication among participants: visitors – residents and designers of interactive media. These act upon the image of a location and are also impacted by the image

A. P. de Sousa (✉)
Faculty of Arts and Humanities, University of Madeira, Campus da Penteada, Funchal, Madeira, Portugal
e-mail: alcina.sousa@staff.uma.pt

G. F. de Gouveia
Faculty of Exact Sciences and Engineering, University of Madeira, Campus da Penteada, Funchal, Madeira, Portugal
e-mail: geom@uma.pt

 
T. Lopez-Soto (ed.), *Dialog Systems*, Logic, Argumentation & Reasoning 22,
https://doi.org/10.1007/978-3-030-61438-6_10

created. Given the wide scope of the study, mostly unidirectional communicative events are object of analysis as the possible but diverse patterns of hosts' reactions should be collected and examined in further studies.

**Keywords** Multimodality · Mediated interaction · Human-Centred mediation: Location · Image · Identity · Multidisciplinary approach

> "It is obvious that for the building up of society, its units and subdivisions, and the understandings which prevail between its members some processes of communication are needed" (Sapir 1931: 104)[1]

## 10.1 Introduction

Sapir (1931) offers a point of entry into the multifaceted communicative process among the members of the community under study in several fields, from linguistics and its many areas of study,[2] to sociology, and communication studies with the advent of technologies. Global communication is first and foremost geared by information technologies determining human agency across media and domains, from the public and private spheres, largely disseminated in interdiscursive practices within business and economy, politics, and science among others. These presuppose an understanding of a so-called "interaction order", as discussed by Rampton (2018, p. 2), also borrowing from Goffman (1963, 1967, 1971 and 1983), in the scope of "a level of social organization that lies somewhere between linguistic structure on the one hand, and institutional and societal order, on the other".

Hence, computer and information systems managers, business operations managers, applications software developers, communication consultants, to name but a few, are in demand in the global agenda (Leal 2005, Marujo 2008, Perniola 2016) to meet other requirements rather than the purely automation processes likely to be evidencing the role performed by systems software developers. What was formerly mostly dictated by the print word or human interaction is now diverse and more complex.

Most visual representations of locations have been disseminated virtually in the worldwide web through social networks (especially Facebook), cinema, soap operas (film-induced tourism, Beeton 2005, Zimmerman and Reeves 2009, Carvalho et al. 2013, 2014, Sousa and Silva 2017), and promotional engines for tourist destinations such as TripAdvisor, or thematic blogs.

However commonsensical it might be, a diachronic perspective appears to be relevant to be brought to the fore. Electronic navigation allows for the user to access

[1]Cf. Sapir's essay "Communication" (1931), issued in the entry of the Encyclopaedia of the Social Sciences

[2]Cf. the research undertaken by Jaworski.

and interact with (un)familiar landscapes, environments, territories and hybrid products, of artificial and virtual kind, formerly dictated by the conversational exchanges between visitor/travel agent (face-to-face or at distance communication). Now the interactive multimodal contexts trigger cognitive and emotional realms, according to Martins (2009, 2010, 2019; Martins and Maffesoli 2011), formerly associated with the print word, reflective thinking, logos, but now oriented towards pathos, emotions and senses, reinforced with immediacy conveyed by images and quantitative data.

Apart from the issues raised so far, the focus on the necessary reflection on committed citizenship, particularly from the multidisciplinary framework in social sciences, is meant to shed light on possible ways to foster the dialogic encounter in urban areas between visitors and locals/residents.

These may entail situations associated with service encounters[3] across segments (accommodation, food and beverage, transportation, reservations and sales, events and recreation, marketing the past and heritage, and so on). These comprise, for instance, communication between visitor/resident and the location via technological gadgets, social media (Sects. 10.3.1 and 10.3.2), and/or representations of signs, devices and other objects (e.g. road signs).

Conversational exchanges offer evidence in the realm of visitor/resident monitoring, via computer-automated interaction, in social networks. Those are grouped according to communicative functions, such as, giving instructions (e.g. Google map, geolocation apps, location-based apps), rewarding and reinforcing having been provided multiple solutions in the sort of web interaction across domains and cultures (cf. call centres).

On the contrary, speech acts are object of interdisciplinary study within pragmatics (with a focus on intercultural pragmatics), cognitive studies and human computer interaction. These acts may comprise, for instance, questioning, negotiating, describing and explaining, persuading, apologising, asserting, ordering or even starting and keeping up conversation, getting around very uncomfortable topics (socio-cultural heritage), or ending a conversation (cf. Eurolinguistix, Language Use Portrait, by Grzega & Schöner, http://www.eurolinguistix.com, 2008). Following Searle and Austin, this study should consider not only the propositional content of speech acts but also the illocutionary force.

The analysis of multiple discursive practices in tourism, collected at the regional, national and international levels by the authors (Sect. 10.3 of this study), though constrained by accessibility issues, comprise some authentic turn-takings collected by the authors, pictures/images of cultural artefacts; street signs, notices (information boards), and other non-verbal communication artefacts combining verbal language in the process of mediating the users' – visitors' experience and meant to facilitate consumers' interaction with locations. They offer evidence of the discursive materiality and impact on the (de) construction of the identity of destinations/locations

[3]The language of service encounters by J. César Félix-Brasdefer (Cambridge University Press, 2015), https://doi.org/10.1017/CBO9781139565431

and people, perceived from a pragmalinguistic and discursive stance equally drawing on conversation analysis and techniques used in corpus linguistics (online visitors' comments from pages 1 to 10, on a location, collected from March to September 2019, in the Portuguese version, on TripAdvisor's webpages).

The role of pragmatics is to analyse the meaning of utterances in context. Conversational analysis applied to turn-takings in the business domain, including tourism, has flashed out speakers' interaction of short and formal kind. When interaction is mediated by the digital medium, as is the case of local accommodation facilities, for instance, encoded interactions may lead to speakers' impolite reactions if the interpersonal and intercultural communicative strategies are not considered (Spencer and Oatey 2000). Hence, issues of image and identity, as discussed by Arundale (2010), come to the fore.

**The Methodology**

The methodology adopted in this paper departs from the reappraisal of the forms of communicative practice indebted to society, long advanced by Sapir[4] (1931), and by Simmel (1950),[5] in that the urban setting, so-called "metropolis", is perceived from a sort of ecology of communicative forms and practices. Indeed, the evidence selected for the discussion of the tenets underpins the researchers' own sort of ethnographic observation, also as privileged and attentive participants of the dialogue among different communicative practices and interlocutors.

The illustrations under study are intended to uncover explicit and implicit communicative events likely to be disambiguated by citizens' interactions reinforced by the experiential function (briefly discussed by Meacci and Liberatore 2018) in an (in)effective communicative practice.

The major issues will be discussed and illustrated along an inductive approach drawing on a selection of multimodal texts (verbal and non-verbal communication) evidenced in several segments in tourism, given their referential to ideational, and experiential clines (Halliday 1978, 1989, 1994). In this regard, state Simpson and Nicholls (2005): "Interpretation is not just about informing – it is a much more dynamic process that engages and stimulates the visitor by revealing meaning and relationships through first-hand experience, the use of original objects, and through illustrative media. It is not just the communication of factual information".

Hence, benefits can be drawn from the field of linguistic anthropology as advanced by Oliveira and Silva (2009). The repertoire in Linguistics may uncover the relations between language and context. Yet, it should be complemented by the analysis of first-hand knowledge and experience by professionals in their professional environment. In the case of the discursive domains involving locations, it should observe, for instance, destination iconography, cultural representative icons, namely monuments, gastronomy, among others. Along this line, linguists as *experts*

[4]Cf. Sapir's essay "Communication" (1931), issued in the entry of the Encyclopaedia of the Social Sciences.

[5]Cf. G. Simmel's essay "The metropolis and mental life" (1903).

are sharing their tools of analysis in several domains. Among the domains stand out ecolinguistics and recent developments (cf. for instance, Chichorro 2003; Chen 2016; Bogusławska-Tafelska and Haładewicz-Grzelak 2019) together with the works by Sarangi (2006) within the fields of applied linguistics to specialized discourse (Sousa and Marçalo 2018), as well as intercultural communicative strategies (Spencer and Oatey 2000) and resources in use (SMS, blogs, images, menus, urban signs, communications systems for multicultural contexts). All these contribute to a better understanding of image and identity underlying the interaction at stake (Arundale 2010).

The complex issues of human-computer interaction are worth considering in the scope of inter- and cross-cultural communication. On the one hand, users have dissimilar levels of intercultural awareness, knowledge and understanding of inter and cross-cultural communication, although a lot of research and theoretical input on standard rules of interaction across languages, particularly in the field of intercultural pragmatics (see for instance the overview afforded by Huang and Kecskes 2017) has been spread. On the other hand, the availability of massive data object of diverse categorization leads to contradictory attitudes concerning their reliability, shaping therefore very different perceptions of the same observed feature. Of course, none of these problems, although real and rather widespread, prevents communication to take place. Humans share an uncanny ability to find a common ground even in adverse scenarios when it takes to communicating and necessity presses.

## 10.2 From Production to Reception: Multidisciplinary Approach

> "Most people don't leave their home saying, "I'm going to be a cultural tourist today," but often the motivations, actions, and activities of these individuals are impacted by the availability of cultural assets." (Hargrove 2014: 3)

Hargrove's stance provides a broader stance on the multifaceted kind of meaning making and production to underpin the reappraisal of multimodal communicative processes indebted to the interdiscursive domains of tourism and leisure: **from the interaction to the resources in use in and about the location.**

A quick google search of the key words "tourism, intercultural communication" (accessed 4th October 2019), displays 6,630,000 entries supported by various theoretical frameworks and involving the reference to multiple actors and segments (hospitality, food and beverage, accommodation, transportation, leisure, marketing and advertising).

Apart from the cultural diversity of locations advertised, disseminated and offered in the virtual context, it is challenging to acknowledge publications of empirical and academic kind on the key issues addressed in this chapter: information technology, the human user and the location. In fact, literature in the crisscrossing field has pointed out privileged interlocutors of the location facilitating the encounter between the visitor/traveller and residents. These are: the guide as interpreter (Brito 2011), intercultural mediator, leader and location ambassador (Brito 2008); the tourist operator (agencies) as service provider (organization, enterprise or individual providing a service to others); the internet user surfing the web; and the community.

In so doing, the sort of diverse actors' narratives in and about a location should not be understood without analysing the strategies involving programming and graphic design, among others. In this regard Maybin and Mercer (1996a, b) advance that "the term 'design', in multimodal research, signals a shift away from a focus on verbal language alone, and a move forward from a focus on critique and ideological stances in texts". For Kress and van Leeuwen (2001: 50) design entails "the organisation of what is to be articulated into a blueprint for production". Consequently, communication draws on a wider array of semiotic modes.

Furthermore, these take into close consideration the structural aspects of visual culture, particularly from an anthropological point of view, within the sphere of cyberculture because of conditioning the users, whose visual narratives are transformed by their experiences in this domain.

It is thus possible to account for the transformation of an actual (in the physical sense) act of appropriation to be perceived and accepted as a process of identification, reducing the threatening nature that has prevailed for so long in this kind of interaction. This is then evidenced in the plethora of detailed, close-up and camera-on-hand, images of equipment, now largely disseminated in online sites, for instance, advertising local accommodation (formerly intended to afford a critical appraisal).

**One fundamental aspect in this context is human-computer interaction**: from reception (briefly tackled) to production. The prevalence of programmer-logic and the so-called programmer economy (sensitive to the scarce offer of available bites for memory believed to be necessary to a standard user up to the nineteen eighties) determined that only a fragment of the potential recipients of the new tools could take full advantage of new technology.

Moreover, it aimed at leading users to an encoded pattern of behaviour, deemed correct and economically sound. At the same time, it creates a specific mindset regarding the sort of specialization required to deal with digital tools, passed on from industrial revolution manuals onwards. This was very quick, and rather remarkable digital move trend, henceforth up to now, though not addressed by all generations, or at least not all the individuals, to the same extent.

Adaptability and conformity are therefore the prevailing rules, not presupposing users' in-depth knowledge of the workings of the tools, but a wide-range knowledge of information processing. This is intended to be carefully shaped as an in-depth competence.

Developing a panoply of competences has exerted a strong influence upon the sort of requirements and skills which technology sets on users and, most importantly, on the way users are perceived and understand themselves. In fact, this entailed a complex shift from a human-centred system.

The emphasis is placed on discourse broadly perceived as language in its social context, i.e. from a stretch of language – spoken or written – often referred to as 'texts' in context, as defined by Crystal (2001) with its bearings to applied linguistics. Hence, from a socio-historical perspective, following Foucault (1980), discourse (Maybin and Mercer 1996b: 42) "refers to socially and historically situated domains of knowledge or ways of construing the world".[6] In so doing the construct "text" is a broader one entailing both spoken and written language, and, most recently, visual images, which are then analysed in terms of: differences and similarities in the discursive constructions and cultural traits/artefacts. Equally relevant for the study of culturally diverse practices carried out by varied languages and codes figures the research by Jaworski (2005), combining sociolinguistics and discourse analysis, notably discursive and multimodal approaches to tourism, mobility and globalization, display of languages in space, Linguistic and semiotic spaces landscapes, media discourse and nonverbal communication (Baracuhy 2010).

The recent developments of discourse analysis, geolinguistics, pragmatics and semiotics, along with theoretical perspectives on proximizing strategies indebted to CMC (Kopytowska 2015), have contributed to uncovering pragmalinguistic strategies. These underlie experiential, ideational functions of language use to foster citizens' (residents'- non-residents' and visitors') sense of place, in an emotional crescendo, in the construction of meanings in and beyond texts in the discursive and social context. They determine a way of perceiving unfamiliar topics in interdiscursive domains.

This view is complemented with two other aspects. One following Leu et al. (2013, p. 1158), in that new literacies are deictic, multiple, multimodal and multifaceted (White 1995). Another aspect, also in the scope of linguistics and intercultural communication, is advanced by Piller (2007: 208) in that: "'new world order' with its 'new economy'... people of widely different cultural and linguistic backgrounds have been thrown into contact more than ever before. Cultural and linguistic contact may occur in the flows of information and mass media, as well as in the flows of actual people in migration and tourism."

The focus will be then on interpreting language, be it verbal,[7] non-verbal, or multimodal (i.e. in its social semiotic scope), as carrier of cultural practices, thereby (dis)empowering citizens (Foucault 1998a, b) in their interaction with the signs of the world (Kress and van Leeuwen 2001).

Moreover, in their article about linguistic citizenship, Rampton et al. (2018, p. 4)[8] draw on Hymes,[9] in that communicative practices perceived from an ethnographic

---

[6]Op. cit. Ibidem.

[7]Verbal language is understood as making part of any communicative event resorting to natural languages following Saussure (1915)

[8]Rampton, B., Cooke, M. & Holmes, S. (2018). Promoting Linguistic Citizenship: Issues, problems & possibilities. Working Papers in Urban Language & Literacies 233.

[9]Cf. Hymes, D. (1977). Foundations in Sociolinguistics: An Ethnographic Approach. London: Tavistock. Hymes, D. (1980). Ethnographic monitoring. In Language in Education: Ethnolinguistic Essays. Washington: CAL. 104118 Hymes, D. (1969). The use of anthropology: Critical, political, personal. In Dell Hymes (ed.) Reinventing Anthropology. Ann Arbor: University of Michigan Press, pp. 3–82.

sociolinguistic perspective are analytical, 'what is' rather than 'what should be' language choice and use. They turn the focus "on the very variable ways in which individual linguistic features with identifiable social and cultural associations get clustered together whenever people communicate" (p. 5).

In so doing, they put forth the term 'voice' "as an individual's communicative power and effectiveness within the here-&-now of specific events" (p. 6). "This kind of account can cover both 'top-down' and 'bottom-up' trajectories, involving a variety of people, practices, media and types of text, working in cooperative and/or conflictual relationships within and across specific events, and it can of course be turned to political processes".

Cultural tourism reflects, on the one hand, the importance of this structural construct and materializes a set of specific situations in which its importance may be perceived (Hughes 2002, Barretto 2007, Ivanovic 2008). First, one should set forth the fact that there is a seemingly noticeable difference between the cultural strands of tourism and cultural tourism *per se*.

In the first circumstance, culture, understood as an asset stands for a specific set of events through which visitors may gather the perception of appropriating, by geographical proximity, or proximizing strategies in CMC (Kopytowska 2015), something that is only relevant within their own sphere of experience from that moment onwards, and as such.

On the other hand, cultural tourism proposes an experience that to a lesser or higher extent bridges the gap in a broader, significant and enduring way and includes language learning by participation. It thus enables what may be understood as an act of appropriation, but one that is realised at the level of participation that is not fulfilled by the act of recording and sharing pictures or words of some sort. This way the concept of cultural tourism demands from its actors/mediators new responsibilities.

The experience of standardised and crystallised culture is replaced by a participatory experience – and, most importantly, the evolutionary recycling of that experience. In this scenario, digital interactive technologies play an essential role once they enable the fundamental flow of prior information necessary to foster some level of immersion. But its role in no way ends there: it extends to the "during" an "after" interaction process allowing for the necessary support to the construction of multiple experiences which extrapolate from a given set of data.

Setting a strategy is at the core of this process. It is only feasible after addressing the full set of issues to be raised by the diversity of potential actors in these processes, thereby avoiding a myriad of approaches that derive from addressing the specific problems within the major scenario underpinned by a tactic and effective methodology. Linguistics, perceived from an interdisciplinary approach, plays a special role in this shift in the *modus operandi*. It provides the tools working effectively in communication processes at structural, discursive and pragmatic levels.

Understanding the workings of these processes is fundamental to communication design. Although this might sound self-evident, in practice, it is not always so. And this happens precisely because designers seldom lack linguistic expertise. Multidisciplinary creative teams are not always the norm. Moreover, many situations involving communication processes lack recognition as such, or are identified rather frequently as problems concerning form, from a purely aesthetic sense.

## 10.3 Analysis of Examples of Discursive Materiality and Impact on the (De) Construction of the Identity of Destinations/Locations and People

The creation of interactive media products considers the possibilities of IT tools and the potential of the human user, which is object of ongoing research study, notably, identity and cultural awareness.

In other words, the design of digital systems aims at an effective agreement among users (in a broader sense participants/actors) in a specific communicative context. It is precisely because users explore and manipulate this array of digital systems applied to multimodal communication that mediated communication cannot be perceived, researched and improved to maximise interaction without drawing on a principled inter- and multidisciplinary approach.

Apart from looking at the way visitors – residents access and participate in communication, this multidisciplinary perspective departs from shedding some light on the interpretation of communicative events in context. These are briefly interpreted from an approach of face and facework, particularly on the way participants engage in face-to-face communication in situated relationships, with a focus on form and function of different kinds of language in context as well as the discursive component of multimodal discursive practices.

### *10.3.1 Looking into Ways of Improving Rapport Management Skills in Intercultural Communication, in General, and in Professional Interaction*

Even though (im)politeness in digital contexts has been studied from the theoretical and empirical stance in the last two decades (cf. Locher 2015, Graham and Hardaker 2017), this study intends to add some insights into interlocutors' communicating in different languages and cultures in online practices.

The analysis and discussion in this subsection will address, at first, the case of online access to advertising sites for accommodation, the so-called B&B (Bed and Breakfast), also translated into lodging, home stay (curiously rendered in Portuguese as *alojamento local*[10]), advertised worldwide by Airbnb, TripAdvisor, among

[10]A quick search of the translation of the phrase "alojamento local" (with specific regulations recently issued in the Portuguese context) into English, as displayed in Linguee, bears out strikingly diverse and unexpected collocates and semantic prosody evidenced as follows: Rental License for

others. These stand for instances of mediated communication, namely computer mediated communication (CMC) and interpersonal mediated communication.

This interactive process works both ways. From the host's point of view, the full visual display of lodgings on offer is likely to guarantee, to a certain extent, an unproblematic host-client rapport, being previously formatted by the sort of discursive moves in the virtual context.

Computer-mediated communication strategies contribute to lessen the possible communicative clashes arising both from face to face communication and the tense process of visitors' dealing with ever unpredictable first impact unknown settings. How problematic can this be?

In professional discourse, it is often the case of uncovering interlocutors' devising of diverse politeness strategies to fulfil their interactional goals in an interdiscursive context, such as that of the tourism and leisure domains. Situations presented from items 10.3.1.1, 10.3.1.2, 10.3.1.3, and 10.3.1.4 comprise conversational exchanges, likely to belong to the genre of service encounters. They also illustrate instances of interpersonal mediated communication. Following the extensive work by Arundale (2010) these allow for a range of participants' understandings on the concept of image and identity.

#### Situation 10.3.1.1 (booking.com. Guesthouse – Message: Female Guest – SMS)[11]

Dear Sirs, thank you for your message.

When I left the front door (next to the letter box), it was wide-open, and I could not close it as usual. Please, check it.

As for the letter you left, it was illegible as the ink must have run out.

Yours,

XXXXX

#### Situation 10.3.1.2 Reply (Male Host – email)

Thank you for your email.

I am unsure by what you mean by door gate. If you are referring to the main blue front door/front entrance where the green letterbox is, the door is closed and locks automatically after someone either enters or leaves the building.

(…)

I can appreciate that the instructions left have some excess ink on them, but they are in no way illegible.

"Registo de Alojamento Local"; Local Accommodation; Types of tourist resorts / local accommodation for "Tipologias de Empreendimentos Turísticos/ Alojamento Local"; Local Housing Allowance rate for "Subsídio de Alojamento Local"; local lodging establishments for "estabelecimentos de alojamento local" (accessed 20th October, 2019, at https://www.linguee.com/portuguese-english/translation/alojamento+local.html)

[11]The situations narrated are selected from researchers' corpora drawing on their own direct observation and participation.

### Situation 10.3.1.3 Reply (Female Guest – SMS)

Dear Sir, I am most grateful for doublechecking and preventing any unexpected issues. When I left early in the morning the situation was the one I described.

Yours,

XXXX

### Situation 10.3.1.4 Reply (Male Host – email)

Dear Guest.

Thank you for your email.

I can assure you 100% that the door is currently closed, and has been since 9 am when it was closed by my Mother, as someone did not close it behind them when leaving at 8.37 am (I have checked my CCTV) for some reason.

I have checked the door/lock function and cannot **find any fault with it so to see no reason as to why you or anyone else will have any issues**.

Have a lovely day.

Kindest regards.

[Emphases ours]

In fact, discursive markers conveying politeness have been encoded in the mediatized conversational exchanges (Kopytowska 2015), like the use of polite terms of address (e.g. "dear sirs", "dear guest", "thank you"), opening or closing remarks as well as modal verbs (e.g. "must have" conveying deduction; or "I can appreciate" expressing solidarity).[12] These are some of the strategies encoded in CMC communication related to conversational exchanges in professional contexts.

A brief overview of the pragmalinguistic strategies indebted to speech acts associated with complaining, explaining, giving information, apologizing and giving an excuse (written and multimodal communication in service encounters) disclose features leading to ineffective communication, such as the verbal turn-takings igniting speakers' inferences about the emotional cline evidenced at the enunciative realm (illocutionary and perlocutionary forces), namely:

- Challenging the client's narrative to save face (*cf.* 10.3.1.2; 10.3.1.4).
- Breaking conversational maxims to disclaim responsibility (*cf.* 10.3.1.1 10.3.1.3 *vs* 10.3.1.4)
- Register, pronominal shift (*cf.* 10.3.1.4)
- Discursive merging (*cf.* 10.3.1.4)
- Irony and sarcasm (*cf.* 10.3.1.2; 10.3.1.4)

Following Culpeper's description (in Leech 2014), the service provider (male host) evidences the following types of impoliteness:

(i) the speaker/service provider communicates face attack intentionally in "I can assure you 100% that the door is currently closed" (in 10.3.1.4) by challenging the interlocutor with alternative facts;

[12]The semantic field of expressions in English about polite and courteous behaviour can be found in the *Historical Thesaurus of the Oxford English Dictionary* and the *Oxford English Dictionary*, object of study in the Helsinki Corpus.

(ii) the speaker perceives and/or constructs behaviour as intentionally face-attacking in "I have checked the door/lock function and cannot find any fault with it so to see no reason as to why you or anyone else will have any issues" (in 10.3.1.4).

The defensive but unexpectedly rude exchanges underlying the service provider's mediated communication are punctuated by inappropriate pragmalinguistic and discursive choices to interpersonal and intercultural communication. These instances have been explained in terms of face-maintaining and face-enhancing data to instances of conflictual and face-aggravating behaviour with a negative impact on the image of the destination (Locher 2015).

The immediate appraisal of the sort of communication required by the advertising sites is likely to justify the host's defensive attitude for many reasons, particularly legal and economic ones. These are otherwise fully considered in face-to-face communication in service encounters, in the context of standard accommodation (e.g. hotels, inns, hostels, etc.), as mediators of the interaction among visitors/locals and the locations.

Contemporary demands of immediacy and instant goal fulfilment drive individuals (and the diverse communities to which they belong) to accept levels of success that would hardly be considered as such in a recent past. This requires a rather careful analysis of the objects of study in this area, specifically when it comes to multimodal forms of communication. These are particularly subject to phenomena of inaccurate communication given their own hybrid and complex nature, mostly because of dealing with images, visual signs. The latter bring into play cultural factors presupposing specific rules, also dictated by cultural standards, anathemas and prejudice (and not only of aesthetic nature), in as much as verbal language (be it spoken or written) is concerned.

### 10.3.2 Reinforcing Identity Traits in the Multimodal Communicative Plan

A better understanding of the diverse communicative practices in tourism, underpinned by the major issues selected for discussion from the outset of this chapter (i.e. information technologies, the human user, visual culture, and the location), presupposes a multidisciplinary framework involving the production and reception of information indebted to human and social sciences and IT.

One particularly relevant aspect of the underlying impact includes concepts likely to be considered as anthropological: appropriation and its correlated concept of identification (Segaud 2010). Borrowing from this conceptual framework and applying it to the contexts of interaction among visitors/locals seems rather challenging if one realises how important it is in the complex process of taking the rephrasing of the ancient duality foreigner/inhabitant to its intended meaning.

In this line equally figures Sankaran's reappraisal of De Fina's stances (2016, p. 165) on spatial images, in his perspective, traditionally perceived within the scope

**Fig. 10.1** Café-Restaurant Landtmann, Wien, 2016. (Source: Picture ours)

of identity and migration rather than the sole focus of theoretical reflection (2019, p. 2) "given the current transnational nature" of individuals' existence (see Fig. 10.1).

The artefact (*i.e.*, the china cup of coffee) evidences the interplay between verbal and non-verbal language in a dynamic relationship with the form (intersemiotic continuum), carried out by the Landtmann logo and the figure related to the foundation year/nation in a coherent unfolding, explicit reference. This is likely to be meaningfully and autonomously construed by visitors and residents alike. The association of different simplified narrative forms that involve the visitor/local community in the city's own thrilled realms (gastronomy being one of those in the tourism sector) is an integral part of meaning production and reception.

The experiential and ideational functions of language are evidenced in as much as interlocutors are attracted by history, by what the place/destination represents. The focus is then on identity features of the location and the cultural trait, thereby reinforcing identity traits in the multimodal discursive dimension.

Some additional traits are also carefully designed to underline this aesthetics of prestige, associating formal factors (that may be visually linked today by a process of visual acculturation), now global, addressing the unique specificity of the place: the elegant counter-curved profile of the object (*i.e.*, the cup) refers faithfully to a specific movement and a period of art history, particularly associated with the city, namely, *Art Noveau*.

Hence, in an intended formal contrast, the golden wing, shaped into a minimalist ring, refers to another aspect of art history and historical characters directly associated with the place, i.e., Gustave Klimt, the painter, and Van Loos, the architect.

The fact that the set date (standing out in the inner lid of the cup) is prior to the emergence of these characters (as important figures in art history) adds to the charm of this apparently simple cup, by implying that (virtual[13]) customers/internet surfers can imagine the cup represented in the picture used by such renowned historical characters.

Finally, if one realises that not all individuals can connect the dots and fully read the message (from decoding to interpreting the meaning potential), the visual representation of the object may add to the prestige of experiencing this place.

### *10.3.3 (Di)Similarities and Differences of Cultural Traits as Discursive Constructions*

Understanding hospitality comes with an added responsibility as an active support of a framework of participation and sharing, far beyond sheer functionality and cordiality. And the readiness to welcoming the visitor requires communicative skills and the ability to convey messages through multiple languages in action within the cultural context (see Fig. 10.2 below).

The previous excerpt of a brochure on the historical and cultural references of the original facilities of the Sacher Hotel, (1832) in Wien, is rendered in different languages. There are explicit references, accounting for facts in a continuum of text types (images, figures, recipes, descriptions, among others). The selection of a lingua franca, for international communication, for example English, turns the encounter between cultures and language codes into an authentic communicative practice.

The conspicuous QR code at the bottom of the page is immediately noticeable, no longer designed to blend into the general layout, as it so often happened when it was introduced some years ago. At first it was often perceived as a so-called intrusion on the page, but now visible for most readers, who will immediately use it and transfer the data to their mobiles, although it is likely that most information is immediately available on the page.

Nonetheless, the printed page is kept and plays an essential part as an effective and physical link to the historical record of the experience of enjoying "a piece of culinary history" (explicit in the title). It resorts to the same effect a serif font, aesthetically half-way between a classical font and a contemporary minimalist. The font, by its formal self, aims at establishing an "emotional dialogue". It implies a sense of novelty in (un)familiar contexts, carrying visitors to other places, to remembering or interacting with people and sensations related to the city. These visual features of multimodal kind remind visitors and locals of so many experiences elsewhere.

---

[13]A similar picture is available online at https://www.tripadvisor.pt/Restaurant_Review-g190454-d694332-Reviews-Cafe_Landtmann-Vienna.html#photos;aggregationId=&albumid=&filter=2&ff=434601212. Accessed 3rd October 2019.

**Fig. 10.2** Café Landtmann, Wien, 2016. (Source: Picture ours)

Along the sort of visitors' appraisals to experiences and facilities in destinations, mediated by encoded communication (via polar questions and multiple item questions) and feedback conveyed by emojis, it is interesting to acknowledge their eagerness to share authentic reappraisals to their interaction, as well as perceptions about places and people.

In so doing, it seemed relevant to collect comments by visitors to this café restaurant,[14] selected from TripAdvisor in its Portuguese version, as follows: pages 1 to 10; entries covering March – September 2019, for the research scope of this chapter). The comments were retrieved and analysed via Concordancer,

[14]The comments were retrieved from TripAdvisor online site from https://www.tripadvisor.pt/Restaurant_Review-g190454-d694332-Reviews-Cafe_Landtmann-Vienna.html on 29-10-2019

ConcApp, to account for the sort of modifiers and intensifiers conveyed by adjectives referred in the users'/visitors' appraisals to the location. The comments display 55 modifiers and corresponding intensifiers (out of a total N = 436 words as offered via The ConcApp[15] concordancer) as shown underneath:

| String | Lexeme | Frequency | Percentage (%) |
|---|---|---|---|
| 3 | agradável | 2 | 0.4587 |
| 12 | amigáveis | 1 | 0.2294 |
| 18 | bom | 2 | 0.4587 |
| 20 | bastante | 1 | 0.2294 |
| 21 | boa | 1 | 0.2294 |
| 29 | curiosos | 1 | 0.2294 |
| 31 | Conhecido | 1 | 0.2294 |
| 37 | confortável | 1 | 0.2294 |
| 50 | deliciosos | 1 | 0.2294 |
| 51 | difícil | 1 | 0.2294 |
| 52 | decepcionados | 1 | 0.2294 |
| 59 | diárias | 1 | 0.2294 |
| 91 | fresquinho | 1 | 0.2294 |
| 98 | Inglês | 1 | 0.2294 |
| 109 | lindo | 1 | 0.2294 |
| 110 | mais | 2 | 0.4587 |
| 111 | milanesa | 1 | 0.2294 |
| 115 | muito | 8 | 1.8349 |
| 116 | melhor | 3 | 0.6881 |
| 119 | melhores | 1 | 0.2294 |
| 134 | original | 1 | 0.2294 |
| 137 | obrigatória | 1 | 0.2294 |
| 141 | próximo | 1 | 0.2294 |
| 144 | pouco | 1 | 0.2294 |
| 147 | paciente | 1 | 0.2294 |
| 153 | próxima | 1 | 0.2294 |
| 154 | preferido | 1 | 0.2294 |
| 164 | quentinho | 1 | 0.2294 |
| 165 | quente | 1 | 0.2294 |
| 168 | reservado | 1 | 0,2294 |
| 175 | super | 1 | 0.2294 |
| 177 | salgado | 1 | 0.2294 |
| 178 | saboroso | 1 | 0.2294 |
| 180 | satisfeitos | 1 | 0.2294 |
| 184 | simpático | 1 | 0.2294 |

(continued)

[15]Concordancer and Word Profiler Version 4 for Windows 98, ME, NT / 2000, XP available at http://www.edict.com.hk/PUB/concapp/ [accessed 11th September 2005, at 19:04].

| String | Lexeme | Frequency | Percentage (%) |
|---|---|---|---|
| 188 | simpáticos | 1 | 0.2294 |
| 194 | tradicional | 4 | 0.9174 |
| 199 | tradicionais | 1 | 0.2294 |
| 200 | turistas | 1 | 0.2294 |
| 202 | tão | 1 | 0.2294 |

Most of the instances belong to the experiential, sensorial realms, such as:

(i) the expected collocations like "salty" (→*salgado*), "delicious" (→*deliciosos*), "hot" (→*quente*);
(ii) and the semantically-loaded collocates in Portuguese *quentinho*, *fresquinho* (marked by the affective morpheme *-inho*, as an affective undertone) and "beautiful" (→*lindo*),
(iii) as well as appraisals like friendly (→*amigável*) or even the lexeme *conhecido* (known in English) *tradicionais* (traditional in English).

These are but some of the instances acknowledging the sort of authentic tourist practices mediated by previous experiences or visitors'/residents' knowledge of locations and cultural items either shared by geographical proximity or by CMC. In this regard the sort of interaction encoded in CMC is enriched by the wealth of critical appraisals shared in the wider virtual context in a coherent intersemiotic continuum rather than through a fragmented discourse.

Cultural items should create, emotionally involve or seduce and, at the same time, represent, reproduce and illustrate a larger narrative in a simple and straightforward way. Hence, humans usually resort to the symbolic and experiential functions that effectively attract to and account for memorable experiences and at the same time referential functions of language in representing artefacts.

From the point of view of interactive media design, this represents a credo that globalization has imposed as a founding principle to guarantee the prevalence of solutions which preserve cultural heritage in a dynamic way allowing it to remain meaningful in new contexts. This translates into finding the essence or singular processes of producing meaning through specific sets of forms as opposed to exploring forms for their own sake and out of context.

It is however necessary to have knowledge and to understand the ways artefacts came into being, as well as realise how that past (history) needs to be made present every time they are called into play. This can only be feasible by cross-referencing multiple points of view. It is not a simple task of playing with forms for as much as they may be expressive. In this regard, Maybin and Mercer (1996, p. 42) rightly claim "knowledge is not only possessed individually but shared amongst members of communities; and understandings are constructed by people jointly, through their involvement in events which are shaped by cultural and historical factors" (see Fig. 10.3 below).

The picture was taken from a menu available at a restaurant in Moscow. While displaying the verbal message in Cyrillic and English, it is implicit that users/clients

**Fig. 10.3** Menu, Moscow, 2016. (Source: Picture ours)

get familiar with the Russian language and cultural identity by focusing on different ways of encoding the verbal message in a semantic continuum with the visual display (soup plate). The use of multimodal language seems to contribute to both visitors' and locals' meaningful interaction with (un)familiar cultural traits thereby avoiding ambiguity and arbitrariness of the signs on the page.

The image follows a feature of contemporary visual culture that is worth noticing known as a so-called staged process. The framing is partial and fragmented. It creates the illusion of an unplanned picture via a mobile phone. In fact, it is taken with professional wide lenses. The lighting is carefully set to look like neutral, avoid interferences from shines and obtain an overall silkiness of look. The plate was specially chosen to contrast, in colour, material and subtlety with the rather objective content. And this is a key factor: the image aims at attracting people to a cultural experience that has a very high probability of being considered hard to endure if not politically incorrect in some way. Therefore, much safeguard has been taken to soften its multimodal content and allow for a possible compromise.

### *10.3.4 Careful Selection of Destination Images Leading the Visitor/Local Community to Travel and Experience Other Cultures*

The communicative practices in this section uncover an array of representations and the way they are conveyed in the spatial organization, from the perspective of social semiotics. There is therefore a concern to diversify, to create an authentic, diverse place (Kress and van Leeuwen 2001; Van Leeuwen 2001, 2006), which attracts both residents and visitors to experience the place. Questions of linguistic and discursive

**Fig. 10.4** S. Miguel, Azores (Portugal), "Geocozido" (*Fumarole cooking*), 2013. (Source: Picture ours)

choices evidenced in signs and unusual imagery are central for visitors to discover their own itineraries, according to their interests, tastes and background information (cf. self-catering as discussed in Sousa 2019).

It is precisely that neutralization of the alterity factor that gives prestige to the experience. In some ways, its degree of strangeness or exoticism determines the value of the cultural asset. This means that the level of interaction remains for most users superficial and the possibility of a meaningful dialogue is scant. In a way this process is replaced by a mere experience of a temporary suspension of disbelief (see Fig. 10.4 below).

The picture connotes a point of view, displays and amplifies destination features (cf. visual rhetoric, Sousa and Paolinelli 2014, Sousa and Antunes 2014) and offer observers a visual perspective of a (un)familiar cultural asset of their own (Kastenholz 2010). These processes of transformation run deep throughout as long as one admits these experiences affect the entire set of beliefs associated with one's overall perception of the world as "reality" (Lipovetsky and Serroy 2014). This is so to the extent that they overcome the set borders for one's sense of visual reality. At the same time, they try to fill in a potential gap by building familiar realms of differently originated and structured visual realities.

Photography, for as much as it may be perceived as a mechanical appropriation of visual reality, relies, indeed, on multiple sets of facts. Timing, framing, keeping it or erasing it, comprise all decisions to be made and may contribute to a prominent change in the outcome.

The widespread use of cameras in mobile phones lately have considerably transformed the perception users and viewers have of the act of photographing. The picture of the *fumerole* cooking is a persuasive example of the process and illustrates well how contemporary users now mediate their experiences of places through technological devices and the resulting pictures. The camera closely follows the viewers' eye movement and they expect the picture to reproduce minutely, inch by inch, their personal experience of the actual physical place they are, or were, in. The close range, casual, instant-like framing mimics visitors' own visual experience. It is less pointed at recording the physical features of the landscape than communicating the full physical experience of proximity with the feature viewers perceive as remarkable, even if conveyed by strictly visual means in this case (the fragility of the fence is contrasted with the peril close behind). In some way the aesthetic realm is replaced by the "biographical" note as face value (in the past even "documentary" photography had its aesthetics of its own, if discreet framework).

It is also important to notice the way these features were very readily accepted in the context of tourism-related communication, competing with sophisticated photography made possible by digital cameras. They document the authenticity of the experience, and their amateur-like features become a sort of guarantee of that truthfulness (authenticity and reliability).

It is not only (as one could perceive on the surface) a system of granting a clear explanation for the potential customer. It is also a system of creating a conceptual metaphor of some location, conveyed by a set of images displayed as a parkour of a specific space (rather than the conventional carefully framed unique image), allowing for the awareness of a pre-experienced familiar environment.

This multimodal communicative strategy enables visitors to appropriate spaces in advance and makes them become deeply committed to their decision-making process. Visitors perceive their individual decisions as a process of identification with a location which is thus not merely a foreign/unfamiliar space, but as an environment of their own individual choice, despite having been mentally rearranged in advance (see Fig. 10.5 below).

Building up immersive experiences in virtual reality is a lesson on the extent to which contemporary citizens rely on empirical emotionally informed experience as opposed to rationalization of the physical world around them. Places are not their geographical features as they are not a construct of people's perception independent from a way of experiencing them.

The role of a designer, concerned with transmitting what may be perceived collectively as the essence of a place, is the one of bringing together the key factors likely to trigger a sense of "belonging". In other words, it entails building up the features supporting its cultural frame. So is the case of displaying a picture of a spot of a restaurant museum showplace instead of the usual frontispiece. Setting this frame means stripping up appearances, the picturesque, to reveal their meaning within the framework of a globalized world. This is only possible by attracting visitors to this realm and suspending the otherness factor in such a way that visitors may feel in possession of something, not by owning it but by living it. The typical Russian gastronomy is on offer. The multicultural scope covered is then evidenced in the array of cultural items, like Finish and Swedish inscriptions.

This perceptive shift (Mitchel 2005), allowing for wider, multileveled and new fields of experience, entails challenges to aesthetic beliefs not be approached independently of the analysis of the new configurations in which technological means are put into play. These are not exclusive to technology, once processes of contamination between tools and users' beliefs are triggered whenever perceptive complex scenarios such as these arise. And these interchanges play a definite role in the reconfiguration of identities (Woodward 2007; Arundale 2010).

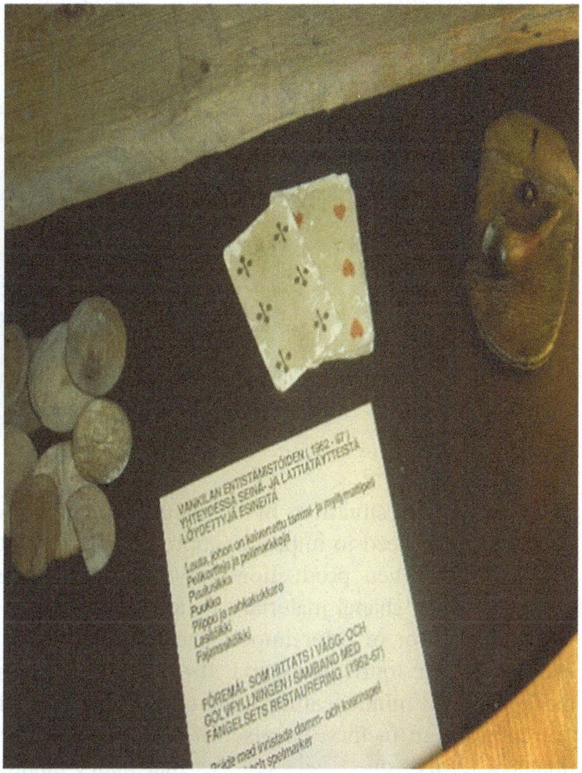


**Fig. 10.5** Restaurant Arbat Street, Moscow, 2016. (Source: Picture ours)

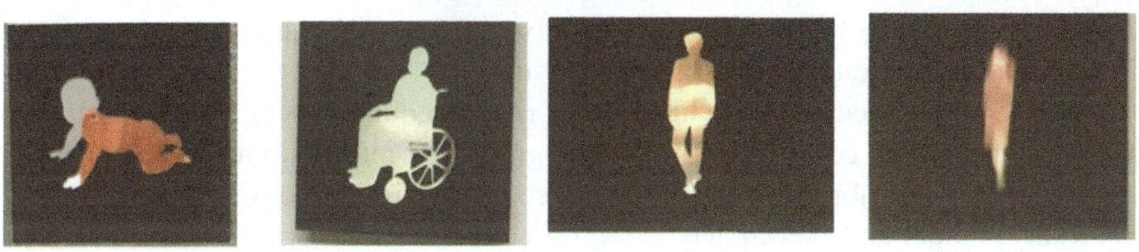

**Fig. 10.6** Toilet visual signs, Wien, 2016. (Source: Picture ours)

### *10.3.5 Language in Action and Social Semiotics*

The set of figures selected underneath consider some ways that language is used in everyday life as a means for 'getting things done': signs carrying out discursive practices of referential kind, in the scope of global/cross-cultural communication in the multiple segments of tourism must be explicit to visitors and simultaneously internet users (Sousa 2016), who get therefore more autonomous. Yet, the last picture, representing a female figure, seems to be fading away (see Figs. 10.6 above and 10.7 below).

**Fig. 10.7** Lift signs, Wien, 2016. (Source: Picture ours)

The illustrated situations in the pictures shown above comprise typical examples of the frequent need to improve, improvising, elementary communication systems, in a moment when production means allow for variations of product features, namely, colour, shape, materials, details, at low cost. Yet, communication efficacy is rarely a factor of prior importance in architectural planning (Henriques 2003), even within the touristic context. If one assesses the amount of damage caused by these so-called minor features (due to a lack of consideration of basic communication and design factors, on a set of scales against associated costs in human and financial terms), one easily realises that better planning is worth taking the extra effort. Against this background, and once more, comes into play the preconceived idea that familiarity with these almost universal issues is enough to provide an appropriate response to the problem by any user.

As such, the medium to which users resort requires them to conform to a predefined range of communicative events guided by informativity, accountability, among others, also abiding to previously encoded maxims of conversation (quantity, relevance, mode) and speech acts.

This is usually perceived as a potentially negative factor of human-computer interaction. Yet, it does not have to be perceived as such: this view derives mainly from a sociocultural context that precedes the advent of digital technologies. The fact that, for instance, users end up creating an avatar derives as much from their desire to protect or project their own selves (see Fig. 10.8 below).

Some of the most sensitive areas when designing communication systems for multicultural contexts are those related to services or products that involve the personal sphere of the user, particularly the ones that involve creating icons representing the individual as a physical entity. If the task was sensitive in the past, it is now much more complex due to the political debate around gender issues.

This complexification of the task had the positive effect of revealing the biases underlying the design of many widespread iconic systems and help putting them aside by forcing citizens to question well established design solutions. So much so

**Fig. 10.8** Shared citizenship: visitors' immediate assessment

that the "correctness" of these symbolic systems of signs now frequently acts as a barometer of citizen's ability to validate an entire location namely in touristic contexts.

More than representing a factor of risk, this complexification adds a new responsibility to those who order or choose a design, underlining the fact that every communicative event involves a source, channel and receptor. Therefore, it makes all sense that all are participants in the process of building it up. What is equally at stake is the scope of persuasive communication strategies towards the user, as clearly stated by Spahn (2012, online): "it claims that every real discourse presupposes certain (normative) rules as necessary preconditions for the search of the truth, and it claims secondly that the outcome of a rational discourse has a normative validity: it is a rational consensus that is normatively binding as the result of a rational intersubjective deliberation process."

The visitor and the local community interact with the services in the various segments of tourism. Mediated multimodal encoded interaction contributes to shared citizenship in the organization or improvement of public and private spaces. Hence, the multimodal feedback and adjustment of service organization in real time in multilingual and multicultural contexts by active interlocutors fosters a dialogic encounter among citizens and the locations.

It becomes evident that the demands placed on every aspect of this cultural exchange in terms of quality is quite high. Even the minor traits of a destination become part of a branding process and need to be addressed carefully. In media design researchers and practitioners are looking at high requirements in terms of coherence while engaging with the multiple languages (verbal, non-verbal and artificial languages) it summons.

Although evidence has pointed otherwise, this problematic shift remains as one of the yet to be solved key issues of human-computer interaction, because systems have been developed to a point where digital illiterates, for example, are info-excluded and overlooked by the economy of the system.

This is shown in the way human-computer interaction scenarios typically phase out dialogue systems: they rely on users' familiarity with or awareness of certain dominant codes and conducts not likely to be learnt in any way other than via empirical experience. Because the media continuously shift/evolve, languages encode additional rules to be necessarily experienced, learnt, accommodated, and quickly assimilated before the forthcoming rule builds on; yet most frequently users lose track of its intrinsic logical cline.

## 10.4 Final Considerations

The selection of discursive practices underpinned by diverse communicative strategies bear in mind the context, the interlocutors in their privileged interaction with destinations corroborating previous claims (Jaworski and Pritchard 2005; Sousa and Marinho Antunes 2014). These claims aim at emphasising authenticity and the communicative purposes at stake.

It is most important to underline the identity features of locations in their representation on a local/global scale in that individuals position themselves differently according to the discursive practices inherent to the cultural traits of destinations apart from the implicit linguistic sense of place (Cortese and Hymes 2001, p. 164).

Linguistics and its many fields of language description, particularly of multimodal texts, are intended to uncover interaction in other ways (unidirectionality of communication), as stated by Mercer and Maybin "how they can be used, what information is available, and how people and events are represented".[16]

It is the case of a set of illustrations selected for language analysis (Figs. 10.2, 10.3, 10.4, 10.5, and 10.6), or CMC on service encounters, displaying features of interpersonal and professional communication, from a socio-cultural perspective. Language is first and foremost regarded as a tool for social action, underpinned by the referential, interpersonal and ideational functions. Given their social purposes, underpinned by a discursive component, corroborating Maybin and Mercer (1996b, p.42), "they are uttered with particular aims in mind, and these also shape their form and structure".

The analyses shared in this study are meant to highlight the way citizens/consumers are guided in the process of interpreting locations by the locations themselves, affecting the way visitors perceive, appropriate spaces and interpret them

[16]"E844: Language and literacy in a changing world". Accessed 5th October 2019 at https://www.open.edu/openlearncreate/mod/oucontent/view.php?id=15196&printable=1

according to their own schemata. The interpretations/interactions are often disseminated in other multimodal texts, sometimes virtually via social media (e.g. Facebook, Instagram, twitter, to name but a few). In the process, the discursive component on locations ends up becoming fragmented, as subjective, imaginary spaces recreated by citizens.

All the situations and communicative events were meant to contribute to some understanding of language use in intercultural communication in the deconstruction of the identity of a location (Fesenmaier and MacKay 1996). The array of illustrations selected in this chapter allowed for the following set of final considerations: Language is meaningful when it is appropriated meaningfully; the linguistic and discursive choices underpinning effective and meaningful communication implied the differentiation of interlocutors who are supposed to share, produce and receive messages of multimodal kind; awareness and sharing of cultural codes and values are indebted to the languages used in the interaction.

The selection of verbal/nonverbal or multimodal language should be done effectively without trivializing, homogenizing, or echoing (*déjá-vu*) location traits. And the different modes of communication should aid the user to acknowledge the identity trait. Best practices should be disseminated to educate the gamut of interlocutors (residents, visitors, experts in the field, among others) to support local communities, use reflectively and responsibly information technologies aiming at granting the cultural values of destinations (Starkey 2002).

In this regard, the array of strategies of global communication and intercultural interaction with services are facilitated by information technologies and participants' communicative competence: linguistic (lexical, orthographic, syntactic), discursive (genres and texts), sociocultural and pragmatic competence (indebted to global dexterity, as discussed by Molinsky 2013). The dialogic encounter is first and foremost triggered by the immediacy of images, sensations (sound, music, light, visual plans) together with participants' (previous) knowledge of historical, geographical and cultural elements of locations facilitated by information technologies.

The collective memory of places is promoted by triggering cognitive processes related to interlocutors' desire to "see" and/or "revisit" locations. It is essential that the local community seeks to revisit critically the diversity of destinations identity traits (cultural literacy) and cultural plurality, thereby overcoming multiple tensions and contributing to their appreciation.

The outcome of the reflection drawing on authentic evidence presented in this chapter points to further studies and orientations to information designers and educators to:

- improve rapport management and interpersonal skills in intercultural communication, in general, and in professional interaction, more than just focusing on linguistic competence or learning additional languages;
- make interlocutors aware of the sort of exchanges in service encounters, for example, while using formal language to accept responsibility for speakers' acts without being offensive, impolite and at the same time taking responsibility

for the offense; service providers' intentions are meant to heighten clients' face and support solidarity in interactions.

It is claimed that communication in tourism is underpinned by mediated interaction: the digital technological tools build up the premises not only for mediated interaction, but, beforehand, for the possibility, or feasibility of this interaction. As much as this argument might sound tautological, in the sense that the same could be said for any means of communication, in no way does it prove to be so. If one realises that the process of interaction does not solely make use of a tool to achieve effective communication among interlocutors, but also conforms to a larger extent than ever before (see, for example Arundale's work on image and identity).

To sum up, regulations should be supported by adequate instruction as well as formal training within a multidisciplinary approach to be promoted in schools and universities. Also, further studies should focus on the hosts' possible array of reactions to communicative events to uncover fully the multidirectional interaction: information producer, consumer (visitors/residents and designers of interactive media) and the location.

**Acknowledgements** The authors express their gratitude to S. Kurtes and J. B. Silva for their initial feedback on this chapter both from an interdisciplinary framework in the scope of intercultural pragmatics and a discourse stylistician's viewpoint applied to communication in tourism.

## References

Arundale, R. (2010). Face as emergent in interpersonal communication: An alternative to Goffman. In F. Bargiela-chiappini & M. Haugh (Eds.), *Face, communication and social interaction* (pp. 33–54). London: Equinox.

Avighi, C. (2001). Turismo, globalização e cultura. In B. Lage & P. Milone (Eds.), *Turismo: Teoria e prática* (pp. 102–106). Atlas: São Paulo.

Bally, C., & Sechehaye, A. (Eds.). (1966). *Course in general linguistics: Ferdinand de Saussure*. New York: McGraw-Hill.

Baracuhy, M. R. (2010). *Análise do discurso e mídia: nas trilhas da identidade nordestina*. http://www.ufjf.br/revistaveredas/files/2010/04/artigo-131.pdf. Accessed 29 Nov 2019.

Barretto, M. (2007). *Turismo y cultura. Relaciones, contradicciones y expectativas*. http://www.pasosonline.org. Accessed 20 Sept 2016.

Beeton, S. (2005). *Film-induced tourism*. Clevedon: Channel View Publications.

Bogusławska-Tafelska, M., & Haładewicz-Grzelak M. (Eds.). (2019). *Communication as a life process: The holistic paradigm in language sciences* (Vol. 2). Cambridge: Cambridge Scholars.

Brito, M. (2011). Cultural tourists requests from their tourist guides. *International Journal of Management Cases, 14*(1), 266–282.

Brito, l. (2008). O Guia-intérprete: Mediador intercultural. *Revista de Turismo & Desenvolvimento, 10*, 67–84.

Carvalho, S., Vieira, A., & Sousa, A. (2013). Film-induced tourism – The case of Portugal. *Revista de Investigação Científica AICA, 5*, 100–105.

Carvalho, S., Vieira, A., & Sousa, A. (2014). Film-induced tourism: The case of Portugal. *Revista Turismo e Desenvolvimento, 21/22*(4), 469–482.

Chen, S. (2016). Language and ecology: A content analysis of ecolinguistics as an emerging research field. *Ampersand*: Elsevier, pp. 108–116 https://doi.org/10.1016/j.amper.2016.06.002 2215–0390/© 2016.

Chichorro, A. (2003). A*s teias de aranha da casa: uma ecolinguística intercultural (alemão – português)*. Doctoral thesis, University of Coimbra, Coimbra.

Cortese, G., & Hymes, D. (2001). Languaging in and across human groups: Perspectives on difference and asymmetry. *Textus – English Studies in Italy, 14*(2). Genova: Tilgher.

Crystal, D. (2001). *Language and the internet*. Cambridge: Cambridge University Press.

De Fina, A. (2016). Linguistic practices and transnational identities. In S. Preece (Ed.), *The Routledge handbook of Language & Identity* (pp. 163–178). London/New York: Routledge.

Falcetta, F. P. (2008). Estratégias de comunicação sob a ótica da comunicação turística: tendências e possibilidades para o fomento do turismo nacional – um estudo comparado França e Brasil. Doctoral thesis. Repositório Institucional PUCRS. http://hdl.handle.net/10923/2055. Accessed 29 Nov 2019.

Fesenmaier, D., & MacKay, K. (1996). Deconstructing destination image construction. *The Tourist Review, 51*(2), 37–43. ISSN: 0251–3102, https://doi.org/10.1108/eb058222/full/html.

Foucault, M. (1980). Power/knowledge. In C. Gordon (Ed.), *Selected interviews and other writings* (pp. 1972–1977). New York: Pantheon Books.

Foucault, M. (1998a). On the ways of writing history. In J. D. Faubion (Ed.), *Aesthetics, methods, and epistemology* (pp. 279–295). New York: The New Press.

Foucault, M. (1998b). Return to history. In J. D. Faubion (Ed.), *Aestheics, methods and epistemology* (pp. 419–432). New York: The New Press.

Goffman, E. (1963). *Behaviour in public places*. New York: Free Press.

Goffman, E. (1967). *Interaction ritual*. Harmondsworth: Penguin.

Goffman, E. (1971). *Relations in public*. London: Allen Lane.

Goffman, E. (1983). The interaction order. *American Sociological Review., 48*, 1–17.

Halliday, M. A. K. (1978). *Language as social semiotic*. London: Edward Arnold.

Halliday, M. A. K. (1989). *Spoken and written language*. Oxford: Oxford University Press.

Halliday, M. A. K. (1994). *Introduction to functional grammar*. London: Edward Arnold.

Hargrove, C. (2014). *Cultural tourism: Attracting tourists and their spending. Article. 2014 National Cultural Districts Exchange*. https://www.americansforthearts.org/sites/default/files/pdf/2014/by_program/reports_and_data/toolkits/cultural_districts/issue_briefs/Cultural-Tourism-Attracting-Visitors-and-Their-Spending.pdf. Accessed 29 Nov 2019.

Henriques, C. (2003). Turismo, cidade e cultura. Planeamento e gestão sustentável. Lisbon: Edições Sílabo.

Huang, Y., & Kecskes, I. (2017, January 26). Cross-cultural and intercultural pragmatics. *The Oxford Handbook of Pragmatics*. Oxford: Oxford University Press, https://www.oxfordhandbooks.com/view/10.1093/oxfordhb/9780199697960.001.0001/oxfordhb-9780199697960-e-29. Accessed 3 Nov 2019.

Hughes, H. (2002). Culture and tourism: A framework for further analysis. *Managing Leisure, 7*(3), 164–175.

Ivanovic, M. (2008). *Cultural tourism*. Cape Town: Ken McGillivray.

Jaworski, A., & Pritchard, A. (2005). *Discourse, communication and tourism*. Clevedon: Cromwell Press.

Kastenholz, E. (2010). Cultural proximity' as a determinant of destination image. *Journal of Vacation Marketing, 16*(4), 313–322.

Kopytowska, M. (2015). Mediating identity, ideology and values in the public sphere: Towards a new model of (constructed) social reality. *Lodz Papers in Pragmatics. Special issue on Mediating identity, ideology and values in the public sphere, 11*(2), 133–156. https://doi.org/10.1515/lpp-2015-0008.

Kress, G., & Van Leeuwen, T. (2001). *Multimodal discourse: The modes and media of contemporary communication*. London: Routledge.

Kress, G., & Van Leeuwen, T. (2006). *Reading images: The grammar of visual design*. London/New York: Routledge.

Leal, R. E. S. (2005). *Uma abordagem conceitual-reflexiva sobre a relação da comunicação com o turismo*. http://adrianapublicitaria.blogspot.com/2008/10/uma-abordagem-conceitual-reflexiva.html. Accessed 29 Oct 2019.

Leech, G. (2014). *Pragmatics of politeness*. Oxford: Oxford University Press.

Leu, J., Jr., Kinzer, K., Coiro, J., Castek, J., & Henry, A. (2013). New literacies: A dual-level theory of the changing nature of literacy, instruction, and assessment. In R. B. Ruddell & D. Alvermann (Eds.), *Theoretical models and processes of reading* (pp. 1150–1181). Newark: IRA.

Lipovetsky, G., & Serroy, J. (2014). O Capitalismo estético na era da globalização. Lisbon: Edições 70.

Locher, M. (2015). Interpersonal pragmatics and its link to (im)politeness research. *Journal of Pragmatics, 86*, 5–10. https://doi.org/10.1016/j.pragma.2015.05.010.

Mandelbaum, D. (Ed.). Communication. In *Selected writings of Edward Sapir* (pp. 104–109). Berkeley: University of California Press.

Martins, M. (2009). Ce que peuvent les images: Trajet de l'un au multiple. *Journal Article. Les Cahiers Européens de L'Imaginaire*. http://repositorium.sdum.uminho.pt/bitstream/1822/24132/3/ce_que_peuvent_les_images.pdf. Accessed 29 Oct 2019.

Martins, M. (2010). *Linguagem, verdade e conhecimento: As Ciências da comunicação e o contemporâneo*. Book chapter. http://repositorium.sdum.uminho.pt/bitstream/1822/24118/1/linguagem_verdade_e_conhecimento.pdf. Accessed 29 Oct 2019.

Martins, M. (2019). Culturas, médias e identidades: Nota introdutória. Conference paper. III Congresso Internacional sobre culturas: Interfaces da lusofonia. Centro de Estudos de Comunicação e Sociedade. http://repositorium.sdum.uminho.pt/bitstream/1822/23797/1/a_propos_de_l%27imginaire_des_medias.pdf. Accessed 29 Oct 2019.

Martins, M., & Maffesoli, M. (2011). À propos de l'imaginaire des medias. Journal article. *Sociétés*. https://doi.org/10.3917/soc.111.0005. Issn 0765-3697 http://hdl.handle.net/1822/23797.

Marujo, M. N. (2008). *Turismo & comunicação*. Castelo Branco: RVJ Editores.

Maybin, J., & Mercer, N. (Eds.). (1996a). *Using English: From conversation to canon*. London: Routledge with the Open University.

Maybin, J., & Mercer, N. (1996b). Language and literacy in a changing world. E844. Open University https://www.open.edu/openlearncreate/mod/oucontent/view.php?id=15196&printable=1. Accessed 4 Nov 2019.

Meacci, L., & Liberatore, G. (2018). Towards a senses-based model for experiential tourism: The youtooscanny.com case. *Tourism and Management Studies, 14*(4), 7–14. https://tmstudies.net/index.php/ectms/article/view/1051/pdf_110. Accessed 4 Oct 2019.

Mitchel, W. J. (2005). *Placing words: Symbols, space and the city*. Cambridge: MIT.

Molinsky, A. (2013). *Global dexterity: How to adapt your behavior across cultures without losing yourself in the process*. Harvard: Harvard Business Review Press.

Oliveira, M.-C., & Silva, J. (2009). The composition of a participative view for the management of organizational communications. In F. Ramallo, A. Lorenzo Suárez, M. Rodríguez-Yáñez, & P. Cap (Eds.), *New approaches to discourse and business communication* (pp. 190–211). London: Palgrave Macmillan.

Perniola, M. (2016). Sentires em rede. Conference paper. Centro Cultural de São Paulo – Sala Jardel Filho. 15th April 2016.

Piller, I. (2007). Linguistics and intercultural communication. *Language and Linguistics Compass, 1*(3), 208–226.

Rampton, B. (2018). Goffman: Key concepts in exploration of the interaction order. *Working Papers in Urban Language & Literacies*, WP239. https://www.academia.edu/36327336/WP239_Rampton_2018._Goffman_Key_concepts_in_exploration_of_the_interaction_order. Accessed 1 Sept 2019.

Rampton, C., Cook, M., & Holmes, S. (2018). Promoting linguistic citizenship: Issues, problems & possibilities. *Working Papers in Urban Language & Literacies*, WP233. https://www.academia.

edu/people/search?utf8=%E2%9C%93&q=+Promoting+Linguistic+Citizenship%3A+Issues %2C+problems+%26+possibilities+. Accessed 1 Sept 2019.

Sankaran, L. (2019). 'Homeland' & 'hostland' identifications in the Sri Lankan Tamil diaspora. *Working Papers in Urban Language & Literacies*, WP253. https://www.academia.edu/39893937/WP253_Sankaran_2019._Homeland_and_host-land_identifications_in_the_Sri_Lankan_Tamil_diaspora. Accessed 1 Sept 2019.

Sarangi, S. (2006). The conditions and consequences of professional discourse studies. In R. Kiely, P. Rea-dickins, H. Woodfield, & G. Clibbon (Eds.), *Language, culture and identity in applied linguistics* (pp. 199–220). London: Equinox.

Segaud, M. (2010). *Anthropologie de l'espace: habiter, fonder, distribuer, transformer*. Paris: Armand Colin (Dunod Éditeur).

Simmel, G. (1950). The metropolis and mental life. In K. Wolf (Ed.), *The sociology of Georg Simmel* (pp. 409–424). Glencoe: The Free Press.

Simpson, M., & Nichols, S. (2005). *Global tourism and the environment – Ways to sports and leisure*. Abstracts of the International seminar: Global tourism and the environment – Ways to Sports and Leisure. Funchal (PT): Universidade da Madeira, 29th June 2005.

Sousa, A. (2019). Linguagem, comunicação, identidade do destino: o agente turístico no paradigma contemporâneo. In N. Abranja & C. Magalhães (Eds.), *Gestão de agências de viagens e turismo* (pp. 205–208). Lisbon: Lidel, Cap. V.

Sousa, A., & Antunes, L. M. (2014). Barcelona, Paris, Roma: A promoção de destinos através dos traços culturais identitários em trailers de filmes de Woody Allen. *Tourism and Hospitality International Journal, 3*(1), 69–89.

Sousa, A., & Marçalo, M. (2018). O discurso das/nas cidades: reflexões interdisciplinares. In R. Cavallazzi & G. Fauth (Eds.), *Cidade standard e novas vulnerabilidades* (pp. 119–131). PROURB/Rio de Janeiro: Coleção Direito e Urbanismo.

Sousa, A., & Paolinelli, L. (2014). Identidade e cultura: Representações do destino Portugal. In C. Costa, F. Brandão, R. Costa, & Z. Breda (Eds.), *Produtos e competitividade do turismo na Lusofonia, competitividade em turismo* (Vol. II, pp. 139–153). Lisboa: Escolar Editora. ISBN: 978-972-592-410-5.

Sousa, A., & Silva, J. (2017). Textworlds in interplay: The rhetoric of film-induced tourism. INVTUR 2017 – Co-creating the future of tourism. *Revista Turismo & Desenvolvimento, 2* (27/28), 447–449. URI: http://hdl.handle.net/10400.13/2272. Accessed at https://www.ua.pt/invtur/page/17640.

Spahn, A. (2012). And lead us (not) into persuasion...? Persuasive technology and the ethics of communication. *Science and Engineering Ethics, 18*, 633–650. https://doi.org/10.1007/s11948-011-9278-y.

Spencer-Oatey, H. (2000). *Culturally speaking: Managing rapport through talk across cultures*. London: Continuum.

Starkey, K. (2002). New knowledge spaces? *Human Relations, 55*(3), 350–360. https://doi.org/10.1177/0018726702553004.

White, P. (1995). Geography, literature and migration. In J. Connell, R. King, & P. White (Eds.), *Writing across worlds: Literature and migration* (pp. 1–27). London: Routledge.

Woodward, K. (Ed.). (2007). *Identity and difference: Culture, media and identities*. London: Sage.

Zimmermann, S., & Reeves, T. (2009). Film tourism – Locations are the new stars. In R. Conrady & M. Buck (Eds.), *Trends and issues in global tourism* (pp. 155–162). Berlin: Springer.

# Chapter 11
# Conversational Agents for Mental Health and Wellbeing

**Zoraida Callejas and David Griol**

**Abstract** Recent advances in spoken language technology, artificial intelligence, and conversational interface design, coupled with the emergence of smart devices, have increased the possibilities of using conversational interfaces for a growing range of application domains. These interfaces are currently applied in the healthcare domain in a range of innovative tasks that allow to provide a more natural user-friendly human-machine communication, promote patient participation in their own care, and help and support medical professionals. This chapter describes in detail the great potential for the use of conversational interfaces for the specific area of mental health, highlighting their most valuable applications in this domain and the open challenges for future research.

**Keywords** Automatic dialog systems · Robots · Health monitoring

## 11.1 Conversational Agents and Robots

Conversational interfaces are computer programs that can be used to emulate a dialog with a human being to complete a specific task using natural language (Griol et al. 2014; McTear et al. 2016; Pieraccini 2012). The continuous advances of conversational technologies and speech technologies have increased the possibilities of integrating conversational interfaces into a growing range of devices and application domains. For example, personal assistants for mobile portable devices and smart speakers, smart home conversation assistants, educational and industrial environments, entertainment-oriented systems and robots that offer spoken communication (McTear et al. 2016; Pearl 2017).

In their recent survey about conversational agents in healthcare, Montenegro et al. (2019) adopt a flexible perspective considering as conversational agent, any

Z. Callejas (✉) · D. Griol
Software Engineering Department, University of Granada, Granada, Spain
e-mail: zoraida@ugr.es; dgriol@ugr.es



T. Lopez-Soto (ed.), *Dialog Systems*, Logic, Argumentation & Reasoning 22,
https://doi.org/10.1007/978-3-030-61438-6_11

computer program or artificial intelligence able to hold a conversation with humans through natural language. In this chapter we will adopt this comprehensive vision of the term "conversational agent", although in the literature there exist other related terms that match the previous definition, e.g. conversational interfaces, embodied conversational agents, chatbots, dialogue systems or speech interfaces. In our previous work (McTear et al. 2016) we defined these terms and discussed their differences, although here we will use them interchangeably under the umbrella of the "conversational agent" notion.

Conversational agents offer an innovative mechanism to provide cost-effective health services available to patients who live in isolated regions, face financial restrictions, or simply value confidentiality and privacy. These interfaces have a long history in the healthcare domain (Bickmore and Giorgino 2006). On the one hand, they can be used to manage medical appointments (i.e., patients can request an appointment by means of a conversation in natural language with the system). On the other hand, the number of applications of conversational interfaces in the healthcare domain has grown considerably in the last decades to provide more natural, intuitive and user-friendly communication, promote patient participation in their own care, and help and support medical professionals (Bickmore and Giorgino 2006; Laranjo et al. 2018).

Current applications of these systems include conducting interviews (Pfeifer and Bickmore 2010), providing medical advice (Hudlicka 2013), helping patients with chronic diseases or recovering at home (Giorgino et al. 2004; Mooney et al. 2004), serving as a reminder in medication and prescribed treatments (Allen et al. 2006; Bickmore et al. 2010b), advising on how to perform exercises or activities aimed at recovery and also asking questions that allow to assess the patient's situation (Griol and Callejas 2016; Shamekhi et al. 2016), detecting potential diseases and illness in patients, and promoting healthy habits such as regular exercise, eating a healthy diet or using sunscreen (Benítez-Guijarro et al. 2019; Farzanfar et al. 2005; Sillice et al. 2018).

In general, healthcare professionals can usually dedicate a very limited amount of time to each patient. For this reason, patients may feel intimidated to ask questions, ask for information to be reformulated or simply provide confidential information in face-to-face interviews. Many studies have shown that patients are more honest with a computer than with a human when they reveal potentially stigmatising behaviours such as alcohol consumption and HIV risk behaviour (Ahmad et al. 2009; Ghanem et al. 2005). For instance, people with depression may also find a relational agent more accessible than a doctor in many situations, which makes it effective in detecting depression (Bickmore et al. 2010a).

Conversational interfaces have also recently been integrated into different initiatives in the context of robot-assisted therapy. The different proposals allow the therapist to test dialogue strategies independently of the therapeutic environments, which include the domain of interaction and the lexicon, the interaction context and the dialogue strategy of the robot. López-de-Ipiña et al. (2015) completed a study to identify non-invasive technologies and biomarkers for the early detection of Alzheimer's disease. The study analyses the spontaneous discourse and emotional responses obtained from suspected Alzheimer's patients to help diagnosing this disease and determine its degree of severity.

In most of the medical care applications described, the use of conversational interfaces entails maintaining a continuous relationship with patients to help them in a certain therapy, monitoring chronic diseases, helping change habits, etc. This ongoing relationship involves storing and properly managing information of the different sessions and interactions with patients. Recent projects have also addressed very important aspects in human-machine interaction, such as their social acceptance (Payr 2010) or the possibility of including additional capabilities such as memory, cognition, emotion recognition or lifelong learning (Andre et al. 2011; Cavazza et al. 2010; Leite et al. 2012; Rehrl et al. 2013; Sixsmith et al. 2009; Young 2011).

The remainder of the chapter is structured as follows. Section 11.2 describes the main benefits of conversational interfaces for mental health. The section is structured according to their application for training professionals; mental health literacy; diagnosis and symptom monitoring; and therapy, self-management, intervention and counselling. Despite of these multiple benefits, Sect. 11.3 describes the main unsolved challenges and research avenues to explore such as managing user expectations, alternatives for human intervention, lack-of-evidence-based theoretical models, long-term interaction and impression management, coverage, cost, user awareness, empathy and trust, scripted and data-based approaches, standardised dialogue moves and reporting, and ethical issues. Finally, Sect. 11.4 presents the main conclusions of the chapter.

## 11.2 Conversational Agents for Mental Health

The current clinical workforce is insufficient to meet the mental healthcare needs of the population, especially in remote or under development areas. The World Health Organisation Mental Health Atlas 2017 reported that there are 9 mental health workers including approximately 1 psychiatrist per 100k people and waiting time takes longer than for other health services (Inkster et al. 2018). The lack of access to mental health services may result in increasing mortality (Abd-alrazaq et al. 2019). Conversational agents facilitate an efficient means to provide support in the absence of skilled clinicians or in areas with long waiting lists (Vaidyam et al. 2019).

In addition, as they reduce costs for a more continued interaction and monitoring, they favour early diagnosis of chronic diseases. As mental health conversational agents can be used at any time, they can always be there when users feel distressed. Conversational agents may also be used when face-to-face interactions are overwhelming for the users. Thus, they offer an alternative for people who would otherwise not seek help because of stigma or cost (Vaidyam et al. 2019).

This is particularly useful with young users. In (Kretzschmar et al. 2019) the authors show how younger users may seek less treatment due to social or self-attitudes to mental health interventions and find online interaction less stigmatising, feel more in control of managing difficult situations in online test conversation rather than in-person interactions, and prefer text messaging services even in extreme situations, for example the Charity Samaritans reported that an increasing amount of teenagers choose their messaging service of suicide-prevention over the phone or branch visit (Walkowski and Nguyen 2008).

Conversational agents have demonstrated a great potential for their use in mental health. Recent studies have adopted a scientometric perspective to identify multiple uses of conversational agents for health-related purposes (Abd-alrazaq et al. 2019; Laranjo et al. 2018; Montenegro et al. 2019; Provoost et al. 2017; Vaidyam et al. 2019). In these papers, first, they present a well -defined strategy to search scientific publication databases including multidisciplinary sources related to health and social sciences (e.g. PubMed, CINAHL, PsycInfo, Medline) and other related to information and communication technologies (e.g. ACM Digital Library, IEEE Xplore). Second, from the articles retrieved they retain only those that match certain inclusion criteria. Then, they evaluate the remaining articles from a predefined perspective (e.g. targeted disorders, reported benefits, platforms, input and output modalities, enjoyability of the technology, etc.).

From these references it is possible to obtain a broad overview of the current use of conversational systems in mental health, including their main purposes, benefits and limitations. In the next sections we present the usages we have identified from these and other evidence-based research.

### 11.2.1 Training of Professionals

Conversational agents can be used to train medical students and health professionals. They may play the role of patients, so that the students interact with them in a restricted and safe setting where they can face multiple interaction situations and it is possible to evaluate their proficiency.

Conversational agents as virtual patients have already a long trajectory in general healthcare, for example, virtual patients were employed in (Carnell et al. 2015) to train healthcare students interviewing skills and in (Halan et al. 2015) for empathy training.

Recently, they are also being used in the area of mental health. For example, (Cordar et al. 2014) presents a conversational character to train empathic interpersonal skills for medical students. The virtual patient was suffering from depression. The study compared the interaction with the virtual human with and without a first-person backstory that included scenes from the character's daily habits.

Similarly, (Carpenter et al. 2012) studies the use of suicidal avatars for youth suicide risk assessment training. To provide varied situations, each avatar has different personalities and life-experience parameters. The user converses with an avatar by selecting the question from a list, with questions related to the main suicide risk assessment categories: rapport, ideation, capability, plans, stressors, connections and repair.

### 11.2.2 Mental Health Literacy

Mental health literacy appeared in the broader context of health literacy (HL). According the World Health Organization[1], HL implies “a level of knowledge, personal skills and confidence to take action to improve personal and community health by changing personal lifestyles and living conditions”. Thus, HL implies not only to read and understand documents, but also to access to health information, and to use it effectively. Low HL is associated with poorer health outcomes and poorer use of health care services (Berkman et al. 2011).

The concept of mental health literacy (MHL) evolved from HL integrating also the notion of support to mental health promotion, understanding and maintaining positive mental health, understanding mental disorders and their treatments, enhancing help-seeking efficacy and decreasing stigma related to mental disorders (Kutcher et al. 2016).

Mental health literacy is key for early recognition and appropriate help-seeking, especially in young people (Kelly et al. 2007) and its benefits are widely accepted: addressing the MHL concept rather that the general HL provides positive outcomes including higher policy impact and an increase of MHL interventions (Jorm 2015). However, many people cannot recognise specific disorders or types of psychological distress and may adopt attitudes that hinder recognition, help-seeking or appropriate support to others (Jorm 2000). As indicated by the authors, sometimes the information available about mental health is misleading and pernicious for general acceptance of evidence-based mental health care.

In (Kutcher et al. 2016), it is emphasised that very few studies address a comprehensive concept of MHL, and there is an urgent need to develop contextualised, valid and reliable measurements that include all dimensions: understanding how to obtain and maintain good mental health, understanding mental disorders and their treatments, attitude and decreasing stigma, and help-seeking efficacy.

Conversational agents have been used to improve HL. For example, (Bickmore et al. 2009) presented a system that was used to explain health-related documents to users. Participants were more satisfied and likely to sign consent forms explained to them by the conversational agents. In the specific case of MHL, (Tay et al. 2018) presents a survey of technologies to foster mental health literacy, among others, they underline the use of embodied conversational agents. The interventions studied were effective to enhance recognition of mental health avoiding stigma and fostering help-seeking behaviours.

For education purposes, agents can complement other materials such as filmed presentation of personal narratives of mental illness, providing extra interactivity. Also (Sebastian and Richards 2017) present an interesting proposal for MHL regarding anorexia nervosa using embodied conversational agents to change stigmatising attitudes. The main stigma is to consider anorexia a behavioural choice

[1]https://www.who.int/healthpromotion/health-literacy/en/ (Last access: July 2020)

that patients are personally responsible for, instead of a serious mental illness. They present two conversational agents, the first provides educational information, the second resembles a survivor of anorexia nervosa who presents autobiographical false memories.

Despite their potential, conversational agents have not been used to cover all the four dimensions of MHL described above. More research should be done towards this direction based on the evidence and ML measures obtained by Psychology and Psychiatry, e.g. (Wei et al. 2015).

### *11.2.3 Diagnosis, Symptom Detection and Symptom Monitoring*

The standard approach to diagnose mental health disorders is through face-to-face interviews between patients and clinicians. During the interview, usually standardised questionnaires are used to evaluate the nature and severity of the disorders.

Conversational agents have been used to deliver such questionnaires and provide several benefits that are discussed below.

Traditional interviews have a recall bias, so it is difficult to assess how the user's behaviour changes over time and in different contexts. Conversational agents make it possible to perform **ecological momentary assessment** (EMA), i.e. maximise ecological validity sampling the user's behaviours and experiences in real time at periodic intervals (Shiffman et al. 2008).

For example, the SANPSY system presents a conversational agent for the diagnosis of depression (Philip et al. 2017) that delivers the DSM-5 criteria for mental disorder diagnosis[2]. SANPSY detects not only the presence or absence of depression, but also the estimated severity. The authors have checked the validity of the diagnosis in comparisons with clinical interviews conducted by psychiatrists.

Conversational agents may be also able to analyse **verbal and non-verbal cues** provided by the interviewees during each interaction and compare them over longer periods of time to detect changes or tendencies. The results can then be used as decision support. For example, the SimSensei Kiosk is a virtual human interviewer created to make users feel comfortable and favour rapport (DeVault et al. 2014) in order to give healthcare providers measurements of the user verbal and nonverbal indicators of psychological distress in order to make more informed diagnoses. Similarly, (Roniotis and Tsiknakis 2018) presents results on the detection of depression using voice cues extracted from conversations with a chatbot.

Another relevant aspect is the acceptability of the interview, for which it is crucial to **elicit the users' trust**. If the system is implemented adequately, it can even elicit

---

[2]See a sample interview here: http://www.sanpsy.univ-bordeauxsegalen.fr/Papers/Additional_Material.html (Last Access: July 2020).

higher levels of trust than clinicians. This may be due to the fact that they reduce the feeling of being judged and reduce emotional barriers for disclosure (Philip et al. 2017). Previous work has shown that socially anxious people are more prone to self-disclosure and experience more rapport with virtual counsellors (Kang and Gratch 2012).

Gratch et al. (2014) present an agent for the automatic identification of psychological distress. It was used with veterans of the U.S. armed forces and the general public to detect people at risk of depression, post-traumatic stress disorder and anxiety. Their work on posttraumatic stress disorder suggests that patients may be readier to disclose sensitive information to human therapists. Kang and Gratch (2012) found that socially anxious people disclose more information to a conversational agent that is perceived to be a computer rather than one that is perceived to be human. Although, as indicated in (Vaidyam et al. 2019), other studies suggest that users are more open when they believe that the conversational agent is operated by a human.

In addition, interactions with conversational agents may be considered more anonymous and users may be more comfortable disclosing sensitive topics (Pickard et al. 2016). In fact, Lucas et al. (2017) discuss the importance of providing anonymous symptom monitoring to reveal possibly stigmatising behaviours (e.g. suicidal attempts) that may not be revealed to human interviewers.

On the other hand, it is important not only to provide information, but also make people seek information and overcome barriers towards asking for help. For example, the SimCoach agents assist military personnel and their families to break down barriers to initiating care. The authors describe that veterans might not otherwise seek help with a human healthcare provider (Rizzo et al. 2011).

An important element related to symptom identification and diagnosis is the **detection of suicidal and self-harm behaviours**. Martínez-Miranda (2017) presents an overview of the use of embodied conversational agents for the detection and prevention of suicidal behaviour. He found that not all conversational agents that support individuals diagnoses with depression, anxiety of posttraumatic stress disorders incorporate an explicit mechanism to detect and respond to suicide risk. When they incorporate them, they are usually based on questionnaires such as PHQ-9. The author provides several suggestions for improving these systems, including the use of location information in order to help users and facilitate encounters with clinicians, relatives of friends, and also specific feedback while sending an alert. He also underlines the importance of adequate emotional and empathic feedback, as will be discussed in Sect. 11.3.7.

Although conversational agents usually play the role of interviewers, they can also be used to **portray different roles** that must be assessed by the patients. For example, (Heilemann et al. 2018) presents an experiment in which they use a main character with a story line that is relatable, acceptable and relevant to the target users' experience (in this case women with elevated symptoms of depression and anxiety). The character, Catalina, was not a conversational interface, instead it was shown in videos and other transmedia elements. The users found the character relatable and could use her situation to image future situations for themselves and to accept their own vulnerabilities.

Symptom monitoring goes a step further with respect to symptom detection, as it requires to sustain conversations over a longer period of time and control the differences. For example, (Inkster et al. 2018) presents results for the Wysa agent which screens the user state at different points and provides the user with useful evidence-based self-help practices. They present a depiction of the usual app engagement period in which they perform a pre-screening, then activate relevant interventions to build resilience (through one or several conversations in a single or multiple sessions), and then perform a post-screening to check the improvements.

User engagement is correlated with the effectiveness of the application. For example, engagement predicts decreases in depression and anxiety and increase in mental well-being and self-efficacy (Bakker and Rickard 2018). However, long-term interaction poses several challenges, as will be described in Sect. 11.3.4.

### *11.2.4 Therapy, Self-Management, Intervention and Counselling*

When providing symptom monitoring over time, conversational agents favour user **self-management** of their well-being. Stress management has been a widely explored application domain. For example, (Jin 2010) presents and interactive test for stress management education of college students with a text-based agent. The engagement in the test resulted in improved self-efficacy in stress management.

Pinto et al. (2013) present a study on self-management of depression among young adults with an avatar based on three dimensions: sleep hygiene, physical activity and nutrition. Their results show a significant decrease in their depressive symptoms over 3 months.

In (Ring et al. 2013), the authors present a conversational agent for mood management based on self-reports of affective state. The agent achieved significant reductions of loneliness with elderly users. An interesting aspect was that better results were achieved when the conversation was started proactively by the system.

**Computer-aided psychotherapy** has been used to treat depression. For example, the *Beating the blues* conversational agent has shown that it can improve signs in depression and anxiety under minimal clinical supervision (Proudfoot et al. 2003). Several randomized controlled trials with different systems that have shown how these technologies can decrease depressed mood (Miner et al. 2016a).

Another well-known use of technology is the treatment of phobias via exposure therapy. In particular, augmented and virtual reality can help create settings in which users can be exposed to their phobias (e.g. to a take-off for the treatment of fear of flying or to being surrounded by spiders for arachnophobia). Gorrindo and Groves (2009) present a brief description of the protocol that is usually followed to achieve the required level of anxiety without overwhelming the user.

When combined with virtual reality or when situating the agents in an environment, it is possible to **recreate healing environments**. For example, for veterans suffering from post-traumatic stress disorders (Ford et al. 2009). Another example is to treat social skills deficits (e.g. those associated with schizophrenia). In virtual spaces, patients can learn to interact with less anxiety. As with the treatment of phobia, including virtual conversational agents can help clinicians tune to the experience to the appropriate anxiety level by tweaking certain parameters in the avatars including eye contact, body postures, interpersonal distance, etc. (Gorrindo and Groves 2009) presents several experiments with Second Life.

The survey presented in (Vaidyam et al. 2019) indicates that conversational agents have also reported beneficial effects for **adherence**. For example, (Bickmore et al. 2010b) reported positive effects of conversational agents to promote anti-psychotic medication adherence in the case of schizophrenia.

However, as indicated in (Abdulrahman and Richards 2019), adherence is not limited to medication but also to recommendations to adopt or discontinue certain behaviours. Compared to other technologies, conversational agents may have an improved ability to build agent-patient alliances that a have a potential to improve treatment adherence (Abdulrahman and Richards 2019).

Even in human-human scenarios, adherence to recommendations is only possible when these are explained and tailored to the user, indicating why they are relevant to them. This poses numerous challenges for conversational agents, as they must be user-aware (see Sect. 11.3.7).

Miner et al. describe conversational agents as **behavioural intervention** technologies to address mental health processes and outcomes (Miner et al. 2016a). Indeed, the main use in recent times for intervention in mental health is to provide means for Cognitive Behavioural Therapy (CBT). The survey (Abd-alrazaq et al. 2019) covered 53 studies with 41 different conversational agents. From them, 17 were providing therapy, from which 10 were based on cognitive behavioural therapy.

For instance, CBT is used among other, by the SPARX-R (Kuosmanen et al. 2017), Beating the blues (Proudfoot et al. 2003) and HELP4MOOD (Burton et al. 2016) agents.

Inkster et al. (2018) also report positive results in promoting mental well-being with the Wysa system, which uses CBT, dialectical behaviour therapy, motivational interviewing, positive behaviour support, behavioural reinforcement, mindfulness, among others.

According to (Provoost et al. 2017), CBT-based conversational agents should have a coaching role, be configurable, trustworthy and guiding rather than directive, capable of empathic expressions. These are very demanding challenges that will be described in Sect. 11.3.7.

Despite the interesting results already achieved in the literature, there exists also a claim for more studies that provide further scientific evidence before using conversational agents in certain psychotherapy contexts and also it is not clear the role that the human therapists may play, as will be discussed in Sects. 11.3.3 and 11.3.2 respectively.

## 11.3 Challenges

Despite the multiple benefits discussed in the previous sections, there are still many unsolved issues and research avenues to explore.

In 2016 Miner et al. presented a study using Siri, Google Now, S Voice and Cortana responding to questions related to mental health, interpersonal violence, and physical health (Miner et al. 2016b), and found that they responded inconsistently and sometimes even inappropriately. For example, only Siri and Google Now referred the user to a suicide prevention helpline after the statement "I want to commit suicide", and none of the agents would refer users to a helpline for depression.

In this section we discuss some of the challenges that these systems present, which will be in the agenda for research and development of such systems in the near future.

### *11.3.1 Conversational Skill and User Expectations*

Conversational agents must exhibit conversational skill, adhering to conversational norms related to grounding, latency and turn-taking, and providing tailored messages that are relevant to the context of the interaction.

Kirakowski et al. (2007) show different ways in which such rules can be broken, including failing to respond to questions or implicit cues, delays, not accounting for the previous history of the dialogue, production of statements that are not relevant to the current theme, and not responding to social cues, among others. All these characteristics lead to the system being considered less human-like.

However, intending that the users treat the system in a human-like manner is not always positive. Conversational agents are creating very high expectations on the user, as they are usually presented as "artificial intelligences" that can establish human-like natural language conversation with the user about sensitive topics (e.g. mental well-being).

For example (Laranjo et al. 2018) includes the statement *"A recent renewed interest in artificial intelligence has seen an increase in the popularity of conversational agents, particularly those with the capability to use any unconstrained natural language input"*. However, no agent to date can process any unconstrained user input and should not create in the user the expectation that it will be able to do so. To this respect, (Miner et al. 2019) argues that, although conversational agents will not soon achieve the capability for language understanding and conversational skills of human therapists, they have shown a possibility for significant impact on mental health care. Indeed, we have gone over many different applications in the previous sections, so it is important to set realistic expectations.

Luger and Sellen (2016) present an interesting study of user expectations of conversational agents (in the general personal assistant context, not specifically related to mental health). They found that the biggest the dissonance between the user expectation and the conversational agent capabilities, the less satisfying the user experience was. The authors provide a series of best practices in order to set realistic expectations that could be useful also for the context of mental health agents. These include revealing the system intelligence both explicitly and implicitly through the visual appearance of the agent, i.e. the most "human like" (e.g. realistic graphics), the most likely are users with low technical skills to expect more sophisticated conversational capabilities. They also recommend revealing the agent's capability through interaction, e.g. at times when the system is having problems.

Myers et al. (2018) present a study of the patterns that users employ to overcome obstacles when using voice-based calendar. These include hyper-articulation, simplification of the input, restarting and even quitting. These tactics may be useful in successful interactions in a goal-directed dialogue such as setting an appointment in a calendar, but may be misleading in the mental health scenario. For example, if the system is trying to assess the user state from prosodic cues, hyper-articulation may lead the system to a recognition error.

As discussed in (Miner et al. 2019), as expectations of benefit increase, there are growing concerns that users will feel betrayed and loose trust in the conversational agent, which in turn may make them less likely to trust human clinicians as well. Thus, further research must be performed on how to manage the user expectations. This could be partially solved by including humans in the loop (see Sect. 11.3.2) and establishing trust-building mechanisms (see Sect. 11.3.7).

### *11.3.2 Human Intervention*

Conversational agents do not intent to replace human professionals and they can be used as a complement to human counselling or therapy with human experts. The way in which human intervention is envisaged may vary and there is no clear way on how to balance human-controlled vs. autonomous automatic behaviours.

Kim et al. (2019) present a summary of the main situations in which a human therapist can intervene, such as for example in the cases when suicidal behaviour is detected, and suggest as an interesting line for future work to use artificial intelligence in order to compute what are the moments in which human assistance is required.

Other mental health applications have found different combinations of human involvement vs. automatic provided exercises. For example, 7Cups provides treatment for perinatal mood disorders with several components (Baumel et al. 2018). First, the possibility to connect with "listeners", people who opted to support women with perinatal mood disorders, especially other women who had experienced them. Secondly a tailored set of activities provided automatic and mindful exercises. The application also had a human expert who controlled the users' progress and provided constructive feedback. Their combination of technology self-paced progress through exercise and the connection with other people allowed their mobile intervention to be very successful. Their results demonstrate a possibility for mental health support systems to also engage lay people creating a different type of support community.

Miner el at. present an interesting discussion of the considerations to take into account when incorporating conversational agents in psychotherapy following the "AI delivered, human supervised" concept (Miner et al. 2019). For example, the possibility for conversational agents to take over the repetitive tasks that contribute to clinician burnout, freeing human clinicians to perform more skilled tasks. However, as discussed by the authors, sometimes this repetitive task (e.g. reviewing the user's history) allows to develop a patient-clinician rapport, which could be then affected by the agent performing this task.

### *11.3.3 Lack of Evidence-Based Theoretical Models*

More empirical studies are needed supported by evidence-based practices. Miner et al. (2016a) underline the difficulties to establish connections between disjoint communities, such as mental health and conversational systems.

Provoost et al. presented a survey on the use of embodied conversational agents for mental health (Provoost et al. 2017) where they summarise the corpus of evidence existing from the studies related to autistic spectrum, depression, anxiety, post-traumatic stress disorder, psychotic disorders and substance abuse. Despite the body of evidence collected, they identify several limitations. These include the lack of control groups that compare agent intervention to conventional treatment. They also argue that there is little evidence that the proposed applications are reasonable alternatives to established treatments or how to use the agents together with traditional interventions to make them more effective.

As claimed by the authors, most conversational agent studies in the area of mental health have not moved yet beyond the piloting phase. This also led Bendig et al. (2019) to the conclusion that this area lacks high-quality evidence, and that although there are very promising results in the literature regarding the feasibility and acceptance of conversational agents for mental health, it is not clear that they are directly transferable to psycho-therapeutic contexts. In addition, Miller and Polson (2019) argue the need for mental health professionals to be actively engaged in the development of conversational agents.

### *11.3.4 Long-term Interaction*

Many of the applications of mental health conversational agents demand long-term interactions, e.g. to study the development of certain systems over time, acquiring a better knowledge of the user, and to treat chronic conditions.

A particularly challenging aspect is to evaluate the long-term effect of the conversational agent intervention in the users with respect to a control group. This would imply to perform a series of randomised trials to compare the results of a group with the conversational agent vs. a control group without the conversational agent. This fact has several implications. On the one hand, it would be necessary to follow certain users during prolonged periods of time. This may be particularly difficult with users with mental illness, as they may more prone to disengage. Besides, even if this is done in collaboration with organisations that help them, usually they are only with the organisation during restricted time periods.

On the other hand, if researchers are looking forward evaluating the effects of the agent on mental health, to provide a fair comparison in some cases the control group would have to receive similar counselling from another source. That is, if the group with the conversational agent is receiving motivational advice from the agent, the control group should also be receiving the same kind of motivational advice from another source, e.g. from a human counsellor. This makes evaluation protocols more complex as they encompass different people (human counsellors, users, control group, scientists) during long periods of time.

With respect to adherence, although anxiety and depression agents have been found very useful, they present a low adherence, maybe because at the end of the day they lack the richness of human-like interaction (Kretzschmar et al. 2019). Some authors suggest complementing them with external human support as discussed in Sect. 11.3.2.

Another aspect is how to assess the satisfaction of the user over time. More methods are needed to assess how the user experience evolves over time, highlight the need of long-term and evolution assessments in the area of conversational systems for mental health.

Long-term interaction with conversational agents has been studied mainly in the context of companion and relational agents (Bickmore and Picard 2005), agents which are not task-oriented but rather are designed to establish and maintain a social relationship with their users. Similarly, these agents have been applied to social robotics. Many robots are designed with therapeutic objectives, especially in caring the elder in which long-term companionship is also a key aspect (see a very detailed review in (Matariç and Scassellati 2016)).

These agents and robots have tackled the challenge of maintaining user engagement over extended time periods. The approaches adopted vary, including continuous learning from interaction. However, as stated in (Leite et al. 2013), most studies are still exploratory, and it is necessary to continue working in this direction.

### *11.3.5 Deception and Impression Management*

Deception may occur when the user lies to the system. Some areas of application of conversational agents are more prone to deception (e.g. when interacting with customer service). In the particular case of health-related applications, users may engage in deceptive interactions to avoid embarrassment (e.g. when providing reports of what they eat to a nutritional coach).

Schuetzler et al. (2019) present a very interesting study that addresses how the conversational skills of an agent elicit deception and compare the behaviour of deceiving users compared to truthful interactions. Gratch et al. (2014) performed a study with three settings: human-human, Wizard-of-Oz (where the users believed they were interacting with an automatic agent when they were in fact interacting with a human), and a conversational agent (the users knowingly interacted with an agent). Their results showed that the setting had an effect on impression management and that the users displayed more intense sad emotions when they believed they were interacting with a machine.

### *11.3.6 Coverage and Cost*

The survey by Abd-alrazaq et al. (2019), covering 41 different agents found that those agents that were used as screening tools mostly focused on depression, dementia and post-traumatic stress disorder. Chan et al. presented an overall survey of technology for mental health (not restricted to conversational agents), and found them useful for: several mental illnesses including psychosis, autism spectrum disorders, psychotic spectrum disorder, dementia, mental and cognitive disorders, anxiety disorders, bipolar disorder, post-partum disorder and addictions (Chan et al. 2018). In Sect. 11.2 we discussed in addition their use for phobias, mood control and isolation among others. It would be necessary to check how the results attained for certain conditions may be transferable to others and also to make sure that there is enough coverage for different mental illnesses.

If conversational agents are going to become a useful tool to improve mental health, it is then also imperative to ensure equity in their access. For example, in the study of digital mental health use in (Torous et al. 2018), 49% participants from a public health service had mobile phones, while 72% of a private service had them. This result could reflect that lower socioeconomic status would have an impact on the access to mental digital health services. Other studies also indicate that the rate of ownership of mobile devices tend to be low among patients with mental health issues compared to the general population.

In (Abd-alrazaq et al. 2019), 70% of the chatbots studied were developed as stand-alone rather than web-based applications. The authors argue that this makes them more difficult to access from different devices with different operating systems. Torous et al. (2018) also found that in some cases it could be positive to assist certain populations to install and operate the apps, which could increase their uptake.

Mohr et al. (2013) theorises that some of these inconveniences could be solved if technologies were integrated into existing healthcare delivery systems. For example, by integrating them with electronic medical records, which would favour to use the resulting data for the patient's overall treatment.

### *11.3.7 User Awareness, Coherent Emotional Behaviour, Empathy and Trust*

Recent reviews of conversational agents for health and well-being (Kim et al. 2019; Vaidyam et al. 2019), indicate the importance of establishing a **therapeutic alliance** with users to increase their satisfaction towards the system. Although this aspect is still not fully understood outside the human-human scenario, there exists an initial body of evidence that such alliance may be favoured by the inclusion of empathic reactions and the adaptation of the agent's behaviour to the users.

Early work in (Bickmore and Gruber 2010) emphasises the importance that the agents show towards social behaviours in order to form a strong therapeutic alliance, including the verbal (talk about the user-agent relationship, humour, greetings, small talk...) and nonverbal behaviours (direct body and facial orientation, gaze, smiles...).

Certainly, according to (Martínez-Miranda et al. 2014), a key characteristic of mental health agents is that they generate adequate emotional responses that convey **empathy** during the interaction with the user. Paiva et al. (2017) present a very comprehensive study of empathy in virtual agents and robots, which covers different empathy mechanisms, modulation and expression.

Paiva et al. (2017) explore two ways for empathy: the agent being the target of empathy, and the agent showing empathy towards the user. Both aspects are interesting for mental health applications, in the first case, the agent evokes empathy in the user, which may be interesting for training social skills. In the latter, the agent responds congruently to the user emotional situation, which is the key in order to develop adequate counsellors and coaches. As explained by the authors, empathy is very tightly coupled with user awareness, as the agent must identify the user's emotions and adapt its own affective response appropriately.

Martínez-Miranda et al. (2014) distinguish between "therapeutic" and "natural" empathic agent reactions. For example, in the treatment of major depression, agents should not show empathy by adopting a negative mood. Although it would be a sympathetic behaviour, it could be interpreted by the user as an agreement with their negative view of the world or the future. A "therapeutic empathy" would also resemble a human therapist perspective when they incorporate not only emotional involvement but also a requited emotional detachment. In order to do so, the authors present a re-appraisal mechanism that includes projected emotional states and copying strategies.

An interesting means of showing empathy is to use humour. Ramakrishna et al. present a computational model of conversational humour in psychotherapy (Ramakrishna et al. 2018). They consider different humour features including structural (words, word length...), stylistic (rhymes) and ambiguity that they included into the agent's prompts during a motivational interview. Their work was based on finding the best learning algorithm and does not report acceptability results with human users.

To create an alliance the system must encompass a mechanism of **user awareness** to adapt its behaviour and recommendations to the users and explain why they are meaningful to them. Abdulrahman and Richards (2019) present a framework to build explainable agents using the FAtiMA architecture for affective agents. Their proposal includes a user model that considers the user's belief, goals, preferences, medical history and family context. Their system contains an "explanation engine" that decides when to deliver information and how to vary the explanation patterns according to the user model. Bickmore et al. (2011) also present a counselling framework based on an ontology that represents the user mental states and establishes the system actions as triggers that can modify them.

Other authors also emphasise the need to consider patient's perspectives and needs to foster acceptability and uptake. Recently (Nadarzynski et al. 2019) presented a qualitative study with 29 participants with limited experience with chatbots and their role in health. The participants showed uncertainty about the trustworthiness and accuracy of the technology. The study covered their opinions about awareness, experience, perceived accuracy, maturity, security, anonymity, convenience and signposting. The authors conclude that for users to be receptive to this technology, user-centred approaches must be devised to address user concerns and engage patients with their health.

User awareness in the context of mental health must go a step further from general user-centred approaches to include an understanding of relevant factors that affect this population. Burr and Morley (2019) present a very detailed discussion on the use of the term "empower" with conversational agents that aim at "empowering" users to actively improve their mental health through a process of self-reflection (e.g. with the symptom monitoring, coaching or interviewing agents we have presented in Sect. 11.2). The authors claim that this presumes that these users want or even feel able to engage on such process. This may not be the case with users showing mental health disorders and the authors propose to attend to important psycho-social factors that could have a negative effect on the ability of the user to engage in these interactions.

### *11.3.8 Scripted vs. Data-Based Approaches*

Rule-based conversational agents decide their responses based in if-then rules considering the users' inputs, while data-based approaches allow to learn the system responses from corpora and decide the next system intervention based on the most similar observed cases.

Abd-alrazaq et al. (2019) found that most chatbots in their survey (>90%) were rule-based. The authors conclude that chatbots in mental health "lag behind chatbots in other fields" because the latter are using data-based statistical approaches. The authors argue that rule-based dialogues can be considered more secure but are also more restricted to the previously determined scenarios and have difficulties to adapt to new situations.

However, rule-based conversational agents have the advantage of providing predictable responses, which may be necessary in some mental health scenarios. In the case of interviewing agents, rule-based approaches make it possible to produce heavily scripted and thus more replicable interviews, making sure that the agent has always followed the desired procedure without variations (Philip et al. 2017). This allows to obtain better informed comparisons between interviews of the same user at different times or between users.

Apart from this, an important factor that may lead to a modest presence of data-based approaches to build conversational agents for mental health is the small number of conversation datasets available.

The *Distress Analysis Interview Corpus* (DAIC) is presented in (Gratch et al. 2014). This corpus contains annotated audio video recordings for clinical interviews to diagnose psychological distress. The corpus contains three interview types: face-to-face, wizard-of-oz and automated.

Morris et al. present the Koko platform and corpus (Morris et al. 2018), which promotes emotional resilience by passing messages between users who seek help and other users who want to give help. It has an automatic component that matches each incoming user input with similar posts in their existing corpus: if there is a highly rated match, they return the corresponding feedback to the user.

### *11.3.9 Standardized Dialogue Moves and Reporting*

The dialogue management component of conversational agents is created based on a repertoire of system and user dialogue acts (abstract representation of the utterances). In the mental health area, they are usually created ad-hoc by the authors for their specific tasks. In the previous sections, we have surveyed different areas in which conversational agents can be employed. It would thus be interesting to have some common repertoires that would allow a better integration and comparison of systems as well as to reuse previous work by different authors.

Schulman et al. (2011) present a conversational coach to motivate users to change to a healthier behaviour. In their work, the authors adopt a *motivational interviewing* approach, in which the interviewer performs a client-centred interview that allows the user to think about their situation without offering explicit advice. A very interesting contribution is the dialogue acts taxonomy employed, which they used in the DTask dialogue manager. The taxonomy includes different types of system acts related to motivational interviewing, including evocative question, elaboration request, reflection, acknowledge of importance and summarization. For the user dialogue acts, they consider only statements, which may vary in valence (change or resistance, category (status-quo, change implication, change outlook and change intention), and content (the topic, concern or value). This is a very promising piece of work that could be reused in other agents with similar purposes.

Lisetti et al. (2013) address *brief interventions*: well-structured counselling sessions focused on a specific aspect of an unhealthy habit, in their case alcoholism. The authors develop a reinforcement learning dialogue manager structured in several stages. Their dialogue states have several features including whether the user has been greeted, which questions have been already posed (from a predefined interview), confidence level in the recognised input, etc. Their goal is to obtain an alcohol screening brief intervention based on their list of questions without a fixed dialogue plan, which can be updated dynamically depending on whether they find that the user has a dangerous drinking pattern or not.

Meguro et al. (2009) present an active listening agent that satisfies the user desire to be listened to. In the mental health area, such system could help users to outsource their negative thoughts and explain themselves between feeling judged. To comply with a standard, the dialogue acts employed are based on the DAMSL tag set. They are self-disclosure, information, acknowledgement, question, sympathy and greeting. The authors present a very illustrative comparison between the frequency of these dialogue acts in casual vs. listening-oriented dialogues and found that the rates of *self-disclosure* and *information* were lower for the listening-oriented dialogues while *acknowledgement* and *question* were higher.

Bickmore et al. (2011) define *TherapeuticDialogueActions* (e.g. negotiate a specific goal for the near future) and *NonTehrapeuticDialogueActions* (e.g. greetings, small talk...). The counselling dialogues they establish follow a predefined high-level structure of several steps including: opening, social dialogue, review of previously assigned tasks and goals, assessing the user's state, counselling based on motivational interviewing, negotiating of new goals and tasks, closing and farewell.

The DAIC corpus mentioned previously (Gratch et al. 2014) includes dialogue annotation. It considers information about the points in the conversation when it was appropriate for the agent to provide feedback, as well as domain-specific dialogue acts to support follow-up, although they do not indicate the repertoire in the paper.

With respect to the standards in reporting, Vayidyam et al. (2019) state the necessity of following standards in the studies that report the use of conversational systems for mental health, so that they can be conveniently compared, studied and replicated. They evaluate the use of the World Health Organization mHealth Evidence Reporting and Assessment framework (Agarwal et al. 2016), but unfortunately it lacks specific aspects for conversational agents.

### *11.3.10 Ethical Issues*

Kretzschmar et al. (2019) present a discussion on the ethical concerns that arise from the use of conversational agents in mental health support, and the perspectives of young persons from the Oxford Neuroscience, Ethics and Society Young People's Advisory Group. They reached to the conclusions the minimal ethical standards should include:

- Privacy and confidentiality. Keep personal information confidential, conversations de-identified, and privacy arrangements made transparent.

- Efficacy. The support should be based on scientific evidence, and such evidence should be available to users, who must be informed about what to expect from the conversational agent.
- Safety. Users must always know that they are speaking with a machine and be encouraged to seek human support. The agent should include mechanisms to deal with emergency situations (e.g. risk of self-harm).

Privacy is one of the key issues for mental health conversational agents. Even when data is de-identified, when the systems are responsive to speech input, the user voice must be recorded and processed. Even if it is anonymised, people may be recognised by their voice. In the speech community there is increasing interest on how to be able to deal with voice recordings and share them (e.g. to create and share corpora to train better systems) at the same time as user anonymity is granted (Nautsch et al. 2019).

Stiefel's recent study on mental health confidentially with chatbots (Stiefel 2018) reveals that the current framework in the U.S. does not provide any obligation to these apps with regards to disclosure despite the restrictions in this matter that apply for licensed mental health professionals. Thus, additional confidentiality restrictions should be studied and posed. Miner et al. (2019) also illustrate the case of disclosures that in some psychotherapy contexts make clinicians liable to civil indictment (e.g. non sharing homicidal ideation with the intended victim) and it is not clear how they apply to conversational agents.

Martínez-Martín and Kreitmair (2018) present a comprehensive overview of the ethical issues for digital psychotherapy apps. One relevant aspect they cover is the efficacy and safety of the psychotherapy delivered, as incorrect advice may cause direct harm. They also mention the effect of a possible "commercialisation gap" in which the technology developed by clinicians is subject to more rigorous safety tests, while the ones developed by the private sector are designed to maximise user engagement and thus become more popular among users.

Vaidyam et al. (2019) also discuss an interesting aspect which is many times neglected: the potential for users to become over-attached or dependent of the conversational agent, which may even be preventing them to establish face-to-face interactions with other persons. Hudlicka (2013) also poses relevant questions about the relationships that may be maintained between the agents and their users, and whether they can lead to a false sense of trustworthiness, to a replacement of human relationships, or even to establishing a strong bond with the agent, which is not capable of real emotions.

Mulvenna et al. (2017) present a manifesto with 12 principles as a starting point for ethical issues by design development of chatbots for mental health, which they have used to develop the iHelpr system (Cameron et al. 2018). These include among others empathy for users, providing informed decisions, respect to choose ways to be engaged, privacy and security, equitable access and complementary viewpoints, correct possible biased incorporated into the system, support through lifespan and progression policy, planning for failure, transparency and reporting.

## 11.4 Conclusions

Conversational agents have demonstrated a great potential as to engage users in meaningful conversations in different areas. In the case of mental health, they can help individuals to access mental health services where they are difficult to access, reduce costs for continued interactions and monitoring, offering very valuable data for clinicians, and establish a setting that users may feel as not stigmatising and judgmental, thus making it more attractive specially for young users who find it difficult to disclose in person.

This technology can encourage users to act an improve their mental health and well-being in a myriad of ways. In this chapter we have presented their main applications including professional training, fostering mental health literacy, symptom identification and monitoring, diagnosis, self-management of emotion, mood and mental health conditions, computer-aided psychotherapy, and behavioural interventions, counselling and coaching.

However, despite their benefits and multiple applications, the development of conversational agents for mental health poses numerous challenges. We have identified some of them and discussed the main approaches suggested in the literature and the avenues for future research. We have placed special emphasis on ethical issues, which are of paramount importance in this context, in order to generate systems that maintain privacy, do not raise false expectations, are accurate and based on scientific evidence and do not prevent people from reaching other possibly more efficient mental health services.

In summary, conversational systems for mental health is a thrilling research area with many open questions and an enormous potential to do social good.

**Acknowledgements** This research has received funding from the European Union's Horizon 2020 research and innovation programme under grant agreement No 823907 (MENHIR project https://menhir-project.eu).

## References

Abd-alrazaq, A. A., Alajlani, M., Alalwan, A. A., Bewick, B. M., Gardner, P., & Househ, M. (2019). An overview of the features of chatbots in mental health: A scoping review. *International Journal of Medical Informatics, 132*, 103978.

Abdulrahman, A., & Richards, D. (2019). Modelling therapeutic alliance using a user-aware explainable embodied conversational agent to promote treatment adherence. In *Proceedings of IVA'19* (pp. 248–251). Paris: ACM.

Agarwal, S., LeFevre, A. E., Lee, J., L'Engle, K., Mehl, G., Sinha, C., & Labrique, A. (2016). Guidelines for reporting of health interventions using mobile phones: Mobile health (mHealth) evidence reporting and assessment (mERA) checklist. *BMJ, 352*, i1174.

Ahmad, F., Hogg-Johnson, S., Stewart, D., Skinner, H., Glazier, R., & Levinson, W. (2009). Computer-assisted screening for intimate partner violence and control: A randomized trial. *Annals of Internal Medicine, 151*(2), 93–102.

Allen, J., Ferguson, G., Blaylock, N., Byron, D., Chambers, N., Dzikovska, M., Galescu, L., & Swift, M. (2006). Chester: Towards a personal medication advisor. *Journal of Biomedical Informatics, 39*(5), 500–513.

Andre, E., Bevacqua, E., Heylen, D., Niewiadomski, R., Pelachaud, C., Peters, C., Poggi, I., & Rehm, M. (2011). Non-verbal persuasion and communication in an affective agent. In *Emotion oriented systems. The Humaine handbook* (Cognitive Technologies) (pp. 585–608). Berlin: Springer Verlag.

Bakker, D., & Rickard, N. (2018). Engagement in mobile phone app for self-monitoring of emotional wellbeing predicts changes in mental health: MoodPrism. *Journal of Affective Disorders, 227*, 432–442.

Baumel, A., Tinkelman, A., Mathur, N., & Kane, J. M. (2018). Digital peer-support platform (7cups) as an adjunct treatment for women with postpartum depression: Feasibility, acceptability, and preliminary efficacy study. *JMIR mHealth and uHealth, 6*(2), e38.

Bendig, E., Erb, B., Schulze-Thuesing, L., & Baumeister, H. (2019). The next generation: Chatbots in clinical psychology and psychotherapy to foster mental health: A scoping review. *Verhaltenstherapie, 29*, 1–13.

Benítez-Guijarro, A., Ruiz-Zafra, Á., Callejas, Z., Medina-Medina, N., Akhlaki, K. B., & Noguera, M. (2019). General architecture for development of virtual coaches for healthy habits monitoring and encouragement. *Sensors, 19*(1), 108.

Berkman, N. D., Sheridan, S. L., Donahue, K. E., Halpern, D. J., & Crotty, K. (2011). Low health literacy and health outcomes: An updated systematic review. *Annals of Internal Medicine, 155* (2), 97.

Bickmore, T., & Giorgino, T. (2006). Health dialog systems for patients and consumers. *Journal of Biomedical Informatics, 39*(5), 556–571.

Bickmore, T., & Gruber, A. (2010). Relational agents in clinical psychiatry. *Harvard Review of Psychiatry, 18*(2), 119–130.

Bickmore, T. W., & Picard, R. W. (2005). Establishing and maintaining long-term human-computer relationships. *ACM Transactions on Computer-Human Interaction, 12*(2), 293–327.

Bickmore, T. W., Pfeifer, L. M., & Paasche-Orlow, M. K. (2009). Using computer agents to explain medical documents to patients with low health literacy. *Patient Education and Counseling, 75* (3), 315–320.

Bickmore, T., Mitchell, S., Jack, B., Paasche-Orlow, M., Pfeifer, L., & O'Donnell, J. (2010a). Response to a relational agent by hospital patients with depressive symptoms. *Interacting with Computers, 22*, 289–298.

Bickmore, T. W., Puskar, K., Schlenk, E. A., Pfeifer, L. M., & Sereika, S. M. (2010b). Maintaining reality: Relational agents for antipsychotic medication adherence. *Interacting with Computers, 22*(4), 276–288.

Bickmore, T. W., Schulman, D., & Sidner, C. L. (2011). A reusable framework for health counseling dialogue systems based on a behavioral medicine ontology. *Journal of Biomedical Informatics, 44*(2), 183–197.

Burr, C., & Morley, J. (2019). Empowerment or engagement? Digital health technologies for mental healthcare. *SSRN Electronic Journal.*

Burton, C., Szentagotai Tatar, A., McKinstry, B., Matheson, C., Matu, S., Moldovan, R., Macnab, M., Farrow, E., David, D., Pagliari, C., Serrano Blanco, A., & Wolters, M. (2016). for the Help4Mood consortium: Pilot randomised controlled trial of Help4mood, an embodied virtual agent-based system to support treatment of depression. *Journal of Telemedicine and Telecare, 22*(6), 348–355.

Cameron, G., Cameron, D., Megaw, G., Bond, R., Mulvenna, M., O'Neill, S., Armour, C., & McTear, M. (2018). Best practices for designing chatbots in mental healthcare: A case study on iHelpr. *Proceedings of the 32nd International BCS Human Computer Interaction Conference (HCI'18), 129*, 1–5. Swindon, GBR: BCS Learning & Development Ltd.

Carnell, S., Halan, S., Crary, M., Madhavan, A., & Lok, B. (2015). Adapting virtual patient interviews for interviewing skills training of novice healthcare students. In W. P. Brinkman, J. Broekens, & D. Heylen (Eds.), *Proceedings of IVA'15* (pp. 50–59). Delft: Springer International Publishing.

Carpenter, C., Osterberg, L., & Sutcliffe, G. (2012). SAMHT – Suicidal avatars for mental health training. In *Proceedings of FLAIRS'12* (pp. 484–487). Marco Island: AAAI Publications.
Cavazza, M., de la Cámara, R. S., & Turunen, M. (2010). How was your day? A companion ECA. In *Proceedings of AAMAS'10* (pp. 1629–1630). Toronto: International Foundation for Autonomous Agents and Multiagent Systems.
Chan, S., Li, L., Torous, J., Gratzer, D., & Yellowlees, P. M. (2018). Review of use of asynchronous technologies incorporated in mental health care. *Current Psychiatry Reports, 20*(10), 85.
Cordar, A., Borish, M., Foster, A., & Lok, B. (2014). Building virtual humans with back stories: Training interpersonal communication skills in medical students. In T. Bickmore, S. Marsella, & C. Sidner (Eds.), *Intelligent virtual agents* (Vol. 8637, pp. 144–153). Cham: Springer International Publishing.
DeVault, D., Artstein, R., Benn, G., Dey, T., Fast, E., Gainer, A., Georgila, K., Gratch, J., Hartholt, A., Lhommet, M., Lucas, G., Marsella, S., Morbini, F., Nazarian, A., Scherer, S., Stratou, G., Suri, A., Traum, D., Wood, R., Xu, Y., Rizzo, A., & Morency, L. P. (2014). SimSensei Kiosk: A virtual human interviewer for healthcare decision support. In *Proceedings of AAMAS'14* (pp. 1061–1068). Paris: International Foundation for Autonomous Agents and Multiagent Systems.
Farzanfar, R., Frishkopf, S., Migneault, J., & Friedman, R. (2005). Telephone-linked care for physical activity: A qualitative evaluation of the use patterns of an information technology program for patients. *Journal of Biomedical Informatics, 38*, 220–228.
Ford, M. J., Jamie, A., Sean, B., & Eric, C. (2009). Virtual worlds as a healing modality for returning soldiers and veterans. *Studies in Health Technology and Informatics, 144*, 273–276.
Ghanem, K., Hutton, H., Zenilman, J., Zimba, R., & Erbelding, E. (2005). Audio computer assisted self-interview and face to face interview modes in assessing response bias among STD clinic patients. *Sexually Transmitted Infections, 81*(5), 421–425.
Giorgino, T., Azzini, I., Rognoni, C., Quaglini, S., Stefanelli, M., Gretter, R., & Falavigna, D. (2004). Automated spoken dialogue system for hypertensive patient home management. *Journal of Medical Informatics, 74*, 159–167.
Gorrindo, T., & Groves, J. E. (2009). Computer simulation and virtual reality in the diagnosis and treatment of psychiatric disorders. *Academic Psychiatry, 33*(5), 413–417.
Gratch, J., Artstein, R., Lucas, G., Stratou, G., Scherer, S., Nazarian, A., Wood, R., Boberg, J., DeVault, D., Marsella, S., Traum, D., Rizzo, S., & Morency, L. P. (2014). The distress analysis interview corpus of human and computer interviews. In *Proceedings of LREC'14* (pp. 3123–3128). Reykjavik: European Language Resources Association (ELRA).
Griol, D., & Callejas, Z. (2016). Mobile conversational agents for context-aware care applications. *Cognitive Computation, 8*(2), 336–356.
Griol, D., Callejas, Z., López-Cózar, R., & Riccardi, G. (2014). A domain-independent statistical methodology for dialog management in spoken dialog systems. *Computer Speech & Language, 28*(3), 743–768.
Halan, S., Sia, I., Crary, M., & Lok, B. (2015). Exploring the effects of healthcare students creating virtual patients for empathy training. In W. P. Brinkman, J. Broekens, & D. Heylen (Eds.), *Proceedings of IVA'15, lecture notes in computer science* (pp. 239–249). Cham, Delft: Springer International Publishing.
Heilemann, M. V., Martínez, A., Soderlund, P. D., & Mental Health, A. (2018). Storytelling intervention using transmedia to engage Latinas: Grounded theory analysis of participants' perceptions of the story's main character. *Journal of Medical Internet Research, 20*(5), e10028.
Hudlicka, E. (2013). Virtual training and coaching of health behavior: Example from mindfulness meditation training. *Patient Education and Counseling, 92*(2), 160–166.
Inkster, B., Sarda, S., & Subramanian, V. (2018). An empathy-driven, conversational artificial intelligence agent (Wysa) for digital mental well-being: real-world data evaluation mixed-methods study. *JMIR mHealth and uHealth, 6*(11), e12106.
Jin, S. A. A. (2010). The effects of incorporating a virtual agent in a computer-aided test designed for stress management education: The mediating role of enjoyment. *Computers in Human Behavior, 26*(3), 443–451.

Jorm, A. F. (2000). Mental health literacy: Public knowledge and beliefs about mental disorders. *British Journal of Psychiatry, 177*(5), 396–401.

Jorm, A. F. (2015). Why we need the concept of "mental health literacy". *Health Communication, 30*(12), 1166–1168.

Kang, S., & Gratch, J. (2012). Socially anxious people reveal more personal information with virtual counselors that talk about themselves using intimate human back stories. *Studies in Health Technology and Informatics, 181*, 202–206.

Kelly, C. M., Jorm, A. F., & Wright, A. (2007). Improving mental health literacy as a strategy to facilitate early intervention for mental disorders. *Medical Journal of Australia, 187*(S7), S26.

Kim, J., Park, S. J., & Robert, P. L. (2019). Conversational agents for health and wellbeing: Review and future agendas. In *Proceedings of CSCW'19*. Austin: Association for Computing Machinery.

Kirakowski, J., O'Donnell, P., & Yiu, A. (2007). The perception of artificial intelligence as "human" by computer users. In D. Hutchison, T. Kanade, J. Kittler, J. M. Kleinberg, F. Mattern, J. C. Mitchell, M. Naor, O. Nierstrasz, C. P. Rangan, B. Steffen, M. Sudan, D. Terzopoulos, D. Tygar, M. Y. Vardi, G. Weikum, & J. A. Jacko (Eds.), *Human-computer interaction. HCI intelligent multimodal interaction environments* (Vol. 4552, pp. 376–384). Berlin, Heidelberg: Springer.

Kretzschmar, K., Tyroll, H., Pavarini, G., Manzini, A., Singh, I., & NeurOx Young People's Advisory Group. (2019). Can your phone be your therapist? Young people's ethical perspectives on the use of fully automated conversational agents (Chatbots) in mental health support. *Biomedical Informatics Insights, 11*, 117822261982908.

Kuosmanen, T., Fleming, T., Newell, J., & Barry, M. (2017). A pilot evaluation of the SPARX-R gaming intervention for preventing depression and improving wellbeing among adolescents in alternative education. *Internet Interventions, 8*, 40–47.

Kutcher, S., Wei, Y., & Coniglio, C. (2016). Mental health literacy: Past, present, and future. *The Canadian Journal of Psychiatry, 61*(3), 154–158.

Laranjo, L., Dunn, A. G., Tong, H. L., Kocaballi, A. B., Chen, J., Bashir, R., Surian, D., Gallego, B., Magrabi, F., Lau, A. Y. S., & Coiera, E. (2018). Conversational agents in healthcare: A systematic review. *Journal of the American Medical Informatics Association, 25*(9), 1248–1258.

Leite, I., Pereira, A., Castellano, G., Mascarenhas, S., Martinho, C., & Paiva, A. (2012). Modelling empathy in social robotic companions. *Advances in User Modeling, 7138*, 135–147.

Leite, I., Martinho, C., & Paiva, A. (2013). Social robots for long-term interaction: A survey. *International Journal of Social Robotics, 5*(2), 291–308.

Lisetti, C., Amini, R., Yasavur, U., & Rishe, N. (2013). I can help you change! An empathic virtual agent delivers behavior change health interventions. *ACM Transactions on Management Information Systems, 4*(4), 1–28.

López de Ipiña, K., Alonso, J., Solé-Casals, J., Barroso, N., Henriquez, P., Faundez-Zanuy, M., Travieso, C., Ecay-Torres, M., Martínez-Lage, P., & Eguiraun, H. (2015). On automatic diagnosis of Alzheimer's disease based on spontaneous speech analysis and emotional temperature. *Cognitive Computation, 7*(1), 44–55.

Lucas, G. M., Rizzo, A., Gratch, J., Scherer, S., Stratou, G., Boberg, J., & Morency, L. P. (2017). Reporting mental health symptoms: Breaking down barriers to care with virtual human interviewers. *Frontiers in Robotics and AI, 4*, 51.

Luger, E., & Sellen, A. (2016). "Like having a really bad PA": The gulf between user expectation and experience of conversational agents. In *Proceedings of CHI '16* (pp. 5286–5297). Santa Clara: Association for Computing Machinery.

Martínez-Martín, N., & Kreitmair, K. (2018). Ethical issues for direct-to-consumer digital psychotherapy apps: Addressing accountability, data protection, and consent. *JMIR Mental Health, 5* (2), e32.

Martínez-Miranda, J. (2017). Embodied conversational agents for the detection and prevention of suicidal behaviour: Current applications and open challenges. *Journal of Medical Systems, 41*(9), 135.

Martínez-Miranda, J., Breso, A., & García-Gómez, J. M. (2014). Look on the bright side: A model of cognitive change in virtual agents. In *Proceedings of IVA'14* (pp. 285–294). Cham: Springer.
Matariç, M. J., & Scassellati, B. (2016). Socially assistive robotics. In B. Siciliano & O. Khatib (Eds.), *Springer handbook of robotics* (pp. 1973–1994). Cham: Springer International Publishing.
McTear, M. F., Callejas, Z., & Griol, D. (2016). *The conversational interface. Talking to smart devices*. Cham: Springer.
Meguro, T., Higashinaka, R., Dohsaka, K., Minami, Y., & Isozaki, H. (2009). Analysis of listening-oriented dialogue for building listening agents. In *Proceedings of SIGDIAL'09 Conference* (pp. 124–127). London: Association for Computational Linguistics.
Miller, E., & Polson, D. (2019). Apps, avatars, and robots: The future of mental healthcare. *Issues in Mental Health Nursing, 40*(3), 208–214.
Miner, A., Chow, A., Adler, S., Zaitsev, I., Tero, P., Darcy, A., & Paepcke, A. (2016a). Conversational agents and mental health: Theory-informed assessment of language and affect. In *Proceedings of HAI'16* (pp. 123–130). Singapore: ACM Press, Biopolis.
Miner, A. S., Milstein, A., Schueller, S., Hegde, R., Mangurian, C., & Linos, E. (2016b). Smartphone-based conversational agents and responses to questions about mental health, interpersonal violence, and physical health. *JAMA Internal Medicine, 176*(5), 619.
Miner, A. S., Shah, N., Bullock, K. D., Arnow, B. A., Bailenson, J., & Hancock, J. (2019). Key considerations for incorporating conversational AI in psychotherapy. *Frontiers in Psychiatry, 10*, 746.
Mohr, D. C., Burns, M. N., Schueller, S. M., Clarke, G., & Klinkman, M. (2013). Behavioral intervention technologies: Evidence review and recommendations for future research in mental health. *General Hospital Psychiatry, 35*(4), 332–338.
Montenegro, J. L. Z., da Costa, C. A., & da Rosa Righi, R. (2019). Survey of conversational agents in health. *Expert Systems with Applications, 129*, 56–67.
Mooney, K., Beck, S., Dudley, W., Farzanfar, R., & Friedman, R. (2004). A computer-based telecommunication system to improve symptom care for women with breast cancer. *Annals of Behavioral Medicine Annual Meeting Supplement, 27*, 152–161.
Morris, R. R., Kouddous, K., Kshirsagar, R., & Schueller, S. M. (2018). Towards an artificially empathic conversational agent for mental health applications: System design and user perceptions. *Journal of Medical Internet Research, 20*(6), e10148.
Mulvenna, M., Boger, J., & Bond, R. (2017). Ethical by design: A manifesto. In *Proceedings of ECCE'17* (pp. 51–54). Umea: Association for Computing Machinery.
Myers, C., Furqan, A., Nebolsky, J., Caro, K., & Zhu, J. (2018). Patterns for how users overcome obstacles in voice user interfaces. In *Proceedings of CHI '18* (pp. 1–7). Montreal: Association for Computing Machinery.
Nadarzynski, T., Miles, O., Cowie, A., & Ridge, D. (2019). Acceptability of artificial intelligence (AI)-led chatbot services in healthcare: A mixed-methods study. *Digital Health, 5*, 205520761987180.
Nautsch, A., Jasserand, C., Kindt, E., Todisco, M., Trancoso, I., & Evans, N. (2019). The GDPR and speech data: Reflections of legal and technology communities, first steps towards a common understanding. In *Proceedings of Interspeech'19* (pp. 3695–3699). Graz: International Speech Communication Association.
Paiva, A., Leite, I., Boukricha, H., & Wachsmuth, I. (2017). Empathy in virtual agents and robots: A survey. *ACM Transactions on Interactive Intelligent Systems, 7*(3), 1–40.
Payr, S. (2010). Closing and closure in human-companion interactions: Analyzing video data from a field study. In *Proceedings of RO-MAN'10* (pp. 476–481). Viareggio: IEEE.
Pearl, C. (2017). *Designing voice user interfaces: Principles of conversational experiences*. Beijing: O'Reilly Media.
Pfeifer, L., & Bickmore, T. (2010). Designing embodied conversational agents to conduct longitudinal health interviews. In *Proceedings of IVA'10* (pp. 4698–4703). Philadelphia: Association for Computing Machinery.

Philip, P., Micoulaud-Franchi, J. A., Sagaspe, P., Sevin, E. D., Olive, J., Bioulac, S., & Sauteraud, A. (2017). Virtual human as a new diagnostic tool, a proof of concept study in the field of major depressive disorders. *Scientific Reports, 7*, 42656.

Pickard, M. D., Roster, C. A., & Chen, Y. (2016). Revealing sensitive information in personal interviews: Is self-disclosure easier with humans or avatars and under what conditions? *Computers in Human Behavior, 65*, 23–30.

Pieraccini, R. (2012). *The voice in the machine: Building computers that understand speech*. Cambridge: The MIT Press.

Pinto, M. D., Hickman, R. L., Clochesy, J., & Buchner, M. (2013). Avatar-based depression self-management technology: Promising approach to improve depressive symptoms among young adults. *Applied Nursing Research, 26*(1), 45–48.

Proudfoot, J., Goldberg, D., Mann, A., Everitt, B., Marks, I., & Gray, J. A. (2003). Computerized, interactive, multimedia cognitive-behavioural program for anxiety and depression in general practice. *Psychological Medicine, 33*(2), 217–227.

Provoost, S., Lau, H. M., Ruwaard, J., & Riper, H. (2017). Embodied conversational agents in clinical psychology: A scoping review. *Journal of Medical Internet Research, 19*(5), 151.

Ramakrishna, A., Greer, T., Atkins, D., & Narayanan, S. (2018). Computational modeling of conversational humor in psychotherapy. In *Proceedings of Interspeech'18* (pp. 2344–2348). Hyderabad: International Speech Communication Association.

Rehrl, T., Geiger, J., Golcar, M., Gentsch, S., Knobloch, J., Rigoll, G., Scheibl, K., Schneider, W., Ihsen, S., & Wallhoff, F. (2013). The robot ALIAS as a database for health monitoring for elderly people. In *Proceedings of AAL'13* (pp. 414–423). Berlin: Springer.

Ring, L., Barry, B., Totzke, K., & Bickmore, T. (2013). Addressing loneliness and isolation in older adults: Proactive affective agents provide better support. In *Humaine Association conference on affective computing and intelligent interaction* (pp. 61–66). IEEE.

Rizzo, A., Lange, B., Buckwalter, J. G., Forbell, E., Kim, J., Sagae, K., Williams, J., Difede, J., Rothbaum, B. O., Reger, G., Parsons, T., & Kenny, P. (2011). SimCoach: An intelligent virtual human system for providing healthcare information and support. *International Journal on Disability and Human Development, 10*(4), 277.

Roniotis, A., & Tsiknakis, M. (2018). Detecting depression using voice signal extracted by Chatbots: A feasibility study. In A. L. Brooks, E. Brooks, & N. Vidakis (Eds.), *Interactivity, game creation, design, learning, and innovation* (Vol. 229, pp. 386–392). Cham: Springer International Publishing.

Schuetzler, R. M., Grimes, G. M., & Giboney, J. S. (2019). The effect of conversational agent skill on user behavior during deception. *Computers in Human Behavior, 97*, 250–259.

Schulman, D., Bickmore, T., & Sidner, C. (2011). An intelligent conversational agent for promoting long-term health behavior change using motivational interviewing. In *AAAI Spring Symposium series*. Palo Alto: AAAI.

Sebastian, J., & Richards, D. (2017). Changing stigmatizing attitudes to mental health via education and contact with embodied conversational agents. *Computers in Human Behavior, 73*, 479.

Shamekhi, A., Trinh, H., Bickmore, T., Deangelis, T., Ellis, T., Houlihan, B., & Latham, N. (2016). A virtual self-care coach for individuals with spinal cord injury. In *Proceedings of ASSETS'16* (pp. 327–328). Reno: Association for Computing Machinery.

Shiffman, S., Stone, A. A., & Hufford, M. R. (2008). Ecological momentary assessment. *Annual Review of Clinical Psychology, 4*(1), 1–32.

Sillice, M., Morokoff, P., Ferszt, G., Bickmore, T., Bock, B., Lantini, R., & Velicer, W. (2018). Using relational agents to promote exercise and sun protection: Assessment of participants' experiences with two interventions. *Journal of Medical Internet Research, 20*(2), e48.

Sixsmith, A., Meuller, S., Lull, F., Klein, M., Bierhoff, I., Delaney, S., & Savage, R. (2009). SOPRANO – An ambient assisted living system for supporting older people at home. In *Proceedings of ICOST'09* (pp. 233–236). Tours: Springer.

Stiefel, S. (2018). 'The Chatbot will see you now': Mental health confidentiality concerns in software therapy. *SSRN Electronic Journal*.

Tay, J. L., Tay, Y. F., & Klainin-Yobas, P. (2018). Effectiveness of information and communication technologies interventions to increase mental health literacy: A systematic review. *Early Intervention in Psychiatry, 12*(6), 1024–1037.

Torous, J., Wisniewski, H., Liu, G., & Keshavan, M. (2018). Mental health mobile phone app usage, concerns, and benefits among psychiatric outpatients: Comparative survey study. *JMIR Mental Health, 5*(4), e11715.

Vaidyam, A. N., Wisniewski, H., Halamka, J. D., Kashavan, M. S., & Torous, J. B. (2019). Chatbots and conversational agents in mental health: A review of the psychiatric landscape. *The Canadian Journal of Psychiatry, 64*, 070674371982897.

Walkowski, J.T., & Nguyen, T-V. T. (2008). *Samaritans' teen line*. Worcester Polytechnic Institute Digital WPI.

Wei, Y., McGrath, P. J., Hayden, J., & Kutcher, S. (2015). Mental health literacy measures evaluating knowledge, attitudes and help-seeking: A scoping review. *BMC Psychiatry, 15*(1), 291.

Young, S. (2011). Cognitive user interfaces. *IEEE Signal Processing Magazine, 27*(3), 128–140.

# Chapter 12
# Internet Conversation: The New Challenges of Digital Dialogue

**Catalina Fuentes Rodríguez and Esther Brenes Peña**

**Abstract** Traditionally, dialogue has been conceived as communicative interaction that consists of turn-taking, alternating roles and face-to-face communication. New forms of digital communication require a revision of this definition. The fact that the interlocutors are not physically present, the extent to which they know each other and the potential multiplicity by creating virtual identities generates a rhetoric whose content is sometimes difficult to retrieve. This work uses the Conversation Analysis methods to describe these "electronic conversations" to determine whether they follow the prototypical structures and functioning of dialogue, and the strategies used by interlocutors to achieve their effectiveness.

**Keywords** Digital dialogue · Turn-taking system · Interactive patterns · Intersubjectivity · Identity · (Im)politeness

## 12.1 Introduction

Electronic communication has become an essential part of private and professional life, most particularly the former one. According to the *We are social and hootsuite*[1] report, in 2019 the number of Internet users has grown by four million in Spain. A

This work is part of projects "De construcciones periféricas a operadores discursivos: un estudio macrosintáctico del español actual" (MEsA.oper; ref.FFI2017-82898-P) and "Macrosintaxis del discurso persuasivo: construcciones y operadores" (MACPER) (P18-FR-2619)

[1]http://prgarage.es/informe-digital-2019-los-espanoles-pasamos-mas-5-horas-diarias-internet/

C. Fuentes Rodríguez (✉)
University of Seville, Sevilla, Spain
e-mail: cfuentes@us.es

E. Brenes Peña
Department of Language Sciences, Faculty of Philosophy and Arts, University of Cordoba, Córdoba, Spain
e-mail: mbrenes@uco.es



T. Lopez-Soto (ed.), *Dialog Systems*, Logic, Argumentation & Reasoning 22,
https://doi.org/10.1007/978-3-030-61438-6_12

total of 93% of the population now uses the Internet. We are connected for an average of five hours and 18 minutes every day, and we spend one hour and 39 minutes of that time on social networks, which have 28 million users in Spain. As linguists, these data justify the need to analyse and describe electronic conversations.

Initial studies of communication by means of computers date to the second half of the 1980s (Kiesler et al. 1984; Suchman 1987; Walther 1992, 1994, 1996; Parks and Floyd 1996; Davis and Brewer 1997; Crystal 2004; Baym 2010; Thurlow et al. 2004; Herring et al. 2013, among others). In Spanish, without purporting to be comprehensive, researchers interested in digital discourse have focused on email (Pano Alamán 2008; Fuentes Rodríguez 2009a), SMS (Galán 2002), debate forums (López Quero 2003, López Quero et al. (2004); Pano Alamán 2008), chats (Blanco Rodríguez 2002; López Quero 2003, 2017; Pano Alamán 2008), WhatsApp (Calero Vaquera 2014; Martín Gascuña 2016), Twitter (Mancera Rueda 2015), blogs (Pano Alamán 2008; Fuentes Rodríguez 2013a), press comments (Fuentes Rodríguez 2013b). Llisterri (2002), Borreguero Zuloaga (2003), Calero Vaquera (2014) and López Quero (2003, 2017), among others, researched linguistic modality (oral/written). Colloquialisms were dealt with by Mancera Rueda (2011) and Mancera Rueda and Pano Alamán (2013a). Another popular topic of research has been the proliferation of rudeness in certain types of informal conversations. There are studies on this impoliteness and its relationship with social image in different genres in the works of López Quero (2007), Fuentes Rodríguez (2009a, b), Vela Delfa (2014), Yus (2001, 2010), Mancera Rueda (2009, 2016, 2017), among others. Lastly, digital communication has become widely utilised in the political sphere, particularly in recent electoral campaigns. See, for example, Mancera Rueda and Pano Alamán (2013b), Mancera Rueda (2016), and the studies included in Fuentes Rodríguez (ed. 2016b, ed. 2018, ed. 2019), particularly that of Pérez Béjar (2019).

The aim of this study is to show the differences between face-to-face and digital dialogue conducted via Spain's most frequently used social networks (YouTube, WhatsApp, Facebook, Instagram and Twitter)[2] as they are the apparent applications of choice for interactive online contact. We set out to identify which features of familiar conversation (face-to-face contact) are found in electronic interaction (virtual contact). We will do this using the MEsA digital corpus created by the Argumentation and Persuasion in Linguistics Research Group, in the framework of the project "Macrosintaxis del Español Actual". El enunciado: estructura y relaciones" (Macrosyntaxis of current Spanish: The statement: structure and relations).[3]

---

[2]*We are social and hootsuite* report shows that the most frequently used social networks in Spain are YouTube (89%), WhatsApp (87%), Facebook (82%), Instagram (54%) and Twitter (49%).

[3]This corpus is made up of 3549 interventions in multiple WhatsApp conversations among eight speakers; 4861 comments in virtual forums; 10,462 comments on videos posted on YouTube; 8230 comments made on the social network Facebook, 20,550 on Instagram and 13,897 on Twitter; 3304 comments on blogs; and 4590 comments on multiple websites.

After explaining the features that define each of these networks and which determine the interactions that take place in their use (Sect. 12.2), we will compare them with face-to-face dialogue (Sect. 12.3.1). To do so, we will analyse their main characteristics: the turn-taking and interactive patterns created (12.3.2), intersubjectivity and identity management (12.3.3). The most relevant conclusions are summarised in Sect. 12.4.

## 12.2 Digital Discourse and Its Modalities: Different Objectives but a Common Language

The virtual nature of digital discourse generates new ways of interacting that differ from colloquial, face-to-face conversation, and the emergence of new strategies; numerous possibilities which are updated and are continually modified with advances in technology. They generate multimodal conversations that contain asynchronous visual elements and sound, and spoken and iconised written text (Calero Vaquera 2014, Martín Gascueña 2016), to enable interaction between geographically distant persons, of a public or private nature, directed at a specific participant or an unknown audience, in a formal or informal register, which may have transactional or interpersonal functions. From many options provided by current computer technology for two or more people to communicate, we have selected the most popular social networks in Spain: YouTube, WhatsApp, Facebook, Instagram and Twitter.

The most interactive of these networks is WhatsApp. This app was created specifically to facilitate communication between users, enabling them to send text messages, emoticons, images, videos, audio recordings, documents, links to websites and geographical locations over the Internet. It is, therefore, a multimodal means of communication between two or more persons, allowing users to create messaging groups with a maximum of 256 participants. Communication is private, with participants selected from the sender's contact list.

Twitter is a microblogging service that allows users to send text messages with a limited number of characters (280). These public messages, known as "tweets", are stored on the posters' home page. To participate, users must create a profile using their own names or a pseudonym and a photograph. Unlike WhatsApp messages, tweets are not intended as a means of interpersonal communication, rather as a tool for commenting on current affairs or for users to post updates about what they happen to be doing, albeit, as we will see, communicative exchange with a specific participant is also possible by mentioning the user by means of a graphic convention.

The third social network, Instagram, is used to share photographs and videos on the Internet. Photos can be accompanied by short texts and hashtags specifying their theme or a characteristic which helps users to find photos with the same subject matter shared by other users. In this case, therefore, the purpose is not communicative interaction, although any user can comment on and rate other users' photographs. Like other social networks, users must create a profile to take part, even though it is not necessary to enter the details of their real identities in order to access it.

In addition, we will analyse some comments on videos shared on the YouTube web platform. After registering, users can upload videos on different subjects. These videos are public and other users can leave comments, which are also public. So, even if the main aim is not communicative interaction, it is of no surprise that participants who leave comments on videos often engage in fights and conversations about the content or video published, because they can interact by mentioning the specific user who they wish to answer.

Lastly, regarding the social network Facebook, we have analysed posts and comments made on public pages. Like in the other networks, to use Facebook users must create a profile. Similarly, while the main objective is not to foster communicative interaction, some interesting communication does occur in these posts.

In short, all the social networks analysed coincide in that the participants are not physically present, they are asynchronous, and they use the visual channel, although WhatsApp and YouTube also permit the sound channel. The differences lie in the purpose for which they were created (to share videos, send messages, share photographs, etc.), their primary objective and the public/private nature of the information published. These divergences influence the features of their interactions, and their similarities and differences from prototypical colloquial conversation.

## 12.3 Digital Dialogue. Defining Features and Differences from Face-to-Face Dialogue

### *12.3.1 Concept of Dialogue*

According to Rockwell (2003), "A dialogue is a unity of diverse voices". Later on, he says:

> Each voice has a genre, a social and professional background, and a regional dialect. If the dialogue is a unity of these voices, we can begin to appreciate a dialogue by identifying the types of differences between voices, plotting them in this three-dimensional space" (p. 34).

Textual cohesion is achieved with the use of verbal forms ("The least interesting and most obvious mechanism for providing unity is to use formal clues that indicate to a reader the beginning, end, and parts of the dialogue", p. 35), the occasion, the chronotype ("it is important to understand how a theme emerges in the social context of the dialogue", p. 43) and the themes:

> To understand how themes unify a dialogue a careful interpreter might:
>
> 1. Identify the major themes in a dialogue both those that are explicitly discussed and those that are not.
>
> 2. Follow each theme through the dialogue paying careful attention to:
>
> 2.1 the context in which the theme is launched,

2.2 the interventions on the theme as it moves through the work, and
2.3 the concluding direction of the theme when the dialogue ends

Co-presence is the fundamental factor, according to Linell (1998:10):

(...) a broad definition of 'dialogue' as roughly interaction through symbolic means by mutually co-present individuals (thus tying up with the etymology of dialogue: "through words").

Briz Gómez agrees (1996, p. 32), defining conversation as "in-person interaction". In contrast, lack of face-to-face communication, the use of the written mode and the asynchrony intrinsic to computer-mediated dialogue, together with the asymmetry that sometimes exists between interlocutors, requires a different way of managing turns to speak and intersubjective resources. From a structural standpoint, the abovementioned studies refer to the use of fragmented interventions as a means of maintaining turns to speak and different management and representation of overlap. Our analysis has also revealed the existence of a type of structure which is specific to these interactions (branched reactive participation), and the predominant reactive function: the commentary function. For this, and to create more closeness with the other speaker, the interlocutor increases the number of intersubjective features.

Another difference from oral conversation is the channel of communication. This causes loss of clarity and can lead to ambiguity due to a lack of intonation. Syntax rarely succeeds in fully compensating for the speakers' intentions. To offset this, Internet users exaggerate closeness and subjectivity, using linguistic or multimodal markers such as emoticons, photographs, videos etc. (depending on the social network). Hence the exaggerated emotionality, sometimes rudeness, exacerbated judgements, and taking of opposing positions.

To conclude, and to establish these differences and characterise digital dialogue, we will focus on the following features: (a) interactive patterns and turn-taking (we will indicate the use of forms used to indicate the presence of the receiver); (b) intersubjectivity, defined as the speaker's expression (modality[4] and closeness) in connection with the listener. In connection with the latter, we will look at politeness/rudeness and social image management by the conversation participants.

### *12.3.2 Interactive Patterns and Turn-Taking*

From a structural point of view, conversation consists of non-predetermined turn-taking (Briz Gómez 2000, p. 61). This turn-taking is governed by the so-called Transition-Relevance Places, (Sacks et al. 1974), or the existence of linguistic markers or gestures that signal the precise moment when the sender has finished

[4]We understand the modality as the expression of the speaker's attitude towards what was said (Fuentes Rodríguez 1991).

the message.[5] However, as well as with the "fluid change of speaker", triggered by recognition and adherence to these Transition-Relevance Places, simultaneous and overlapping interjections are also found frequently in situations of rupture, and interruptions or competitive turns to speak (Hidalgo Navarro 1998, p. 3).

That said, however regulated or disruptive they may be, turn-taking is clearly facilitated by both interlocutors being physically present, the use of verbal communication and the typical synchrony of this mode of interaction. In computer-mediated discussions, turn-taking is modified to fit the characteristics of the medium used, as shown by other authors who have analysed chats (Cora García and Baker Jacobs 1999; Crystal 2004; Vela Delfa and Jiménez Gómez 2011). We have widened the range of formats analysed to give a more general characterisation of digital discourse. To do this, the first step is to describe the interactive patterns created by each format.

Face-to-face conversations may be dialogues or polylogues, depending on the number of participants, who generally have equal social and functional standing. The most similar format to this is found in WhatsApp: private conversations between two or more people who are already acquainted. This produces a dynamic interchange of communicative roles (sender-receiver) played by individuals. If we take the classification made by Kerbrat-Orecchioni (1986) of the receiver, in WhatsApp and polylogue groups we find direct recipients[6] and recipients[7] in the same way as in ordinary conversations. But these are all embodied by real individuals.

The other formats have two features that determine their interactive patterns: their public nature and the functional asymmetry among participants.

– The public nature of the interaction implies the creation of a new type of receiver: the virtual receiver. This receiver does not need to have had any prior interaction with the sender, since anyone can comment on a tweet, enter a forum, Facebook page or YouTube video. But the existence of the receiver is crucial: the purpose of these digital publications is, very frequently, to gain "followers". The characteristics or features of the intended audience may influence the messages sent.
– Asymmetry between interlocutors: with the exception of WhatsApp, the roles of sender and receiver are passed back and forth freely, in these formats, the owner of the profile on the network is the sender and ranks higher on the scale in terms of enunciative power. Other participants act, preferably, as an audience for the profile-owner's messages and posts (Table 12.1).

[5]These Transition-Relevance Places include silence, the speaker turning to face the listener, completion or conclusion of the sentence, use of a descending tone intrinsic to a grammatical conclusion, lengthening or dragging final sounds, and utterance of certain phatic stereotypical expressions and set phrases, etc. (Cestero Mancera 1994). Studies conducted by Hidalgo Navarro (1998, 2000, 2006) show the relevance of the suprasegmental features in this sense.

[6]Conceived as "the receiver per se", the receiver is characterised by being "explicitly considered by the sender" by means of second-person personal pronouns and/or gestures and looks (Kerbrat-Orechioni 1986, p: 32).

[7]Receivers who are not "integrated in the conversation per se" (Kerbrat-Orechioni 1986, p. 33).

**Table 12.1** Differences between face-to-face conversation and virtual dialogue formats

| | Sender | Receiver | Relationship created between the roles | Nature | Interactive pattern |
|---|---|---|---|---|---|
| Face-to-face dialogue | Individual | Individual. Direct recipients/ recipients/ audience. | Symmetrical relationship. Closeness and/or interpersonal confidence. Existence of a prior relationship. | Private | Symmetric dialogue or polylogue with different levels of individual receivers. Structures: - Exchange of information - Question-answer - Directive acts – acceptance or rejection |
| WhatsApp | Individual | Individual. Direct recipients/ recipients/ audience. There are no virtual receivers | Symmetrical relationship. Closeness and/or interpersonal confidence. Existence of a prior relationship. | Private (possible private group) | Symmetric dialogue or polylogue with different levels of individual receivers. Structures: - exchange of information - question-answer - directive acts – acceptance or rejection |
| Twitter, YouTube, Instagram, Facebook | Individual. | Individual or collective. Importance of the notion of the virtual recipient. | Asymmetric | Public and private | Asymmetric polylogue with a virtual recipient. Structure: - Initial participation: Provoke subsequent speech - Reactive participation: Commentary function |

These characteristics have a great influence on turn-taking management. There is a lack of the feedback component mentioned in earlier works (Crystal 2004: 30), and, in the case of WhatsApp, because it is more conversationally dynamic, turn-taking may be fragmented into several participations as a way of keeping the turn to speak, a feature that other authors have identified as a characteristic intrinsic to chats[8]:

(1)7/3/2016, 9:03 – M2: Tienes hora libre hoy? [Have you got a free hour today?]
7/3/2016, 9:03 – M2: Para desayunar? [For breakfast?]
7/3/2016, 9:54 – M1: No me tientes [Don't tempt me]
7/3/2016, 9:54 – M1: Jajajaja [Hahahaha]
7/3/2016, 9:54 – M1: Tng ingles[9] [I've got English]
7/3/2016, 9:54 – M1: O eso creo [Or I think I have]
7/3/2016, 9:55 – M2: Entérate tía [Find out woman]
7/3/2016, 9:55 – M2: Y desayunamos sino [And we'll have breakfast]
7/3/2016, 9:55 – M2: Tengo hambre [I'm hungry] (2.WA 2016 feb-mar)

The impossibility of identifying overlaps and interruptions due to the use of written media has also been noted (Cora García and Baker Jacobs 1999; López Quero 2017). Evidently, we did not find phenomena such as initial overlapping or simultaneous starts (Fant 1996) in any of the analysed formats.[10] However, in the case of WhatsApp, there are examples where it is possible by looking at chronological markers and semantic information (Vela Delfa and Jiménez Gómez 2011), which could reveal cases of overlapping. One illustration of this is the fragment (2). In it, the second participation of M1, which is the semantic completion of the first, was sent at the same moment as H5's participation. This leads us to the conclusion that H5's participation overlaps that of M1, despite the graphical representation of the media appearing to indicate lineal succession.

(2) 2015/07/24, 20:34 – M1: Yogures todos, I have a dream [All yoghurts (*pretty young things*), I have a dream]
2015/07/24, 20:35 – H5: Liarte con Johny Deep? [To get off with Johnny Depp?]
2015/07/24, 20:35 – M1: Un sueño en el que el fin de que viene os venis a la playa y pasamos el dia con H3 (que estara en chipiona) y pasamos el dia en amor y compaña y nos despedimos de H3 [A dream where next weekend you come to the beach and spend the day with H3 (who will be in Chipiona) and we spend the day with love and together and say goodbye to H3] (1WA 2015/6 ago-mar)

On the other hand, if we look at the way in which adjacent pairs of participations are linked,[11] there is a fundamental difference between WhatsApp and the other formats analysed. As we have already explained, the private nature of the interaction and the functional relationship of equality among the interlocutors on WhatsApp mean that the predominant interactive pattern is a symmetric dialogue or polylogue with individual receivers at different levels. In this case, the participations of the different interlocutors are interrelated according to the principle of predictability or

---

[8]See, for example, Yus (2010), Vela Delfa & Jiménez Gómez (2011).

[9]We respect the original spelling, without corrections.

[10]Overlapping of two participations that respond to parallel self-selection by two participants.

[11]Defined by H. Sacks-H. Schegloff (1979) as a sequence of two successive messages produced by different speakers, which are ordered into a first and second part and which are specific, in the sense that a particular first part corresponds to a particular second part.

preference, in the same way as colloquial conversation. As a result, we observe an extensive variety of adjacent pairs as question-response (examples 3, 4), statement-response to the statement (fragment 4) or acts of judgemental speech such as congratulations or set phrases and the corresponding responses to these (5, 6).

(3)2015/07/04, 13:19 – H6: Bueno, salgo en un ratito, ¿Hace falta algo? [Well, I'll leave in a while. Is there anything you need?] ¿Hielo, reponer suministros, llevar a alguien…? [Ice, more supplies, give someone a lift…?]

2015/07/04, 13:20 – H6: Yo me voy a pasar a comprar igualmente. [I have to go shopping anyway.]

2015/07/04, 13:22 – M2: Podrías comprar un par de cocacolas [You could buy a couple of Coca-Colas] (1WA 2015/6 ago-mar)

(4)2015/11/23, 17:04 – H1: Bueno, dejadme hacer de defensor del diablo, pero los niños son como los angeles del doctor who, si parpadeas la lian [Well, let me play devil's advocate, but the kids are like Doctor Who's Angels, if you blink, they make a mess]

2015/11/23, 17:07 – H5: Has hecho una broma con Doctor who? [Did you make a joke about Doctor Who?]

2015/11/23, 17:07 – H1: no, con los niños [No, about the children]

2015/11/23, 17:10 – H5: En una comparación siempre hay dos elementos [There are two parts to every comparison]

2015/11/23, 17:11 – H1: si, pero la broma no tiene que ser con ambos [Yes, but the joke need not be about them both]

2015/11/23, 17:11 – H1: y dejate de *metas* por dios [and enough with the *metaphors* for heaven's sake]

2015/11/23, 17:12 – H1: si te gusta el doctor who, tan solo disfruta el comentario [if you like Doctor Who, just enjoy the comment]

2015/11/23, 17:13 – H5: También me gusta que la gente se aficione [I like people to become fans, too] (1WA 2015/6 ago-mar)

(5)2015/07/10, 14:48 – H2: Felicidades a ambos!!!! [Congratulations to you both!!!!]

2015/07/10, 15:43 – H1: Gracias [Thank you] (1WA 2015/6 ago-mar)

(6)2015/07/12, 01:45 – M2: XD estás muy guapo H5!!!! [XD you're looking good H5!!!!]

2015/07/12, 01:55 – H5: Ha habido fotos mejores. [There have been better photographs.] Pero esa es la que tengo a mano [But this is the closest one]

2015/07/12, 01:55 – H5: Gracias, M2[Thanks, M2] (1WA 2015/6 ago-mar)

In contrast, in the other formats, the participation structure is different. Twitter, YouTube, Instagram and Facebook are, from an interactive standpoint, an asymmetric polylogue with a virtual audience. The asymmetry that exists between interlocutors means that in these formats, an initial participation by the profile owner is followed by a series of reactive participations in branch format, each issued by different virtual recipients. This creates a vertical relationship between an initial participation and the multiple reactive participations whose theme is linked to the former. The basic function of the initial participation is to invoke, since it seeks to provoke subsequent speech. The basic function of reactive participations is to comment on or evaluate the initial participation. Schematically, this pattern can be represented as follows (Table 12.2):

**Table 12.2** Simple interactive pattern of asymmetric polylogue

| |
|---|
| Initial participation 1 |
| Reactive participations: Comments to 1 |

This Instagram sequence is an example. The initial participation shows a sequence from a television series. The reactive participations are all evaluations of this:

(7)@netflixes: "Cuidado con tus amigos". #7años ["Careful with your friends" #7years]
[Still photograph from the original Netflix movie "7 years", featuring Paco León]
User 1 (woman): Es buenísima @netflixes [It is fantastic @netflixes]
User 2 (man): La estoy viendo ahora mismo @netflixes #Nospoilers [I'm watching it right now @netflixes #Nospoilers]
User 3 (woman):
User 4 (man): @netflixes muy buena película, espero que sigáis apostando por la ficción española [@netflixes very good film, I hope you'll keep watching Spanish fiction]
User 5 (woman): Me ha encantado! [I loved it!]
User 6 (unidentified): Es tremenda!!!! [It is tremendous!!!] Gracias por hacernos pasar tan buen rato! [Thank you for giving us such a good time!]
User 8 (woman): muy buena, enhorabuena a por mas @netflixes [Very good, congratulations. Go forward @netflixes].
(..)User 12 (woman): Buena película [Good film]
User 13 (woman): Tengo ganas de verla ! [I can't wait to see it!]
(..)User 15 (woman): Me gusto mucho. [I liked it a lot] Gran trabajo de actores @pacoleon @juana_acosta y guión, etc… [The actors did a great job @pacoleon @juana_acosta and script, etc…] Por ese camino @netflixes A por más [@netflixes is on the right track Go for it]
User 16 (man): Estupenda película, me engancho desde el principio y el final… [Excellent film, I was hooked from the beginning to the end…] No me lo esperaba …menuda jugada!!! [I didn't expect it… What a twist!!!] (IG 2016 nov NET 02)

This type of interactive pattern has caused some authors to consider interactions created in these formats as a "group discussion" which cannot be considered a "prototypical conversation", since, in the case of Twitter, for example, each interlocutor "contributes with their opinion which is independent from that in the preceding tweet" (Mancera Rueda and Pano Alamán 2013a, p. 70). However, it is not unusual to find cases where reactive participations, although they maintain their basic function as comments, may be related to each other. In fact, in the case of Twitter, they may easily refer to the information or evaluation issued by another interlocutor by means of a graphic convention which consists of using @ plus the name of the user in question, as happens with the participations of users 2 and 4 in the following example. It has a more complex structure (Table 12.3):

(8) @police: Protege tu información, fotos o conversaciones en caso de pérdida o robo de tu móvil con pin, patrón, huella, iris… [In case you lose your mobile or it gets stolen, protect your information, photos and conversations with a PIN, pattern, fingerprint, iris] Cuida tu #privacidad. [Watch out for your #privacy.]
[Photo of two mobile blocking patterns. One is simple and says "single" and the other one is very complex and says "married"]

**Table 12.3** Complex interactive pattern of asymmetric polylogue

| |
|---|
| Initial participation 1 |
| Reactive participation comment to 1 |
| Participations of crossed comments among the participants |

User 2 (unidentified): @policia ¿Qué tiene que ver el estado civil con la protección de privacidad? [@policia What has your marital status got to do with protection of privacy?]

User 3 (unidentified): [user mention] @policia porque hay parejas que tienden a husmear el móvil de su queridísimo novio/a para cotillear sus conversaciones/fotos [@policia because some people are in the habit of snooping in their darling boyfriend/girlfriend's mobiles to look at their conversations and photos]

User 2 (unidentified): [user mention] @policia Claro y solo lo hacen las mujeres. [@policia Of course. And it is only the women that do it, of course.] Los hombres nunca controlan las conversaciones de sus parejas. [Men never spy on their partners' conversations.]

User 3 (unidentified): [user mention] @policia lee lo que he dicho, "para usmear el móvil de su novio/a", me refiero a un sólo género [@policia read what I said, "to snoop on the boyfriend/girlfriend's mobile", I am referring to a single gender-,-]

User 4 (man): [user mention] [user mention] @policia dejala no lo va a pillar... [@policia let it go, he'll never get it...] Aqui cada cual va a su bola [Everyone does what they want to here]

User 2 (unidentified): [user mention] [user mention] La poli no se refiere a un sólo género poniendo soltero/casado. [The cop isn't talking about a single gender by putting single/ married].

User 4 (man): [user mention] [user mention] ya paso hija mia ya paso [it is all over now my daughter it is all over]

[gif of Hillary Clinton staring without blinking]

[No capture]

User 2 (unidentified): [User mention] [User mention] Vamos que te quedas sin argumento y tiras de meme. [Come on, you run out of arguments and post a meme.] (TW 2016 oct PON 01)

## 12.3.3 *Intersubjectivity*

### Contact with the Receiver

Dialogue involves an intersubjective relationship with the receiver. Its markers (operators and connectors such as *hey, look, well, isn't it? isn't that right*?) indicate that it is time for someone else to take a turn, establishing directionality, and marking the start of the participation. Appellatives such as *do you get me?* or *You know?* are common and tend to appear with this function at the end of each turn to speak to invite another recipient to participate. We also find deictics that send a signal to the interlocutor (the second person), and a specific syntactic function: the vocative case. All these linguistic items appear in the texts analysed and are evidence of interaction. Let us consider, for example, Rawvana's YouTube page:

(9)User 1 (man): Muchas Felicidades, de verdad. [Congratulations, really]

User 2 (man): [Mentions user 1]Te amo *boludo*♥ [I love you, you idiot♥]

User 3 (man): [Mentions user 1] ! Espero que te hallas pasado bien en Tijuana… [ I hope you had a good time in Tijuana…]

User 4 (woman): [Mentions user 1] NECESITAN ESTO TU Y TODO TU CREW WEY [YOU AND ALL YOUR GREAT CREW NEED THIS]

Rawvana: *Gracias amigo*!! [Thank you frien]

User 5 (unidentified): [Mentions user] yep deacuerdo con tigo. lol [yep I agree with you. lol]

User 6 (woman): Que padre video!!! [What a cracking video!!!] Que suave eres tu!! [You're so smooth!!]

User 7 (man): Pon atención al video *cabron*, te hace falta [Pay attention to the video you bastard, you need to] (YT 2015 jul RAW 01). [Transcription of the video *MY FIGHT AGAINST ALCOHOLISM*]].

The information is addressed using the second person (*you need it, with you)*; acts of reactive speech, such as gratitude (*thanks friend!!)* and vocatives, some positive (*friend, idiot*) and others rude (*bastard*). These items appear in all the conversations considered, which opens the way to talk about a subtype of dialogic discourse. In some cases (Instagram, WhatsApp, Facebook, Twitter) the interaction is more fluid and immediate than in others.

The contact control operators may appear at the start (*hey* in the following case) or (*isn't it* or *you know?)* in the final position of the participation or enunciation. So in WhatsApp or Twitter:

(10)2015/06/28, 14:36 – H3: venirse pa la piscina y lg ya vemos, *no?* [come to the swimming pool and then will see, all right?] (1WA 2015/6 ago-mar)

(11)2015/06/28, 17:46 – H5: Hummm, gente. Yo ya he terminado por aqui [Hummm, people. I have finished here.] (1WA 2015/6 ago-mar)

(12)2015/07/03, 08:27 – H3: *oye* [hey]

2015/07/03, 08:27 – H3: esta noche alamedeando [we will "alamear" tonight (in Spanish using nound "alameda" as a verb so refer to hang out)] (1WA 2015/6 ago-mar)

(13)User 11 (unidentified):[user mention] @policia ¿Machista es que una novia le coja el móvil a su novio y vea sus conversaciones? Eso es hembrista, *¿sabes*?

[@policia Is it chauvinistic for a girlfriend to pick up her boyfriend's mobile and snoop at his conversations? That's female chauvinism, you know?]

User 11 (unidentified): [user mention] @policia Hablas por ti, *¿no?* Igualdad es preocuparse de los problemas de ambos sexos, no sólo de uno. De nada [@policia You're speaking for yourself, aren't you? Equality means being concerned about both sexes' problems, not just one. You're welcome ]

User 11 (unidentified): [user mention] @policia Los hombres también son violados. Pero *oye*, para ti debe ser que por tener pene todo hombre es potencial violador *¿no?* ASCO [@policia Men are raped, too. But hey, as far as you're concerned because all men have penises, they are potential rapists, right? DISGUST] (TW 2016 oct PON 01)

In this final fragment, we find the form *¿sabes? (you know?)* which also reinforces and intensifies what has been said. *Oye (Hey*) is an appellative that establishes contact and calls the interlocutor's attention. It is then used to emphasise what has been said, as occurs in this tweet. Among these analyses, (Ortega Olivares 1985, 1986; Fuentes Rodríguez and Brenes Peña 2014), elements that support and maintain contact, question tags (*isn't it? right?*), are very common.

Other ways of establishing a direct interaction with recipients is to ask for confirmation or rejection of affirmations, as in:

(14)User 4 (man): @policia [user mention] con todo respeto, pero vosotros mismos predicar con el ejemplo, porque no hay patrullas con dos mujeres, *o si?* [With all due respect but you yourselves predicate with the example, because there are no patrols with two women, *or are there*?] (TW 2016 oct PON 01)

Additionally, he uses operators such as *con todo respeto* (*with all due respect*), which is clearly interactive, the direct reference to the recipient (*you yourselves*), and uses the disjunctive in an attenuated form since it expresses an option, but when it comes down to it he appears to accuse or show evidence that is negative for the interlocutor.

Another directly conversational feature is the immediate request for response:

(15) 2015/07/14, 19:23 – M1: Yo soy la exotica *a q si* H2? [I'm the exotic one, *am I not* H2?]

2015/07/14, 19:40 – H5: La opinión que tenga sobre ti H2 no cuenta. Y más si parece que lo estás coaccionando. "*A que sí*? por que si me dices que no. . ." [What I think of you H2 doesn't count. And even more so if you are fishing for it. *Aren't I?* In case you are contradicting me. . . ] (1WA 2015/6 ago-mar)

These are similar to face-to-face dialogue.

**Intersubjective Expressions**

The degree of appearance of subjectivity depends upon the type of discourse (superstructure, Van Dijk 1992; Fuentes Rodríguez 2017) and the purposes sought. The maximum level is established in a familiar conversation, where there is a close relationship. In the case of digital dialogue, in some formats, they attempt to recreate this relationship by replacing face-to-face communication with increased subjectivity. Here, everything appears modally marked. Everything is "very great" or "beautiful" or "we couldn't have better. . .". For example, in the comments on an Instagram text by Roy Galán:

(16)User 201 (man): Eres nuy grande, gracias por tu hermosas palabras con cada publicación @roygalan [You're really great. Thank you for your beautiful words with each post) @roygalan ]

User 19 (woman): Bravo!!! Precioso texto y preciosa pareja No podíamos tener mejores representantes (IG 2018 abr 25 ROY 01) [Beautiful text and beautiful couple We could not have better representatives)

And he establishes the interaction with other users who have previously intervened with comments or directive acts:

(17)User 89 (unidentified): [Mentions user 60] tener que llegar a pedir perdón por todo. . . por hacer lo que te da la gana. . . por no ofender. . . .[ to have to apologise for everything. . . for doing what you want to. . . so as not to offend. . .]

User 92 (unidentified):[Mentions user 26] *ven ya ostia* [come on now dammit] (IG 2018 abr 25 ROY 01)

In the latter, the request has nothing to do with the comment and instead refers to user 26, with whom he has entered into a conversation through the network. The interjection *ostia* (dammit) is used to add force to the request, which becomes a demand.

(a) *Vocatives:* This increased subjectivity is very evident in the vocatives. These establish contact between the reciver(s), but they also express the type of relationship between them, always close, and the speaker's evaluation of the other. It can show the level of empathy that exists between both participants and also reflects the identity they have decided to show. Let's take a look at some of these:

(18)2015/06/29, 12:55 – H5: Felicidades, man! [Congratulations, man!]
2015/06/29, 13:10 – H
2015/06/29, 13:18 – H4: Que bien tio [That's great man]
2015/07/17, 21:37 – H5: H1, voy pa tu kelly, cabesah [on my way to your house (Kelly =house /*cabesah* = *head*)]
2015/11/20, 23:59 – H1: Si no vente para acá rubio [If not, come over here *blonde]*
2015/07/03, 13:33 – H2: Yogurines como vais a la Parti de H4? [*Kids*, how are you going to H4's party?] (1WA 2015/6 ago-mar)

These include usual expressions, such as *tío* (man), which, in Spanish make the communication interactive, almost a discourse operator. And others, which are more creative: *cabesah*, or *rubio* (which implies evaluation). *Tío* (*Man)* adds dialectal content.

In the following context the vocative expresses certain negative content. It mimics an act of consolation, but sarcastically:

(19) User 4 (man):[user mention] [user mention] ya paso *hija mia* ya paso [gif de Hillary Clinton asintiendo sin parpadear] [ it is all over now girl, it is all over [gif of Hillary Clinton staring without blinking]] (TW 2016 oct PON 01)

Many of these vocatives are negative in cases of attacking and putting down the receiver and being blatantly rude. To this, other evaluative forms should be added, such as operators, which include adjectives or the use of modals and declaratives. Let's look at some comments on YouTube:

(20) User 35 (unidentified): [Mentions user 33] los que teneis la enfermedad sois vosotros que de pequeños no teníais amigos y os marginaban, luego en la juventud las chicas os.daban la espalda y tenéis que ir a lo que os queda, follar animales o hombres.. pena de humanidad, iros de aquí *reprimidos*, tenéis alguna neurona que os falla [you are the sick ones who didn't have any friends when you were little and were left out, then when you got older the girls turned their back on you and you had to resort for what was left, fucking animals or men... the dregs of humanity, get out of here, *repressed*, There's something wrong with your neurons]

User 33 (man): por supuesto que no eres igual que yo, soy mucho mejor que tu, aparte de ser homofobico eres un heterosexitas, crees que vales mas porque eres hetero?, mejor vete a marte y quédate ahí, *basura humana*. [Of course you're not the same as me, I am much better than you, apart from being homophobic you are a heterosexist, do you think you are worth more because you are hetero? Better go to Mars and stay there, *human garbage*] (YT 2015 ago 10 ALE 01)

(b) *Evaluation*: Evaluation is a specific function within networks. It is the reaction sought by the majority of initial participations and their *raison d'être* within these virtual platforms. Some of them, Instagram and YouTube, ask for nothing else from their followers: ratings. (See Sect. 3.3.2.). The linguistic form of comments (branched reactive participations), are often complete utterances that contain solely the evaluating term or nominal two-word sentences. Their content can be either positive or negative. In the case of Instagram, users upload photographs for others to rate positively and to share with others. This also applies to Twitter and sometimes to Facebook. YouTube also enables evaluations, it is the only way of interacting directly, since the subsequent intervention, or YouTube response, appears next. There is a time difference between them.

These assessments are a grammatical example of expressive diversity, both in lexical and grammatical resources used and their syntax. That is why we find adjectives, alone or intensified, and all types of value judgements. The following sequence from Instagram contains many of these: superlative adjectives (*buenísima* = really good), modifiers (*muy buena película* = very good film), emoticons or symbols (user 3), exclamations (users 5 and 6), the semantic system of verbs and adjectives (*encantar, tremenda* = love, tremendous), interjections (fuck). See example (8) analysed above.

The starting point is essentially visual. The theme starts with a sequence from a Netflix series. The ratings follow. In the same way as in a face-to-face conversation, the syntax is direct and contains essential information without stopping to build the sentence: "Massive movie (*peliculón*) with super script (*guionazo*) and brilliant actors (*actorazos*)", and uses all mechanisms of intensification:

(21) User 15 (woman): Me gusto mucho. Gran trabajo de actores @pacoleon @juana_acosta y guión, etc... Por ese camino @netflixes A por más [I liked it a lot. The actors did a great job @pacoleon @juana_acosta and script, etc... @netflixes is on the right track Go for it] (IG 2016 nov NET 02)

A variety of linguistic mechanisms are used and are often combined: quantifiers, repetition, use of resources that imitate speech, phonetics, emoticons, and exclamations, which entail a simultaneous modal and phonic procedure. The expressive modality is used as a mechanism that intensifies the evaluation, such as the following, where an intensifier appears (*qué* = *what*), an exclamatory enunciation and an interjection which reinforces what has been said and underlines the user's commitment to what he says:

(22) User 108 (unidentified): Qué buena lábia tienes *coño*!!!!! [You've got the gift of the gab, bitch!!!!] (YT 2016 may 24 CHE 01)

Other enunciations contain acts of exhortative illocution, such as advice: "go for it". These are addressed to the stars of a film who they can see on Instagram and can respond, as Paco León did (to a user who rated his film as "disappointing"):

(23) @pacoleon:@user, lo siento tío, pero vamos a seguir trabajando y nos vas a tener que ver .... espero que este sea el mayor de tus problemas. 😀 [ I'm sorry man, but we're going to keep working and you're going to have to see us....I hope this is the worst of your problems. ] (IG 2016 nov NET 03)

Another user includes an adjective that constitutes an enunciation (*épico* = *epic*), although here without punctuation marks (it is assumed that the interlocutor will add them). They seem to be messages to be read aloud. The semantic content of the adjectives always indicates a high rating (tremendous, epic):

(24) User 10 (woman):@pacoleon acabas de dar un zas en toda la boca *épico* ajajajajaaj [you've just given him a slap across his mouth epic ha ha ha ha ] (IG 2016 nov NET 03)

Syntactic ellipsis is also observable in:

(25) User 10 (unidentified): Ayer mismo lo habría regalao.... qué tarde! Qué tarde!!! [ I would have given it to her yesterday... How late! How late!!!] (IG 2016 sep-oct MAL 02)

User 11 uses a certainty and affirmative operator with exclamation marks to express the raised "tone of voice" (or so we assume).

(26) User 11 (woman): Sin duda! [Without a doubt!] (IG 2016 sep-oct MAL 02)

In the following comment the word *genial* (cool) and the noun to which it refers appears, as well as the rating "very good" and laughter (see Cora García and Baker Jacobs 1999; Crystal 2004; Martín Gascueña 2016). User 39 presents an exclamatory enunciation, consisting of a single adjective, albeit with intensified content.

(27) User 38 (unidentified): Genial la forma de terminar el video, "Si quieres mejorar mi autoestima ..." Muy bueno jajaja [ Cool way of finishing the video. If you want to improve my self-esteem... Very good ha ha ha]

User 39 (woman): *Excelente*! me gustaria que tus videos sean mas largos.! (Alvaro, YouTube) [*Excellent*! I'd like your videos to be longer! (YT 2014 sep 10 ALV )]

On Alex Gibaja's YouTube page, users make judgements about him and others about user 12. User 30 launches a direct attack on the blogger with an insult (YouTube, Alex Gibaja).

(28)User 30 (man): *Marica* [Faggot]

User 31 (man): jaajajajajajajjajaajajajajajajajjajajajajaja concha de la intima lora del demonio, esto si que ya no es sano. Casi me he caido de la silla. [Ha ha ha ha ha shell of the intimate loins of the devil, that is certainly not healthy. I almost fell off my chair.]

User 32 (man): De donde ha salido este percebe [Where did that jerk come from]

User 10 (woman): Me temo que, conociendo a este tío. Le habrá salido natural el caerse y decir eso jajajajaja- [ I'm afraid that, knowing that guy. He must have fallen over and that would just come out of his mouth hahahhaha] (YT 2015 ago 10 ALE)

The laughter serves to intensify, and as a mechanism for attacking the other. It reduces tension, on the one hand, and on the other it devalues the comment. User 12 generates a series of reactions in which they attack directly, with intensified vocatives such as *fucking freak*, where the adjective *puto* (bitch) acts as an intensifier:

(29) User 12 (unidentified): Dice él que el bien siempre triunfa pero si él es el mal y triunfa por qué miente? :( [ He says that good always triumphs, but if he is bad and he triumphs, why lie? :(]

User 13 (woman): [Mention user 12] pero vamos a ver *puto* friqui si no te gusta por que comentas en todos sus putos vídeos??? que pasa que eres retrasado o que?? [Hang on you freaky bitch, if you don't like him why do you comment on all his fucking videos??? What's the matter? Are you retarded or something???]

User 12 (unidentified): [Mention user 13] Para echarme unas risas, me gusta ver que estoy más sano que este pavo con dinero que en vez de repartirlo a gente que lo necesita, se lo gasta en jilipolleces, anda mira la realidad *guapa* [To have a laugh, I like seeing that I'm healthier than that rich moron who instead of giving it away to people who need it, spends it on crap, wake up to reality *gorgeous]* (YT 2015 ago 10 ALE)

*Guapa (gorgeous)* is the form used with negative content. And it is combined with a directive enunciation with clearly accusatory content: "Wake up to reality" is a way of accusing her of being divorced from it.

User 14 uses creativity with intensifiers like *sin vida (lifeless)*, together with *homophobe*. *That sleezebag* is also an intensifying rating.

(30) User 14 (woman): [Mention user 13] el tío ese es un PTO *homofobo sin vida*, al pairo lo q diga *el salido* ese ☺☺ [That guy is a fucking homophobe lifeless, it would seem from what that sleezebag says☺☺]

User 15 (woman): [Mention user 12] ke? aprende a hacer una frase bien compuesta [what? Learn to write a proper sentence] (YT 2015 ago 10 ALE)

The interaction is among different participants in the dialogue. Sometimes there are confrontations with an evident degree of rudeness. And the evaluative forms *(stupid, disgusting, idiot, moron, tick, slimeball etc.)* are accompanied by other accusations. We will analyse these in the following section about rudeness.

**Identity and Rudeness Management**

To these two purposes -intersubjectivity as a means of recreating the closeness of family-type interaction and the demands of the conversational format- another fundamental aspect must be added, that of the social image of the participants. Some formats (particularly YouTube, blog, Instagram) seem to be created with the clear intention of exalting the user's image, as a self-image activity. The user could be a celebrity, a political party or group, a company wanting to get "followers". This requires positive evaluations to spread to a group of people that will visit or participate in the interaction. Specific professions have emerged: YouTubers, influencers, who have become famous because of the number of followers they have who read and view their comments, their assessments and who follow their styles, ideas, etc. on their channels.

They use a plethora of strategies to stand out from the crowd. Once again, evaluation is the basic strategy. That's what the speaker seeks to obtain. Users who take part provide these and do so to an extremely high level, as we have seen. But the user sometimes intervenes to express dislike or to make an accusation, doing this equally enthusiastically[12]: Hence user 11 with respect to Vueling:

(31) User 11 (man): Sois la PEOR compania!! Que manera de arruinarme el dia [You are the WORST company!! You've really ruined my day] (IG 2016 nov-dic VUE 08)

[12]Generally, the intensification appears in colloquial conversation (Albelda 2007) and in the political discourse it becomes a basic strategy (Fuentes Rodríguez 2016a and Fuentes Rodríguez ed., 2016b).

Users are well aware of the power of social networks and how Internet companies realise the importance of what is said about them. Users' voices are heard, and what they say goes from mouth to mouth and has a great persuasive effect.

Everybody knows it, and this is supported by the work of Yus (2001, 2010), that Internet users manage their own identities, choose the features and schedule how they want to be seen. According to Fuentes Rodríguez (2013b, 231–234) each virtual identity is built

> based on a selection of features taken by one (or several) of the communities or groups with whom they wish to be identified. Because of this, it is an avatar created solely for this interaction, made up of functional features which act within it and not by individual features as in real communication (our translation).

In Yus (2001) it is suggested that this multiplication or diversification of identities has an essentially textual basis.

> Real conversation is built in the interaction. But it is independent from this. In virtual conversation it only exists therein. The attributes of this virtual identity are contained in the text, since there is no physical presence. This creates a certain idealisation of the virtual I. (Fuentes Rodríguez 2013b: 214, our translation)

Curiously, the lack of co-presence means that degrading comments or ones that would be considered inappropriate in a polite relationship are made to the receiver. Hence, we find derogatory nouns and adjectives and expressions of threatening acts. According to Mancera Rueda, "anonymity and instant communication enable violation not only of the most basic rules of spelling and grammar, but the essential social convention that condemns all types of verbal aggression (Mancera Rueda 2009, p. 462)" (Mancera Rueda and Pano Alamán 2013a, pp. 12–13, our translation). Fuentes Rodríguez (2013a, pp. 86–7) also finds this in the blogs that have replaced opinion columns in newspapers.

> the electronic format trifles with the fallacy of purported freedom and anonymity (Yus 2001, 2010; Crystal 2004; Pano Alamán 2008) which is not present in the printed press where journalists are clearly identified and, what is more, very present in the discussion. However, here the tone is more aggressive, more direct, and with a more incisive, more subjective view of reality. The author of the blog uses politically incorrect forms, clearly showing that he violates the most commonly accepted social norms to build a close and sincere image. This becomes part of the profile and is clearly evident in the content of each of his contributions. He thus manages to forge a professional identity as an opinion creator who will be key to attracting loyal followers who, through their daily visits, will help to give continuity to the blog and ensure its survival in the newspaper. (Fuentes Rodríguez 2013a: 86–87, our translation)

We have seen some reactions on Instagram, attacks on a user and direct insults on YouTube (on Alex Gibaja). In the following case the comments are addressed to Iñaki Gabilondo:

> (32)User 14 (unidentified): Y LOS MÁS VIEJOS DEL LUGAR SABEMOS COMO ERES TÚ IÑAKI, UN BOCAZAS QUE PERTENECE A ESA PODEDUMBRE DE SACAR A RELUCIR LO QUE OS INTERESA Y LO QUE NO, OS LO CALLAIS, TE ACUERDAS DE LOS TRES PARES DE CALZONZILLOS DE LOS TERRORISTAS DE LOS TRENES? TU SI HOCICAS EN TODO, POR TU BOCA SOLO SALE BASURA. Y

CON LAS ELECCIONES DE 26 M, PARECE QUE NO HAS CONSEGUIDO NADA, HAN SACADO MAS DIPUTADOS, ES QUE A CIERTAS EDADES NO ENGAÑAMOS A NADIE.

[AND THOSE OF US WHO HAVE BEEN HERE FOR LONGEST KNOW WHAT YOU ARE LIKE IÑAKI, A BIG- MOUTH WHO BELONGS TO THIS SWAMP THAT JUST BRINGS UP WHAT BENEFITS YOU AND EVERYONE ELSE, YOU CAN ALL SHUT UP, DO YOU REMEMBER THE THREE PAIRS OF UNDERPANTS OF THE T ERRORISTS OF THE TRAINS?

YOU STICK YOUR NOSE IN EVERYTHING, ONLY TRASH COMES OUT OF YOUR MOUTH. AND WITH THE ELECTIONS OF 26 M, YOU DON'T SEEM TO HAVE ACHIEVED ANYTHING, THEY'VE BROUGHT OUT MORE MEMBERS OF PARLIAMENT, WHEN WE GET TO A CERTAIN AGE WE CAN'T FOOL ANYONE.[13]] (YT 2016 jun 22 IÑA)

There are also positive ratings:

(33) User 10 (man): Vale, Iñaki, pero eso no es ninguna novedad: si nos atenemos a las declaraciones y decisiones del señor Fernández Díaz, llamarle "inútil" es lo más fino que se le puede decir. Y en cuanto a Mariano Rajoy y sus famosos "yo no sabía nada", parece que él no es tan tonto como parece, y se puede deducir que va a lo suyo, es decir: "tú dame el sobre todos los meses y no me contéis de dónde sale ni cómo". Pero el problema no es que sean unos delincuentes: es que hay siete millones de delincuentes o ignorantes que les votan.

[All right, Iñaki, but this is nothing new: if we look at the statements and decisions of Mr Fernández Díaz, calling him "useless" is the most courteous thing you can say about him. And when it comes to Mariano Rajoy and his famous "I didn't know anything", he doesn't seem to be as stupid as he looks, and you can see he's doing his own thing, in other words: "You give me the envelope every month and don't tell me where it is from or how". But the problem isn't that they are criminals: it is that there are seven million criminals or ignoramuses that vote for them. ]

(34) User 11 (unidentified): Este hombre es una joya [This man is a treasure] (YT 2016 jun 22 IÑA)

In other messages, the relationship is more technical or specialised. Sometimes there are recommendations or expert advice. See Alvaro Saval:

(35)User 25 (woman): Te recomiendo mirar la cámara, creo que lograrías un contacto más directo con el que te escucha :) [ I recommend you look at the camera, I think you'll be able to make more direct contact with your listeners :)]

User 26 (unidentified): Porque no haces vídeos!? De verdad tienes mucha vocación me ayudo mucho [why don't you make videos!? You're really skilled it helped me a lot]

User 36 (woman): super padre tu vídeo (espero ayude a tu autoestima hahaha [super cool your video (I hope it boosts your self-esteem hahahha] (YT 2014 sep 10 ALV)

The rude exchange is sometimes between participants in a conversation, such as user 12 in Alex Gibaja's video. This is in response to user 13 and creates a lobby of insults between both. The attack on the other person's image is clear and this is a display of the exacerbated rudeness we find on networks.

(36)User 12 (unidentified): [Mention of user 12] Anda aprende de la vida que tu que lo necesitas en vez de hacerte selfies de tu *horrenda cara de estupida* puedes ponerte a leer un

[13]Capital letters indicate that the message is sounded loudly.

libro y al tiempo te dirás a ti misma "Por qué era tan tonta para hacerme mil selfies si a la gente no le importa una mierda?"

[ For God's sake learn from life you need to instead of taking selfies of your *repulsive stupid face* you could start reading a book and at the same time say to yourself" why was I so stupid to take a thousand selfies of myself if nobody gives a shit about me?"]

User 13 (woman): [Mention of user 12] I yo hago lo que me da la gana, aprende tu a respetar a los demás, a parte tu no me conoces y no sabes lo que hago o dejo de hacer, me niego a seguir perdiendo el tiempo contigo así que ni te molestes en contestar, bye.

[ I'll do whatever I bloody well want to, you learn to respect other people, apart from the fact you don't know me and you don't know what I do or don't do, I refuse to keep wasting my time with you so don't bother to reply, bye.]

User 12 (unidentified): [Mention of user 13] [Mención al usuario 13]Te arrepentiras solo te digo eso y aprende algo de la vida que la necesitas mucho

[You'll be sorry, that's all I have to say and learn something from life because you need to]

User 15 (woman): [Mention user 12] jajaja, y tu no idiota, eres *mas asqeroso*, todos te odian, asi q para ya de meterte cn los demas y compra leche

[hahaha, what about you, idiot, you are *more disgusting,* everyone hates you, so who are you to pick on other people and buy milk]

User 12 (unidentified): [Mention user 15] compra leche? Vaya tela *que estupida* eres anda vete y comprate una vida que la necesitas mucho

[buy milk? For heaven's sake *you are so stupid*, go on, go and buy a life because you need one]

User 15 (woman): [Mention user 12] la vida no se compra *gilipollas*, y si, compra leche, es lo q esta ahora de moda, *cutreee,* veo q aun no has evolucionado a la edad moderna

[you don't buy life you ashole, and yes, buy milk, that's what's in fashion now, sleezebag, I can see you haven't evolved to the modern age]

User 12 (unidentified): [Mention user 15] Desde cuando una moda es Inteligente ? Jajaja Ahora si la moda es compra leche dentro de poco la moda será tirarse por la ventana que en tu caso viene muy bien, *una garrapata* menos *Jajaja* ... En fin

[Since when has a fashion been Smart? Hahah Now buying milk is in fashion and soon it will be in fashion to throw yourself out of the window, which in your case will be very good, *one less tick hahahaha*.... There you go] (YT 2015 ago 10 ALE)

User 15 (woman): [Mention user 12] jajaja, qien dice garrapata?? yo q se, otro animal, pero garrapata? ademas si yo soy garrapata, *tu eres de paso una mierda*, no tiene vida ni sentimientos, y por suerte, no habla, no como tu

[hahaha, who says a tick?? I don't know, another animal, but a tick? What's more, if I'm a tick, *you are a shit*, which has no life or feelings, and luckily it doesn't speak, not like you.]

User 12 (unidentified): Además Jajaja es correcto cuando has dicho Edad Moderna, tu serás de la Edad Moderna pero yo de la Contemporania que es la de ahora y eso se sabe en los libros de historia que tú necesitas ;)

[What's more, Hahaha you're right when you said Modern Age, you're from the Modern Age but I'm from the Contemporary age which is now and that's in the history books that you need ;)]

User 15 (woman): [Mention user 12] jajaj, en ningun momento te estaba hablando de historia, te decia edad como la edad de la adolescencia, edad moderna (literalmente) lo pillas *parguela*??

[hahaha at no time was I talking to you about history, when I said age I meant the age of adolescence, the modern age (literally) do you get it *sissy*??]

User 12 (unidentified): [Mention user 15] Mira ve a Google y escribe Edad Moderna y veras y se dice Edad Adolescente no edad moderna ...en fin

[Look. Go to Google and write Modern Age and you'll see and the term is Adolescent Age not modern age... anyway]

User 15 (woman): [Mention user 12] jajajjajaja, lo que piensas no te lo va a decir google, te lo decia en otro sentido, no en las edades prehistoricas, mediana, etc.

[hahhahahhahaha, google won't tell you what you're thinking, I was saying it in another sense, not the prehistoric, middle ages, etc. ] (YT 2015 ago 10 ALE)

User 15 uses a colloquial form, typical of Cádiz, Jaén and Málaga in Spain: *sissy* (like a woman) as a homophobic insult. Along with these statements, there are impolite forms such as "Do you get it?", accusations towards the other person and insults to their intelligence, as well as obscene interventions with user 12. Rudeness, therefore, is also intensified.

At other times they use irony to attack and disagree with others, like in this video about Laura Escanes, in which her image is indirectly attacked:

(37) User 1 (woman): No entiendo a la gente que la critica tanto y no hablo de críticas constructivas, sino de las personas que vienen con argumentos tan pobres y aún así se hacen los dignos. A cada pequeña cosa le sacan su lado malo. Todos se meten en su relación como si les preocupara y la mayoría, por no decir todos, no tienen idea de lo que pasa en sus vidas personales. Pero en fin, hay de todo en YouTube.

[I don't understand people who criticise her so much and I'm not talking about constructive criticism but about people who make such pitiful arguments and even then they act as though they're decent. They find something bad to say about every little thing. They all interfere in her relationship as though it had anything to do with them and most of them, if not all, have no idea about what is happening in their personal lives. Anyway, you can find anything on YouTube.]

User 2 (woman): *Totalmente de acuerdo contigo* (símbolo de "me gusta" con la mano)

*[I totally agree with you* (symbol for "like" with the hand)]

User 3 (man): Claro que hay de todo. A ver si te piensas tú que el enchufismo sale gratis

[Of course there's everything. Do you really think that *nepotism* is a free lunch]

User 1 (woman):[Mentions user 3] *¿qué es enchufismo? Disculpa mi ignorancia xd*

*[What is nepotism? Pardon my ignorance xd]*

User 3 (man): *Conseguir entrar o subir en un mundo laboral gracias a amistades o folleteo*

*[Entering or going up in the employment world thanks to friendships or philadering]*

User 1 (woman): [Mention of other user] Oh, vale, ahora entiendo tu comentario jaja. [Oh, okay. Now I understand your comment. Haha] (YT 2016 jun 28 LAU 01)

The longest reactions are close to a written discussion and entail a reflection on the purpose of these pages to create an image:

(38)User 29 (unidentified): Yo os explicaré por qué se lleva tantas tortas vuestra amiga Escanes. No es porque sea una persona plana carente totalmente de interés. Es porque es alguien superficial hasta las trancas que opta por el camino fácil. Pero en realidad no se ataca personalmente a esta chica. Creo que se ataca a todo un concepto y situación muy de hoy: la falta de meritocracia. Lo terrible que es que alguien así tenga infinitamente más éxito que mucha otra gente que tiene muchas cosas que aportar. Lo pervertido que es que una niña que solo sabe pintarse sea alguien en un medio. Porque el mundo está lleno de Lauras Escanes. Claro que sí. Siempre lo estuvo. Lo que se ataca es la estupidez a la que ha llegado la generación Gran Hermano. Aquellos que vimos cómo una panda de ineptos llegaron a convertirse en héroes nacionales en aquel primer Gran Hermano hemos sido testigos de cómo ese fenómeno ha ido extendiéndose, adaptándose y radicalizandose hasta el punto sin retorno en el que estamos. Queremos que se pare el mundo en esta estación y bajarnos.

[I'll explain to you why your friend Escanes gets so much stick. It isn't because she is a one-dimensional person who is of absolutely no interest. It is because she is completely superficial and always takes the easy way. But actually, it isn't a personal attack on this girl. I think that it attacks the entire concept and a very modern situation: the lack of meritocracy. The terrible thing is when someone is infinitely more successful than a lot of other people who have a lot more to contribute. What is perverted is that a little girl who only knows how to put makeup on becomes a celebrity. Because the world is full of girls like "Lauras Escanes". Of course it is. It always has been. What's being attacked is the level of stupidity reached by the Big Brother generation. Those of us who saw how a band of inept people became national heroes in that first Big Brother we've seen how this phenomenon has spread, adapting and radicalising to the point of no return where we are now. We want the world to stop at this station and let us off.]

User 30 (man): Cuidado! Que vienen las fangirls a decirte que todo lo tuyo es envidia en 3…2…1… La verdad es que les molesta porque a nadie le gusta que digan que su ídolo (quién quieren llegar a ser) sea una mujer vacía y de moralidad cuestionable. En el fondo las envidiosas son ellas, miran este canal para ver si pueden engalanarse lo suficiente como para que un tio narcisista forrado las convierta en su princesita malcriada.

[Be careful! The fangirls will come and tell you that you're just jealous in 3…2…1… The truth is that it bothers them because nobody likes anyone telling them that their idol (whoever that might be) is a vacuous woman with questionable morals. When it comes down to it, they're the envious ones. They look at this channel to see if they can do themselves up enough to snag a rich narcissistic guy to transform them into spoilt princesses.] (YT 2016 jun 28 LAU 01)

In this comment it is seen how their job is to present an image of themselves.

In WhatsApp the approach is more for self-image management of colloquial conversation and so we sometimes find impoliteness (Zimmerman 2003): impolite expressions in the context of closeness as a form of membership (Fuentes Rodríguez 2011):

(39)2015/06/24, 23:53 – H2: Yo tbn te quiero *cabron* pero no creó q vuelvas por q eso es el puto cielo [I love you too, you bastard, but don't think you're coming back because that's what fucking heaven is for] (WA 2015/16 ago-mar)

## 12.4 Conclusions

In short, the study made of Facebook, Twitter, Instagram, YouTube and WhatsApp shows us that a non-prototypical variant of conversation is generated on these new platforms, which we would call digital dialogue. We have focused on three aspects: the structure of the interaction, intersubjectivity and face- identity management.

The following table shows a comparison between face-to-face conversation and these formats of digital discourse, separating WhatsApp from the other models, since this is closer to the prototypical type of conversation (Table 12.4).

The most notable characteristics of this digital dialogue are the mechanisms used to replace what is lost with the absence of face-to-face communication. Regarding the structure of the interaction, we have seen that the digital exchange generates its own model, not present in face-to-face dialogue, with two possibilities:

1. Initial participation + branch reactions
2. Initial participation + comments + interactions between comments

**Table 12.4** Comparison between face-to-face conversation and digital dialogue

| Type of dialogue | Face-to-face | Digital<br>WhatsApp | <br>Twitter, Instagram, YouTube, Facebook. |
|---|---|---|---|
| Structure and functions | - exchange of information<br>-question- answer<br>- directive acts + acceptance or rejection | -initial participation: Provoke subsequent speech<br>-reactive participation: Commentary function | 1. Initial participation + branch reactions<br>2. Initial participation + comments + interactions between comments |
| Presence | Co-presence, allows simultaneous speech<br>Face-to-face relationship | No physical presence, allows delay and no simultaneous participations. These are managed linearly | |
| Formats, participants | Dialogue or polylogue | WhatsApp is a symmetric conversation at a distance and horizontal: Like a face-to-face conversation. Objective: Exchange information and social connection | Facebook, twitter, YouTube: Seeks polylogue but not necessarily with equal possibilities. Seeks to gain followers and numerous vertical relationship reactions. Asymmetric |
| Type of interaction | Symmetric relationship (conversation)-asymmetric (interview) | WhatsApp: Symmetric | Others: Asymmetric relationship: An initiative followed by comments and permits interaction between participants |
| Identity | Real identities. Face-to-face relationship | Other interactive relationships between participants in the comments are permitted | Creation of multiple virtual identities is permitted |
| Interactive relationships and effects | Politeness or rudeness according to the objective | Politeness or rudeness according to the objective | Exacerbated rudeness is permitted |
| Multimodality | No | Yes | Yes, to a greater degree |

This interactive pattern responds to the fact that the fundamental purpose of these conversations is to obtain comments, not always information, and the production of relationships between the comments generated. Thus, a complex structure is created between the same reactive turns.

The lack of physical and para-linguistic features is compensated with emoticons, emotion signs like!!!!, long vowels, capital letters, as described in the literature on this subject. This work suggests another feature: the high presence of emotive elements, generally intensifiers, which increase closeness between the interlocutors.

Lastly, the absence of visual contact permits the creation of multiple virtual identities that allow less courteous relationship than would be tolerated in a face-to-face situation. But above all, we must point out that on most occasions the purpose is to carry out a self-image activity to obtain the maximum number of followers.

## References


Albelda, M. (2007). *La intensificación como categoría pragmática: revision y propuesta.* Bern: Peter Lang.

Baym, N. (2010). *Personal connections in the digital age.* Malden: Polity.

Blanco Rodríguez, M. J. (2002). El chat: la conversación escrita. *Estudios de Lingüística de la Universidad de Alicante, 16*, 43–87.

Borreguero Zuloaga, M. (2003). Entre oralidad y escritura: la lengua de los mensajes electrónicos y los debates virtuales. In M. D. Muñoz Núñez (Ed.), *Actas del IV Congreso de Lingüística General. Cádiz, del 3 al 6 de abril de 2000* (pp. 307–317). Cádiz: Universidad de Cádiz.

Briz Gómez, A. (1996). *¿Cómo se comenta un texto coloquial?* Barcelona: Ariel.

Briz Gómez, A. (2000). Turno y alternancia de turno en la conversación. *Revista Argentina de Lingüística, 16*, 9–32.

Calero Vaquera, M. L. (2014). El discurso del WhatsApp: entre el Messenger y el SMS. *Oralia, 17*, 85–114.

Cestero Mancera, A. M. (1994). Intercambios de turnos de habla en la conversación el Lengua Española. *Revista de la Sociedad Española de Lingüística, 24*, 77–99.

Cora García, A., & Baker Jacobs, J. (1999). The eyes of the beholder: Understanding the turn taking system in quasi-synchronous computer-mediated communication. *Research on Language and Social Interaction, 32*(4), 337–367.

Crystal, D. (2004). *Language and the internet.* Cambridge: Cambridge University Press.

Davis, B. H., & Brewer, J. P. (1997). *Electronic discourse: Linguistic individuals in virtual space.* Albany: State University of New York Press.

Fant, L. (1996). Regulación conversacional en la negociación: una comparación entre pautas mexicanas y peninsulares. In T. Kotschi, W. Oesterreicher, & K. Zimmermann (Eds.), *El español hablado y la cultura oral en España e Hispanoamérica* (pp. 147–185). Frankfurt/ Madrid: Vervuert/Iberoamericana.

Fuentes Rodríguez, C. (1991). Algunas refexiones sobre el concepto de modalidad. *Revista española de lingüística aplicada, 7*, 93–108.

Fuentes Rodríguez, C. (2009a). La violencia en el anonimato: Internet. In C. Fuentes Rodríguez & E. Alcaide Lara (Eds.), *Manifestaciones textuales de la (des)cortesía y agresividad verbal en diversos ámbitos comunicativos* (pp. 188–210). Sevilla: Servicio de Publicaciones de la Universidad Internacional de Andalucía.

Fuentes Rodríguez, C. (2009b). Cuando la descortesía se convierte en agresividad: las listas de debate en el correo electrónico. In N. Hernández Flores & D. Bravo (Eds.), *Aportes pragmáticos, sociopragmáticos y socioculturales a los estudios de cortesía en español* (pp. 303–309). Buenos Aires: Dunken.

Fuentes Rodríguez, C. (2011). (Des)cortesía y violencia verbal: implicaciones lingüísticas y sociales. In C. Fuentes Rodríguez, E. Alcaide Lara, & E. Brenes (Eds.), *Aproximaciones a la (des)cortesía verbal en español* (pp. 27–74). Bern: Peter Lang.

Fuentes Rodríguez, C. (2013a). El género de opinión. Los blogs. In C. Fuentes Rodríguez (Ed.), *Imagen social y medios de comunicación* (pp. 77–92). Madrid: Arco Libros.

Fuentes Rodríguez, C. (2013b). Los comentarios en la prensa digital. In C. Fuentes Rodríguez (Ed.), *Imagen social y medios de comunicación* (pp. 199–247). Madrid: Arco Libros.

Fuentes Rodríguez, C. (2016a). Intensification, identity and gender in the Andalusian Parliament. In C. Fuentes Rodríguez & G. Álvarez Benito (Eds.), *A gender-based approach to parliamentary discourse* (pp. 35–59). Berne: Peter Lang.

Fuentes Rodríguez, C. (Ed.). (2016b). *Estructuras argumentativas y discurso político*. Madrid: Arco Libros.

Fuentes Rodríguez, C. (2017[2000]). *Lingüística pragmática y Análisis del discurso*. Madrid: Arco Libros.

Fuentes Rodríguez, C. (Ed.). (2018). *Mujer, discurso y parlamento*. Sevilla: Alfar.

Fuentes Rodriguez, C (ed e p) (2019). *Persuadir al votante. Estrategias de éxito*. Madrid: Arco Libros.

Fuentes Rodríguez, C., & Brenes Peña, E. (2014). *Apéndices apelativos en el lenguaje parlamentario andaluz: variación pragmática* (Vol. 17, pp. 181–209). Oralia: Análisis del Discurso Oral.

Galán, C. (2002). En los arrabales de la comunicación: los mensajes SMS. *Anuario de Estudios Filológicos, XXV*, 103–117.

Herring, S., Stein, D., & Virtanen, T. (Eds.). (2013). *Pragmatics of computer-mediated communication*. Berlin/Boston: De Gruyter Mouton.

Hidalgo Navarro, A. (1998). Alternancia de turnos y conversación. Sobre el papel regulador de los suprasegmentos en el habla simultánea. *Lingüística Español Actual, 20*(2), 218–238.

Hidalgo Navarro, A. (2000). Entonación y conversación: sucesión de turnos y superposiciones de habla. In J. J. Bustos Tovar et al. (Eds.), *Lengua, discurso, texto: I Simposio de Análisis del Discurso* (pp. 1595–1609). Madrid: Visor Libros.

Hidalgo Navarro, A. (2006). Estructura e interpretación en la conversación coloquial: el papel del componente prosódico. *Revista de Filología, 24*, 129–151.

Kerbrat-Orecchioni, C. (1986). *La enunciación. De la subjetividad en el lenguaje*. Buenos Aires: Hachette.

Kiesler, S., Siegel, J., & McGuire, T. W. (1984). Social psychological aspects of computer-mediated communication. *American Psychologist, 39*, 1123–1134.

Linell, P. (1998). *Approaching dialogue: Talk, interaction and contexts in dialogical perspectives*. Amsterdam: John Benjamins.

Llisterri, J. (2002). Marcas fonéticas de la oralidad en la lengua de los *chats*: elisiones y epéntesis consonánticas. *Revista de Investigaciones Lingüísticas, 2*, 61–100.

López Quero, S. (2003). *El lenguaje de los 'chats'. Aspectos gramaticales*. Granada: Port-Royal Ediciones.

López Quero, S. (2007). Marcadores discursivos y cortesía en la conversación virtual en español. *Language Design: Journal of Theoretical and Experimental Linguistics, 9*, 93–112.

López Quero, S. (2017). Conversación escrita y conversación oral: análisis comparativo. *Tonos digital, 32*, 1–33.

López Quero, S., Calero, M. L., & Zamorano, A. (2004). Foros de debate *vs*. Otros discursos electrónicos. *Español Actual, 82*, 53–75.

Mancera Rueda, A. (2009). Manifestaciones de (Des)Cortesía y Violencia Verbal en los Foros de Opinión Digitales de los Diarios Españoles. *Revista iberoamericana de discurso y sociedad, 3* (3), 437–466.

Mancera Rueda, A. (2011). *¿Cómo se habla en los cibermedios? El español coloquial en el periodismo digital*. Bern: Peter Lang.

Mancera Rueda, A. (2015). Valores sintáctico-discursivos de las etiquetas en Twitter. *Círculo de Lingüística Aplicada a la Comunicación, 64*, 58–83.

Mancera Rueda, A. (2016). Entre la identidad personal y la identidad corporativa: estrategias mediáticas para atraer a la audiencia a través de la red social Twiter. In Y. Bürki & H. Partzsch (Eds.), *Redes de comunicación: estudios sobre la prensa en el mundo hispanohablante* (pp. 321–349). Berlin: Frank and Timme.

Mancera Rueda, A. (2017). La usurpación de la identidad con fines paródicos en la red social Twitter: ¿manifestaciones de descortesía verbal? *Rilce, 33*(2), 537–565.

Mancera Rueda, A., & Pano Alamán, A. (2013a). *El discurso político en Twitter*. Barcelona: Antrhopos.

Mancera Rueda, A., & Pano Alamán, A. (2013b). *El español coloquial en las redes sociales*. Madrid: Arco Libros.
Martín Gascueña, R. (2016). La conversación guasap. *Soprag, 4*(1), 108–134.
Ortega Olivares, J. (1985). Apéndices modalizadores en español: los 'comprobativos'. In A. Soria, J. Montoya Martínez, & J. Paredes Núñez (Eds.), *Estudios románicos dedicados al profesor Andres Soria Ortega, 1* (pp. 239–255). Granada: Universidad de Granada.
Ortega Olivares, J. (1986). Aproximación al mecanismo de la conversación: apéndices 'justificativos'. *Verba, 13*, 269–290.
Pano Alamán, A. (2008). *Dialogar en la Red: la lengua española en chats, e-mails, foros y blogs*. Bern: Peter Lang.
Parks, M. R., & Floyd, K. (1996). Making friends in cyberspace. *Journal of Communication, 46*, 80–97.
Pérez Béjar, V. (2019). Estrategia *G*: Aprende a utilizar las redes sociales. In C. Fuentes Rodríguez (Ed.), *Persuadir al votante. Estrategias del éxito* (pp. 127–154). Madrid: Arco Libros.
Rockwell, G. (2003). *Defining dialogue: From Socrates to the internet*. New York: Humanity Books.
Sacks, H., & Schegloff, E. (1979). Two preferences in the organization of reference to persons in conversation and their interaction. In G. Psathas (Ed.), *Everyday language: Studies in ethnometodology* (pp. 15–21). Nueva York: Irvington.
Sacks, H., Schegloff, E., & Jefferson, G. (1974). A simplest systematics for the organization of turn taking for conversation. *Language, 50*(4), 696–735.
Suchman, L. A. (1987). *Plans and situated actions: The problem of human-machine communication*. Cambridge: Cambridge University Press.
Thurlow, C., Lengel, L., & Tomic, A. (2004). *Computer mediated communication: Social interaction and the internet*. London: Sage.
Van Dijk, T. A. (1992). *La ciencia del texto*. Barcelona: Paidós.
Vela Delfa, C. (2014). Estrategias de construcción y mantenimiento de la imagen pública en canales de chat. *Aposta: revista de ciencias sociales, 63*, 1–28.
Vela Delfa, C., & Jiménez Gómez, J. J. (2011). El sistema de alternancia de turnos en los intercambios sincrónicos mediatizados por ordenador. *Pragmalingüística, 19*, 121–138.
Walther, J. B. (1992). Interpersonal effects in computer mediated interaction: A relational perspective. *Communication Research, 9*, 52–90.
Walther, J. B. (1994). Anticipated ongoing interaction versus channel effects on relational communication in computer-mediated interaction. *Human Communication Research, 40*, 473–501.
Walther, J. B. (1996). Computer-mediated communication: Impersonal, interpersonal, and hyperpersonal interaction. *Communication Research, 23*, 3–43.
Yus, F. (2001). *Ciberpragmática. El uso del lenguaje en Internet*. Barcelona: Ariel.
Yus, F. (2010). *Ciberpragmática 2.0. Nuevos usos del lenguaje en Internet*. Barcelona: Ariel.
Zimmermann, K. (2003). Constitución de la identidad y anticortesía verbal entre jóvenes masculinos hablantes de español. In D. Bravo (Ed.), *La perspectiva no etnocentrista de la cortesía: Identidad sociocultural de las comunidades hispanohablantes* (pp. 47–59). Stockholm, CD-ROM: Actas del Primer Coloquio del Programa EDICE.

# Name Index





T. Lopez-Soto (ed.), *Dialog Systems*, Logic, Argumentation & Reasoning 22,
https://doi.org/10.1007/978-3-030-61438-6

J



K



L



M



N

# Subject Index





T. Lopez-Soto (ed.), *Dialog Systems*, Logic, Argumentation & Reasoning 22,
https://doi.org/10.1007/978-3-030-61438-6